Markus Schmitz
Transgressive Truths and Flattering Lies

Für Gini

Markus Schmitz teaches Comparative Literary and Cultural Studies at Münster University, Germany. His research revolves around (Anglophone) Arab Representations, Relational Diasporic Studies, Theories of Cross-Cultural Comparison, Forced Migration and Border Regimes, and (Counter-)Archival Arts.

Markus Schmitz

Transgressive Truths and Flattering Lies

The Poetics and Ethics of Anglophone Arab Representations

[transcript]

Bibliographic information published by the Deutsche Nationalbibliothek
The Deutsche Nationalbibliothek lists this publication in the Deutsche National-
bibliografie; detailed bibliographic data are available in the Internet at http://
dnb.d-nb.de

First published in 2020 by transcript Verlag, Bielefeld
© **Markus Schmitz**

Cover layout: Maria Arndt, Bielefeld
Cover illustration: Larissa Sansour, »Space Earth«, C-Print (2009)

Print-ISBN 978-3-8376-5048-8
PDF-ISBN 978-3-8394-5048-2
https://doi.org/10.14361/9783839450482

Contents

Acknowledgements

Some will argue that a non-Arab critic working in Germany who tries to construct an Anglophone Arab poetics and ethics must be conscious of his intrinsic inadequacies. He doesn't have first-hand experiences of being Arab in a world of anti-Arab racism and he doesn't really know the heavy burdens of English as a former colonial language that one has to carry to get oneself across. To intervene into the academic sub-field of Anglophone Arab literatures, arts and cultures from such positionality almost automatically risks disenfranchising oneself from the debate. I cannot but see it as an epistemological privilege to imagine myself as a tolerated houseguest who labors under such slightly embarrassing predicament. I boldly assume that I too am among the implied readers of these cultural texts—and yes, I claim to being among these works' implied critics. It is perhaps in my partial silence on the issue of identity politics, my refusal to speak morally, and my mere failure to write with the authentic authority of an insider about the collective value of Anglophone Arab representations that something of the *true* ethics resulting from my own intersectional limitations is articulated.

Most critical writings begin with some affirmative idea toward which they strive. I am afraid this project first and foremost was set in motion by my discomfort toward dominant readings of contemporary Anglophone Arab discourse. However, in the course of writing against other critics' attempts to locate this discourse in a reality which does not allow for fantasy, inconsistency, and dissonances, the initial idea of alternative interpretive approaches underwent profound transformations. The idea itself was constantly caught up in its actualization—in re-reading and re-writing. Such continuing actualization took the form of imagined and real exchanges. The book's various chapters reflect the immediacy of these textual and/or personal encounters. I have benefitted from each and every of them.

I am deeply grateful to a number of people—writers, artists, critics, colleagues, students, and friends—who helped me each in their own way to traverse the fiction of truth and counter-truths in literary and cultural criticism and who encouraged me to write this book. I wish to thank Rabieh Alameddine in particular for the tender smile of his narratives' metafictional wisdom as well as for a conversation on

writing and the birds' non-qualification for ornithology at the Berlin Gemäldega-
lerie. Works of concept and performance art played an important role in shaping my
ways of reading and seeing Anglophone Arab articulations. Emily Jacir and Walid
Raad's artistic tracing of the regularly harsh adjustment, transformation, and re-
moval of historical meaning and Larissa Sansour's apparently playful dystopian
imaginaries were particularly instructive for my undertaking. I appreciate Larissa's
kind permission all the more to use one of her visual works for this book's cover
design. I wish to thank Ella Shohat whose ways of re-thinking Arab diasporic relations have decisively inspired my own critical project.

Sofian Merabet, Katja Sarkowsky, Tobias Döring, and Mark Stein reviewed the
habilitation thesis from which this book derives. I have a long-standing debt to
my colleague and friend Franziska Quabeck who has generously spared time from
her own scholarly work to read and criticize the manuscript in every stage of its
drafting. I am particularly obliged to Sofian for his thoroughly reading and his
many very helpful comments. Last but not least my wife and intellectual companion
Regina Göckede, was among those rare swans that I am proud to call my earliest
readers and critics.

A book like the one at hand would not have been possible without the material
basis of a research position and the respective support of an institution. An earlier
version of this study has been filed as a post-doctoral (habilitation) thesis at the
University of Münster. I particularly have to thank Mark Stein at whose chair I was
affiliated during the period of the book's fabrication.

I wish to thank Anita Kaul who did an excellent copy editing and Anke Poppen
from transcript for her professional management of the publishing procedure.

Maria Arndt and Philip Radowitz helped me to implement my ideas for the
design of the cover.

The book's open-access dissemination is financially supported by the publication fund of the University of Münster.

Although I have constantly tried to circumvent a too-rigid notion of truth and
lie I do now strongly believe one can describe, if not what truths and lies are, at
least what they do, in literary fiction, in works of art, in the world, and between
worlds. In any case it is my hope that this book can contribute to the critical
reconceptualization of the two notions. Yet, it goes without saying that no one is
expected to believe in this study more than I have believed in its writing.

This book is dedicated to Gini, who shared with me its changeful genesis just
as she is my irreplaceable partner in the unpredictable circling of our joint worlds.

Kiel, 2019

0. Setting in Motion: The Trans-Location of Anglophone Arab Cultures

In season 5, episode 2 of the popular American television series *Homeland*,[1] the former CIA officer Carrie Mathison, now in her new job as a security advisor to a hyper-humanitarian German oligarch, is escorted by Hezbollah militants through a Syrian refugee camp in Lebanon. The buildings and walls of the filmic setting are excessively covered with Arabic graffiti (fig. 1 and fig. 2). Among the messages spray-painted on the film set's walls are "al-watan 'unsuri (*Homeland* is racist)," "mafish watan (There is no *Homeland*)," and "al-watan batikh (*Homeland* is a watermelon)."[2] One of the graffiti shows the Arabic transcription of the English words "Black lives matter." What happened to the film set?

Although the respective episode is set in an imagined Arab refugee camp, it was shot on an old factory site on the outskirts of Berlin. In the summer of 2015, the series' producers hired a collective of Egyptian street artists to add authenticity to the camp's location design. The artists known as Heba Yehia Amin, Caram Kapp, and Don Karl aka Stone used the unexpected opportunity to vent their political discontent with the controversial series.[3] The drama was not only known for being one of President Barack Obama's favorite TV shows but has also garnered the reputation of being among the most bigoted series for its undifferentiated and highly biased depiction of Arabs and Muslims. Although it supposedly questions America's war

---

1 "The Tradition of Hospitality," *Homeland*, season 5, dir. Lesli Linka Glatter, Keith Gordon et al., perf. Claire Danes, Mandy Patinkin, Rupert Friend et al., Showtime, 2015.

2 Dan Bilefsky and Mona Boshnaq, "Street Artists Infiltrate 'Homeland' with Subversive Graffiti," *The New York Times* 15 Oct. 2015, 30 Oct. 2015. <http://www.nytimes.com/2015/10/16/world/europe/homeland-arabic-graffiti.html?_r=0>.

3 Eric Hynes, "Interview with Heba Yehia Amin, Caram Kapp, and Don Karl of 'Homeland is not a Series'," *Field of Vision* 20 Dec. 2015, 22 Dec. 2015 <https://fieldofvision.org/interview-with-heba-yehia-amin-caram-kapp-and-don-karl-of-homeland-is-not-a-series>. Heba Amin has by now received international recognition as a concept and performance artist and participant of the 10th Berlin Biennale; see "Heba Y. Amin discusses her work in the 10th Berlin Biennale for Contemporary Art," *ARTFORUM* 5 June 2018, 11 July 2018 <https://www.artforum.com/interviews/heba-y-amin-discusses-her-work-in-the-10th-berlin-biennale-for-contemporary-art-75675>.

against terror at home and abroad, the series essentially affirms the dominant representational formula of Islamophobia and anti-Arab racism. What it adds to the known screen image of Arabs and to the established cinematic scripts of homeland-paranoia is the notion "that Arabs are so dangerous that even all-American White men can be corrupted by them and become equally dangerous to America."[4] Against this background, the artists expected to add Arab authenticity to the set braced themselves with critical slogans that comment on the ideological nationalist and racist contiguities hidden behind the series' real-Middle-Eastern decoration. The supplementary visual backdrop detail of Arabic script was thus turned into a tool to smuggle a subversive message into the filmic representation's main text.

Figure 1: Heba Amin, Caram Kapp, and Don Stone, Graffito "Al-watan 'unsuri (Homeland is racist)", 2015. Photography of the film set, Homeland, Seaon 5, episode 2. On the top left, "#gasusu"—a reference to an Egyptian Abla Fahita puppet which stands for the critique of the Egyptian regime spying on its citizens.

4   Joseph A. Massad, "Homeland, Obama's Show," *Aljazeera Online* 25 Oct. 2012, 30 Oct. 2015 <http://www.aljazeera.com/indepth/opinion/2012/10/2012102591525809725.html>.

Figure 2: Heba Amin, Caram Kapp, and Don Stone, Graffito, "Black lives matter" [phonetically English, yet in Arabic transcription], 2015.

The artistic intervention into a German location that was meant to provide the Middle Eastern setting for an American-produced television show is rich in dislocations. The Egyptian street artists' use of Arabic script for the semantic transgression of an Anglophone filmic text broadcast worldwide further multiplies their transgression's disorienting effects. The signs of critical comment only directly address those viewers who read Arabic. Hence, the message *"Homeland is racist"* is not primarily directed at the makers and consumers of the American TV series but first and foremost criticizes the artists' homeland and Egyptian nationalism. This meaning is further underlined by the reference to "#gasusu" (fig. 1), a puppet character on Egyptian social media which stands for the critique of a regime that spies on its own citizens. Yet shortly after the episode was broadcast on October 11, 2015, the critical Arabic intervention was covered up and translated to a global English-speaking audience by European and American mass media. In sum, these graffiti can be read as the critique of both the TV series *Homeland* and of the nationalist notion of homeland (security). They articulate a powerful critique of any form of nationalism and racism, by anyone, anywhere.

What makes these messages particularly relevant to my project is that they simultaneously express and criticize the structural limitations of their subversive endeavor. Their cross-cultural meaning can be fully grasped only in a relational reading that transcends both analytical frameworks of national cultures, linguistic belongings, and ethnic identity as well as the neatly fenced off geographical allocation of disciplinary cognizance and expertise. Although the Arabic transcription of a phonetically English phrase like "Black lives matter" (fig. 2) does not exactly fit into the cultural practices with which my study is primarily concerned, it nevertheless shares these practices' regularly conflictual genesis and transgressive effects in various ways. Formed out of and within the tension of cross-cultural and translational misrepresentation, the TV series' equally transnational and post-national Arab subtext is therefore an appropriate symbolic point of departure from which to set my project in motion.

The twenty-first century began with two major events of global relevance: the terrorist attacks of September 11, 2001 and the Arab uprisings of 2011. I do not need to elaborate on the contextual importance of these events for a study like the one at hand. They had somehow already set my project in motion before I had set foot on its topical terrain. Depending on our individual geographic location and intersectional positionality, they continue to influence our daily lives to different extents. Both the supreme fictions of the-West-versus-the-Rest as well as alternative representational modes of global identification are tied to the worldly dynamic of history. And the Middle East, Arabs, and Islam continue to fuel controversy. Since at least the late eighteenth century, these collective significations have been at the center of cross-cultural power struggles around distorted knowledges, reductive images, and often mutually ignorant polemics. The many conceptual mutations within recent academic and extra-academic debates on secular versus religious identity, cultural alterity, or terror and counter-terror do not indicate a foreseeable end to these tensions.

Although I cannot fully escape from epistemo-ideological precedents that suggest a calendrical ground zero for literary and cultural studies, my project is not intended as a contribution to the transdisciplinary field of post-9/11 studies or the expanding academic industry of intercultural/interreligious dialogue and terror-expertise. Without excluding works produced by Muslims or works that are identified as Islamic, for that matter, my project primarily explores secular discourses. Those readers who expect me to expose the Anglophone Arab writer's, artist's, or critic's true self, her or his Arab mind, her or his soul, or the socio-historical truths of her or his community will be equally disappointed. This study is not concerned with the individual Anglophone Arab intellectual's psychology or authentic cultural self-identification but with the psychology and originality of her or his work. I treat both the entity of a literary, critical, or audio-visual representation as well as the individual author or artist first and foremost as a communicative function. I have selected Anglophone Arab representations according to their topical and aesthetic specificity and with a view to their interventionist quality. It is not my intention to trace any original truths of those that represent or are (mis-)represented. The works that I discuss do not speak for the Arab world. If my project pursues any psychoanalytic interest, it approaches individual works as symbols and critical vehicles for the recognition of a disavowed writing across cultures.

Transgressive Truths and Flattering Lies aims at tracing the production and circulation of contemporary Anglophone Arab discourses as well as literary and artistic responses to the modern history of Arab-Western (trans-)migrations, misrepresentations, and translations, frictions, and cohabitations across various cultural sites against the historical backdrop of cross-cultural flows between what we have become accustomed to call the Arab world and the Anglophone West. It tries to interpretatively grasp the paradoxical situation of Anglophone Arab representations both in the US and Europe, where Arab voices and bodies are desired and rejected, ideologically assimilated and legally excluded, spectacularly exposed and discursively silenced, and within the Middle East, where Anglophone works increasingly gain importance as carriers of internal critique and external self-representation. Based on selected readings of Anglophone Arab representations of various geographic origins and genres ranging from early 20th century Arab American *Mahjar* writings to recent artistic practices of transnational Palestinian resistance, this study pursues multiple objectives: It explores individual and collective sociopolitical struggles from which Anglophone Arab representations emerge, it traces these artistic-literary works' multiple cultural beginnings and intertexts, it analyses their aesthetic devices and ethical contents, and it describes the multidirectional spectrum of the recursive effects of these interventions. The works of Anglophone Arab literatures, audio-visual arts, and critique that I discuss do not only respond to Western discourses that position the Middle East, Arabs, or Arabness as consumable objects but also offer more radical queries of our understanding of (self-)representation, authenticity, cross-cultural translation, or inter-subjectivity. Dissonances of cross-cultural encounters and inconsistencies of transmigratory identifications are not only unavoidable but of direct conceptual and interpretive evidence for my project. I have chosen my material first and foremost with a view to its particular narrative capacity, its inherent poetic and ethical transgressivity, and its metafictional quality regarding the representation of these cross-cultural dissonances and inconsistencies. Personal preferences and political leanings have surely fed into the selection procedure. The selection at hand does not claim any collective representativeness in terms of cultural or generic specificity. It instead claims a particular critical value in (sometimes violently) partial accounts.

Charting the shifting significations of overlapping forms of Orientalism and Occidentalism, *Transgressive Truths and Flattering Lies* addresses Anglophone Arab cultural practices (diasporic and non-diasporic alike) from a transnational perspective that brings the methods of postcolonial cultural studies together with Arab American studies, Arab British studies, and Middle Eastern studies. My relational (diasporic) approach to Anglophone Arab studies intends to disentangle the conventional separation of regions and cultural realms, moving beyond the binary notion of here and there to reveal the interconnectedness of cultural geographies. For this endeavor I draw on Ella Shohat's conceptualization of an interdisciplinary polylogue, an understanding of interdisciplinarity that transcends narrow linguistic, ethnic, or nation-state analytical frameworks prevalent in regional studies and ethnic immigrant studies approaches.[5] Although I explore representations produced by immigrants and/or members of minority groups, I am not concerned primarily with questions of immigrant literatures and minority literatures. If my study contributes to the field of American studies, it does so from a transnational American studies perspective. If it is designed as a contribution to British studies, its conceptual design is a decisively transnational one. And if my approaches and findings are of relevance for scholars of Middle Eastern studies, they are so because they allow a better understanding of either Arabic Middle Eastern cultural articulations generated in exchange with Anglophone Arab diasporic actors or representations by Middle Eastern intellectuals who choose English as the primary tool of their cultural enunciations. In other words, I place my comparative project at the disciplinary intersections of these academic fields without claiming my subject matter for any of these disciplines.

The prominent placement of the notion of translocation in the title of this introduction first and foremost underlines the disciplinary translocation of my project as a relational study project. It also indicates an interest in the representational practice of spacing, imaginaries of other spaces, physical and discursive movements between places and across borders, as well as in the spatial politics of identity.[6] In addition, the notion of translocation applies to the individual works' shifting fields of reference and utterance and to the scandal of unpredictable cross-cultural translations. It hence carries direct methodological implications: according to my understanding of Anglophone Arab literary and cultural studies, the analysis of cultural representations of lived or imagined spatial transgression needs to be complemented with reflections of the inherent poetic and ethical transgressivity of literatures and arts themselves. Questioning established ethics of reading the

---

5   See Ella Shohat, "The Sephardi-Moorish Atlantic: Between Orientalism and Occidentalism," *Between the Middle East and the Americas: The Cultural Politics of Diaspora*, eds. Evelyn Alsultany and Ella Shohat (Ann Arbor: U of Michigan P, 2013) 42-62.

6   See Marga Munkelt, Markus Schmitz, Mark Stein, and Silke Stroh, "Introduction: Directions of Translocation—Towards a Critical Spatial Thinking in Postcolonial Studies," *Postcolonial Translocations: Cultural Representation and Critical Spatial Thinking*, eds. Marga Munkelt et al. (Amsterdam: Rodopi, 2013) xiiv-ix.

Anglophone Arab literary text, audio-visual work, or performance, my study interrupts the acquired epistemological claims of unconditional intercultural truthfulness and intentionally displaces what is usually seen as the *correct* politics of crosscultural interpretation. The partial readings presented in this study do not aim at formulating a coherent ethics of Anglophone Arab representations. Neither is it my primary goal to trace unique formal and stylistic innovations that allow us to speak of genuine Anglophone Arab aesthetics. While I cannot see any contraction in addressing moral and extra-moral issues or questions of style related to my material, I do believe that poetical and ethical queries can be applied to the interpreted and to the act of interpreting in equal measures.

The transgressive character of my subject matter repeatedly forced me to revise my own interpretive positionality. Reading Anglophone Arab representations triggers an ongoing questioning of the conventional notion of a firmly located reading ego and can lead to a growing suspicion regarding one-sided disciplinary consistencies. This study intentionally undermines the all-too-often overstated and in my view misleading question of authenticity or cultural origin in debates revolving around global cultural production. Drawing on Elias Khoury's notion of critical correlation[7] and Édouard Glissant's relational poetics,[8] I suggest an understanding of literary and artistic creativity and critical reading, for that matter, which acknowledges contemporary Arab writers' and artists' capacity for narrative, audio-visual, or performative identifications that express the tensions involved in Arab encounters with the West while at the same time blurring those boundaries that for too long regulated discursively this encounter's representation. Such relational criticism aims at transcending the ethno-cultural fragmentation of creative expression and interpretation alike. It ultimately presumes a translational dynamic at work in Anglophone Arab representations which cannot be traced in the binary terms of originality and plagiarism. The dissonances and inconsistencies addressed and/or expressed in the representations that I explore require the critic to challenge and maybe to unlearn the consensual conceptions of moral aesthetic boundaries which usually determine the limits of corporate identification. They equally urge us to question both our own subject position and that of our respective cultural other. Such questioning necessarily goes beyond the dual critique of Orientalist and Occidentalist misrepresentations. Writing from the geographical and epistemic positionality of a white German scholar with a decisively cross-disciplinary background who is working outside the English-speaking world and who can hardly claim to be an Arab (if not by choice), I have adapted the notion of relational reading to facilitate a bi-directional critique of Anglophone Arab cultural resemblances that

---

7   Elias Khoury, "Reading Arabic," *DisOrientation: Contempory Arab Artists from the Middle East* (Berlin: Haus der Kulturen der Welt, 2003) 10-13.
8   Édouard Glissant, *Poetics of Relation*, trans. Betsy Wing (Ann Arbor: U of Michigan P, 1997).

involves more than simply questioning established Western truths by paternalistically giving voice to alternative Arab truths.

I argue that the particular aesthetics and ethics of Anglophone Arab resemblances cannot be exhaustively explained with the tension between competing notions of veracity and beauty. The allegorical and performative strategies at work in the ongoing Anglophone rearrangement of individual and collective Arab selves regularly speak a language that is at the same time both inside and outside the topological structure of figurative Arabness and Westerness. Our critical practice, however, seriously connected to historical contextualization and socio-political interpretation, is not free from frictions between the figural, the performative, and the ethical side of the cultural text that it seeks to interpret. In my view, Western scholars of Anglophone Arab representations, should they not want to entirely suspend the idea of self-critical cultural reading, must sometimes take the liberty to respond allegorically to the Orientalist/Occidentalist system of tropes they seek to debunk. This is better done with ironic exposure of one's own interpretive paradoxes than with earnest pathos. In other words, whoever wants to read Anglophone Arab representations as signs of cross-cultural translations must be aware that such signs might contain more traces of what they do not mean than of what they actually mean. Literary and cultural criticism thus understood is an impossible translational process that is aware of what Gayatri Chakravorty Spivak calls the "violence of culturing".[9] There is a degree of this violence at work in any Western interpretation of Arab articulations in Arabic and Anglophone Arab articulations alike.

Reading Anglophone Arab representations is therefore conceptualized in this study as an act of responsible transcoding rather than enriching explaining. At times I use the allegorical fragmentation of a given cultural text to transfer a socio-political meaning which is not necessarily intrinsic to that text. The question of cultural translatability is not primarily approached as a sociolinguistic problem. In theoretical alliance with Spivak, I do not believe that the process of semiotic regression can ever be fully reversed. Instead, the interpretive undertaking must sometimes shift its focus from the question of a particular text's readability, from the search for some original meaning or the echo of such original meaning, to the question of the critic's own reading-ability in relation to the respective cultural text. Such mode of interpretation is skeptical with regard to both the self-proclaimed insider's belief in translational authenticity and the outsider's all-too-often disclaimed interpretive matrix of cultural exoticization. *Transgressive Truths and Flattering Lies* therefore participates in the comparative translocation rather than in the identitarian relocation of Anglophone Arab discourse.

---

9   Gayatri Chakravorty Spivak, "Translation as Culture," *An Aesthetic Education in the Era of Globalization* (Cambridge, MA: Harvard UP, 2013) 244.

Please do not get me wrong! I am not saying that there are no real places and real bodies involved in the making of this discourse or that there is no Anglophone Arab identity other than an allegorical one—how could I do so without claiming to be a real Arab at the same time? What I argue is that the identities narratively and performatively iterated in contemporary Anglophone Arab representations are predominantly stylized from various cultural signs and socio-historic experiences that cannot be easily resolved in any conceptual unity of form and meaning. They are regularly characterized by the fragmentariness, arbitrariness, and discontinuity of allegory. Consequently, the referential systems necessary for their interpretation can significantly exceed the place and text of their own articulations. In order to decode such representations, the critic cannot strictly confine herself or himself to the search for authentic archival hints intrinsic to these works' central signifiers or for consistent counter-archival references. Drawing on Paul de Man, one could argue that allegory, beyond its function as rhetorical trope, itself advances to a mode of reading in such project.[10] In *Transgressive Truths and Flattering Lies*, critical reading is understood as an interpretive way of transgressing the notion of Anglophone Arab symbolic totality. It goes without saying that such responsive transgression of the reading-writing binary necessarily involves transgressing the differentiation between the poetics of an individual work, the theoretical implications of its metafictional dialectics, and the ethical insights offered in that work self-critically and in equal measure. In other words, reading Anglophone Arab representations demands a (co-)relational rethinking of how meaningful (cross-)cultural critique can be approached today. My study wishes to contribute to precisely such rethinking.

I have tried to methodically incorporate my discomfort with the idea of rationalizing Anglophone Arab arts and literatures as products that are either intrinsically linked to an equally exotic Arab cultural essence or a shadow reflex of hegemonic Western culture. One way to overcome this unease is the redemptive step into and multiplication of the uncertainties of tentative endings, open-ended beginnings, and (occasionally very) distant intertexts which blur such simple binaries. Since I claim to treat both my subject matter and my critique as discursive events in their own right, the Foucauldian notion of discourse is of direct relevance here. I neither claim to place myself outside or on the other side of the discourse that I explore, nor do I pretend to always know exactly how to differentiate strictly between a work's inner identity and its discursive structuration or external codification. As Julia Kristeva has demonstrated, the comparative axis that connects a text to another text is constantly crossed and altered by the axis that connects a

---

10   See Paul de Man, *Allegories of Reading: Figural Language in Rousseau, Nietzsche, Rilke, and Proust* (New Haven: Yale UP, 1979) and Paul de Man, *Blindness and Insight: Essays on the Rhetoric of Contemporary Criticism*, 2nd ed. (1971; Minneapolis: U of Minnesota P, 1983) 187-228.

text and its reader.[11] And of course my readings cannot fully escape the discursive rules of interpretive inclusion and exclusion that they seek to lay bare.

One of the key-arguments of this study is that the narrative and performative strategies at work in Anglophone Arab writings go beyond both the questioning of the factual accuracy of Western truth claims and the stretching of essential Arab truths. Although I trace counter-discursive strategies of writing back and other dialogical dynamics at work in Anglophone Arab representations, I am equally interested in the tension of lies and counter-lies. In my view, the cultural practices of counter-lying, representational inaccuracy, the performative invention of half-truth or risky truth, of *matters of act*, strategic opacity, unreliability, and incoherence, the practices of faking, forging, and counterfeiting, have been badly neglected in Anglophone Arab literary and cultural studies. The reasons for such reluctance are manifold. One reason certainly lies in the enduring discursive afterlives of the racist Orientalist trope of the Lying Arab. Another can supposedly be grounded in the plain identity-political or institutional necessity to speak (or pretend to do so) one's people's truth to whatever hegemonic power. So far, only (and one might add significantly) Victorian literature's lies have been systematically explored.[12] The idealistic scholarly disregard for Anglophone Arab cultural statements that willingly risk being (or being seen as) paradoxical with a view to universalized (or self-universalizing) standards of morality, however, results in the marginalization of works that do not feel inclined to become visible in their true existence; works that do not believe in the identity of truth-bearing, truth-telling, and truth-making. Many of the Anglophone works that I discuss fall into this category.

While the epithets of post-truth and post-fact were being declared words of the year by various dictionaries in 2016, this study is not concerned with the dialectics of enlightenment, the popular rhetoric of alternative facts, or the politics of post-truth.[13] It starts from the premise that the dominant truths of the so-called Oriental, of Islam or of the Arab world never spoke for themselves from the point of view of those represented in these very truths,[14] although the new discomfort with a post-factual present naively presumes a factual past. Given the not-at-all-new critique of power-knowledge and the identification of universal truth claims as dogmatic claims made by those who control the representational means to rule

---

11   Julia Kristeva, *Desire in Language: A Semiotic Approach to Literature and Art*, ed. Leon S. Roudiez, trans. Thomas Gora, Alice Jardine, and Leon S. Roudiez (New York: Columbia UP, 1980) 69.

12   John Kucich, *The Power of Lies: Transgression in Victorian Fiction* (Ithaca: Cornell UP, 1994). *See also* Andrew Hadfield, *Lying in Early Modern Culture: From the Oath of Supremacy to the Oath of Allegiance* (Oxford: Oxford UP, 2017).

13   Cf. Matthew D'Ancona, *Post-Truth: The New War on Truth and How to Fight Back* (London: Ebury P, 2017).

14   Edward Said, "Permission to Narrate," *Journal of Palestine Studies*, 13.3 (1984): 27–48.

out ambiguity, this assumption must come as a surprise. Whereas normative philosophical theories of truth seldom transcend their own fact/value dichotomy to reflect the practice of knowledge within the aesthetic realm, aesthetic theories in turn are often based on the convergence of meaning and its empirical manifestation.

Instead, I am interested in the poetic and interpretive devices that produce meaning, in the historically shifting discursive structures that evolve and devolve systems of Anglophone Arab meaning-making, and in the synecdochic capacity of individual poetic interventions for more than distorted substitutions. My interest in Anglophone Arab writers' and artists' particular imaginative faculty of translating a perceived reality into significance partly draws on Jacques Derrida's insight "that each time an event has been produced, for example in philosophy or in poetry, it took the form of the unacceptable, or even of the intolerable, or the incomprehensible."[15] Understanding events of art and literature as prospective with a view to alternative articulations of experiences of impossibility (articulations of experiences which otherwise due to a lack of agreement cannot be represented), I willingly risk to give up the illusion of absolute candor in cross-cultural representations and my own relational criticism alike. I am interested in analyzing a poetics and ethics in which producing and circulating dissonant set-ups appears almost inescapable for those who want to effectively undermine a hegemonic representational system that is blocking their truth claims. I argue that Anglophone Arab representations have a particular capacity to transgress one-sided fact-claims and creatively imagine counter-lies that tell other truths. Under conditions in which so-called objective truths do not correspond with the subjective experience and in which not everybody can find herself or himself in that truth, these representations intentionally blur the orthodox division between the objective and the subjective. As a consequence, what appears as blatant lies for some can *in fact* be expressions of necessary truths of individual experiences and collective aspirations for others. It goes without saying that Friedrich Nietzsche's genealogy of (extra-)morality, Jean-François Lyotard's concept of the *differend*,[16] and Michel Foucault's archeology of (un-)reason are of direct relevance for theoretically grasping such dynamics of transgressing dominant idioms in Anglophone Arab rough truth-speaking and flattering lying. I draw in particular on an important link that exists between these critics constituted by their critique of interiority and intersubjectivity. Following this strand of theory, the question is not: does this literary or artistic work carry a truth? But: does it work? What is its operational quality? What lies does it lay

---

15   Jacques Derrida, "Passages—from Traumatism to Promise," *Points... Interviews 1974–1994: Jacques Derrida*, ed. Elisabeth Weber, trans. Peggy Kamuf et al. (Stanford, CA: Stanford UP, 1995) 387.

16   Jean-François Lyotard, *The Differend: Phrases in Dispute*, trans. G. Van Den Abbeele (Minneapolis, MN: U of Minnesota P, 1988).

bare, and what portion of truth does it cover? What power-truth does it denunciate? What social antagonisms and historical contradictions does it represent? What alternative sensations and perceptions does it open up? How does it counter the truth of our learned dispositives? What new thoughts and enunciations does it make possible? And how is the event of its emergence (of its *ecriture*) marked by the discursive ambivalences of that very process?

The Anglophone Arab representations that I explore rather perform than represent selectively extended translations of Arabness to make themselves heard without promising to mirror any real presence transparently. If they conceal an essential truth-claim, it is not simply transferred to the reader. In order to smuggle their message into the dominant historical, political, and ethical discourse effectively, while escaping from the threat of disciplined integration, these traveling narratives repeatedly desert from normative modes of telling truth and take refuge in false translations. In these moments, their transgressive poetics of breaking free are ones of *real doing* rather than of representing the real. They imagine opponents of dominant truth-claims and express the whole force of the difficulty which would be felt by anybody attempting to think, narrate, and act the Anglo-Arab encounter differently. They thus creatively investigate the dense relations of the factual and the fantasmatic in both political rhetorics and literary poetics.

Transgressive Truths and Flattering Lies is subdivided into five chapters. The first and second can be read as extended introductory chapters. The sections of the fifth chapter represent various experimental travails into areas of cultural practice that are not secured by the traditional focus on works of literature in Anglophone Arab studies. The sharp contrast that the readings of this final chapter mark in relation to the previous sections directly results from my chosen source materials' generic location (theory, popular literature as well as concept and performance art) and their specific medialities (film and other audio-visual devices). However, the impression of difference might also derive from some of the discussed works' particular historical and political places of emergence (i.e. Palestine).

Chapter one makes the issue of discontinuity my beginning question. To underline the complex correlations of Anglophone Arab narrative beginnings with the world of cross-cultural representations, I use two quasi-unending narratives by 'Abd al-Rahman Munif (*Endings*, 1977/88 and *Cities of Salt*, part 1, 1984/87) as points of departure and literary vehicles to address key questions that will repeatedly be encountered in the course of my systematic discussion. This short chapter is intended to sensitize the reader and complicate the notion of beginnings for writing about Anglophone Arab representations. It explains why Anglophone Arab representations can neither be located within a clearly demarcated sphere of first Anglophone articulations by ethnically Arab writers nor can they be understood as necessarily diasporic, ethnic immigrant, or transmigrant representations.

Against this background, chapter two focuses on several semi-inaugural works, quasi-initiating starting points, or decisive stop-overs for the formation of the discursive field with which I am dealing. The chapter traces Anglophone Arab representations' plural beginnings and thus revises models of clear transitivity or direct influence. Focusing on early and particularly innovative ways of making Anglophone Arab meaning, the discussion involves historical, theoretical, and practical issues in equal measure. It relates the literary and cultural discourse of the so-called Nahda (Arab renaissance) of the nineteenth and early twentieth century to cross-cultural contacts between the Arabic-speaking world and the English-speaking world since the early modern period. Without arguing for comparative narrative morphologies between early Arabic popular fiction and early Anglophone Arab writing, this chapter provides prerequisites for a transnational interpretation of Anglophone Arab representations which disrupt the conventions of West-Eastern representational accountability. In addition, it explores the conditions of (im-)possibility of tracing translocal, translinguistic, and translational correlations in a historical perspective.

Chapter three forms the kernel part of this study. Here I use Ameen Fares Rihani's 1911 novel *The Book of Khalid* as a vehicle for carving out the spectrum of discourses informing contemporary Anglophone Arab representations. Closely re-reading a text that is perceived as the inaugural text of Arab writing in English, I am less concerned with cultural characteristics, ethnic spirit, and direct or indirect artistic borrowings from either Arabic or Anglophone works than with historical contexts, topical motives, narrative devices, and structural affinities. Drawing on the poet Adonis, I am particularly interested in those aesthetic innovations that allow replacing concepts of authentic roots or heritages by multiply interrupted, intentionally confused, and mutually incomplete ongoing relational tensions. In this spirit, I place the novel within the long history of transnational encounters which go back to early modern Arab immigration to Britain, encounters that continue even after the events of September 11, 2001. I read *The Book of Khaled* as an equally self-critical and ironically mocking confrontational imaginary instead of interpreting it as a prototypical literary representation of immigrant secularization. With this reading, I take my first concrete steps into the direction of a radical politics of interpretation that does not confine itself to the idealist claim of cognitively controlling and reconciling competing truth claims and that is sensitive to the strategic use and (im)moral economy of lies. I do so by stressing the narrative's anti-hero's experience of humiliation and oppression, his resistive excess of real and symbolic destruction, or his desperate posture of revolutionary prophethood. The novel is interpreted as a reciprocation of the false promise of assimilation and the social practice of discrimination. Stressing the close link between the social and the discursive directly incorporated into the novel's mode of emplotment, I describe the paradoxes and power of strategic imitations and inauthentic self-enactments against the background of the Arab *Mahjar* movement and American racism. These enactments are explained as early incidences of the social struggles, identity politics, and cultural practice of Arab (diasporic) intellectuals that have shaped Arab American experiences of not-quite-whiteness and ambivalent racial identifications throughout the twentieth century and beyond.

Discussing topical and performative tools of strategic subversion, critical revision, and correlative identification, I shall then use the example of *The Book of Khalid* to re-construct a transnationally expanded interpretive geography for the study of diasporic discourses in relation to Middle Eastern cultural politics. Consequently, I spend a separate sub-chapter on the exploration of those portions of the novel, which are set within the Middle East. Here I place particular focus on the spatial alteration of the story's fictional landscape. The chapter's last section explores the novel's narrative discourse to lay bare tensions between representational reliability and strategic inaccuracy in cross-cultural representations within and between the Middle East and the West. Thus the question of narrative structure is directly related to the metafictional *dialogics* of authorship, narrative authority, readership pre-disposition, and strategic (mis-)translation at work in Anglophone Arab discourses of critical correlation. Using Miguel de Cervantes' *Don Quixote* as a particularly important intertext, I include a classic that not only represents a visionary mode of telling lies in order to tell the truth, but that can be seen as the Andalusian mother of the modern novel. By relating it to contemporary Anglophone Arab narrative discourse, I place my discussion of Anglophone Arab meta-narratology in a translocal literary sphere that cannot be firmly assigned to either the West or the Middle East and that transgresses the historical period of my primary material. The examples of Assia Djebar, Abdelkébir Khatibi, Édouard Glissant, and Ngũgĩ wa Thiong'o help to illustrate how under the historical condition of (post-)coloniality, strategic translation, selective translation, or even non-translation can become a form of resistive identification and how the strategic multiplication of non-transparency and ambiguity form the narrative devices in the Anglophone Arab discourse. Drawing on a more contemporary comparison, the notion of cross-cultural translation itself gets radically questioned in order to make sense of partial translational endeavors, inventive pseudo-transfers, strategic opacities, or fake transmittings in the literary figuration of Arab truth. In addition, the Spanish classic's Andalusian chronotope helps one to grasp literary instances of Anglophone Arab reverse-plagiarisms as flights from the unbearable situation of being translated by Westerners.

The fourth chapter voyages from the Shahrazadian trope derived from the *The Arabian Nights* (the European novel's Arabic grandmother) to the Saidian quasi-trope as disparate literary and critical intertexts of contemporary Anglophone Arab representations. It traces varying Anglophone Arab appropriations of the *Nights* that have turned the classical narrative into a powerful metafictional weapon that goes beyond sole aesthetic preoccupations. In some cases, this regaining of Shahrazad as a narrative guide for resisting (neo-)patriarchy and countering hegemony is openly performed. In other cases, the recourse to the *Nights* rather takes the form of an oblique allegory. These different developments ask the contemporary reader to take the transgeneric and transnational genesis of nocturnal writings into consideration. With a view to modern Arabic writing, I stress the importance of the so-called post-Mahfouzian novels such as Emile Habibi's *The Secret Life of Saeed, the Ill-Fated Pessoptimist* (1974/1982) or Elias Khoury's anti-heroic epic *Gate of the Sun* (1998/2006) as intertexts for Anglophone Arab writings. In addition Jorge Luis Borges and Gabriel García Márquez's oeuvres are read both as products of a literary intercourse with the Shahrazadian narrative and as important pretexts for contemporary Anglophone Arab writers. Salman Rushdie's 1980 novel *Midnight's Children* is used as another example of the widely ramified voyage of the Shahrazadian trope and her nocturnal mode of stretching the truth.

After reading Jabra Ibrahim Jabra's 1960 novel *Hunters in a Narrow Street* as an early example of an Anglophone Arab text written by a person living and working within the Middle East, I discuss Tayeb Salih's 1966 *Mausim al-hijra ila-sh-shamal* as an Arabic text that had an immense impact in its English translation. At the same time, I read *Season of Migration to the North* (1969) as the depiction of the tremendous bi-directional effects of Europe's constant denial of the non-Europeans' humanity, leading to the violation of the idealist humanist notion of communicative reason. I demonstrate how this narrative imagines lies and counter-lies as speech acts that are intrinsically linked to the colonial and postcolonial appropriation of cross-cultural authority. It is against this background that I re-visit Joseph Conrad's partial affirmation of colonialist-racist ethics in *Heart of Darkness* (1899–1902), as an antecedent of *Season*'s anti-imperialist project. Arguing that the novel depicts the verbal act of lying as a given practice under the socio-historical condition of coloniality, I interpret the lying of Salih's anti-hero, Mustafa, as a resistive strategy that rehabilitates the strategic use of partial truths as justifiable forms of political agency and that in a similar way guides the transgressive syntax and correlational narrative techniques of Anglophone Arab truth-making. Against the background of earlier ideological adaptations of Shakespeare's *Hamlet*, I then describe the Hamletization of the Arab political and literary hero for the interrogation of current post-heroic regimes inside the Arab world. It is at this point that I re-read Edward Said's oeuvre as that of an Anglophone Arab critic and as an important intertext for Anglophone Arab representations as well as an Anglophone Arab studies text in its own right. By doing so, I confess his criticism's importance for my own critical endeavor and profess those dissonances between his and my approach that cannot be resolved in theoretical harmony.

Chapter five enters a different sphere of Anglophone Arab enunciations in order to discuss the complex nexus of blocked and forced visibility, discrepant concepts of (non-)belonging and identity, competing representational modes of alterity, mutually exclusive archives, and the limits of enunciability. Including popular literature, theory, and the audiovisual arts, the cross-cultural analysis goes beyond the still-predominant focus on literature to underline the continuing topical and structural overlaps across genre divides. More than early Anglophone Arab literary representations, recent works of Anglophone Arab concept and performance art explicitly admit to being shaped by the representational norms that they anticipate. More openly than the former, they perform the mechanisms of their own adjustment of meaning. Thus they represent what I see as a particularly parafictional strand of Anglophone Arab representations.

Reading the novelist and screenplay writer William Peter Blatty alongside the postmodern literary theoretician Ihab Hassan, the first section of chapter five focuses on the discursive practices of assimilation and non-assimilation. By selectively exploring the writings of two Americans who are usually placed in the margins or outside of the Anglophone Arab discourse, I interpret their texts against the grain. I interpret Blatty's auto-fictional narrative *Which Way to Mecca, Jack?* (1958) with a view to its engagement in the psychology of impossible assimilation and its narrative strategies of resisting the assimilationist paradigm of identification. I suggest seeing the invisible violence resulting from the horrors of discriminatory assimilation as a missing link between this piece of popular fiction and the best seller *The Exorcist* on which Blatty's success as an American mainstream writer is based. My psychoanalytic reading interprets the 1971 horror novel as an allegory of a much more horrific and ambivalent intra-psychic struggle related to the assimilationist pressure to exorcise the Arab within. I argue that *The Exorcist* additionally carries the unsettling suggestion that the act of exorcism is directed at those to be assimilated. The interpretation of the text as an Anglophone Arab Gothic allegory of the horrors of Arab experiences of assimilation in the West uses Kristeva's notion of abjection to lay bare the fictional representation's deeper allegorical meaning related to the dynamics of racialized subject-constitution and the fears of reverse colonization and miscegenation. Against this background, the section revisits Hassan's rigorous refusal of any Arab ethnic identification. Without re-claiming Hassan's theoretical work for the corpus of Anglophone Arab studies, I partly explore the hidden (non-)Arab contiguities of postmodernism. Relating the theoretical notion of *indetermanence* (indeterminency + immanence) as the quasi-ethos and post-moral episteme of postmodern theory to Hassan's writings at the intersection of autofiction and theory [*Out of Egypt* (1986)], I ask for both these writings' poetics and ethics of self-concern and the psychic inconsistency of rigorous identitarian indeterminacy. The discussion then shifts to Hassan's critique of postcolonial theory and his counter-notion of spiritual interculturalism. Exploring the strengths, psychological implications, and conceptual contradictions of his notorious anti-

Arab polemics, I stress the political ambivalence of Hassan's farewell-to-the-roots talk.

The following subchapter uses the literary writings of Rabih Alameddine and the concept and performance art of Walid Raad as examples of Anglophone Arab transmigrant works that blur boundaries between fiction, metafiction, and parafiction. Questioning the notions of stable morality, factual history, and sexual normativity, the discussion stresses the sordid anger of tragic memories and the fragile wisdom of unstable truths. The section opens with a reading of Alameddine's 1998 literary debut *Koolaids*, a novel that relates situational, cross-cultural settings of physical deterioration to graphic depictions of bodily love and that juxtaposes public mediations with private musings. Transgressing the referential system by which we usually position ourselves against others, this queer narrative not only unsettles our heteronormative convictions and one-sided cultural identifications but also questions our own geographic, historiographic, and epistemic self-locations as readers and critics. Alameddine's third novel, *The Hakawati* (2008), shares this radically disorienting strategy of crossing dividing-lines of belonging. The text is presented as metafiction about storytelling that draws on both the counter-narrative power and the hegemonic commodifications of the Shahrazadian trope. It expresses a fundamental skepticism regarding the narrative capacity to represent factual truth. The discussion then switches to the audio-visual and performative spheres of Anglophone Arab cultural production, using an example in which the performative adjustment of authority is particularly evident: the Atlas Group forms the constant basis for the concept artist Walid Raad's multimedia performances. The project is interpreted as a pseudo-scientific laboratory that mimics and thereby exposes the mechanisms of the archive as a place where the production of historical knowledge happens and which thus questions the claims of archival truth. The projects selected for my analysis undertake a performative reversal of translational power by working with faked documents presented as *art-facts* rather than as artefacts.

The last chapter focuses on recent transformations within Palestinian transnational cultural resistance across genres. Starting with a discussion of the long-term concept and performance project, *Material for a Film* (2005–ongoing), by Emily Jacir, a project that sheds light on the lost and obscured fragments of a murdered Palestinian activist to expose the archival violence involved in the production of historical evidence, I illustrate how the local struggle for liberation is transposed into the domain of Western representation. In addition, I demonstrate that this work transgresses a morality of counter-truth that long dominated the Palestinian resistance paradigm of narrating back. Interpreting the project as an artistic research project that is concerned with the aesthetics of *formativity* rather than the aesthetics of form, *Material for a Film* is presented as encapsulating a poetics of post-romantic lies rather than an ethic of counter-truth. The remaining section traces similar frictions of truth and fiction in Anglophone Palestinian representations, with a particular focus on questions of space, place, and (im)mobility. Using a geocritical approach, I read Raja Shehadeh's *Palestinian Walks* (2007) as an anti-travelogue that counters imperial, military, or tourist mappings of the occupied territories and its people. Drawing on the independent online project *Electronic Intifada*, the section stresses the importance of the internet as a transnational space of counter-journalistic activism. Reading selected audio-visual works of art that respond to the experience of spatial restrictions alongside the practices of traceurs in Gaza, the discussion culminates in a dystopian interpretation of Larissa Sansour's 2009 *A Space Exodus*, a mixed-media installation that turns the exilic experience of Palestinian deterritorialization into a vision of impossible escape and loss in outer space.

The concluding chapter recapitulates my reading's main findings, drafts the spectrum of desiderata and possible future research directions in Anglophone Arab studies, and discusses my project's general theoretical and methodological implications with a view to the future of the broader field of postcolonial literary and cultural studies and comparative cultural theory. It stresses in particular the need for an extra-moralistic re-conceptualization of lies and counter-lies in our theoretical stance towards postcolonial archival dissonances.

Although *Transgressive Truths and Flattering Lies* is first and foremost carried (and sometimes carried away) by the creative works that it explores (and at other times exploits), it regularly carries across other critics' interventions. Ella Shohat's scholarly work functions as a constant model for the disciplinary decentering of my own critical endeavor, not failing to (trans-)locate this study in relation to the various disciplines' approaches. I have learned from Fanon and Glissant that the search for cross-cultural conviviality cannot possibly end up in the construction of depoliticized transculturality or trans-difference. Freud and Kristeva have taught me, each in her or his own way, that there is no relational reading without at least a certain dynamic of narcissistic transference involved. From a different disciplinary perspective, Clifford Geertz states that "it has become harder and harder to separate what comes into science from the side of the investigator from what comes into it from the side of the investigated."[17] Against this post-factual approach, Spivak was a constant reminder that postcolonial allegorical readings, if they claim to be responsible, necessarily demand relating one's own intersectional positionality to the text to which one claims to respond. My first teacher, Munasu Bonny Duala M'bedy, brought to my attention that the so-called O/other, too, has a political existence and that, therefore, the cultural analysis of the dynamics of selving and othering needs

---

17   Clifford Geertz, *After the Fact: Two Countries, Four Decades, One Anthropologist* (Cambridge, MA: Harvard UP, 1995) 135.

to go beyond the interpretation of cultural sign systems.[18] Said, who was always somehow present, agreed and allowed for some strategic simplifications and essentialisms. Last but not least, Nietzsche showed up (often in Foucault's baggage) on the most unexpected occasions, insisting that I be true to myself against all conventions. I resisted as much as I could at some points, but allowed him to seduce me at others though I knew well that this could easily end up in a slightly contradictory undertaking.

However, the critical voice in the text that you read is basically my own. It is I who selected, re-composed, and interpretively reciprocated other people's representations. Hence, it is I who is responsible for the effects involved in such transposing. If I occasionally switch from the first person singular to the plural form 'we', this is not to place, or even hide, myself within an abstract academic *communitas* and thus to exonerate my own truth-claims from the inescapable epistemological nexus of intersecting positionalities, power relations, and knowledge production. I rather use the first person plural pronoun in the most naïvely inclusive sense to imagine a conversation *across* that does not disavow historically generated differences. It is up to the reader to selectively feel herself or himself included in such an interpersonal conversation or to resolutely reject the respective interpretive inclusion. It goes without saying that this study is not designed to trigger any unconditional interpretive identification with my arguments. In fact, it leaves my own relation to some positions unresolved. In these situations, I prefer to use the depersonalized subjunctive "one could" which, together with a vague "or," turns the notion of final statements and interpretive resolutions into one-sided preconceptions.

Again, my readings do not claim to inaugurate formerly unknown truths of local or translocal Arabness in relation to a clearly located Anglophone Westernness. Instead, they suggest alternative ways of relating oneself and responding to Anglophone Arab articulations. They are first and foremost meant to provide some theoretical, methodical, and interpretive innovations. That is what characterizes the different fragments of this book as essayistic offerings for hopefully continuing conversations on matters of shared interest across discrepant ethnic self-identifications, geographical and disciplinary locations, epistemological and linguistic filiations, or ideological pretentions. The absence of resolution or theoretical consistency is generic. For myself, reading Anglophone Arab representations marked a significant break with what I had done until that point as a literary and cultural critic, both regarding the project's extended frame of theoretical reference and interpretive tools as well as with a view to the particular extra-moral interest in the political poetics of art and literature. The following readings and theoretical mus-

---

18   Munasu Duala-M'bedy, *Xenologie: Die Wissenschaft vom Fremden und die Verdrängung der Humanität in der Anthropologie* (Freiburg: Alber, 1977).

ings, therefore, ask to be approached as documents of a necessarily open-ended starting out—a setting in motion...

A note on my spelling of Arabic names and terms: There are different approaches to the transcription and spelling of Arabic in Latin characters. In my view, no system works perfectly in all literary and extra-literary contexts. I have generally used the spellings of names and words as used by Anglophone Arab writers and artists themselves. If such spellings were not available, I have tried to approach a less-formal modern pronunciation that non-Arabic readers should find somewhat familiar and pronounceable. The avoidance of institutionalized academic transcriptions results from my conviction regarding the contemporariness of Anglophone Arab representation. My decision stresses these representations' modern, postmodern, and postcolonial worldliness instead of invoking that they are coming from a different world, a so-called classical Arabic and pre-modern literary tradition. The exception that proves this rule is the use of more formal spelling when pre-modern Arab writers and works are mentioned.

1. Endings as Desert(ed) Starts

> "I take a long breath, the air of anticipation."[1]

This is how Rabih Alameddine's 2013 novel *An Unnecessary Woman* ends. After Aliya, the fragile and equally eloquent Lebanese character at the center of the novel, has narrated her own tragic life story—the story of a lonely producer of unpublished (hence seemingly useless or at least *unnecessary*) Arabic literary transferences from English and French translations of works originally written in German, Italian, or Spanish—she decides for the first time to do direct translations of French or English novels into Arabic. No longer allowing the two former colonial languages to allegorically demarcate the limits of her own socio-psychological world, the elderly woman leaves the determination of what her next project will be to chance. The only thing she seems confident about is that she will give up translating from a second-order distance that doubly removes her from the source text. The toss-up regarding her next translational endeavor is between J. M. Coetzee's *Waiting for the Barbarians* (1980)[2] and Marguerite Yourcenar's *Mémoires d'Hadrien* (1951).[3] It shall be decided by a neighbor's way of stopping at her door: "If she rings my doorbell, my next project will be *Hadrian*, if she knocks, then it's *Barbarians*."[4] The reader does not learn what happens next. We are informed neither about the Arabic translator's future nor about her next translation's afterlife. Instead, the ending perpetuates the very moment of beginning a translation. Anticipating the possibility of other post-novelistic beginnings, it stresses the tension between the narrating self and the act of narrating itself.[5]

I will elaborate on the particular non-conclusiveness and importance of narrative beginnings in Alameddine's writing in a later chapter, and I shall repeatedly come back to the scandal of unpredictable cross-cultural translations throughout this study when discussing the various Anglophone Arab ways of managing the

---

1   Rabih Alameddine, *An Unnecessary Woman* (New York: Grove P, 2013) 291.
2   J. M. Coetzee, *Waiting for the Barbarians* (London: Secker & Warburg, 1980).
3   Marguerite Yourcenar, *Mémoires d'Hadrien* (Paris : Plon, 1951).
4   Alameddine, An *Unnecessary Woman* 291.
5   On the notion of the "postnovelistic," see Edward W. Said, *Beginnings: Intention and Method* (New York: Columbia UP; Basic, 1975) 18.

crisis of impossible filiation. At this point, however, it seems fair enough to use Alameddine's novel as a hint to pause and ask about the relevance of endings for our understanding of Anglophone Arab beginnings. In order to scrutinize what makes these beginnings unique, what they have invented or innovated, and if they are still charting possibilities of new inventive orders, I make the issue of discontinuity my initial question. To further underline the complex correlations of Anglophone Arab narrative beginnings with the world of cross-cultural representations and to sensitize oneself to their ambivalent estrangement or even dislocation from other Anglophone representations as well as their correspondence with non-Anglophone Arab discourses, I will first draw on two quasi-unending narratives by one of the most renowned and influential Arab writers of the 20th century. The literary fragments chosen for the following section do not comprise my final object of inquiry. They are literary vehicles to display certain issues that will be repeatedly encountered in the course of my systematic discussion of Anglophone Arab beginnings.

An-Nihayat (*Endings*) was first published in 1977.[6] 'Abd al-Rahman Munif's novel tells the story of the people of al-Tiba. Divided into two parts, each with a different narrative strategy and style, it eludes simple classification. The first part functions as an elaborated frame narrative for the polyphonic stories presented in the second part. The primary setting is liminal, both with regard to its geographical and environmental location and with a view to the socio-historical dynamics in which it is placed. An exact definition of place is not provided. Al-Tiba is a small village located right at the edge of a desert somewhere in the Arab world, sometime around the middle of the 20th century. Governmental authorities have ignored the vital needs of the patient villagers for generations. The fictional village's inhabitants urgently await a dam project that has been repeatedly postponed. Al-Tiba suffers from extended seasons of deadly drought and from the young generation's exodus to the newly emerging cities of the modern nation state. Thus, the village not only marks the beginning of the desert but also represents a social space radically changed by external ecological, political, and economic dynamics. The extradiegetic-heterodiegetic narrator's decisively detached, almost ethnographic descriptions are clearly of limited omniscience. S/he constantly speculates on different versions of the things and events s/he sets out to narrate, and s/he ruminates on plausible explanations for the many turns of those events. When the narrator describes social and ecological relationships without reciprocity, s/he does so not to resolve them in harmony but to evoke their endings as forces of change. Very early, the reader is warned that when "changes start occurring, no one can afford to make snap judgments."[7] It is only after a radical rupture provoked by the tremendous death of the

---

6   'Abd al-Rahman Munif, *An-Nihayat* (Beirut: Mu'assasa al-'Arabiyya lil-Dirasat wal-Nashr, 1977). 'Abd al-Rahman Munif, *Endings*, trans. Roger Allen (London: Quartet, 1988).

7   Munif, *Endings* 3.

solitary hunter, 'Assaf, that the initial narrative devices are significantly unsettled and the novel's second part begins. The village's eccentric outsider, who lives alone with his dog, dies in a sandstorm while reluctantly guiding visitors from the far city to the desert's over-exploited hunting spots. During the following "Remarkable Night"[8] of collective mourning, anonymous stories of grief take command to fully emancipate from the main narrator's account of what has happened. Now the reader is immersed in a narrative conglomerate of a particular quality that is already announced in the novel's opening section: The people of al-Tiba have a "special narrative technique,"[9] they "know how to turn a story in that incredible way which makes everything seem to be of primary importance."[10] Sorrows without end lead to multiple narrative beginnings. Series of tales of human and non-human beings, of stark differences and violent cohabitations, are told without any information being given on the individual narrative voices or their respective stories' origins. Instead of directly explaining why and how the half-nomadic 'Assaf had to meet his end, the novel's quasi-fabulous second part provides allegorical versions of the dead protagonist's individual history and al-Tiba's past. The anti-hero's ending not only leads to the collective tracing of local histories but also triggers stories that, by imagining relationships across seemingly intrinsic differences, test the boundaries of traditional spaces of belonging. In view of 'Assaf's death, storytelling becomes a practice of survival and transgression. The reader is informed about rich people from the city and other strangers who came to the village "from heaven knows where"[11] with dreadful Land Rovers. We hear of foreigners turning into demons who transform the desert into a space crisscrossed with roads, pierced by artificial light, and shattered by the roar of engines. We learn about local men turning into animals, about Bedouins who let themselves be corrupted by foreigners, as well as about guests from the city who are in charge and villagers who are never willing to say outright what they really want. The story of Al-'Azni, a crazy hunter from a neighboring village, is recounted—his tears, after having killed a goat, transform the surface of the desert. A feud between a dog and a crow is narrated along with tales of close relations between a dog and a shaykh and between a village-major and a dog. Stories of other animal-man relations that no one really wants to tell are only evoked, and fragments of stories that everyone always remembers are narrated. We listen to the story of a cat that commits suicide by throwing herself into an open fire. We hear fables from the *Kitab al-Hayawan* (*The Book of Animals*) by ninth-century Arabic polymath, Al-Jahiz,[12] and learn about the book's diverse

---

8   Munif, *Endings* 78.
9   Munif, *Endings* 7.
10   Munif, *Endings* 8.
11   Munif, *Endings* 79-80.
12   Abu 'Uthman 'Amr Ibn Bahr (born 776), known as Al-Jahiz, was a prose writer and author of more than two hundred theological, political-religious, polemical, and zoological works. His

sources.[13] Finally, the fourteenth and final story makes a full circle from the rumor of a relationship between an old woman and a dog, narrated by someone who had always had "deep-seated contempt for dogs in general,"[14] through the memory of an anonymous Arab narrator, whose love affair to some English woman called Linda finds its abrupt ending after they sleep together for the very first time, back to the novel's frame narrative, where 'Assaf's laid-out corpse creates an aura of endless storytelling.

Whereas the people of al-Tiba realize that the strange figure of 'Assaf proves almost prophetic with a view to what really endangers the community's life, the reader understands that silence does not necessarily mean a final ending: After "the longest night in al-Tiba's history went by,"[15] the corpse of the by now highly respected hunter is escorted to the village's graveyard. When the equally magical yet dignified ceremony of 'Assaf's burial ends, the men from al-Tiba and its neighboring villages set out for the city to put forward their political and infrastructural demands "for one last time."[16] The uncanny, almost exilic non-conclusion of the final paragraph invites the reader to stop and anticipate other stories set in other spaces and maybe told in other languages: "Once again silence reigned. All that could be heard was the sound of the cars on the asphalt road as they headed for the city."[17]

Munif's tentative *Endings* remind us that death is not the end and that a beginning necessarily follows an ending. It does so literally, allegorically, as well as metafictionally. Although the frame narrative comes to an end, there is no definite close. Instead, this novel's ending without closure enables the imagining of futures with the possibility of (narrative) beginnings across and amongst divides. This beginning-vision of a shared community in the face of difference placed in the book's final pages is the equally simple yet striking message of *Endings*.[18] On a metafictional level, the novel calls for a relational Arab literature that *begins* to engage creatively with what is usually juxtaposed as strange and foreign within and beyond the so-called Arab world. As I will demonstrate in the following chapters, this particular concern with the inevitability and pitfalls of narrative or performative beginnings across and amongst allegedly fixed cultural dispositives—the will

---

        Book of Animals is a seven-volume encyclopedia of philosophical anecdotes, poetic representations, and fables describing over 350 varieties of animals and an early theory of biological evolution.

13   For details, see James E. Montgomery, *Al-Jāḥiẓ: In Praise of Books*, Edinburgh Studies in Classical Arabic Literature (Edinburgh: Edinburgh UP, 2013).

14   Munif, *Endings* 127.

15   Munif, *Endings* 134.

16   Munif, *Endings* 139.

17   Munif, *Endings* 140.

18   Mary N. Layoun, "Endings and Beginnings: Reimagining the Tasks and Spaces of Comparison," *New Literary History* 40.3 (2009): 583-607.

to begin and begin again in order to create new meaning of correlational ways of being in and between worlds—is at the core of many Anglophone Arab representations.

For Munif, the "Arabian Master"[19] of multiple Saudi, Jordanian, Algerian, Yugoslavian, French, Iraqi, Lebanese, and Syrian (af)filiations,[20] *Endings* was to be the prelude of his celebrated five-part work, *Mudun al-Milh* (*Cities of Salt*).[21] While the American writer, John Updike, denounced his Arab colleague as "insufficiently Westernized to produce a narrative that feels much like what we call a novel,"[22] the monumental Arabic narrative has been praised by the late Edward Said for being "the only serious work of fiction that tries to show the effect on a gulf country of oil, Americans and local oligarchy."[23] It is particularly the quintet's widely read first novel, *Al-Tih* (*The Wilderness*), that traces this cross-cultural encounter.[24] A cursory reading of the pentalogy's inaugural book already shows many of the topical foci, discursive references, and representational devices that one regularly encounters in contemporary Anglophone Arab narratives. Mainly written in Parisian exile and set in an unnamed Gulf kingdom in the 1930s, *Al-Tih* addresses the socio-political changes that have determined the region's modern history following the discovery of oil there. By doing so, it fictionally reclaims fragmented versions of an Arab past largely neglected in both dominant Arab and Western representations. On the surface, this alternative script of recent Arab history simply provides a tribal saga of loss and radical transformation. But, by narrating "the triumph of one particular tribe over the others through treachery, violence, manipulation of religious dogma and the enlisting of foreign support,"[25] this novel of mixed grotesque-mythopoetic style articulates a barely hidden critique of the House of Saud[26] and its Western allies. At the same time, it places local or localized texts in relation to a larger global

---

19   Sabry Hafez, "An Arabian Master," *New Left Review* 37 (Jan.-Feb. 2006): 39-66.

20   On the details of Munif's multilayered private, political, and professional life across five countries, see Hafez, "An Arabian Master," 39-54.

21   Only three of the five novels were translated into English: 'Abd al-Rahman Munif, *Cities of Salt* (*Cities of Salt*, vol. 1), trans. Peter Theroux (New York: Random House, 1987); *The Trench* (*Cities of Salt*, vol. 2), trans. Peter Theroux (New York: Pantheon, 1991); *Variations on Night and Day* (*Cities of Salt*, vol. 3), trans. Peter Theroux (New York: Pantheon, 1993).

22   Updike reduces the novelist's many narrative voices to one: "that of a campfire explainer." John Updike, "Satan's Work and Silted Cisterns," Rev. of *Cities of Salt*, by Abdelrahman Munif, *New Yorker* 17 Oct. 1988: 117-21.

23   Edward W. Said, "Embargoed Literature," (17 Sept. 1990), *The Best of The Nation: Selections from the Independent Magazine of Politics and Culture*, eds. Victor Navasky and Katrina vanden Heuvel (New York: Thunder's Mouth P / Nation Books, 2000) 57.

24   'Abd al-Rahman Munif, *Al-Tih* (Beirut: Mu'assasa al-'Arabiyya lil-Dirasat wal-Nashr, 1984). In the following, I quote from Munif, *Cities of Salt* (*Cities of Salt*, vol. 1), trans. Peter Theroux (New York: Vintage, 1989).

25   Hafez, "An Arabian Master," 56.

26   Saudi Arabia's ruling family/tribe.

text. Telling the story of a fictional oasis community, its subsequent disruption, and its diasporic relocation in the new dual Arab/American city of Harran, Munif's petrofiction[27] illustrates what the writer himself has described as the main factors "that led to the collapse, confusion, and consequently to the suffering lived by Arab societies in their search for the road to modernity."[28]

Soon after the first engineers of an American oil company arrive with their translators, and after their "hellish machines,"[29] supported by the local emir, have destroyed the oasis of Wadi al-Uyoun, the demolition of the old coastal town, Harran, begins. In its place grows a city-space with two strictly separated sectors. American Harran is the new port location of the oil company's headquarters, a gated community of extraterritorial Western exceptionalism. New Arab Harran, in turn, represents the local life of an emerging emirate floating on oil money. The narrated world is a hierarchical world divided into mutually excluding compartments. This almost Manicheistic socio-spatial order is further intensified by the barbed-wire-fenced barracks of uprooted Bedouins, foreign Arab workers, and other migrant laborer located between the two Harrans. The camp is controlled by the emir's men by means of constant surveillance and repressive persuasion. The forcibly segregated and exploited migrant workers are made desolate prisoners of two communities which are already imprisoned in themselves. Munif, who, at least since his 1975 novel, *Sharq al-Mutawassit (East of the Mediterranean)*,[30] has advanced to the prototypical proponent of so-called Arab torture and prison fiction,[31] multiplies the literary trope of imprisonment in *Al-Tih*, rendering a new allegorical dimension:

> The depression was never deeper than when the workers looked around them to see, in the east, American Harran: lit up, shining and noisy, covered with budding vegetation; from afar they could hear the voices of the Americans splashing in the swimming pools, rising in song or laughter. On some nights they filled the

---

27   Amitav Gosh, "Petrofiction: The Oil Encounter and the Novel," *The New Republic* 2 Mar. 1992: 29-33.

28   'Abd al-Rahman Munif, Interview, "Unpublished Munif Interview: Crisis in the Arab World—Oil, Political Islam, and Dictatorship," by Iskandar Habash, trans. Elie Chalala, *Al-Jadid Magazine* 2003, 14 May 2015 <http://www.aljadid.com/content/unpublished-munif-interview-crisis-arab-world-%E2%80%93-oil-political-islam-and-dictatorship>.

29   Munif, *Cities of Salt* 184.

30   'Abd al-Rahman Munif, *Sharq al-Mutawassit* (Beirut: Mu'assasa al-'Arabiyya lil-Dirasaat wal-Nashr, 1975).

31   In fact, the trope of imprisonment, although not completely new, would become one of the most prevalent in modern Arabic literature after Munif's *East of the Mediterranean*; see Elias Khoury, "Writing the Novel Anew: East of the Mediterranean and now and here or East of the Mediterranean once again," ed. Sonja Mejcher-Atassi, *MIT Electronic Journal of Middle East Studies: Special Focus Writing: a 'Tool for Change': 'Abd al-Rahman Munif Remembered* 7 (2007): 70-76.

sky with colored fireworks, particularly when new groups of Americans arrived. To the west were the houses of Harran, from which smoke rose at sundown and the sounds of human and animal life came. Last of all they saw the barracks they lived in and this dry, harsh, remote life, at which point memories flooded back and their hearts ached with longing, and they found endless pretexts for quarrels and sorrow, and sometimes tears.[32]

The oil-encounter's diverse worlds exist in an unequal relationship of fetishistic identification and discriminatory enunciation of intrinsic difference. The novel traces the splitting of a sometimes reluctantly globalizing Arab self which, although made entirely knowable and visible in its difference, is totally disavowed regarding its own subject position within the Westerner's stereotypical monologue. These dynamics first become obvious when a massive American ship with glittering lights and seemingly naked women and men dancing on its deck to the rhythms of party music drops its anchor at the shore of Harran at sunset. The events that follow dramatically turn from moral shame, laughing surprise, and voyeuristic desire to hopeful expectations, uncertain worries, and deep fears regarding the local community's future. Right after the villagers and the men from the worker's compound come to the beach to follow the procession of celebrants entering American Harran, it becomes clear that their longing gaze is not returned by those who are gazed at: "'The American sons of bitches!' said one man angrily. 'They don't even mind if we watch—we are not better than animals to them.'"[33] The psychological and political implications of Arabs looking at Americans without being seen as humans by those very same Americans are manifold. On the one hand, the narrative fragment represents the pain of symbolic castration caused by being denied the force of one's own gaze and by the lost object of re-gazing alterity. On the other hand, it illustrates the modalities of a neo-imperial hegemony that works through absence and invisibility rather than through voyeuristic exhibitionism. In addition, the narration of impossible narcissistic identification clearly has a moment of sexual perversion. The Arabs of Harran both resist and insist upon being fixed as passive objects of "to-be-looked-at-ness"[34] and scopic knowledge by reversing the spectacle of Orientalist voyeurism. In this context, the local baker Abdu Mohammad's passion for collecting and exhibiting pictures from foreign magazines and his painfully imagined love affair with one of the female pinups has a particular fetishistic quality. The hashish smoker and user of other narcotics is worshiping a picture of a woman which he has found in a magazine and which he claims is a picture of one of the women on the American ship:

---

32   Munif, *Cities of Salt* 295.
33   Munif, *Cities of Salt* 216.
34   I borrow this term from British feminist film theorist, Laura Mulvey, "Visual Pleasure and Narrative Cinema," *Screen* 16.3 (1975): 6-18.

"As soon as she landed she looked at me. She left all the rest of them and looked at me. She did not leave me!" He paused and then went on as if talking to himself. "She was smiling happily, she was laughing. The day the ship left she left the others and kept looking at me and smiling. Even when the ship was sailing away she kept waving and smiling."[35]

The arrival of what the people of Harran variously coin "King Salomon's ship" or "Satan's ship"[36] marks a narrative turn and the beginning of a new era: "[M]ost people have no memory of Harran before that day."[37] The city's infrastructural and organizational growth is characterized by the people of Arab Harran's highly ambivalent exchanges and their often contradictory relationship with the American presence.

The remaining parts of *Cities of Salt* narrate how the oil company uses local leaders to gradually expand its power while keeping ordinary Arabs outside their gated private world. The Americans spend most of their time in "their air-conditioned rooms whose sick wall curtains shut everything out: sunlight, dust, flies and Arabs."[38] At the same time, they are not only intensifying their endeavors of classifying, controlling, and disciplining the workers of the camp but also frequently visit Arab Harran. In these situations, the Americans behave like hybrids of small children and professional anthropologists, taking photographs, asking naïve questions, and making notes on every detail. When a group of extraordinarily excited Westerners attends a wedding in new Harran, the Arab men sing sad songs of Harran's bygone days: songs "of a life that was coming to an end."[39] To the foreign guests, these singing men immersed in sorrow "become creatures of another species."[40] The American Sinclair, who pretends to understand Arabic and the Arab mind, explains to his fellow Americans:

Weeping relieves them, but they are hard people, and stubborn. They weep inside—their tears fall inside them and are extinguished again by the shouting and lamentations they call song." [...] A moment later he added sarcastically, "They call this music!" [...] "You never know whether they're sad or happy [...] Look, look—now they are expressing happiness!" After listening for a while he added, "They're like animals—jostling each other and moving around in this primitive way to express their happiness. Imagine!"[41]

---

35   Munif, *Cities of Salt* 249.
36   Munif, *Cities of Salt* 223.
37   Munif, *Cities of Salt* 215.
38   Munif, *Cities of Salt* 391.
39   Munif, *Cities of Salt* 264.
40   Munif, *Cities of Salt* 266.
41   Munif, *Cities of Salt* 267.

At another occasion, a sword-dance is performed for the American guests of the emir. But this time the latter does not permit his men to sing for the foreign guests: "'If we sing for them today, then tomorrow they'll want us to dance for them, like monkeys'."[42] The Arab American party finds its sudden end.

The radical challenge of the oil-encounter has two presumably mutually exclusive but interdependent effects. On the one hand, it increasingly transforms Harran into a heterogeneous international non-place and thus questions the traditional notion of clearly located and distinguishable forms of belonging. On the other hand, the very dynamics of radical displacement cannot be lived out on dialogically equal terms. Neither Arabs nor Americans find cultural and political articulations for their complex coexistence.[43] There is a decisive reluctance on all sides to express the experience of multiple identitarian dislocations, either in representational or in organizational forms. This leads to the affirmation rather than to the dissolving of simple binary constructions of mutually exclusive collectivities: "The Americans are godless. They are infidels, they know nothing but 'Work, work, work. Arabs are lazy, Arabs are liars, Arabs don't understand.'"[44] With the passage of time and the retelling of Arab-American encounters, the image of the respective other is distorted further. The novel does not provide coherent accounts of such cross-cultural encounters but narrates how the people of Harran recount them. The problem of intertwined but mutually exclusive stories is not restricted to the difference between Arab and American narratives of what happened but also concerns competing versions of a single event within each group.[45]

Al-Tih ends with a labor strike triggered by the murder of an Arab worker and violently quelled by the emir's police with the help of the newly installed American emergence unit.[46] Although portending a basically open and unreadable future, the bloody ending of the local conflict signals the danger of continuing conflicts between and among cultural divides. At least at one moment, the narrative anticipates a cross-cultural encounter and potential conflict that significantly transgresses the boundaries of the novel's primary linguistic mode and geographical setting. When the Arab workers are interviewed by the Americans to determine their functional classification and political-ideological stance, some are asked if they could imagine going to the US for professional training and to learn English. Ibrahim, one of those interviewed, answers that question with a clear "No."[47] To the

---

42   Munif, *Cities of Salt* 282.
43   Cf. Gosh, "Petrofiction: The Oil Encounter and the Novel," 29-33.
44   Munif, *Cities of Salt* 415.
45   See, for instance, Chapter 40, which depicts the emir's visit to American Harran and the American reverse-reception as well as the ways these events are remembered and commented upon by the people; Munif, *Cities of Salt* 277-83.
46   Munif, *Cities of Salt* 603pp.
47   Munif, *Cities of Salt* 326.

repeated enquiry regarding the reasons for his adamant refusal of the American oil company's generous offer, he responds, laughing loudly: "The jackal is a lion in his home country."[48]

Munif's way of storytelling has inspired younger writers throughout the Arab world and beyond. Given his enormous popularity with Arab readers and literary critics, his vision of splitting subjectivities and his anticipation of translocal double visions must surely have had an impact on Anglophone Arab representations as well.[49] I cannot exhaustively recapitulate Munif's many Arabic narrative endings which conceivably anteceded Anglophone Arab arts and literatures. My highly selective reading of Munif's fiction aims instead at complicating the notion of beginnings as something one thinks about as a logical point of departure for writing about Anglophone Arab representations. It is meant to sensitize the reader to the importance of endings or the illusions of endings (Arab and non-Arab alike) as the condition for any Anglophone Arab beginning. The brief excursion into Munif's narrative stopovers aims at directing particular attention to those tentative endings that, instead of marking narrative closure, open up imaginary spaces for stories not yet told. It might be true that beginnings are by definition pregnant with narrative possibilities, and many critics will further agree with the idea that every beginning is necessarily the beginning of an end. But narrative endings, archival breaks, discursive pauses, and other forms of cultural discontinuities do anticipate a much broader spectrum of possible futures; critics working in the field of Anglophone Arab studies should keep that in mind. In my view, there is a particular need to see that the beginnings of Anglophone Arab representations cannot possibly be located within a clearly demarcated sphere of first Anglophone articulations by ethnic Arab writers. Nor can we restrict our critical endeavor to the study of Anglophone Arab culture as a necessarily diasporic, ethnic immigrant, or transmigrant culture. Only if one first truly grasps what cannot and should not be definitely grasped in terms of cultural originality and authenticity, authorial ethnicity, contextual genesis, or linguistic specificity can one then go on to try it anyway and ask what an Anglophone Arab beginning is or ought to be. Thus, let me begin again.

---

48   Munif, *Cities of Salt* 327.
49   Tariq Ali, "A Patriarch of Arab Literature," *Counterpunch* 1 Feb. 2004.

2. Beginnings as Cultural Novelties: Intertexts and Discursive Affinities

How can one locate the beginning of the particular Anglophone Arab cultural sphere that this study seeks to explore? Can one at all designate such a single point zero or point of departure for the complex representational dynamics at stake? Should one really try to isolate any particular moment in time or any individual work retrospectively? Given the many historical ruptures, suppressed histories, and counter-memories, cultural discontinuities and ahistorical absurdities, self-totalizing truth claims, non-senses, and counter-knowledges that have molested Anglophone Arab representations and that have formed and informed these representations' particular non-essentialist quality, it seems rather misleading to raise the question of originality as a beginning question. However, in order to understand these cultural articulations as decentered responses to the crisis of presumably clearly located origins, linear filiations, unquestioned authenticities, and universal authorities, one cannot thoroughly avoid re-turning to at least some semi-inaugural works, quasi-initiating starting points, or decisive stop-overs. If one seriously wants to treat Anglophone Arab representations as equally creative and critical interventions—as distinctive (re-)assemblings of texts, images, and narrative modes which are formed and performed under shifting socio-historical conditions—then one needs at least to acknowledge their plural beginnings. Without arguing for a logic of first steps from which a coherent cultural practice linearly develops and without evoking any clear transitivity or direct influence, this chapter designates selected literary beginnings as early and particularly innovative ways of making Anglophone Arab meaning. Neither does it aim at rediscovering or inventing a unique tradition nor does it claim to lay bare individual and collective agencies or to recapitulate the respective works' immediate worldly effects.

Such historical tracing of narrative directions of accomplishments in the Anglophone Arab production of difference—one might call these directions cultural novelties—will ultimately, if sometimes involuntarily, raise questions of contexts, and of by no means exclusively Anglophone inter-texts. Moreover, it will evoke considerations of authorship and authority or trigger perspectives on genres, generations, influences, translations, and disseminations. The discovery of insights with regard to these aspects is not my primary purpose. However, since the endeavor of locating Anglophone Arab beginnings as acts of *différance* is closely related to the problem of discursivity and competing notions of criticism,[1] the following discussion necessarily involves historical, theoretical, and practical issues in equal measure. While my interest in Anglophone Arab beginnings is somehow paradoxically the result of not believing that any singular origin can be located, the rationale for the quasi-substitutional undertaking presented here derives from the attempt to place both this study's main subject matter and my own ways of reading within the historical conditions of their mutual appearance. By connecting cultural representation and its critique to the sociopolitical discourses around both practices of which they are a part, I try to unite my own critical intention with a method.[2] If the practical need of naming beginnings at the same time opens possibilities of theoretically (re-)framing and allegorically (re-)reading or even strategically misreading Anglophone Arab representations (early and contemporary ones alike) with a necessary portion of selective blindness and critical insight,[3] then this chapter has more than fulfilled its initial function.

2.1   Pulling Apart or Pushing Together: Relations of Alterity and Critical Instrumentality

Of course, there have been entextualizations of Anglo-Arab encounters long before 'Abd al-Rahman Munif set out to find a literary expression for the American-Arab oil encounter of the 20th century. And one can certainly find examples of similar textual encodings produced much earlier than the temporal setting of Munif's narrative encounters suggests. Most literary and cultural critics—Arab and Western

---

1   This question is at the core of Edward W. Said's still underestimated and, within postcolonial criticism, all-too-often neglected study, *Beginnings: Intention and Method* (New York: Columbia UP; Basic Books, 1975). Said's important theoretical study must surely have fed into my own approach, here and beyond, more than surreptitiously. I will elaborate on my by no means unconditional affiliation to Said's criticism in a later section of this study. For a detailed discussion of *Beginnings* and its importance for the cross-cultural genesis and impact of Said's oeuvre, see my *Kulturkritik ohne Zentrum. Edward W. Said und die Kontrapunkte kritischer Dekolonisation* (Bielefeld: Transcript, 2008) 98–118.

2   Said, *Beginnings* 380.

3   On the use of the concept of allegory as a reading strategy (a way of reading and interpretation that self-critically takes into consideration competing assertions of truth or falsehood linked to specific modes of figuration), see Paul de Man, *Blindness and Insight: Essays on the Rhetoric of Contemporary Criticism* (New York: Oxford UP, 1971) and Paul de Man, *Allegories of Reading. Figural Language in Rousseau, Nietzsche, Rilke, and Proust* (New Haven: Yale UP, 1979). See also, on the notion of misreading or literary misprision related to the reader's specific location, Harald Bloom, *The Anxiety of Influence: A Theory of Poetry* (New York: Oxford UP, 1973).

alike—would actually argue that the emergence of modern Arab culture in general and the rise of the Arabic novel in particular are to a large extent determined by the encounter with non-Arab conceptions of (literary) modernity. According to these scholars' unidirectional teleology, early novelistic writing in Arabic was essentially a late 19th century derivative from Europe. Following their literary historiography, it was only with the 1913 publication of Muhammad Husayn Haykal's *Zaynab* that Arab writers started to produce *real* Arabic novels, thus arriving at the stage of its self-realization as a properly national genre.[4]

For the purpose of my study, I see no need to discuss the misleading question of whether the Arabic novel must be seen as an intrinsically Western genre imported into Arab narrative culture. In my view, not only does such a question risk simplifying the dynamic process of acculturation and transculturation but it is also grounded in an organizational and interpretive system of national literatures produced by writers who can be clearly identified as national subjects. The tentative questioning already takes for granted the very conventional colonial-nationalist ideology of cultural belonging, which is radically questioned in many Anglophone Arab representations and in this study.[5] As manifest, for instance, in the autobiographies of the Egyptian icon of modern Arab literature and criticism, Taha Hussein,[6] early modern literary articulations in Arabic draw directly from the simultaneous experience of discrepant modernities. However, they cannot be grasped as a one-way process of imitating incorporation. Sure, early modern Arab articulations have often been formed between competing epistemological, ideological, and linguistic worlds—worlds that seemed to pull those seeking to articulate themselves in equally different directions. However, Hussein's work illustrates how the often unbearable challenge of seemingly splitting identities within de facto increasingly overlapping worlds at the same time triggered a complex transgression of learned

---

4   See the influential essay by H. A. R. Gibb, "Studies in Contemporary Arabic Literature," *Bulletin of the School of Oriental and African Studies* 7.1 (1933): 1-22. For more recent discussions, Ibrahim Abu-Lughod, *The Arab Rediscovery of Europe: A Study in Cultural Encounters* (Princeton, NJ: Princeton UP, 1963); Issa J. Boullata, *Critical Perspectives on Modern Arab Literature* (Washington: Three Continents, 1980); Sabry Hafez, *The Genesis of Arabic Narrative Discourse* (London: Saqi, 1993); Roger Allen, *The Arabic Novel. An Historical and Critical Introduction*, 2nd ed. (1982; Syracuse: Syracuse UP, 1995).

5   For an alternative poststructuralist tracing of Arab (literary) modernity and the critique of the dominant derivative thesis with a particular focus on the often neglected or devaluated popular fiction, see Samah Selim, "The Nahdah, Popular Fiction and the Politics of Translation," *MIT Electronic Journal of Middle East Studies* 4 (2004): 71-89.

6   Taha Hussein, *Al-Ayam*, 1-3 (Beirut: Dar al-Kitab al-Lubnani, 1982); *The Days*, trans. E. H. Paxton, Hilary Wayment, and Kenneth Cragg, 2nd ed. (Cairo: AUC P, 2000).

boundaries of thought and narrative practice that was decisively more than just the result of any unidirectional cultural adaptation.[7]

As Radwa Ashour's 2003 allegorical-historical novel, *Qit'a min Urubba: Riwayya* (A Part of Europe: A Novel),[8] impressively testifies by fictionally tracing Cairo and Egypt's relationship to Europe, the historical quest of Arab modernity was concerned very early on with the question of whether or not and—if so—how to emulate Western models of modernization without affirming these models' colonial-orientalist aspirations. In fact, since at least the early 19th century, such a search for a distinctive Arab modernity based on the selective appropriation of European science and technology was at the core of the Arab *Nahda*, the literary and cultural discourse of the so-called Arab renaissance in what Albert Hourani coined the *Liberal Age*.[9] Rifa'a at-Tahtawi's inaugural publication of the reformist movement, *Takhlis al-Ibriz fi Talkhis Bariz*,[10] already proved the importance of educational travels to Europe and translations from European writings for Arab intellectuals. Drawing on his four-year stay in France as the religious head of a group of young Egyptian scholars sent to study in Paris by Mohammad 'Ali, the 1834 publication offers a transgeneric mix of travel account, memoir, and social anthropological treatise. The book's topical framework ranges from descriptions of everyday Parisian life and a detailed analysis of the French educational system to the critique of the host country's political (dis-)order, including the events of the revolution of July 1830. The French writers directly addressed in this seminal *Nahda*-text include Montesquieu, Voltaire, and Rousseau. After his return to Egypt, at-Tahtawi would advance to an eminent Arabic translator of French technological, historical, political, and legalistic works, including the Code Napoléon.[11]

In the context of my discussion, Jamal Ad-Din al-Afghani's later exilic voyage into the center of Western learning has quite a different and even more paradigmatic quality. His critical response to Ernest Renan's 1883 lecture, "L'Islamisme et

---

7   Hussein, *The Days* 232; on Hussein's autobiographical writing, see Fedwa Multi-Douglas, *Blindness & Autobiography: Al-Ayām of Tāhā Ḥussain* (Princeton: Princeton UP, 1988) as well as Ed de Moor, "Autobiography, Theory and Practice: the Case of Al-Ayyām," *Writing the Self: Autobiographical Writing in Modern Arabic Literature*, eds. Robin Ostle, Ed de Moor, and Stefan Wild (London: Saqi, 1998) 128-38. On Hussein's criticism, see Louay M. Safi, *The Challenge of Modernity. The Quest of Authenticity in the Arab World* (Lanham, MD: UP of America 1994).

8   Radwa Ashour, *Qit'a min Urubba* (Cairo: Dar ash-Shouruq, 2003).

9   Albert Hourani, *Arabic Thought in the Liberal Age 1798–1939* (London: Oxford UP, 1962).

10   Rifa'a at-Tahtawi, *Takhlis al-Ibriz fi Talkhis Baris aw al-Diwan al-Nafis bi-Iwan Baris* (1834; Beirut: Mu'assasa al-'Arabiyya lil-Dirasat wal-Nashr, 2002). The title translates as: The extrication of gold in summarizing Paris, or the valuable collection in the drawing room of Paris. For an annotated English translation, see Daniel L. Newman, *Rifā'ah Rāfi' Ṭahṭāwī. An Imam in Paris: Account of a Stay in France by an Egyptian Cleric (1826–1831)* (London: Saqi, 2004).

11   Muhammad Hijazi, ed., *Usul al-Fikr al-'Arabi al-Hadith 'inda at-Tahtawi — Tahtawi and the Roots of Modern Arab Thought* (Cairo: Al-Hay'a al-Misriya al-'Ala lil-Kitab, 1974).

la science," appeared in Sorbonne University's prestigious *Journal des débats*.[12] The pan-Islamic modernist, anti-colonial theorist, and transnational public intellectual was particularly upset by the prominent French Orientalist's Eurocentric notion of a transhistorical *homo islamicus* who is by definition incapable of rational scientific thinking. In his short open letter, Al-Afghani frankly accused Renan of reducing the long and diverse history of Islamic thinking to a quasi-biological essence and thus constructing an image of Arabs and Muslims who, due to their intrinsic lack of rationality, are cursed to stagnate in backwardness unless they are liberated by the germ of Western reason. Afghani's broadly received refutation of Renan's colonialist-racist argument probably marks the first dissenting intervention by a Middle Eastern intellectual into the until then almost completely self-referential discourse of European Orientalism. What is significant about the Arab critic's critique in the context of my study is that Afghani intervenes from within (and in the language of) that very discourse.[13]

Given the increased prominence of the British as a major colonial power in the Middle East since the early 19th century and the growing US-American involvement in the region during the 20th and 21st centuries, it does not come as a surprise that, within the debates on Arab modernity and cross-cultural contacts, the English-speaking world, too, was (and is so to this day) a particularly important point of reference. The early modern period, when England laid the groundwork for its global empire, already offers a wide range of economic, political, and cultural contacts and forms of coexistence between Arabs and Britons. In fact, Arabs and other Muslims "represented the most widely visible non-Christian people on English soil in this period."[14] At the time of Queen Elizabeth I's government, Britain had very close relations with both the Ottoman Empire and various North African states, whether this took the form of Ottoman ambassadors visiting London and Arab merchants coming to Dover or of British privateers shipping off the coast of Tangier and English merchants held in captivity in Algiers. Although these early encounters surely must have fed into inner-Arab and diasporic Arab representations of cultural otherness and cross-cultural contact both in Arabic and the English language, the available sources consist chiefly of accounts of ambassadors and royal

---

12   Renan's Sorbonne lecture, *L'Islamisme et la science*, has been translated by Sally P. Ragep as *Islam and Science: A Lecture Presented at La Sorbonne 29 March 1883 by Ernest Renan, 2nd Edition* (Montréal: McGill U, 2011). For Afghani's Renan critique, see Nikki R. Keddie, "Response of Jamal al-Din to Renan," *An Islamic Response to Imperialism. Political and Religious Writings of Jamal al-Din al-Afghani*, by Nikki R. Keddie, new ed. (1968; Berkeley: U of California P, 1983) 181-89.

13   Nikki R. Keddie, "Afghānī, Jamāl al-Dīn (1838–1897)," *The Oxford Encyclopedia of Philosophy, Science, and Technology in Islam*, Vol. 1, ed. Ibrahim Kalin (Oxford: Oxford UP, 2014) 9-14.

14   Nabil I. Matar, *Turks, Moors and Englishmen in the Age of Discovery* (New York: Columbia UP, 1999) 3.

scribes, official reports of historical events like Christian invasions or Muslim captivity in Christendom, as well as early geographical studies and travelogues. More recent microhistorical subaltern studies of Arab-European encounters show that the Arabic-speaking communities of North Africa had already formed a non-elite multi-vocal narrative of the Europeans from the late 16th century onwards. Yet, early modern Arab representations of the West remained by far narrower in scope than Western representations of the Arab world.[15]

While early modern British cultural production ranged from translations of Arabic religious, alchemic, astronomic, and philosophical texts to Christian anti-Muslim polemics and eschatological fantasy or Renaissance plays dealing with Arabs and Muslims and Euro-Arab exchanges, there is hardly any fictional representation of cross-cultural encounters by Arab writers in English before the early 20th century.[16] One would indeed have to undertake a separate archival study of Arab diplomatic history and Arab popular accounts to trace the perspectives of those who from the early 16th century onward began to be categorized as barbarians by British and other European writers alongside the natives of North America so that "by the end of the seventeenth century the Muslim 'savage' and the Indian 'savage' became completely superimposable in English thought and ideology."[17] Indeed, the records and writings of Britons who spent time in North African captivity before arriving in what they called New England have been retrospectively incorporated into early American national narratives as quasi proto-national texts.[18] Such imaginative superimposing of distant Anglo-Arab encounters onto the new world's narrative topography would be supplemented after American independence in 1776 by first hand-experiences of life in so-called Arab Barbary captivity or the related Barbary Wars, such as the Tripolitan War (1801–1805) or the war of Algiers (1815–1816), as well as by the cultural incorporation of those experiences into the national archive.[19] What is however rarely acknowledged in debates about Arab-American migrations is that Arabic-speaking Africans arrived

---

15   Nabil I. Matar, *Europe Through Arab Eyes, 1578–1727* (New York: Columbia UP, 2009) 3-28.

16   For the early modern representation of Islam and the Muslim-British encounter in English, see Nabil I. Matar, *Islam in Britain, 1558–1685* (Cambridge: Cambridge UP, 1998) as well as Geoffrey Nash, *Writing Muslim Identity* (London: Continuum, 2012); for the representation of Europe in the Arabic letters and accounts of Arab travelers, captives, and diplomatic chroniclers, see Nabil I. Matar, ed. and trans., *In the Lands of Christians: Arabic Travel Writing in the Seventeenth Century* (New York: Routledge, 2003) and Matar, *Europe through Arab Eyes, 1578–1727*.

17   Matar, *Turks, Moors and Englishmen in the Age of Discovery* 155.

18   Nicole Waller, *American Encounters with Islam in the Atlantic World* (Heidelberg: Winter, 2011) 45-130.

19   Waller, *American Encounters with Islam in the Atlantic World* 131-70.

in both Americas long before the late 19th century Arab immigration from the provinces of the Ottoman empire.[20]

My study cannot possibly cover Arab representations of Europe, the US, and Australia in the *longue durée*. It will only address the enormous corpus of 20th and 21st century literary fiction and artistic production in Arabic, dealing with the so-called East-West encounter very selectively.[21] Particularly the hidden (non-public and/or non-canonized) dispositive of this encounter is much more complex than one would expect. Recent archival discoveries demonstrate that there is still a vast archive of forgotten Arabic popular literary texts, polemics, and pamphlets on the Anglo-Arab encounter that might allow rethinking 19th century Arab literary history in its relation to Western literature and questioning the basic binary premise of the European origin of Arab modernity. Again, my study does not aim at contributing to the ongoing scholarly debate on the historical formation of modern novelistic writing in Arabic. It does not ask when the genre emerged in the Arabic language.[22] What my readings nevertheless have in common with recent attempts to critically revisit and transgress the Western-Orientalist and Arab-nationalist literary canon of Arab modernity is the interest in cultural representations that are bypassing or mutilating these canons' equally essentialist conceptualizations of subjectivity. Of course, such shared interest alone does not allow for the formulation of comparative narrative morphologies between early Arabic popular fiction and early Anglophone Arab writing. But it seems to me to be a necessary prerequisite for any transnational interpretation of Anglophone Arab/Arabic beginnings that seeks to disrupt the institutional and moral conventions of West-Eastern representational accountability. Whereas I will show that some Anglophone Arab works indeed participate in the real or fictional re-discovery and reinterpretation of lost and forgotten or excluded archives that elude simple cultural locations, I myself did not go to the national libraries of Egypt and Lebanon or to the rare books collections of the regions' universities to search for such subaltern Arabic or English documents. Nor was it my aim to comprehensively trace the flourishing of Anglophone Orientalist portrayals of Arabs and Anglo-Arab encounters in Western visual arts and litera-

---

20   See Michael Gomez, *Black Crescent: The Experience and Legacy of African Muslims in the Americas* (New York: Cambridge UP, 2005).

21   Rasheed El-Enany, *Arab Representations of the Occident: East-West Encounters in Arabic Fiction* (New York: Routledge, 2006).

22   See, for instance, Samah Selim, "The Nahdah, Popular Fiction and the Politics of Translation," *MIT Electronic Journal of Middle East Studies* 4 (2004): 71-89 and Rebecca C. Johnson, "Importing the novel. Arabic literature's forgotten foreign objects," *On the Ground: New Directions in Middle East and North African Studies*, ed. Brian T. Edwards (Northwestern U in Qatar, 2015) n. pag. <http://ontheground.qatar.northwestern.edu/uncategorized/chapter-7-importing-the-novel-arabic-literatures-foreign-objects/>.

ture, travel accounts, plays, ethnographies, histories, or political rhetoric since the 18th century.

While early Arab discourses of alterity and notably early Arab articulations of diasporic experiences must still be seen as a severely understudied and at best emergent field, the bi-directional nexus between modern Western representations of Arabs and the execution of imperial power has been extensively explored by scholars of diverse disciplinary backgrounds.[23] For the purpose of my study, Western Orientalist texts or images and Arab Occidentalist representations naturally make up an important, almost trans-historic matrix of overlapping (mis-)representations within and against which many of the more recent Anglophone-Arab articulations (still have to) position themselves. When directly indicated in an individual work and if necessary for my argument, the respective narrative pixels of this broader discursive formation will be selectively referred to in the following chapters.

At this point, however, my search for beginnings and intertextualities within 20th century Anglophone literary articulations of cross-cultural Arab trajectories is primarily directed at self-positionings and narrative strategies that cannot be easily classified by a clear-cut Orientalist/Occidentalist binary or exhaustively explained by the legacies of British colonialism and American imperialism or the resistance to them. Such multidirectional tracing of discursive and narrative conjunctures does not always do justice to an individual representation's explicitly proclaimed or performed referential system, and it will rarely allow organizing the discussed works according to culturally and linguistically specific traditions or the geographic spaces of their historical genesis. But it does serve my own interpretive intention. It goes without saying that the manifest language(-traditions) and the local contexts in which an Anglophone Arab work is produced are of analytical importance. And no one will seriously question the impact of the individual cultural producer's identification, both in terms of externally constructed, negated, or chosen ethnicity and with a view to her or his political location within real or imagined collectivities. It is, however, my argument that by solely focusing on these aspects, one would not only underestimate the very translocal, transhistorical, and translinguistic (or translational) correlations that these works inform but, in addition, one would also

---

23   For a selective overview, see Zachary Lockman, *Contending Visions of the Middle East. The History and Politics of Orientalism*, 2nd ed. (Cambridge, UK: Cambridge UP, 2010); Abdur Raheem Kidwai, *Literary Orientalism: A Companion* (New Delhi: Viva, 2009) and Geoffrey Nash, *Writing Muslim Identity* (London: Continuum, 2012). Jack G. Shaheen, *Reel Bad Arabs: How Hollywood Vilifies a People* (New York: Olive Branch P, 2001); Barbara Harlow and Mia Carter, eds., *Imperialism and Orientalism: A Documentary Sourcebook* (Walden, MA: Blackwell, 1999). The relevance of Said's seminal *Orientalism* (1978) as well as of his *Covering Islam* (1981) and *Culture and Imperialism* (1993) for this field of studies is obvious.

neglect one's own responsibility for responding by transposing their reference systems.[24]

I count it as the privilege of my own interpretive positionality, although I of course do not (fully) account for myself, that I do not feel the need to claim Anglophone Arab representation either for Arab (diasporic) culture or for Anglo-American (immigrant) culture. Nor do I see any reason to firmly place my study's subject matter as a clearly assigned and commonly recognized branch into one of the institutionalized academic fields of Middle Eastern Studies or Arab American or Arab British Studies. Yet, although I can imagine myself not to be the primarily implied reader of the cultural texts that I am reading and thus not as their primarily liable critic, I do not refuse to relate to these representations. In making sense of what is written, spoken, or performed, no one can fully escape from assuming such articulations to be destined for oneself. Hence, while I do *identify* with Anglophone Arab texts and images, I do so as an implied reader/gazer of a second order. I hope such worldly-cum-theoretically inspired self-degradation will allow for other ways of being *seduced* by Anglophone Arab representations and for other responses than the academically established ones.

While my resonating with these representations hardly contributes to their conclusive relexicalization and commodification as signs of clear belonging or definite non-belonging, it helps to transgress my own inherited interpretive reference system and to test out alternative possibilities of complicity without the complacency of clear filiation. By doing so, I hope to contribute to an amplified relational approach to Arab diasporic studies that transcends both the analytical frameworks of national culture, linguistic belonging, and ethnic identity as well as the neatly allocation of disciplinary expertise.[25]

I'd like to think that such testing out of alliances across difference and disciplines is one of the key functions of comparative literary and cultural criticism today: a critical project that is only conditionally an ethical undertaking—one that does not hesitate to question the conventional notion of a firmly located reading

---

24   I am referring here to Gayatri Chakravorty Spivak's vision of reading responsibility. See Gayatri Chakravorty Spivak, *Readings* (London: Seagull, 2014).

25   Such a relational approach is directly inspired by Ella Shohat's ongoing re-conceptualization of Middle Eastern/Arab Diasporic Studies. See, for instance, Ella Shohat, "Columbus, Palestine, and Arab-Jews: Toward a Relational Approach to Community Identity," *Cultural Readings of Imperialism: Edward Said and the Gravity of History*, eds. Keith Ansell-Pearson, Benita Parry, and Judith Squires (New York: St. Martin's P, 1997) 88-105, and her more recent "The Sephardi-Moorish Atlantic. Between Orientalism and Occidentalism," *Between the Middle East and the Americas: The Cultural Politics of Diaspora*, eds. Evelyn Alsultany and Ella Shohat (Ann Arbor: U of Michigan P, 2013) 42-62. See also Evelyn Alsultany and Ella Shohat, "The Cultural Politics of 'the Middle East' in the Americas," *Between the Middle East and the Americas: The Cultural Politics of Diaspora* 3-41, here particularly 17-25.

ego and that willingly takes the risk of becoming an almost transvestite project.[26] Such a project cannot but trust in the principle human capacity of leaving behind the straightjackets of reasoning, which conventionally define us and which we are used to defining for ourselves. It necessarily presupposes an altered identity politics of cultural interpretation and maybe a new ethics of reading. It resists ending up as a self-serving dead end because it is not only contrapuntally aware of its inherited reading positionality and learned perceptional certainties but it also knows its own transitive interests, abstracting instrumentality, and inevitable contradictions. If such criticism claims to read identities without neglecting differences and particularities, it obviously risks an accusation of naïve exoticism, decadent Orientalism, or even moral hypocrisy. However, cultural critique understood in this post-moralistic way is more concerned with the practical substitution of interpretive paradigms of dominant identifications than with re-writing identities or returning to(wards) authentic origins. At the same time, to look contrapuntally at Anglophone Arab beginnings as Arabs (by choice) and Westerners (by choice)[27] necessitates the obvious: to critically watch ourselves looking while being aware of the political ambivalence of the very assertion of becoming someone else.[28] I will illustrate what I have in mind here by closely re-reading a fictional narrative that is regularly presented as marking the birth of the Anglophone Arab novel. I will read this narrative not only for the sake of fully grasping its equally innovative and paradigmatic quality for the formation of the Anglophone Arab cultural sphere but also in order to use it as a vehicle to revisit other beginnings, intertexts, and discursive precedents of importance for my study.

---

26   Here I refer to Kamal Abu Deeb's understanding of critical reading as an equally transitive and transvestite act; see my "Re-Reading Said in Arabic: (Other)Worldly Counterpoints," *Edward Said's Translocations: Essays in Secular Criticism*, eds. Tobias Döring and Mark Stein (London: Routledge, 2012) 101-102.

27   On the notion of (reading-)identity by choice, see Edward W. Said, "By Birth or by Choice?" *Al-Ahram Weekly* Oct. 28–Nov. 3, 1999: 13 and Schmitz, "Re-Reading Said in Arabic: (Other)Worldly Counterpoints," 101-102 and 107.

28   I do well remember being interviewed during the final stage of an application procedure for the postdoctoral fellowship of a well-known private German research foundation when one member on the selection committee suddenly asked me to elaborate on my research project's ultimate relevance for Germany and its particular Germanness. I was shocked then (call it naive if you want) by the blatantly enunciated demand of a national(ist) added value promised by any project to be founded by the Volks(Wagen)Foundation; I guess this paragraph would have been a possible strategic response, if not a responsible one.

3. Khalid's Book and How Not to Bow Down Before Rihani

First published in 1911, Ameen Fares Rihani's *The Book of Khalid*[1] has long remained neglected in the intellectual history of both the Arab world and North America. In 2012, it was republished by Melville House's Neversink Library, thanks to the efforts of Todd Fine and his *Project Khalid*, a campaign to commemorate the book's centennial anniversary.[2] Written in English by a self-identified Arab, the novel is usually perceived as the inaugural text of Arab-American immigrant literature and is thus hastily assimilated into the gradually expanding national canon of so-called ethnic literatures.[3] Additionally, other critics reclaim *The Book of Khalid* for Arab cultural history by placing it among the first modern Arab novels, thereby implicitly affirming the Eurocentric devaluation of earlier novelistic writings in Arabic.[4]

It is probably correct to say that the narrative anticipates many of the challenges related to the experience of geographic dislocation and the dynamics of translocal identification that are addressed in later Anglophone Arab migratory

---

1   Ameen Fares Rihani, *The Book of Khalid* (New York: Dodd, Mead & Company, 1911).
2   Ameen Rihani, *The Book of Khalid* (New York: Melville House, 2012); with an afterword by Todd Fine. In the following, I refer to this edition. Fine is also the co-founder of the Save Washington Street effort. For the *Project Khalid*, founded by Fine to commemorate the novel's anniversary in 2011 by republishing it and celebrating it as the first Arab-American novel as well as advancing its author's reputation as an important Arab-American figure, see website *Project Khalid*, "Welcome to Project Khalid: The 100th Anniversary of the First Arab-American Novel," 2010, 12 Mar. 2014 <http://projectkhalid.org/>.
3   See, for prominent examples, Waïl S. Hassan, "The Rise of Arab-American Literature: Orientalism and Cultural Translation in the Work of Ameen Rihani," *American Literary History* 20.1-2 (2008): 245-75; Waïl S. Hassan, *Immigrant Narratives: Orientalism and Cultural Translation in Arab American and Arab British Literature* (New York: Oxford UP, 2011) 38-58; Evelyn Shakir, "Arab American Literature," *New Immigrant Literatures in the United States: A Sourcebook to Our Multicultural Heritage*, ed. Alpana Sharma Knippling (Westport, CT: Greenwood P, 1996) 6; or Lisa Suhair Majaj, "Arab-American Literature: Origins and Developments," *Arab American Literature and Culture*, eds. Alfred Hornung and Martina Kohl (Heidelberg: Winter, 2012) 62-63.
4   See, for instance: Nijmeh Hajjar, *The Politics and Poetics of Ameen Rihani. The Humanist Ideology of an Arab-American Intellectual and Activist* (London: Tauris Academic Studies, 2010) 4.

and/or diasporic representations. However, due to the novel's almost encyclopedic and sometimes over-bursting use of translinguistic intertextualities and its multi-layered topical and structural correspondences, it can also function as a vehicle for provisionally carving the spectrum of many other discourses informing the Anglophone Arab representations that I am interested in here. In what follows, I am less concerned with cultural characteristics, ethnic spirit, and direct or indirect artistic borrowings from either Arabic or Anglophone works than with historical contexts, topical motives, narrative devices, and structural affinities.

As Nijmeh Hajjar argues in her 2010 study devoted to the Arab American intellectual's humanist politics, "as a man of letters," Rihani certainly "marks many 'beginnings.'"[5] Looking at the immense impact of his early poetic production in both English and Arabic, published from 1905 onwards, he can be regarded among the pioneers of free verse poetry (al-shi'r al-hurr) and prose poetry (al-shiþr al-manthur) in the Arabic language. Rihani's 1905 English poetry collection, *Myrtle and Myrrh*, can be seen as the first collection of Anglophone Arab poetry.[6] The English language drama, *Wajdah*, written in 1908 and posthumously published in 2001, is regularly considered the first Arab American play. At least one of his more innovative political plays written in Arabic was staged in Beirut as early as in 1909.[7] Those who also consider Rihani's early political and journalistic writings in Arabic, collected in his 1910 publication *Ar-Rihaniyat*,[8] as well as his sometimes semi-fictional travel writing in Arabic and English[9] even present him as an early Arab(-American) proponent of transmigrant critical cosmopolitanism that fuses an emerging humanist nationalism of pan-Arab identity with liberal ideas of global citizenship and multiple belonging.[10]

---

5   Hajjar, *The Politics and Poetics of Ameen Rihani* 49.

6   Rihani's first Arabic poem, "Life and Death: Fall and Sunset in Lebanon," was published in 1905 in the Egyptian literary and cultural journal, *Al-Hilal*. In the same year, he published *Myrtle and Myrrh* (1905; Washington, DC: Platform Intern., 2005). His collected Arabic free verse poetry was first published in 1955 as *Hutaf al-Audiya* and translated into English in 2002 as *Hymns of the Valleys*, trans. Naji B. Oueijan (Piscataway, NJ: Gorgias P, 2002). On Rihani's impact on Modern Arabic poetry, see Shmuel Moreh, *Modern Arabic Poetry: 1800–1970* (Leiden: Brill, 1976) 297-99.

7   Hajjar, *The Politics and Poetics of Ameen Rihani* 5.

8   Ameen Rihani, *Ar-Rihaniyat* [the Rihani essays] (Beirut: Dar al-'Ilmi, 2010).

9   See, for instance, Ameen Rihani, *Muluk al-'Arab au Rihla fi Bilad al-'Arabiya* [Kings of the Arab or a Voyage to the Arab World] (Beirut: Yusuf Sadir, 1924) and Ameen Rihani, *Arabian Peak and Desert: Travels in Al-Yaman* (London: Constable, 1930).

10   See Nuwar Mawlawi Diab, "Ameen Rihani's Vision of Globalization," *Ameen Rihani: Bridging East and West: A Pioneering Call for Arab-American Understanding*, eds. Nathan C. Funk and Betty J. Sitka (Lanham, MD: UP of America, 2004) 93-101 and Hajjar, *The Politics and Poetics of Ameen Rihani*.

Therefore, one cannot be surprised that Rihani's work and name are instrumentalized on all sides and to various ends. Nor does it seem inappropriate against this background that his bust was set up to bow down before at the beginning of the 21st century both in Lebanon and the US (fig. 3, fig. 4).[11]

Figure 3: The unveiling of a large bust of Ameen Rihani in the presence of the Lebanese ministers of culture and education, parliament members, and other representatives. Metn region, Lebanon, on 28 July 28, 2011.

In 2007, William McGurn, a *Wall Street Journal* editorial writer and chief speech-writer for US president George W. Bush, rediscovered Rihani as a genuine Arab champion of American-style global freedom and democracy and as a powerful rhetorical vehicle to promote Arab-American political, economic, and military collaboration in times of the nation's global war on terror. McGurn stumbled upon Rihani's name while reading an openly anti-Arab book by Michael B. Oren, Israel's would-be ambassador to the United States, and in January 2008, persuaded Bush to use a short, second-hand quote from the *Ar-Rihaniyat* for one of his speeches

---

11   In 2004, an Ameen Rihani bust by the Lebanese sculptor Pierre Karam was unveiled at
      Tufts University, Boston. See website *Ameen Rihani*, "Ameen Rihani's Statue in the United
      States of America," 13 Sept. 2015 <http://www.ameenrihani.org/newsevents.php?archive=
      bustattufts>. In 2011, a much larger bust of Rihani was unveiled in Metn, Lebanon in the
      presence of the Lebanese ministers of culture and education, parliament members, and other
      representatives. See "Unveiling Rihani's Bust at a New Memorial in Lebanon," 13 Sept. 2015
      <http://www.ameenrihani.org/newsevents.php>.

*Figure 4: The Rihani bust by the Lebanese sculptor Pierre Karam
was unveiled on December 1, 2004 at Tufts University, Somerville,
MA, USA.*

given during a visit to the United Arab Emirates.[12] At the time of his book's publication, Oren was senior fellow at the Shalem Center for the diplomatic and military
history of the Middle East, located in Jerusalem. In May 2009, he was appointed
ambassador of Israel to the United States. As a consequence, an American president who had chosen Albert Camus' famous 1942 novella about a Frenchman who
kills an Arab Algerian, *L'Étranger*, for his summer holiday readings on the beach

---

12   See William McGurn, "An Arab for Ground Zero," *The Wall Street Journal*, 24 May 2011, 23 Sept.
      2013 <http://www.wsj.com/articles/SB10001424052702304066504576341401418827660>.
      For McGurn's reference, see Michael B. Oren, *Power, Faith, and Fantasy. America in the Middle
      East, 1776 to the Present* (New York: Norton, 2007).

only two years earlier[13] closed his remarks in Abu Dhabi by reminding his Arab audience of the Lebanese intellectual's call for introducing America's equally liberal and liberating values into the Middle Eastern discourse: "When will you turn your face toward the East, O Liberty?"[14] It was again McGurn who in 2011, now inspired by Todd Fine and his *Project Khalid*, recommended erecting a memorial for Rihani close to New York City's Ground Zero site. According to him, ten years after 9/11, against the background of the events around the so-called Arab spring, and in accordance with president Barack Obama's new Middle Eastern diplomacy, there was a need for a monument of an "Arab-American immigrant [...] who believed the Arab world's destiny was freedom for its people and friendship with America."[15] To this day, the Rihani memorial destined for Manhattan has not been erected.

Many of Rihani's multi-generic qualities of innovation and invention seem to converge in *The Book of Khalid*. His only novel does indeed lend itself to reclaiming him as a pioneer. But whatever one thinks regarding the narrative's right place within a general Arab literary history, the history of American ethnic writing, and American-Middle Eastern diplomatic history or the author's bust's appropriate public placement, it seems almost impossible to escape from the discursive precedents that are consistently claiming Rihani as the founding father of a literature that is "Arab in its concern, culture and characteristic, English in language, and American in spirit and platform."[16] Concern, cultural characteristic, language, and spirit: these are the primary criteria of analysis used to categorize *The Book of Khalid* and to place it on the proper bookshelf either among other early modern Arab writings and/or among so-called hyphenated-American immigrant and minority literatures.

An interpretive way out of the narrow ideological concepts of heritage and authenticity might be offered by the Syrian poet Adonis (Ali Ahmad Said) in his preface to Nathan C. Funk and Betty J. Sitka's edited volume *Ameen Rihani: Bridging East and West*.[17] His short statement on Rihani's symbolic importance as an intellectual and literary writer seems to be productively out of place, not solely because it was

---

13   John Mullan, "Bush Takes Camus to the Beach," *The Guardian* 17 Aug. 2006, 24 Oct. 2010
        <http://www.theguardian.com/world/2006/aug/17/usa.bookscomment>.

14   George W. Bush, "Remarks in Abu Dhabi, United Arab Emirates, Jan. 13, 2008," *Public Papers
        of the Presidents of the United States: George W. Bush 2008-2009*, Book I – Jan. 1 to June 30, 2008
        (Washington: United States Government Printing Office, 2012) 79.

15   McGurn, "An Arab for Ground Zero," n. pag.

16   This quote is from the website of the Ameen Rihani Organization: *Ameen Rihani* 18 May 2014,
        23 Aug. 2014 <http://www.ameenrihani.org/index.php>. The organization supports the pub-
        lishing of Rihani's work, research on the writer and intellectual, as well as the Rihani Museum
        in Freike, Lebanon.

17   Adonis, "A Cultural Symbol," *Ameen Rihani: Bridging East and West: A Pioneering Call for Arab-
        American Understanding*, eds. Nathan C. Funk and Betty J. Sitka (Lanham, MD: UP of America,
        2004) xiii-xiv.

written in Berlin: "Today, we celebrate, in the person of Ameen Al-Rihani, a cultural symbol originating not so much from the past as from the future."[18] Using Rihani's importance for the formation of prose poetry in Arabic as a point of departure, Adonis reads Rihani's many beginnings as beginnings of something that has not yet happened. For him, Rihani's work marks an unfinished disorder of transcultural aesthetic innovation that replaces older ideological concepts of authentic roots or heritages to be rediscovered by multiply interrupted, intentionally confused, and mutually incomplete ongoing relational tensions. By doing so, he presents Rihani as one of the forebears of a future poetics and political ethics which rather blur than bridge both Western and Arab tracks of modernity alike.[19] I'd like to genuflect before Khalid's book—rather than before Rihani—by reading it from the perspective of such unknown futures.

3.1   An Arab (Drago)man in New York and the Cultural Imaginary of Confrontation

"The response is in the fire."[20]

Presenting itself to the reader as a composition of dubious Arabic and French sources in translation, selected and commented upon by an equally dubious editor-narrator, *The Book of Khalid* tells the turn-of-the century story of two young Arab men, Khalid and his friend, Shakib. The two flee from the familial and political oppression in Greater Syria (ruled by the Ottoman Empire) to immigrate to New York City. The kernel part of the novel tells the story of these two Arab peddlers in Manhattan. In this regard, it seems to follow the classical immigrant paradigm of coming to America and re-inventing oneself as American. However, re-reading *The Book of Khalid* today as a literary articulation of Arab American crossovers has more to offer than just proving a manifestation of a well-known narrative mode. Such a reading can help to better elucidate the complex dynamics between the so-called West and the so-called Middle East that lead into our own times. In fact, the novel places itself within the long history of transnational encounters which goes back to early modern Arab immigration to Britain and which continues even after flying objects navigated by suicidal Arab terrorists' hands hit New York's World Trade Center on September 11, 2001.

---

18   Adonis, "A Cultural Symbol," xiv.

19   See also Adonis, *Ash-Shir'iya al-'Arabiya* (1985), trans. Catherine Cobham as *An Introduction to Arab Poetics* (1990; Cairo: AUC P, 1992) 101 and Adonis, *Muqaddimah lil-Shi'r al-'Arabi* [Introduction to Arab Poetry] (1971; Beirut: Dar al-'Awda, 1983).

20   Gayatri Chakravorty Spivak, "Terror: A Speech after 9/11," *An Aesthetic Education in the Era of Globalization*, by G. Chakravorty Spivak (Cambridge, MA: Harvard UP, 2013) 378.

What has been regularly overlooked in the American post-9/11 controversy about the presence of Muslims in Lower Manhattan that has ensued over plans for a new 13-story Islamic Cultural Center[21] (fig. 5) is that such a presence is not at all a recent phenomenon (fig.6).

The postcolonial critic, Gayatri Chakravorty Spivak, also underestimated or intentionally understated the continuities of Arab immigration and anti-Arab discrimination when she revised her 2002 lecture on "Terror"[22] almost 10 years after it was first presented at Columbia University's "Responding to War" Symposium[23] for its inclusion in the essay collection, *Aesthetic Education in the Age of Globalization.*[24] In the prequel to her 2012 version of this post-9/11 speech, Spivak explains the debate over the Islamic Cultural Center first and foremost as an issue that "is being used to discredit Barack Hussein Obama and to bring down the Democratic Party," although any rationally abstracting observer would easily grasp that conflict as one between "the right to build on private property" and "the outrage of the families of the victims, whose lives were casually extinguished, apparently in the name of Islam."[25] Given the feminist critic's deconstructivist-materialist training, her strict focus on the here and now as the primarily relevant context for explaining the ideological mapping persecuted within the Ground Zero mosque debate may come as a surprise—the absence of historical dialectics in Spivak's contextualization is rather non-Marxist.[26] Nevertheless, some of her "ruminations [...] in response to America's war on terror"[27] can be applied to the present situation's pre-history and thus might be a helpful interpretive matrix for re-visiting Rihani's 1911 novel as an

---

21   The Islamic community center, Park51—originally called Cordoba House and sometimes labeled Ground Zero mosque—was planned in 2009 to be erected as a community center plus mosque two blocks from the World Trade Center site in Lower Manhattan, New York City. The planned community center advanced to a controversial key issue of nationwide debates during the political campaigns of the 2010 midterm elections. In September 2011, the center provisionally opened in a 3-story building at a site that had housed a Burlington department store before it was damaged in the 2001 attacks. To this day, the original project has not been realized due to strong public outrage by Islamophobic activists allied with right-wing politicians.

22   Spivak, "Terror: A Speech after 9/11," 372-98.

23   The symposium was organized in September 2002 by Columbia University's Institute for Research of Women and Gender with the aim of critically responding to the dominant "War on Terror" debate; see *Feminist News* 21 (Sept. 2002): 8-9, 16-19.

24   Gayatri Chakravorty Spivak, *An Aesthetic Education in the Era of Globalization* (Cambridge, MA: Harvard UP, 2013).

25   Spivak, "Terror: A Speech after 9/11," 372.

26   Of course, Spivak must be aware of this debate's long discriminatory pretext related to Arab-Muslim immigration. One could in fact argue that her stressing of Obama's distinctively Muslim middle name, "Hussein"—one that has been systematically deleted from public discourse—hints to that very pretext.

27   Spivak, "Terror: A Speech after 9/11," 372.

Figure 5: Rendering of Park51 Muslim Community Center by SOMA Architects, 2010.

equally self-critical and ironically mocking "confrontational imaginary."[28] Such a reading of *The Book of Khalid* sees in it a double vison of multiple broken belongings, failed exchange, and destructive revenge rather than—as most critics want to have it—a literary immigration by way of self-orientalizing ingratiation or a pioneering fictional bridging of East and West in the name of tolerance, inter-cultural dialogue, and mutual understanding.[29]

---

28   Spivak, "Terror: A Speech after 9/11," 379.
29   For the critique of self-orientalization, see Waïl S. Hassan, "The Rise of the Arab American Novel: Ameen Rihani's The Book of Khalid," *The Edinburgh Companion to the Arab Novel in English: The Politics of Anglo Arab and Arab American Literature and Culture*, ed. Nouri Gana (Ed-

Figure 6: The Syrian Colony, Washington Street, undated drawing by W. Bengough of a turn-of-the-century New York street scene not far from the spatial focus of the debate over the Park51-project.

By using Spivak's text on terror as a point of departure, I defect from Geoffrey Nash's interpretive script at the same time. The renowned scholar of Arab writings in English is quite aware that "[t]here are of course multiple ways of reading Ameen Rihani's *Book of Khalid*,"[30] ranging from biographical and contextual approaches to perspectives with a focus on intertextuality and linguistic innovation. But although he aims at revealing his own reading from the dominant Orientalist and anti-Orientalist interpretive chains of either celebrating the novel for its cross-cultural bridging and synthesizing capacities or blaming it for the failure of that very synthesis, Nash's interpretation of the novel as a representation of "the secularization of the Arab soul" completed through "the Muslims' migrations of the twentieth century"[31] plays out the very essentialist construction that strictly divides between

---

inburgh: Edinburgh UP, 2013) 39-62; for the bridging-thesis, see Nathan C. Funk and Betty J. Sitka, eds., *Ameen Rihani: Bridging East and West: A Pioneering Call for Arab-American Understanding* (Lanham, MD: UP of America, 2004).

30   Geoffrey Nash, "Beyond Orientalism: Khalid, the Secular City and the Transcultural Self," *The Edinburgh Companion to the Arab Novel in English: The Politics of Anglo Arab and Arab American Literature and Culture*, ed. Nouri Gana (Edinburgh: Edinburgh UP, 2013) 63.

31   Nash, "Beyond Orientalism: Khalid, the Secular City and the Transcultural Self," 66.

religious identification and tribal solidarity within the intrinsically traditional Oriental town on the one hand and the techno-political urban society of Western secular modernity on the other. One wonders what precisely Nash means with "the Arab soul" (the Arab mind?) or how exactly the baptized Khalid's journeys to and from the paradigmatic early 20th century technopolis relate to the immense spectrum of multidirectional migrations of Muslims of later decades. Moreover, one misses a postcolonial perspective on the doctrine of secularism and the cultural boundaries of moral belonging that have shaped the *Formations of the Secular*.[32] Nash presents Khalid as Rihani's alter ego. He sees both the author and his auto-fictional literary character as avant-garde secular Arabs revolting against the "obscurantism of the East" and "American materialism"[33] alike. According to Nash, the two men finally succeed in negotiating both strands of their divided selves (their two souls?) by creating a modern secular yet spiritually authentic identity. Now, this notion of a hyphenated East-Western, transcultural, or hybrid identity not only comes very close to the dominant interpretive paradigm of bi-cultural synthesis criticized by Nash, it also draws on an Orientalist binary in which traditional Islam, lacking the idea of (urban) community, constitutes the West's primary Other. The secular literary critic seems to dress Khalid (and implicitly Rihani) with the stereotypical clothes of the essential *homo islamicus* who is ontologically incapable of separating the public from the personal and the state from religion just to demonstrate how living in the Western metropolis turns him into an emancipated Arab cosmopolitan of bi-directional non-alliance.

I do agree with Nash's argument that the reductionist adaptation of the critique of Orientalism can easily lead to consigning Khalid to "an ineffectual mimicry of orientalist discourse."[34] But I do not think that Nash fully himself emancipates from the episto(-ideo)logical prison of Orientalist secularism. In this context, it is significant that he draws on Harvey Cox's 1966 theological study, *The Secular City*,[35] to explore the importance of the Western urban setting for Khalid's spiritual secularization instead of using a much more skeptical work of urban sociology by a contemporary of Rihani as his reading's interpretive matrix: Georg Simmel published his seminal "The Metropolis and Mental Life"[36] in 1903. While Cox, from the

---

32   Talal Asad, *Formations of the Secular: Christianity, Islam, Modernity* (Stanford, CA: Stanford UP, 2003).

33   Nash, "Beyond Orientalism: Khalid, the Secular City and the Transcultural Self," 65.

34   Nash, "Beyond Orientalism: Khalid, the Secular City and the Transcultural Self," 73.

35   Harvey Cox, *The Secular City: Secularization and Urbanization in Theological Perspective* (1965; Princeton, NJ: Princeton UP, 2013). Nash refers to Cox on page 64 to 72.

36   Georg Simmel, "Die Grosstädte und das Geistesleben," *Die Grossstadt. Vorträge und Aufsätze zur Städteausstellung der Gehe-Stiftung Dresden Vol. 9*, ed. Th. Petermann (Dresden, 1903) 185-206; "The Metropolis and Mental Life," *Classic Essays on the Culture of Cities*, ed. Richard Sennett (Englewood Cliffs, NJ: Prentice-Hall, 1969) 47-60.

perspective of a privileged white urbanite, argues that the city can be a space where people of all faiths fulfill their potential and that God is present in both the secular and in formal religious realms, the sociologist Simmel focuses on the individual's inevitable struggle "to maintain the independence and individuality of his existence in the face of overwhelming social forces, of historical heritage, of external culture, and of the technique of life."[37] Where the American Baptist theologian believes the Western city is a place of expanded religious freedom, the offspring of German-Jewish converts, a secular social theorist of urban culture, is rather interested in the oppressive contiguities of modern metropolitan life, in the negative psychological effects related to the urban gains of freedom, and in the resistance of the individual urbanite "to being leveled down and worn out by a social technological mechanism"[38] of the city. I do not think Nash had read Simmel's profoundly influential essay on the pitfalls of the urban condition's liberating promises. If he had, he would have paid more attention to the socio-historical fact that the city, secular or otherwise, feels quite different to those for whom its emancipatory promise turns out to be a cruel deception, and that, particularly for Arab immigrants, the great Western city can in fact turn into the site of sophisticated humiliations. If Nash had read "The Metropolis and Mental Life," maybe he would have also incorporated Simmel's reflections on the sociological form of "The Stranger,"[39] first published in 1908—not even three years before *The Book of Khalid*. In this short essay, Simmel tries to grasp theoretically the particular social spatiality of the stranger as a person who, for those being or feeling fixed at home, embodies nearness and distance at the same time. He not only acknowledges the stranger's potential freedom for the objective critique of a formerly closed social group's perceptual sureties and self-certitudes and stresses the high degree of ideological independence and intellectual individuation related to this positionality but also shows how the stranger's strangeness can easily give rise to dangerous tensions of institutionalized non-relations, prejudices, de-individualization, and dehumanization.

When reading *The Book of Khalid*, one should not underestimate Khalid's individual freedom of coming and going. But the celebration of the experience of immigration's liberating effects should not lead us to ignore the threat that the Arab immigrant represents to the various groups he encounters. In addition, one cannot but consider Khalid's own vulnerability conditioned by his being more than only a "*potential* wanderer."[40] When the Orientalized immigrant (the immigrant of Muslim and/or Middle Eastern background or any person of color who is racialized as Muslim) enters the Western metropolis, s/he does not easily fit the secular

37   Simmel, "The Metropolis and Mental Life," 47.
38   Simmel, "The Metropolis and Mental Life," 47.
39   Georg Simmel, "The Stranger," *The Sociology of Georg Simmel*, ed. and trans. Kurt H. Wolff (Glencoe, IL.: Free P, 1950) 402-408.
40   Simmel, "The Stranger," 402.

notion of the abstract citizen. S/he enters as a stranger. Just like her or his political presence sits uncomfortably with the imagined community of the Western nation state or the Western city, her or his cultural self-representation (i.e. in the form Arab/Muslim immigrant literatures or art) is regularly placed outside the articulations of those who see themselves as naturally at home. It seems the imaginative boundaries of Orientalism crossed Anglophone Arab representations long before they were assimilated into Western criticism. Searching for the transcultural authenticity of Khalid's journey within these boundaries not only adds a certain quality of Western exceptionalism to the concept of authenticity but also necessarily narrows the interpretation of the literary character's agency to the idealist notion of the autonomous intentional ego revolting against both traditionalism and modernity with the aim of defending individual uniqueness.[41]

Reading *The Book of Khalid* instead as an imaginary of multiple confrontational encounters reveals Khalid's fictional activities as discursive effects and counter-discursive responses—that is, as re-actions to external conditions of selving rather than autonomous acts of authentic self-expression. Such an equally postcolonial and post-secular reading is a first step in the direction of a radical politics of interpretation that does not confine itself to the idealist claim of cognitively controlling and reconciling competing truth claims. Instead, it is equally interested in the strategic use and (im)moral economy of lies as well as in the aesthetic abstraction and symbolic representation of counter-lies.

In her essay on terror, Spivak quotes from Mahasweta Devi's short story, "Douloti the Bountiful," to stress the importance of confrontational imaginaries for our understanding of the enchantment and excess of planetary confrontations: "There are people for passing laws, there are people to ride jeeps, but no one to light the fire."[42] If the American ideology of world peace through trade was a lie, the deadly attack on the World Trade Center as the symbol of the US's economic imperialism was based on a lie, too: the false liberating promises of the extra-state physical violence called terror. And if such terrorism, in turn, is used to legitimate the globalization of military interventionism and so-called peacekeeping missions, the traditional ethical difference between war and peace is swept away beyond any theoretical pursuit of peace or justice. Khalid and his friend, Shakib, come to America more than a hundred years before we have seemingly come to accept the moral oxymoron of planetary confrontation in the name of world peace.[43] As a confrontational imaginary, the novel depicts both the immigrants' experiences

41   Cf. Nash, "Beyond Orientalism: Khalid, the Secular City and the Transcultural Self," 75-77.

42   Mahasweta Devi, "Douloti the Bountiful," *Imaginary Maps: Three Stories*, ed. Mahasweta Devi, trans. Gayatri Chakravorty Spivak (New York: Routledge, 1995) 88, quoted by Spivak, "Terror: A Speech after 9/11," 377-78.

43   Spivak, "Terror: A Speech after 9/11," 378-83.

of humiliation and oppression as well as the resistive excess of real and symbolic destruction. In the case of Khalid, the confrontation with the socio-political environment of New York City as the symbolic center of techno-political imperialism almost takes the form of a self-annihilating confrontation between himself and himself. I am not suggesting that his auto-erotic violence is proto-terrorist. But, looking at the equally ironic and scary mix of Khalid's inner-worldly tasks and his transcendental referencing, one can read this part of the novel as an imaginative exercise in suicidal resistance.[44] Khalid knows how to light fire!

The immigrant's seemingly naïve secular optimism is not at all always harmoniously paired with the search for post-materialistic transcendence or philosophic truth. His path of spiritual resistance and ethical reasoning regularly leads to consistent transgressions into the worldly domain of angry confrontations and thus disturbs the illusion of East-Western harmony. In these moments, Khalid's story rather represents the despair of radical self-judgement and the dissenting anger of "rigorous morality"[45] than social assimilation or psychological balance. That he knows how to make fire first becomes obvious after the newly immigrated young Arab man "sets himself to the task of self-education."[46] Forced to live together with his friend, Shakib, and their fellow immigrant surrogate mother, Im-Hanna, an excellent cook of popular Syrian dishes, in a rented cellar "as deep and dark and damp as could be found,"[47] Khalid makes his life as a peddler selling trinkets like crosses, prayer beads, or scapulars claimed to be relics from the Holy Land. In his free time, he watches the "light-heeled, heavy-hunched women of Battery Park."[48] During the night, he begins digging into the intellectual and spiritual depth beyond his learned scholarly make-up. The Arab immigrant in America becomes a foreign student of both Western ideas and New York's everyday life. This simultaneous investigation into the celebrated ideals and attractive distractions of Western culture allows him to quarrel selectively before burning his idols' book. Never studying more than one book at a time before warming his hands at its flames, the "barbarously capricious" reader "would baptise the ideal in the fire of the real."[49] Khalid goes through Blaise Pascal's *Pensées* (1670), a defense of the Christian faith, and withdraws from it with a resolute "au-revoir."[50] He re-reads the Bible, but misses musical ecstasy and other joys in it. And he invites his friend, Shakib, to warm himself with the flames of Tom Paine's classic deistic pamphlet, *The Age of Reason* (1793-94).

---

44   Cf. Spivak, "Terror: A Speech after 9/11," 384-85.
45   Rihani, *The Book of Khalid* 76.
46   Rihani, *The Book of Khalid* 53.
47   Rihani, *The Book of Khalid* 43.
48   Rihani, *The Book of Khalid* 54.
49   Rihani, *The Book of Khalid* 53.
50   Rihani, *The Book of Khalid* 58.

First consuming and then destroying the carriers of Western culture, the Arab student in New York allegorically anticipates other local and global confrontations to come. One hundred years after Khalid's fictional travails, a group of young Arab men would cross the Atlantic to destroy the symbol of global capitalism, political imperialism, and US military power: "the temple of Empire."[51] The young Arab men of the so-called Hamburg cell who executed the attacks of September 11, 2001 were graduates from German universities. Khalid's self-educational Manhattan undertaking is directly set in this very symbolic temple. Although he is not primarily concerned with questions of political, economic, or military injustice, his transcendental struggle is also inspired by an almost excessive rejection of one-sided American materialism. Every day, he visits a second-hand bookshop located in a cellar close to the stock exchange. Its Arab owner is nicknamed "second-hand Jerry"[52] by Khalid. The old man advances to an important authority for his secondary education. It is in the city's financial district that the Arab student is fired "with free-thought literature"[53] before he gradually develops his own dissenting ideas and radical interventionist strategies. After failing to convince Jerry either to sacrifice his second-hand books to "the god of Trade"[54] by setting them on fire in front of the stock exchange or at least to burn up his off-Wall Street-bookshop, Khalid starts attending political meetings of atheists. Soon turning away from this group's infidel dogmatism, he decides from then on to unseal his mind from any external authority.

On his last peddler tour to the Bronx, he publicly burns his peddling-box filled with fake scapulars to underline his new ethical stance: "Here are the lies, now turned to ashes." [55] While Im-Hanna believes that Khalid has gone insane, Shakib recommends that his friend burns himself as the logical consequence of rigorous morality. He tells him "to pour a gallon of kerosene over his own head and fire himself out of existence."[56] Khalid, however, instead of carrying out such an act of suicide, is carried off by his own self-critical integrity and freedom of mind. To test out his emergent "theory of immanent morality,"[57] he takes up an apprenticeship in a lawyer's office just to be discharged for openly expressing his radical views on the legally binding will of the dead or the deadly pettifogging of the dominant legal order.

---

51   Spivak, "Terror: A Speech after 9/11," 374.
52   Rihani, The Book of Khalid 61.
53   Rihani, The Book of Khalid 64.
54   Rihani, The Book of Khalid 64.
55   Rihani, The Book of Khalid 75.
56   Rihani, The Book of Khalid 76.
57   Rihani, The Book of Khalid 80.

Following this experience, Khalid decides to spend his time "with the huris."[58] Turning himself into a long-haired dervish-gigolo, he wanders from one spiritual meeting of New York City's many "Don't Worry Circles of Metaphysical Societies"[59] to another. When he first enters into a liaison with a bohemian woman, she is drawn to his Middle-Eastern background. Soon "his dark eyes and her eyes of blue" seem to "flow and fuse."[60] In the course of an extended "tête-à-tête [...], the stranger is made a member of the Spiritual Household"[61] and "she, in an effort to seem Oriental, calls the Dervish, 'My Syrian Rose,' 'My Desert Flower,' 'My Beduin Boy,' [...] always closing her message with either a strip of Syrian sky or a camel load of the narcissus." The American woman who presents herself as an esoteric medium imagines herself as a future Bedouin queen traveling ancient desert kingdoms and thus resuscitating the Orient's former greatness. Despite her rather ripe age "at the threshold of her climacteric,"[62] she knows to preserve her beauty. Although she infantilizes Khalid by calling him her "prodigal child,"[63] she in turn "does not permit him to call her, 'mother'."[64] The editor-narrator warns: "Ah, but not thus, will the play close."[65] The Arab American anti-hero soon gets into a second erotic relationship with a female writer, another "huntress of male curiosities, originales" who "only skims the surface of things."[66] After "a hectic uprush about pearly breasts, and honey-sources, and musk-scented arbours," she "withdraws from the foreigner her favour" only to narratively exhibit him in the "magazine supplement of one of the Sunday newspapers" for which she works. There the Arab American immigrant is made a stereotypical Orientalist copy, "thrown into the cauldron along with the magic herbs. Bubble–bubble."[67] The humiliating experience of being performatively exoticized and consumed against his will gives a clear hint at the uncontrollable side effects of the immigrant's strategic self-orientalization. The narrative fragment on erotic attraction turning into sexual exploitation and representational commodification at the same time allegorically explains the particular

---

58   That is the title of chapter VIII of Book One; see page 83. The term huri/huris derives from the
      Koranic-Arabic *hur*, signifying a person with pure eyes of intense whiteness and blackness.
      The word has often been reductively interpreted as a paradisiac promise to male believers.
      It has entered the English language of Romantic Orientalism during the 18th century as a
      decisively erotic female figure. Here Rihani seems to refer to the Orientalist dispositive.
59   Rihani, *The Book of Khalid* 85.
60   Rihani, *The Book of Khalid* 83.
61   Rihani, *The Book of Khalid* 84.
62   Rihani, *The Book of Khalid* 84.
63   Rihani, *The Book of Khalid* 90.
64   Rihani, *The Book of Khalid* 84.
65   Rihani, *The Book of Khalid* 88.
66   Rihani, *The Book of Khalid* 86.
67   Rihani, *The Book of Khalid* 89.

ambivalence of a cross-cultural relationship that is framed by the dynamics of mutual desire and repulsion: "The fire-eating Dervish, how can he now swallow this double-tongued flame of hate and love?"[68] Khalid at least once considers curing his pain by burning the enchantress who turned into a typewriting witch just as he had already consigned many second-hand books to flames. But instead of killing her, he decides on a less murderous and more dosed variety of continuing revenge. Turning ritualized emotional violence of sexist counter-abuse against all the American women he meets in his many erotic short-affairs, Khalid's self-proclaimed immanent morality risks being seriously damaged. As I will show, the narrative motive of gendered revenge by feminized and infantilized Arab men against non-Arab women, against the counter-feminized West as such, or even targeted at Arab women reappears in diverse Anglophone Arab representations to this day. Rihani's *The Book of Khalid* provides an early literary example of this motive. The novel for the first time depicts the more readily neurotic than erotic attempt to regain Arab self-esteem triggered by complex social confrontations and humiliations. Khalid's desperate efforts to feel that he is the agent of (sexual) power, instead of its passive object, rarely come with relish. They rather take the form of an auto-erotic act of purposive self-destruction.

When the Arab anti-hero nearly loses his self within the dynamics of (sexually) abusing American women and being (sexually) abused by them, he and his friend, Shakib, decide to return to their native land. Since the latter has in the meantime become a successful local merchant who first needs to wind up his various business involvements, their remigration is however postponed. During election time, a fellow immigrant and Tammany Hall politician offers Khalid the post of a canvasser of New York's Syrian district to manipulate the Arab immigrant community's votes in favor of the Democratic Party, and the young man enters the corrupt machine of minority patronage and power politics.[69] His new role within New York City's leading political organization ultimately turns out to be one of a strategic trader of speeches conducted on the market principle of "supply and demand."[70] The hyper-moralistic poetic orator accidentally "potted in Tammany Land"[71] is pelted by the Arab American audience with rotten tomatoes and eggs. Shocked by the angry missiles of his fellow-immigrants as well as by the intrigues of the pseudo-demo-

---

68   Rihani, *The Book of Khalid* 89.

69   The Democratic Party's Tammany Hall was, from the mid-19th century until the early 1930s, New York City's leading political organization. The organization's power drew particularly upon the support of the city's growing minority communities. For details, see Daniel Czitrom, "Underworlds and Underdogs: Big Tim Sullivan and Metropolitan Politics in New York, 1889–1913," *The Journal of American History* 78.2 (1991): 536-58.

70   Rihani, *The Book of Khalid* 102.

71   Rihani, *The Book of Khalid* 100.

cratic "Reality Stock Company"[72] of Tammany Hall, Khalid gives honest expression to his disgust and publically complains about the organization's lack of honesty. As a consequence, he is first insulted by his openly racist boss for being a "brazen-faced, unmannerly scoundrel" preaching the naïve morality of "mountain peasants or other barbarous tribes"[73] and then falsely charged for misappropriating party funds. It is against the background of this humiliating experience in a prison cell of the free world's symbolic capital that he hallucinates about America's world-ruling future role and his own transnational destiny. Re-reading Jean-Jacques Rousseau's proto-revolutionary educational treaty, *Émile* (1762), and Thomas Carlyle's collection of lectures, *On Heroes, Hero-Worship, and The Heroic in History* (1841), a magic transformation accompanied by painful spasms and rioting visions of biting irony sets in: "something was going on in him—a revolution, a *coup d'état*, so to speak, of the spirit."[74] Khalid emphatically predicts a global change in the course of which Americans, the "true and honest votaries of Mammon,"[75] would radically question their national quasi-deity of the dollar to rediscover the forgotten aspirations of their souls. It is such a renewed American secularism, blending the ideal of material progress with the universal aspiration of spiritual growth, from whence the imprisoned philosopher-prophet expects inspirations for "every race-traveller on the highway of emancipation."[76]

Khalid's desperate posture of revolutionary prophethood is almost post-moralistic regarding its open contempt for Western-style reformist democracy. Although his vision of an American superman of transcultural inspiration and universal validity seems to be more inspired by the transcendentalism of Ralph Waldo Emerson, Henry David Thoreau, and Walt Whitman[77] than by Friedrich Nietzsche's post-humanistic genealogy of European morality,[78] there is an equally arrogant and ironic boast at work in Khalid's mimicry of prophecy that is reminiscent of Zarathustra's as well as other Nietzschean philosophizing voices' particular talent to sense oneself as a good message to the future world.[79] The transcultural

---

72 Rihani, *The Book of Khalid* 102.
73 Rihani, *The Book of Khalid* 107.
74 Rihani, *The Book of Khalid* 115.
75 Rihani, *The Book of Khalid* 108.
76 Rihani, *The Book of Khalid* 110.
77 On Rihani's reception of American transcendentalist writers, see Walter Edward Dunnavent III., "Rihani, Emerson, and Thoreau," *Ameen Rihani: Bridging East and West: A Pioneering Call for Arab-American Understanding*, eds. Nathan C. Funk and Betty J. Sitka (Lanham, MD: UP of America, 2004) 55-71.
78 Friedrich Nietzsche, *Zur Genealogie der Moral: Eine Streitschrift* (Leipzig: C. G. Naumann, 1887); Friedrich Nietzsche, *Also sprach Zarathustra. Ein Buch für Alle und Keinen* (Chemnitz, Ernst Schmeitzner, 1883–91).
79 Friedrich Nietzsche, *Ecce Homo: wie man wird, was man ist* (Leipzig: C. G. Naumann, 1889).

formula for mankind's coming to its higher self is presented as a direct result of the Arab prisoner's individual transmigrating mind:

> From his transcendental height, the Superman of America shall ray forth in every direction the divine light, which shall mellow and purify the spirit of Nations and strengthen and sweeten the spirit of men, in this New World, I tell you, he shall be born, but he shall not be an American in the Democratic sense. He shall be nor of the Old World nor of the New; he shall be, my Brothers, of both.[80]

This is probably not the right place to discuss whether the transcendentalist call for American individuals to undergo a change from economic materialism of strategic reason to the intuitional wisdom of nature and spirituality before collectively changing world society has been politically reciprocated by the American majority. What seems to be, however, quite obvious is that Khalid's prophecy of a global secular order characterized by the peaceful coexistence of individual spiritualism, artistic innovation, and technological progress has not yet been fulfilled.

In 1971, exactly sixty years after the first publication of Rihani's novel, a Syrian-Lebanese poet, writing in the distant wake of the fictional character Khalid, still laments the unresolved relational tensions between Europe, America, and the non-Western world. Adonis' openly anti-American free verse poem, "The Funeral of New York,"[81] directly addresses the champion of democracy, Whitman, to inform him of what has become of his beloved city and the world, only to allegorically bury him under the wreckage of modern-day New York. The doubly exiled poetic voice assumes the role of a multiply fragmented self that with courage asks "the prophet's questions"[82] regarding New York City's hopelessly demised liberal tradition and its altered symbolic meaning against the background of the American empire's contemporary global impact. New York is described as a "rag called liberty with one hand / and strangling the earth with the other."[83] At the same time, the poem proliferates dark prophecies of violent confrontations: "An eastern wind uproots tents and skyscrapers."[84] Although Whitman's voice is at first hard to find, a direct reference to "The clock" from "Song of Myself," which "indicates the moment,"[85] is taken up to announce a new time to New York and suggest an alliance between the Arab poet and the American bard with the potential of historical change toward global justice. However, in this New York of the early 1970s, Whitman seems to be just as out of place as the turn-of-the-century Khalid: "And you, Walt Whitman, /

---

80   Rihani, *The Book of Khalid* 110-11.
81   Adonis, "The Funeral of New York." *The Pages of Day and night*. Trans. Samuel Hazo (Marlboro, VT: Marlboro P, 1994): 57-74.
82   Adonis, "The Funeral of New York," 67.
83   Adonis, "The Funeral of New York," 57.
84   Adonis, "The Funeral of New York," 60.
85   Walt Whitman, *Leaves of Grass* (1855; New York: Dover Pub., 2012) 61.

stay exiled like an immigrant. / Have you become a bird unknown in the American sky?"[86] Adonis does not manage to convince Whitman of the urgent need to join him and the world's current emancipatory movements: "the absent god hears nothing."[87] Due to his simultaneous awareness of Western and non-Western 20th century lived realities, the Arab visitor sees what the American poet newer saw, and he knows what the dead proponent of democratic transcendentalism "could never know."[88] The poem ends with the lyrical *I* leaving New York and returning to Beirut.[89]

Khalid, too, after being released from prison with the help of his friend, Shakib, hears "the call of his own country."[90] Anticipating America's "true dawn,"[91] he now more than ever wants to return to his native Lebanon. But the story does not end at this point. The New York immigrant who was offended by almost everything he encountered in the US and who in turn offended nearly every American with his revolting honesty and violent outbursts now discovers in himself "the chosen Voice!"[92] of the Arab people. He prepares for a trans-atlantic voyage over the course of which he will revolt against both his people's dominant political ethics and his own inner morality. Up until this re-migrational turn, Rihani's confrontational imaginary can hardly offer a narrative model for East-Western coexistence or an ethical blueprint for the mutual understanding between Arabs and Americans. The narrative constantly shifts between radical individualism and pan-Arab vision, transmigrant universalism and spiritual transcendence, self-Orientalizing role play and counter-Orientalist mockery. If it is true that Khalid is an early prototype of the literary dragoman translating the Arab self from within and to the West, as many critics argue, one cannot miss that his project diverges significantly from the script—a script that, almost unchallenged, prefigured and regulated the unidirectional procedures of West-Eastern (mis-)understandings at the turn of the century. The novel's anti-hero does neither aim at fulfilling the West's expectations, nor is he the immigrant representative of his nation, the agent of his people's fate, or the cultural ambassador of any other collectivity's claims. It might be true that Khalid regularly sells a well-established image of the Arab, but he is not selling himself. His strategic constructions and deconstructions of himself as an Arab in

---

86   Adonis, "The Funeral of New York," 71.
87   Adonis, "The Funeral of New York," 57.
88   Adonis, "The Funeral of New York," 71; note again the direct reference to Whitman's "Song of Myself."
89   See also Roger Asselineau and Ed Folsom, "Whitman and Lebanon's Adonis," *Walt Whitman Quarterly Review* 15.4 (1998): 180-84.
90   Rihani, *The Book of Khalid* 121.
91   Rihani, *The Book of Khalid* 125.
92   Rihani, *The Book of Khalid* 125.

New York are presented as the interpretations of a self-critical ironist of mutually excluding imagined alterities rather than articulations of a self-Orientalizing mimic-man or cross-cultural interpreter of his original culture. Yes, Khalid might be presumed to be a hyperactive narcissistic dragoman escorting us through the overlapping worlds of orientalist-occidentalist misperceptions, but he is decisively a dragoman for his own sake. His strategic self-display as an exaggerated Orientalist copy demonstrates that this copy has no original in the world. Khalid's traveling performances first and foremost follow from the care for himself and his will for personal freedom, but they are inescapably framed by competing collective politics of identifications.[93] It is this equally political and ethical concern of the self within representational formations, which decisively go beyond the individual level of subjectivity, that are so characteristic of many more recent Anglophone Arab works.

Khalid's rhetoric of violence regularly reciprocates the false promise of assimilation and the social practice of discrimination. The close link between the social and the discursive is thus directly incorporated into both the novel's mode of narrative emplotment and the plot's linguistic figuration. Looking at the Arab immigrant's continuing struggle between strategic self-exoticization and the revolt against involuntarily being exoticized as addressed in *The Book of Khalid*, the complex relation of social violence and cultural imaginary sometimes seems to be reversible indeed. Just like hegemonic American perceptions and representations of Khalid turn him into a social object of Orientalist humiliation, the immigrant's rhetoric strategies of social individuation and his performative attempts of becoming the agent of his own story repeatedly participate in the bi-directional discourse of cross-cultural violence. By rendering visible the particular discursive conditionality and strategies of its own narrative and rhetorical direction, the novel brings to the surface those dishonest assumptions that underlie the idealist rhetoric of integration, assimilation, intercultural dialogue, or multiculturalism. While there is a certain risk in seeing social and representational violence as an inherent and indeed constitutive component of *The Book of Khalid*—remember that "you can get burned when you are touched and called by the other"[94]—there lies in my view a larger danger in accepting statist interpretive responses that deny the presence of this very historical violence. When reading Anglophone Arab representations, one cannot afford to ignore many of these representations' particular concerns with the predicament of their own violent adjustment. Rihani's novel is an early example of this metafictional tendency. It is first of all this quality that marks it as an

---

93   Michel Foucault, "The Ethics of the Concern for Self as a Practice of Freedom," *Ethics: Subjectivity and Truth. The Essential Works of Michel Foucault 1954–1984*, Vol. 1, ed. Paul Rabinow, trans. Robert Hurley (New York: The New P, 1997) 281-301.

94   Spivak, "Terror: A Speech after 9/11," 378.

important intertext for any reading of Anglophone Arab articulations that is attentive to the political and ethical implications of the works it chooses. The study of
competing aesthetic framings of planetary conflicts, the exploration of the trivializing modes of Orientalist objectification, or increased interpretive attention to
the victims of Occidentalist counter-representations alone do not bring an end to
the social suffering inflicted by global violence. The urgent need to produce conditions of peaceful coexistence intensifies the need to develop modes of cultural
criticism which make the conditions from which cross-cultural violence continues
to arise intolerable. My readings of conflictual imaginaries presented in the course
of this study, ranging from William Peter Blatty's horror-narrative, *The Exorcist*, to
the Palestinian concept artist Emily Jacir's Sydney performance, *Material for a Film*,
share this aim.

3.2   Post-Gibran Before *The Prophet*: Khalid's Figurality and Performative Arabness

"They are so proud of Gibran. Probably the most overestimated writer in history.
I don't think that any Lebanese has ever read him. If they had, they would keep
their mouth fucking shut."[95]

This is how Mohammad, the main narrative voice in Rabih Alameddine's 1998
novel, *Koolaids*, refers to probably the best-known representative of the early
émigré school of Arab American writing. The decisively unfilial fictional comment
on Kahlil Gibran's[96] literary work and its dominant Lebanese reception does not
at all represent a rare exception within contemporary Anglophone Arab writing.
In fact, the majority of representations with which I am concerned in this study
regularly take up an implicit or explicit critical stance toward what is known in
the Arab world as *Adab al-Mahjar*.[97] The need to go beyond what is seen as the

---

95   Rabih Alameddine, *Koolaids. The Art of War* (London: Abacus, 1998) 243.
96   Gibran's name was changed from Gibran Khalil Gibran to Kahlil Gibran during a registration
       procedure when he first entered a Boston school at the age of twelve. In his English-language
       writings, he would use this bureaucratically domesticated and Americanized abbreviation of
       his name. See Hassan, *Immigrant Narratives: Orientalism and Cultural Translation in Arab Amer-
       ican and Arab British Literature* 64.
97   *Adab* is the Arabic word for "literature". *Mahjar* translates as "place of immigration or exile."
       The term Adab al-Mahjar (Literature of Exile) is used in the Arabic-speaking academic world
       for the late 19th- and early 20th-century diasporic literary production nurtured by Arab immi-
       grants in the Americas, particularly in Sao Paulo, Buenos Aires, and New York. On Anglophone
       Mahjar writings, see Nadeem Naimy, *The Lebanese Prophets of New York* (Beirut: American U of
       Beirut P, 1985) and Geoffrey Nash, *The Anglo-Arab Encounter: Fiction and Autobiography by Arab
       Writers in English* 32-47.

self-Orientalizing confirmation of Western expectations presumably prevalent in early Arab American writing has by now been widely accepted among literary writers, artists, and critics alike. In 1999, Khaled Mattawa and Munir Akash edited an anthology of new Arab American short poems, prose, auto-fictional writing, and critical essays under the title *Post-Gibran*.[98] The volume is particularly concerned with a more recent body of literature which intentionally moves beyond both the equally essentialist and reductionist mode of Arab immigrant articulations associated with the Arab American *Mahjar* school and with those writings in its immediate wake. As Mattawa puts it in his own poetological contribution on the multiple sources, predicament, and potentials of Arab cultural self-locations within the US context,

> [...] the staples of grandmotherly aphorisms, thickly accented patriarchal tradi-
> tionalism, culinary nostalgia, religious dogma, belly dancing and adoration for
> Kahlil Gibran are meager nourishments for cultural identity, let alone a cultural
> revival and subsequent engagement with the larger American culture.[99]

The project recommended here has quite ambivalent implications regarding its literary politics of cultural identification. On the one hand, it presents itself as being inspired by Adonis' poetological call for re-discovering the Arab-Islamic cultural heritage's inherent modernity and innovative capacities outside the politico-cultural model of Western modernity[100] rather than by what is seen as a solely spiritual model of trans-civilizational renewal exemplified by *Mahjar* intellectuals like Gibran.[101] On the other hand, the notion of diasporic creativity, although clearly identifiable as Arabic in character, is placed within and against the dominant social order and already-established symbolic patterns that regulate the Western repertory of defining non-Western alterity. Without further specifying their criteria of selection, Mattawa and Akash claim some truly Arab presences in contem-

---

98 Khaled Mattawa and Munir Akash, eds., *Post-Gibran: Anthology of New Arab American Writing* (Syracuse, New York: Syracuse UP, 1999).

99 Khaled Mattawa, "Freeways and Rest Houses: Towards an Arab Location on the American Cultural Map," *Post-Gibran: Anthology of New Arab American Writing*, eds. Khaled Mattawa and Munir Akash (New York: Syracuse UP, 1999) 61.

100 See Adonis, *Introduction to Arab Poetics* 81.

101 It might be noteworthy here that Mattawa's own English-language poetry was decisively influenced by his work as a translator of Arabic poetry. Aside from the obvious influence of the Palestinian national poet, Mahmoud Darwish, Adonis' poetic model seems to have been particularly exemplary for Mattawa. In 2010, he published a substantial volume with his own translations of works by Adonis; *Adonis: Selected Poems*, trans. Khaled Mattawa (New Haven: Yale UP, 2010). For his poetry, see also Khaled Mattawa, *Tocqueville* (Kalamazoo, MI: New Issues P/Western Michigan U, 2010); *Amorisco* (Keene, NY: Ausable P, 2008); *Zodiac of Echoes* (Keene, NY: Ausable P, 2003) and *Ismailia Eclipse: Poems* (Riverdale-on-Hudson, NY: Sheep Meadow P, 1996).

porary Arab American re-presence: an equally ethical and aesthetical "system of values, attitudes, and manners" that can be traced back as far as the ancient epic of Gilgamesh and that persists in affecting current literary production in Arabic.[102] Such post-Gibranian self-representations are expected to invalidate a false image of Arabs, Arab Americans, the Arab world, the "'Arab-American' world," and Arab "destiny," the design of which has been "created by the American imagination"[103] and has for too long been re-created and consequently affirmed by Arab American writers. Thus, the cultural articulation of a critically renewed Arab American identity is not only directed against American misrepresentations but also "needs a basis of eloquent and thorough social critique of its own subculture."[104] The "Post" in the anthology's title first and foremost suggests new directions of voicing divergent Arab American subjectivities that, while bearing witness to the rich cultural heritage of what the editors variously call "our spirit of Arabness" or "our Gelgamishian [sic!] spirit,"[105] do not allow for comfortable notions of ethnic Arab literature, both in relation to Western mainstream perceptions as well as regarding the impossibility of some absolute return to an authentic origin. However, *Post-Gibran* neglects to reflect thoroughly on its very point of negative reference.

If literary critics aim to explore the so-called "Gibran Phenomenon," as Waïl S. Hassan does in his 2011 study, *Immigrant Narratives*,[106] they try to explain the enduring popularity of the Lebanese-American writer rather than "his works themselves, which [according to Hassan] do not reward rigorous analysis."[107] At best, they acknowledge Gibran's sly strategic use of "the trope of visionary Romanticism [...] to negotiate the market from within the institutions of power"[108] to achieve acknowledgment as well as economic success through the representational channels of Western mainstream discourse. At worst, scholars of Anglophone Arab literature diagnose "the failure of his project on the personal, social, and intellectual

---

102 Khaled Mattawa and Munir Akash, Introduction, *Post-Gibran: Anthology of New Arab American Writing* xi.

103 Mattawa and Akash, Introduction, xi.

104 Mattawa, "Freeways and Rest Houses: Towards an Arab Location on the American Cultural Map," 60.

105 Mattawa, "Freeways and Rest Houses," 60.

106 "The Gibran Phenomenon" is the title of Chapter 2 of Hassan, *Immigrant Narratives: Orientalism and Cultural Translation in Arab American and Arab British Literature* 59-77. The respective chapter is devoted to Gibran's work and his immensely successful reception in the West.

107 Hassan, *Immigrant Narratives: Orientalism and Cultural Translation in Arab American and Arab British Literature* 62; see also Waïl S. Hassan, "Gibran and Orientalism," *Arab Voices in Diaspora: Critical Perspectives on Anglophone Arab Literature*, ed. Layla Al Maleh (Amsterdam: Rodopi, 2009) 65-92.

108 Richard E. Hishmeh, "Strategic Genius, Disidentification, and the Burden of *The Prophet* in Arab-American Poetry," *Arab Voices in Diaspora: Critical Perspectives on Anglophone Arab Literature*, ed. Layla Al Maleh (Amsterdam: Rodopi, 2009) 96.

levels."[109] Following both views, Gibran's Anglophone cultural pseudo-translations regularly take the form of self-exoticizing esoteric cogitations, which at least implicitly affirm the anti-Arab racial and cultural chauvinisms of early 20th century American mainstream representations. Accordingly, his writings contributed to the affirmation of the dominant discourse of American Orientalism at a time when European colonial powers were redrawing the entire Middle Eastern map rather than opening new discursive spaces for a critical dialogue between cultures or a future Anglophone Arab translational poetics.

When first reading *The Prophet*,[110]—a collection of prose poetry which became Gibran's by far most successful work ever written in English, was translated into more than fifty languages since its first publication in 1923, and has been consistently placed on best-selling lists around the world—one cannot but agree that this *Mahjar* writer indeed knew how to address the Western and Westernized global audience's expectations. Written at a historical moment when all things Oriental were particularly *en vogue* in American fashion, marketing, film, popular music, and fine art, the sociohistorical experience of first-generation Arab immigration to the US seems to be almost totally neglected in this book. However, the mystic visions of universal humanity and transcendental connectivity presented by Gibran are framed by a narrative (and articulated through the words) of an Oriental would-be re-migrant called Almustafa (The Chosen One). The prophet-like hero of the short frame story is only blurrily marked as a representative of some mysterious Arabic-Islamic conglomerate East. Having lived in the foreign city of Orphalese for twelve years, he is about to board a ship which is to take him home, a place of origin not further specified. Shortly before his departure, Almustafa is stopped by local women and men. They ask him to explain the deeper meaning of the human condition. His elaborations on the spiritual dimensions of love, marriage, children, joy, pain and sorrow, crime and punishment, reason, freedom and law—the philosophical and mystical preaching of the frame character—turn into the poetic voice of the collection's main part.[111]

I am not interested here in analyzing the formal or topical details of *The Prophet*'s short, almost aphoristic chapters. Nor do I aim at tracing the Arabic-Islamic sources, Baha'i influences, or Persian pretexts of Gibran's instant mysticism.[112] What I am instead concerned with is the particular discursive (pre)figuration

109   Hassan, *Immigrant Narratives: Orientalism and Cultural Translation in Arab American and Arab British Literature* 77.
110   Kahlil Gibran, *The Prophet*, new annot. ed. (Richmond: Oneworld, 2012).
111   Gibran, *The Prophet* 7.
112   For this, see Suheil Bushrui, Introduction, *The Prophet*, by Kahlil Gibran (Richmond: Oneworld, 2012) xiii-xiv.

of the literary prophet in relation to Khalid's "figurative Arab-ness"[113] created by Rihani. Looking closely at the selective adaptation of the character of Khalid in Gibran's performative dressing-up allows an alternative assessment of the paradoxes and power of strategic imitations and inauthentic self-enactments within Anglophone Arab representations beyond the strict division between a pre-Gibran and a post-Gibran discourse.

Khalid claims to be the chosen revolutionary voice of the Arab while still imprisoned in New York. Thus, his prophetic announcement to return to his place of birth and to liberate the Arab world comes with an equal portion of shivering arrogance and ironic boast.[114] In fact, we do not learn whether anybody has stopped him on his repeatedly postponed journey aboard the transatlantic carrier of pan-Arab liberty or if any American has ever asked him for his spiritually inspired political visions and worldly-triggered hyper-moralistic truth. Given the tragic anti-hero's rather conflictual relation to his ultimate socio-economic surrounding, this seems rather unlikely, and the question is probably almost irrelevant for the following plot of remigration. For my argument, it is just as irrelevant whether Khalid's fictional prophethood finds its key inspiration in the experience of America's secular liberalism[115] or if it instead lies in the "spiritual values of the East."[116]

I rather wonder whether the hallucinating Arab prisoner's first distressed prophetic enunciation could indeed have inspired Gibran's successful literary self-invention, *The Prophet*, or his performative embodiment of the chosen arch-Oriental writer-prophet. Could Rihani's fiction of Anglophone Arab prophecy have functioned as a sort of role model for Gibran and his early English-language collections of Sufi-style parables like *The Madman* (1918) and *The Forerunner* (1920)? Is it possible that Khalid's angry farewell to New York anticipated *The Prophet*'s mild address of welcome directed at an English-reading global audience, an address that would soon advance to Gibran's most successful poetic conglomeration of esoteric Orientalism? And, if so: what went wrong, either in the respective process of selective adaptation or within most literary critics' degrading reception of Gibran's famous work?

Rihani and Gibran are regularly placed side by side in distinctive sub-files into the virtual *Mahjar* archive of early Arab American major literary figures: the first as

---

113   Jacob Berman, "Mahjar Legacies: A Reinterpretation," *Between the Middle East and the Americas: The Cultural Politics of Diaspora*, eds. Evelyn Alsultany and Ella Shohat (Ann Arbor: U of Michigan P, 2012) 66.

114   Rihani, *The Book of Khalid* 123-25.

115   Geoffrey P. Nash, *The Arab Writer in English. Arab Themes in a Metropolitan Language, 1908–1958* (Brighton: Sussex Academic P, 1998) 28-29.

116   Ameen Albert Rihani, "The Book of Khalid and The Prophet. Similar Universal Concerns with Different Perspectives: A Comparative Study," *PALMA* 7.1 (2001): 33.

an early pioneer of Anglophone Arab writing across the genres, the latter as the internationally best-known and economically most successful producer of what could be coined Arab American kitsch-Orientalism. Both men belonged to the so-called first wave of Arab, largely Maronite-Christian immigration to the US from the Syrian province of the Ottoman Empire. Both immigrated to the US at an infantile age. Rihani arrived in New York in 1888 at the age of eleven. He moved from his native Freike, a village near Beirut, with his father, his brother, and his sister.[117] Gibran grew up in the Lebanese mountain village, Bisharri, and in 1895, at the age of twelve, immigrated with his mother, his brother, and his two sisters to Boston.[118] The two first met in 1910 in Paris.[119] They were already friends when Gibran followed Rihani's advice and rented a studio in Manhattan in 1912.[120] The seven drawings made by Gibran to illustrate *The Book of Khalid* testify their early personal contact and intellectual collaboration (fig. 7).

The two proponents of disparate Anglophone Arab (pseudo-)prophetic writing, Gibran and Rihani, were founding members of *Ar-Rabita al-Qalamiya* or *Rubiyat al-Qalam* [The Pen League], a book-club-like diasporic literary organization established New York City in 1920 by intellectuals of Arab descent, among them Levantine immigrant writers like Mikhail Naimy, Ibrahim Rihbany, Abdul Masih Haddad, and Wadi Bahout. Gibran would later emerge as the president of that very organization. Although the majority of these men never received formal education in either Arabic or English, they often wrote in and experimented with both languages. While most of their English-language works remained unnoticed by a wider English-reading public in the West, the group members' impact on diasporic Arab journalism, transnational political activism, and the transformation of Arabic literary practice within the Middle East was significant. The diasporic identification of early Arab immigrants is particularly evident in the diverse Arabic-language newspapers and journals that had come into existence since the 1890s.

---

117   On Rihani's biography, see "Biography of Ameen F. Rihani" and "Timetable of Events in Ameen F. Rihani's Life and in the World," *Ameen Rihani: Bridging East and West: A Pioneering Call for Arab-American Understanding*, eds. Nathan C. Funk and Betty J. Sitka (Lanham, MD: UP of America, 2004) 151-63. Berman and Hassan argue that he immigrated at the age of twelve with his uncle and teacher. Berman, "Mahjar Legacies: A Reinterpretation," 66 and Hassan, *Immigrant Narratives: Orientalism and Cultural Translation in Arab American and Arab British Literature* 40.

118   On Gibran's biography, see Suheil B. Bushrui and Joe Jenkins, *Kahlil Gibran: Man and Poet. A New Biography* (Oxford: Oneworld, 1998).

119   Todd Fine, Afterword, *The Book of Khalid*, by Ameen Rihani (New York: Melville House, 2012) 320.

120   Suheil Bushrui, Introduction, *The Prophet*, by Kahlil Gibran (Richmond: Oneworld Pub., 2012): xiii.

121   On Rihani's authorial strategy of inventing an editor-narrator who claims to draw on various manuscripts and other sources in translation, see 3.4 of this study.

Figure 7: Detail from the cover illustration by Kahlil Gibran for Ameen Rihani's The Book of Khalid, 1911. This illustration shows in Arabic letters the novel's title, Kitab Khalid, as well as the year of its first publication. The illustration could alternatively be interpreted as showing a fragment of the cover of the fictional/original Khedival library manuscript that the literary narrative claims to be based upon.[121]

Often sectarian in their editorial composition and readership, periodicals like *Al-Hoda* (Guidance), *Kawkab Amrika* (The Planet of America), *Miray'at al-Gharb* (Mirror of the West), or *Al-Funun* (The Arts) functioned as particularly important platforms for the formation of a distinctive transnational "public sphere linking *mahjar* to *mashriq*."[122]

While establishing new patterns of diasporic politics, these periodicals also had to respond to the pressures of a heavily discriminatory and assimilationist US context. The first generation's attempt to preserve an Arab identity against such pressures increasingly clashed with the socio-political needs and practical

---

122   Stacy Fahrenthold, "Transnational Modes and Media: The Syrian Press in the *Mahjar* and Emigrant Activism during World War I," *Mashriq & Mahjar* 1.1 (2013): 30. The geographical term *Mashriq* refers to the region east of Egypt.

predicaments of legal inclusion and economic participation. Particularly among the first American-born generation, exclusively diasporic-oriented debates on Arab-American identity were no longer seen as adequate for giving sufficient answers to urgently pressing questions of local everyday life in which this generation found itself caught up. The threat of being excluded and discriminated against within the US on the basis of racial definitions of American identity and citizenship rights was directly related to intense debates on who was and who was not a free white person according to the Naturalization Act of 1790. Before the 1920 census classified Syrians and Palestinians under the racial category "foreign-born white population," Arab immigrants had to prove their eligibility for citizenship in a series of individual petitions and court cases: hence, the practical need for individual immigrants and ethnic groups to perform cultural whiteness and non-Asiatic identity. However, such performative strategy could easily collide with both the Mahjar intellectuals' broader political goal to promote a sense of diasporic ethnic identity among the Arab-American community living in the United States and the American majority's perception of Arabs as intrinsically non-European, non-Christian, and non-white.[123]

Arab Americans share this experience with other late 19th-century immigrant groups (non-European as well as European) initially cast as nonwhites. As with the Irish, Italians, and Jews, Arab whiteness was a socially and culturally constructed category that proved infinitely malleable as a political tool of either inclusion or exclusion. But the predicament of the Arab American's *Whiteness of a Different Color*, of their particular not-quite-whiteness,[124] and the various conscious and unconscious attempts at either escaping into impossible invisibility or critically exploiting the status of always being out of place on both sides of "the color-line"[125] continued to shape social struggles, identity politics, and cultural practice of Arab (diasporic) intellectuals throughout the 20th century.

---

123   Alixa Naff, *Becoming American. The Early Arab Immigrant Experience* (Carbondale: Southern Illinois P, 1985) and Gregory Orfalea, *The Arab Americans: A History* (Northampton, MA: Olive Branch P, 2006).

124   Here I am not only referring to Matthew Frye Jacobson's seminal *Whiteness of a Different Color: European Immigrants and the Alchemy of Race* (Cambridge, MA: Harvard UP, 1998) and Homi Bhabha's by now classical psychological definition of colonial mimicry in his 1984 essay "Of Mimicry and Man" [Homi Bhabha, "Of Mimicry and Man: The Ambivalence of Colonial Discourse," *October. Discipleship: A Special Issue on Psychoanalysis* 28.2 (1984): 126, 132]. I first and foremost draw on Jamil Khoury's and Stephen Combs's (dirs.) film documentary *Not Quite White: Arabs, Slavs, and the Contours of Contested Whiteness*, ADF/Typecast Films, 2012. The film integrates scenes from Khoury's 2010 stage play, *WASP: White Arab Slovak Pole*, as well as interviews with scholars and activists from the Arab American and Polish American communities to critically reflect on the racialized history of these communities and particularly on the ambivalent history of their whitening through the use of anti-Black racism.

125   W.E.B. Du Bois, *The Souls of Black Folk* (1903; Oxford: Oxford UP, 2007) 15.

Though classified as racially white according to the official census and most affirmative actions, Arabs have nonetheless been discursively constituted as a distinctive non-white group. The ongoing history of the dominant anti-Arab discourse shows a strange, almost fetishistic fixation on the Arab bodies' non-whiteness as the visible indicator of their intrinsic cultural alterity and the political threat to national security that these bodies represent.[126] Therefore, one cannot be surprised to find in Anglophone Arab representations to this day a constant concern with both the ambivalence of (partial) recognition and racist subjection as well as forms of resistance against being transformed into a normalized, that is Westernized, Oriental Other. Such countering of the equally ambivalent and authoritative Orientalizing discourse does by definition enter the representational spheres of politics and social activism. As I will show, Anglophone Arab attempts to lay bare the contradictions and destabilize the discriminatory paradigms of repressive integration also take place on the tropic axis between allegory and metonymy. This axis is of particularly importance to literary narratives and performative arts.

With the re-racialization of Islam and Middle Easterners after September 11, 2001, the contradictory articulations of Orientalizing desire and fear would not only turn out to be alarmingly well-preserved but would also involve a rather unexpected dynamic of global hyper-visibility and legal violence that demands critically renewed emancipatory strategies.[127] It is against this highly ambivalent background of instable racial identification and the often mutually excluding socio-cultural exigencies resulting from these identifications that one needs to evaluate early Arab American writers' strategies to engage the American audience. On the one hand, these writers found themselves in a discursive situation that demanded the reduction of their writings' cultural distance from European and Western narrative traditions. On the other hand, they quickly learned that any commercially successful address of a broader readership required marketing their works' tropological proximity to mainstream Americans' imaginaries of the Oriental. The employment of ancient-Eastern images, biblical rhetoric, and Christian spirituality was certainly a consequence of early 20th century Arab American self-representations' both racist and assimilationist discursive prefiguration. The literal or implicit self-distancing of Arab immigrant writers from the political actuality of (pan-)Arab nationalist political movements or contemporary Islam was another strategy of proving their successful assimilation into American mainstream culture and rendering themselves less alien.

---

126   Keith Feldman, "The (Il)legible Arab Body and the Fantasy of National Democracy," *MELUS* 31.4 (2006): 33-53.

127   Amaney A. Jamal and Nadine Christine Naber, eds., *Race and Arab Americans Before and After 9/11: From Invisible Citizens to Visible Subjects* (Syracuse: Syracuse UP, 2008). See also Salah Hassan, "Arabs, Race and the Post-September 11 National Security State," *Middle East Report* 224 (2002): 18.

One particularly promising way for Arab American intellectuals of the 1910s and 1920s to perform the difficult task of presenting oneself as a clearly identifiable transhistorical arch-Oriental representative while denying any relation to the socio-economic actuality of what contemporary Americans now called the Middle East was to cast themselves and their literary characters in the role of an essentially depoliticized spiritual Eastern prophet. As Evelyn Shakir has put it, "[t]he first generation of Arab-American writers [...] dressed carefully for their encounter with the American public, putting on the guise of prophet, preacher, or man of letters."[128] This seems to be precisely the performative and poetic formula used by Gibran. His prophet's tremendous success is that of a non-threatening exotic stranger coming from an imaginative, spiritual East, situated at the same time both far away and close, who could be easily assimilated into the dominant American narrative without undermining the nation's white-liberal-secular self-perception. As previously stated, Gibran's Almustafa is preaching in the harbor of a fictional city named Orphalese. Against the historical context of *The Prophet*'s genesis, one tends to see this urban setting as a clear literary reference to New York City. But the poetic frame setting does not overtly signify any real socio-historical place. The city's name might hint to the mythological worlds of the ancient musician-poet Orpheus. It could also be interpreted as drawing on the Aramaic name of Jerusalem, *Urshalim*, the City of Peace. But the brief narrative depiction of *The Prophet*'s urban setting allows for little comparison with any American or non-American metropole in the early 20th century. Orphalese rather seems to represent an almost primordial or *Urphallic* spatiality of the prophet's visionary eruption,[129] an equally mythical and sacred nowhere of the poetic hero's prophecy. If one insists on locating this city, one would have to locate it in the imagined geography of some mystical East. The place of Almustafa's temporary exile and the isle of Almustafa's birth seem to represent one and the same place. Therefore, his prophetic voyage home is not a physical but a spiritual one; it concerns the transcendental spatiality of the human soul rather than the cultural geography of East and West. Gibran's prophet, in other words, departs from a city that he seems to have never lived in, and he seemingly stays within what his pre-prophetic self could never enter.

There are few literary traces of Gibran's personal history within *The Prophet*, and the references to Khalid's multiply broken path to prophecy are at best superficial. We do not learn much about this other Almustafa's exilic experience, of his socioeconomic life before he turns away from the materialist world to turn himself into

---

128   Evelyn Shakir, "Arab American Literature," *New Immigrant Literatures in the United States: A Sourcebook to Our Multicultural Heritage*, ed. Alpana Sharma Knippling (Westport CT: Greenwood P, 1996) 6.

129   This would be a third (admittedly one-sided psychological) reading of the fictional city name.

an Oriental prophet. The latter cannot "go in peace and without sorrow […] without a wound in the spirit," and he remembers "days of pain" as well as long "nights of aloneness" which he spent within the city's walls.[130] There are remains of a certain ill-tempered energy, maybe even a residual-worldly anger, in Almustafa's voice when he speaks of the spiritual uselessness of "burning your law books."[131] Although the reader can find some abstract memories of real-world suffering and respective regrets, the prophet Almustafa obviously succeeds in overcoming these materialist difficulties. Leaving behind his "heart made sweet with hunger and with thirst,"[132] he finally speaks out those rather pedestrian eternal truths, that—critics of Anglophone Arab literature may like it or not—to this day are recited all over the world and in various languages by lovers of esoteric poetry on occasions of weddings, funerals, or birthdays, not to speak of innumerable esoteric blogs that pseudo-spiritually molest the World Wide Web.

Although Rihani created the Arab-American transmigrant, Khalid, more than one decade before Gibran let Almustafa preach shared spiritual humanity at his universal exilic non-place, the two narratives are clearly connected through more than their authors' biographical linkage, Gibran's visual framing of Rihani's novel, a shared concern with universal spirituality, or the common use of a prophetic mode of emplotment. Both literary projects are deeply grounded in the immigrant experience with and the anticipation of West-Eastern misrepresentations. They work through and re-resemble essentially the same anticipations and representations, but they represent two significantly different directions of responding to their shared discursive prefiguration. The dilemma of having to prove themselves worthy within a hegemonic Western discourse which insists that Arabs perform some strictly prefigured cultural difference while at the same time disavowing any sociopolitical claim of difference has continued to molest and inspire later generations of Anglophone Arab artists, writers, and critics. Most post-*Mahjar* intellectuals have seemingly opted for Rihani's narrative pronouncement of a disturbing multiplicity of Arabness rather than for Gibran's model of staging disciplined and clearly located Arab difference. I do, however, argue—and will further show in the course of my study—that the two strategies are not always as strictly separated as some critics want to have it. The mutual effects of self-Orientalizing mimicry and counter-Orientalist mockery are sometimes very slippery, frequently hard to control, and by definition contested by the effects of (consciously or unconsciously) failed imitation. If Khalid's non-harmonizing excess of partial imitations seems more appropriate to disrupt Western Orientalist representations' authority, this is first and foremost due to the moral inappropriateness of his excess. His repetition

---

130 Gibran, *The Prophet* 3.
131 Gibran, *The Prophet* 54.
132 Gibran, *The Prophet* 48.

of stereotypes leads to the confusion of cross-cultural priorities and thus to what Homi Bhabha calls "the strategic production of conflictual [...] 'identity effects'."[133]

Let me briefly elaborate on the splitting effects of Rihani's literary figuration of Khalid before revisiting Gibran's posing. Although *The Book of Khalid* shows a particularly creative exaggeration of the very prophetic Orientalness assigned to Arab immigrant writers that was so strictly adopted by Gibran, Rihani's mode of narrating allows much more imaginative varieties of immigrant Arabness. Khalid's assumingly naïve endeavor to envisage a universal humanity free from racial and cultural chauvinism[134] willingly clashes with American perceptions of Middle Eastern American presences and finally leads to his remigration. The part of the novel set in the US not only directly addresses the particular diasporic organizational conditions of its own emergence—one of Khalid's many jobs is that of the local Democratic Party's "Agent to the editors of the Syrian newspapers of New York"[135]—but also depicts early 20th century Arab immigrant everyday experiences of institutionalized discrimination. Khalid is repeatedly sanctioned on the basis of cultural and racial prejudices. When his Tammany Hall boss calls him a "brazen-faced" descendant of "mountain peasants or other barbarious tribes" and recommends that Khalid should rather preach his inner morality "to the South African Pappoos,"[136] the insult obviously goes beyond the diagnosis of inappropriate political rhetorics or a lack of communicative manners. The Tammany boss's choice of words clearly refers to the Arab immigrant's racialized socio-cultural status as an intrinsically non-Western person of color.

At this point, it is important to remind ourselves that Khalid's first occupation is not that of a preacher or prophet. Before he, with little success, tries the professional roles of the self-educating anti-capitalist student, the womanizing darwish-bohemian, the hyper-moral assistant lawyer, or the public Tammany orator, he, together with his friend, Shakib, makes his life as a street peddler. It is this social role more than any other that marks him as a degraded, lower-class Arab immigrant. As a peddler, he is highly visible on the streets of New York. By using the figure of the "Street Arab,"[137] Rihani's novelistic representation plays out the dominant American discourse' stereotypical trope of Oriental identity around the turn of the century, a trope that hardly responded to the *Mahjar* intellectuals' self-image. The narrative foil of immigrant Arabness in need of normalizing eradication had already been proffered by popular writers of European descent in books like Horatio

---

133   Bhabha, "Of Mimicry and Man: The Ambivalence of Colonial Discourse," 131.

134   See Naji Oueijan, "The Formation of a Universal Self," *Ameen Rihani: Bridging East and West: A Pioneering Call for Arab-American Understanding*, eds. Nathan C. Funk and Betty J. Sitka (Lanham, MD: UP of America, 2004) 83-92.

135   Rihani, *Book of Khalid* 57.

136   Rihani, *Book of Khalid* 61.

137   Berman, "Mahjar Legacies: A Reinterpretation," 69.

Alger Jr.'s 1871 children's series *Tattered Tom, or, The Story of a Street Arab*.[138] In 1890, Jacob Riis had captured the figure of the New York Street Arab in a collection of photographs (fig. 8 and fig. 9) entitled *How the Other Half Lives*.[139]

Figure 8: Jacob A. Riis, A Peddler Sits on his Bedroll, 1888, photography.

In these visual and textual narratives, Arab immigrants appeared as forming an ethnically unique group of poor illiterates who, despite their culturally determined "wild independence"[140] and "biblical code of ethics,"[141] nevertheless worked hard to climb the social ladder and enter the American mainstream. Khalid inhabits exactly this role and thus acts as a representative of the hegemonic narrative's essentialism. At the same time, he disrupts the linear discourse of diagnosing socio-cultural shortcomings and prescribing unconditional assimilation. His repeated inversion and reversal of the Arab street figure and his sturdy multiplication of alternative self-identifications far beyond that figure do not allow for any

---

138   Horatio Alger Jr., *Tattered Tom, or, The Story of a Street Arab* (Boston: Loring, 1871).

139   Jacob A. Riis, *How the Other Half Lives. Studies among the Tenements of New York* (New York: Charles Scriber's & Sons, 1890).

140   Alger Jr., *Tattered Tom, or, The Story of a Street Arab* 104, quoted from Berman, "Mahjar Legacies: A Reinterpretation," 69.

141   Berman, "Mahjar Legacies: A Reinterpretation," 70.

Figure 9: Jacob A. Riis, Street Arabs in Night Quarters, 1888– 89, photography.

either/or-fixation of abstract Anglophone Arabness. Khalid's constant juxtaposing of discursively presumed ontological being and de-facto performed cultural self-making radically questions the truth claim of any pre-figurative Arab identity. His abortive immigrant story instead stresses the inescapably performative modality of being Arab within and against those codes that have prefigured dominant Western perceptions of how Arabs are supposed to feel, think, and act. Even when he finally takes up the role of the Arab prophet, he is not willing to mask this masquerade's internal contradictions. The narrative of Khalid's many selves instead highlights the subversive power of performative contradictions. His decisively politicized and frankly ludicrous interpretation of the imprisoned prophet figure has little to do with the distilled exotic trope of the dignified Oriental mystic-prophet for which Gibran opted. It is this insight into what Jacob Berman calls the "sophisticated strategies of figurative self-representation,"[142] as a tropic and performative tool of strategic subversion, critical revision, and correlative identification, that characterizes many Anglophone Arab representations after Gibran.

---

142   Berman, "Mahjar Legacies: A Reinterpretation," 74.

In my view, we cannot blame Rihani's Khalid for Gibran's Orientalizing self-inventions. Nor should we blame Rihani for his fellow immigrant's highly selective adaptation of only one sub-facet of the literary character. If it is at all true that "Gibran adopted for himself Khalid's role,"[143] he only followed some of Khalid's deceptively genuine Orientalizing side-steps. I do, however, equally hesitate to over-hastily judge Gibran for marketing a poetically abstracted and obviously stereotypical Arab image as the image of his true individual self. It seems to me naïvely essentialist to lament that this image does not truthfully represent him or his particular ethnic community's authentic cultural heritage. Even if one agrees with those critics who, for good reasons consider it a mistake to understand Gibran's English-language writings "as representative of *mahjar* literature's overall characteristics,"[144] we cannot deny his immense visibility as a representative of this very Arab American cultural sphere. Gibran has obviously found "a truth"[145] among the different performative facets of Khalid's lies: one that taught him how to sell his exotic attraction to a Western reading public. If today's literary critics miss Khalid's powerful pain of multiply queered identifications in Almustafa's straightforward sermons, this might indicate Gibran's reluctance to follow the arduous fictional way that Rihani has paved for him. But this absence does not say anything about the possibly no-less-bumpy path that led to Gibran's public conspicuousness or about *The Prophet*'s relation to the broader *Mahjar* experience.

Looking closely at photographic portraits of the Arab American immigrant teenager taken around 1898 by his surrogate-paternal friend and early mentor, Fred Holland Day, while in addition scrutinizing with equal iconographic rigor the poet-painter's self-portrait, drawn in the 1930s (fig. 13), might offer an alternative interpretive hint. Examining the photographs today, one cannot but sense both the symbolic contradictions and the tragic performative irony of Gibran's prophetic literary gestures and publically generated images. Although some of these portraits were frequently reproduced by both Gibran himself as well as his critics as a means of (self-)representation, none of them depict the historical agent Gibran at the age of approximately fifteen. They do not represent his independently defined late 19th-century social likeness but the photographer's power and his camera's potential to capture and visually freeze a theatrical staging.

While the first two images (fig. 10 and 11) present the result of a slightly homo-erotic and explicitly exoticist Orientalist imaginary projected onto the immigrant

---

143   Ameen Albert Rihani, "The Book of Khalid and The Prophet. Similar Universal Concerns with
       Different Perspectives: A Comparative Study," 34. See also Nash, *The Arab Writer in English* 38.
144   Berman, "Mahjar Legacies: A Reinterpretation," 73.
145   I do refer here to Gibran, *The Prophet* 55: "Say not, 'I have found the truth', but rather 'I have
       found a truth'".

Figure 10: Photographic portrait of Gibran by Fred Holland Day, ca. 1895.

boy's defenseless body staged in front of the studio-camera, the significantly dis-similar depiction of Gibran with a book in his hands, dressed in the costume of a self-learning patrician student (fig. 12), already anticipates the young reader's later career as an artist and literary writer. Gibran's own drawing (fig. 13), projecting the poetically engrossed self-image of an intellectual pilgrim and religious mystic wrapped in white cotton drapery, seems to selectively combine both poles of the earlier photographs' pictorial semantics. In this drawing, the visual trope of the beautiful Arab/Bedouin boy appealing to Western sexual fantasies has apparently made room for the iconic consolidation of more spiritually oriented Orientalist desires. Taken together, the four images allow for visually tracing the history of the self-Orientalizing merchandizing brand that the world-famous artist and poet would become. In my view, they can open up an alternative perspective on the fine line between strategic self-Orientalization and the (self-)exploitation by or of Orientalized people. In addition, these images invite the spectator to discuss the

Figure 11: Photographic portrait of Gibran by Fred Holland Day, ca. 1897.

related post-moralistic question regarding the instable gap between the morally illegitimate affirmative use of Orientalist signs and their post-moralistically justifiable resistive insertion.

When Gibran first got in contact with the wealthy Bostonian publisher and artist, Fred Holland Day, the Arab boy had already lost his Arabic first name, Khalil. Now Kahlil risked losing, if not his innocence, the right to control his own image, the right of his photographic copy, too. The much older photographer[146] dressed the young immigrant in burlesque oriental clothes and placed him in a chair covered with the coat of a wild cat. He alternatively enwrapped him in outsized Bedouin fabric before executing his proto-celebrity shots. Day was well known for his rather

---

146   Fred Holland Day was born in 1864 in Norwood, MA.

Figure 12: Photographic portrait of Gibran by Fred Holland Day, 1897.

eccentric understanding of photography as an allegorical artistic practice. The co-founder of the progressive publishing firm, Copeland and Day, was a close friend of Oscar Wilde and Stephen Crane. As the mentor to avant-garde photographers like Alvin Langdon Coburn and Edward Steichen, he was a central figure in artistic circles on both sides of the Atlantic. Since Day began making photographs in the late 1880s, he saw himself determined to promote photography as genuine fine art practice. By the turn of the century, he had established an international reputation as a key figure in the so-called pictorialist movement. This approach to photography embraced labor-intensive processes such as platinum prints, which yielded rich, tonally subtle images. It emphasized the role of the photographer as craftsman and countered the argument that photography was solely a mechanical

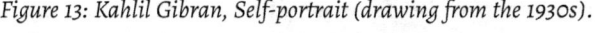

Figure 13: Kahlil Gibran, Self-portrait (drawing from the 1930s).

mimetic medium. Pictorialist photographic works instead claimed to be produced like any painter's canvas and to be as skillfully constructed as any graphic artist's rendering. Day had mounted the first important exhibition of American pictorial photography in 1900 at the Royal Photographic Society in England but was never affiliated with any American artist group.[147]

---

147 The second-generation German-Jewish immigrant, Alfred Stieglitz, was the most prominent spokesperson for pictorialist photographers in America. In 1902, he and several like-minded associates founded the New York Camera Club. Day chose to maintain independence from the New York group. On Day's photography, see Patricia J. Fanning, *Through an Uncommon Lens: The Life and Photography of F. Holland Day* (Amherst: U of Massachusetts P, 2008). On Gibran's relation to his early mentor 69-71.

In order to understand why Gibran attracted the Boston photographer's extraordinary patronage, one needs to ask further what discursively inspired and contextually enabled Day to make the Arab immigrant his model and protégé. Day, like many pictorialists, displayed a particular interest in non-Western cultures and artistic styles, most notably Japanese, Arab, and Native American art. His photographic work was especially controversial for its frequent employment of young male nudity and its glaring homoerotic aesthetics.[148] He regularly used underprivileged youths of ethnic minorities for his pseudo-ethnographic costume-driven depiction of mythical and religious subject matters. As we can learn from Jean and Kahlil Gibran, Day "would dress up young street urchins from the Slums of Boston's South End in ethnic garments."[149] During the first years after his immigration to America, Gibran was one of those underprivileged "young street urchins," a street Arab. Literary critics tend to affirm a quite euphemistic interpretation of Day's photographs of black, Asian, and other minority or immigrant children of color. They stress the philanthropic intention behind the act of turning ghetto teenagers, who suffered in their everyday lives from economic poverty and socio-cultural exclusion, into visual signs of Oriental nobility in front of the camera. It might be true that, in Gibran's particular case, photographic exoticization was indeed his entry into real-world educational and artistic support, so that within a short period Gibran managed to fortify a significantly improved image of his self that was decisively distanced from the slum conditions in which he had previously been. One could even argue that this experience triggered a process at the end of which Gibran finally "live[d] up [to] the grand illusions which Day had caught."[150] The pictorialist photographer was indeed well known for having supported the education of underprivileged youths from ethnic minorities in the Boston area and beyond. It was he who funded and guided the early American education of young Kahlil, encouraging him to study William Blake's drawings, to read Walt Whitman and Maurice Maeterlinck, and to publish his first drawings. But although the Lebanese immigrant surely must have taken note of his American mentor's artistic crossdressings for his own subsequent professional dressing-up, there is a notable absence in these early photographic images of Gibran. When gazing at these visual representations, it is not only important to note that they belong taxonomically to a particular colonial sub-genre of late 19th- and early 20th-century photography—that

---

148   On the homoerotics of Day's Orientalist photography of Gibran, see Joseph Allen Boone, *The Homoerotics of Orientalism* (New York: Columbia UP, 2014) 386-87.

149   Jean Gibran and Kahlil Gibran, *Kahlil Gibran: His Life and World* (Boston: New York Graphic Society, 1974) 54.

150   Jean Gibran and Kahlil Gibran, *Kahlil Gibran: His Life and World* 55. See also Hassan, *Immigrant Narratives: Orientalism and Cultural Translation in Arab American and Arab British Literature* 65.

of ethnographic or racial types.[151] The critical spectator, in addition, needs to see that these portraits obscure the ultimate social and cultural conditions from which they emerged. The Oriental type that Gibran is turned into has a role to play in the intellectual dandy's proto-modernist project of artistic self-innovation.[152] He is not intended to interrupt the authority of the very racist discourse upon which this innovation draws. The photographs thus represent first and foremost the repressive power-relations of racial and social alterity. Day's sublime shooting is an act of symbolic violence. It transforms the street Arab Gibran into an exotic image controlled through the exercise of artistic force, and it produces a visual knowledge of Gibran that he could not have produced himself.[153]

But although there is overt social violence *within* and *of* these images,[154] Day's visualized imaginary involves more than a violent agent and a violated object. It might be due to the particular pictorialist quality of the photographs that one is invited to speculate on an individual presence beyond the artistic re-presence. We know that Gibran would go on make quite a career by selectively cultivating and further developing the role assigned to him in these photographic stagings. With a view to his later career as the author of *The Prophet*, the necessarily selective iconological reflection presented here also needs to consider Day's 1898 series of photographs portraying the passion of Christ. In this series, the photographer himself poses as Jesus (fig. 14). Day had trained for this role by losing weight and letting his hair and beard grow. A group of seven self-portraits, known as "The Seven Last Words of Christ," directly refers to Jesus' statements from the time of his crucifixion until his death. In each single shot, the photographer, in character, assumes what he felt were facial expressions consonant with the prophet Jesus' ordeal. At the same time, he clearly draws aesthetically on a long-established Christian iconography of European paintings.

Could it be that Day was not only his own studio model, but that his photographic proclamation of the artist as the visually re-enacted Christian prophet also functioned as a role model for Gibran's performative prophethood of the 1920s

151   On ethnographic or racial types in colonial photography and the general relationship between colonial racism and the visual technologies of photography, see Arjun Appadurai, "The Colonial Backdrop," *Afterimage* 24.5 (1997): 4-7 and Deborah Poole, "An Excess of Description: Ethnography, Race, and Visual Technologies," *Annual Review of Anthropology* 34 (2005): 159-79. On racial typologies in the visual archives of anthropology, see also Marcus Banks and Richard Vokes, "Introduction: Anthropology, Photography, and the Archive," *History and Anthropology* 21.4 (2010): 337–49.

152   Trevor Fairbrother, *Making a Presence: F. Holland Day in Artistic Photography* (Andover, MA: Addison Gallery of American Art, 2012).

153   On the inherent violence of photographic representation, see Susan Sontag, "In Plato's Cave," first published in 1977; here Susan Sontag, *On Photography*, 1st electronic ed. (New York: Rosetta, 2005) 10.

154   Jean-Luc Nancy, *The Ground of the Image* (New York: Fordham UP, 2005) 20.

Figure 14: Fred Holland Day, The Last Seven Words of Christ, 1898. Series of self-portraits as Christ with crown of thorns.

and 1930s, especially for his strategic iteration of Orientalist stereotypes and his Anglophone poetic imitation of Oriental spirituality? I suggest looking at Gibran's self-Orientalizing strategies against the background of his studio experience. If we use this experience as a point of departure, should we then not see in Gibran's later self-representation, and his literary voices' prophetic role-play, a purposefully mimetic repetition of a religious-Orientalist trope first encountered in a Boston photographic studio rather than simply despising this roleplay and holding him responsible for his unconscious continuation of Orientalist exploitation? In other words, could we take Gibran's ambivalent experience of the pictorial mode as an interpretive point of departure for looking at Anglophone Arab self-Orientalizing strategies? Seen through the interpretive *lens* of Day's photographic experiments, the Anglophone Arab writer Gibran seems to have successfully adapted the early experience of pictorialist-Orientalist photography's expressive potential of making meaning beyond simply reproducing the outlines of the worlds around him. His mentor's camera had powerfully demonstrated to Gibran that an artistically and commercially successful representation of Arabness could decisively diverge from the Arab immigrant world or the Arab Middle Eastern world that he knew. In addition, this experience suggested the incorporation and artistic re-interpretation of the trope of biblical prophecy. In order to assimilate Day's artistic modalities of proto-modernist Orientalist photography into his own literary performances of Oriental prophethood, Gibran had to use quite different technical devices. He had to transform the experience of being photographically turned into an object of symbolic possession to instead take form as a symbolic representation possessed by himself.

I argue that the Arab American poet-artist did not simply reproduce hegemonic Orientalist representations to sell himself but rather cultivated a unique Orientalizing technique of selectively manipulating the presentation of information in his very own interest. Just as the pictorialists manipulated their photographic negatives and thereby injected their own aesthetic will into the beholder's

perception of visual images, Gibran imbued his self-image with Orientalist meaning, pictorial and non-pictorial alike. Whether intentionally or not, his American
mentor's photographic construction of visual meaning seems to have encouraged
or even forced Gibran to commodify the figure of the Oriental prophet-poet self-
consciously, without corrupting his self. I am not saying that such notorious poetic entrepreneurship can effectively test or even transgress normative ranges of
early 20th-century American Orientalism. But the Anglophone Arab avant-gardist's
performed embodiment of spiritually loaded poster-Orientalism is characterized
by a particular historical semantics in which the contrasting pattern of Orientalist discrimination and artistic self-grounding in Orientalist tropes overlap. While
Gibran's poetic politics of ethnic self-dressing and his literary engagement of religious tropes might not have the transgressive power of Rihani's fluxional narrative
figuration of Arabness, his performance of prophecy invites today's students of Anglophone Arab literature to critically grasp the contradictions at work within the
Mahjar discourse and Anglophone Arab writings after Gibran. Instead of avoiding
the tropes of alterity used by Gibran, they can be misused as vehicles of an active
critical commentary on their immediate discursive surroundings and continuing
effects.

The struggle for autonomy, equally aesthetic and ethical, in opposition to the bi-
directional narratives of intrinsic difference and unquestionable authenticity discussed in the previous section could not and has not at all been resolved within
more recent Anglophone Arab representations. Rather, it is my general methodological argument that the tensions between externally produced images and inner
illusions as well as the diverse narrative lines of escape resulting from these tensions should not be resolved or made invisible in the interpretation of these representations. As I will demonstrate below, the production of aesthetic and ethical
resemblances formed out of such tensions not only constitute the conceptual core
of various Anglophone Arab works to this day but are also decisively responsible
for these works' particular cross-referential and metafictional richness. In my view,
any progressivist conception that seeks to differentiate strictly between self-debas-
ing Gibran-like and emancipatory post-Gibran representations risks idealistically
planishing such conflictual dynamics and thus cannot fully decode the allegorical
and performative strategies at work in the ongoing rearrangement of individual
and collective Arab selves.

If contemporary Anglophone Arab representations gain a good portion of their
correlative aesthetic pleasures, post-moralistic pains, and critical gifts[155] from a

---

155   I use the words "pleasure," "pain," and "gift" here to indicate Anglophone Arab representa-
      tions' ambivalent quality both as documents of the socio-historical pain of being externally
      re-presented and self-reliant narratives persistently enunciating the aesthetic pleasures of
      toxically-biting critical revisions.

rather decentered mode of self-enacting, such resemblance of cultural signs and historical archives cannot be interpretively restricted to the use of any interior Arab system of reference or any authentically signifying inside. Nor can it persist in the contextual reconstruction of what is imagined as exceptionally non-Arab references. Those who aim at theoretically grasping Anglophone Arab representations as cross-cultural translations triggered by respective physical migrations, as Waïl S. Hassan does,[156] sometimes suggest that the originals of these translations can and should be fully recovered. However, in my view Anglophone Arab cultural translations, like any other cultural translation, more readily signify the irreversible loss of such original content. At best, they allow tracing an erasure in which the imagined original idiom, image, or sound was lost forever.

To further complicate the epistemological dilemma of reading Anglophone Arab works of literature and art, one needs to admit that it is equally impossible to create an analytical text with a pure metacritical language strictly derived from outside the analyzed tropological structure of figurative Arabness. Our critical practice, no matter how seriously connected to historical contextualization and socio-political interpretation, is not free from frictions between the figural and the grammatical sides of the text that it seeks to interpret. Nor is it free from the tension between the performative and the ethical at work in such a text. The scholar of Anglophone Arab representations, if s/he does not want to entirely suspend the idea of critical reading, must sometimes, like Khalid and Gibran do in quite different narrative and performative ways, take the liberty of participating in the Orientalist/Occidentalist system of tropes that s/he seeks to debunk with all necessary (unmasking) earnestness, (ironic) pathos, and (strategic) paradoxes. When s/he, at the same time, allows herself or himself to read literary or artistic representations as signs of cultural translations, s/he better does so in full awareness of the fact that such signs might contain more traces of what they do not mean than of what they do. Literary and cultural criticism thus understood is an impossible translational process that is aware of a certain "violence of culturing"[157] at work in any Western interpretation of Arab articulations. The critique of Anglophone Arab representations, therefore, needs to be conceptualized as a way of *reading-as-transcoding* that scrupulously uses the poetic dimensions and allegorical fragmentation of a given cultural text to transfer a socio-political meaning which is not necessarily intrinsic to that very text. In such poetics of translation, the question of cultural translatability is not primarily approached as a sociolinguistic problem. I do not believe that the process of semiotic regression can ever be fully

156   Hassan, *Immigrant Narratives: Orientalism and Cultural Translation in Arab American and Arab British Literature* 28-37.

157   Gayatri Chakravorty Spivak, "Translation as Culture," *An Aesthetic Education in the Era of Globalization*, by G. Chakravorty Spivak (Cambridge, MA: Harvard UP, 2013) 244.

stopped or reversed in our critical practice. Instead, the interpretive undertaking must sometimes shift its focus from the question of a particular text's readability, from the search for some original meaning or the echo of such original meaning to the question of the critic's own reading-ability in relation to the respective cultural text. What is at stake, then, is the critic's ability to respond to a text by imposing meaning on it. Such responsibility in turn demands a mode of interpretation that breaks with both the self-proclaimed insider's belief in translational authenticity and the outsider's all-too-often disclaimed interpretive matrix of cultural exoticization.[158] It violates the insider's privileges without claiming a knowledge that the represented subject can never have of herself or himself or turning its essential truth into an object of interpretive possession. If there is any moral promise left in such an interpretive act, it is the interpreter's critical frankness regarding the crude ethics of her or his own post-mimetic transposition of meaning.

I do not at all argue that there is no Anglophone Arab identity other than an allegorical one—how could I do so without at the same time claiming to be a real Arab? What I do, however, believe is that the identities narratively and performatively iterated in the contemporary Anglophone Arab representations I am interested in are predominantly allegorical. They are stylized from different cultural signs, they are composed out of various socio-historical experiences, and they are produced against discrepant historical narratives with a view to competing utopian visions. These resemblances, instead of seeking the perfect union of form and meaning, are characterized decisively by the fragmentariness, arbitrariness, and discontinuity of allegory. They not only derive from the past archives of their original emergence but exist in potentially endless future relations. Consequently, the referential systems necessary for their interpretation can significantly exceed the here and now of their own articulations. In order to decode them, the critic cannot confine herself or himself to the search for authentic archival hints intrinsic to these works' central signifiers or for consistent counter-archival references. New interpretive archives must be continuously produced in which allegory is not only conceived of as a rhetorical trope but also used as an interpretive mode.[159] Such archives might not contribute to the affirmation of the static symbolic coincidence between a particular Anglophone Arab representation and the world. But they have, like Khalid's figurative self-representations and to some extent like F. H. Day's pictorialist pho-

---

158 See also Richard Jacquemond, "Towards an Economy and Poetics of Translation from and into Arabic," *Cultural Encounters in Translation from Arabic*, ed. Said Faiq (Clevedon, UK: Multilingual Matters, 2004) 126.

159 This understanding of allegory as a mode of reading is inspired by Paul de Man's writings on allegory. See Paul de Man, *Allegories of Reading: Figural Language in Rousseau, Nietzsche, Rilke, and Proust* (New Haven: Yale UP, 1979) and de Man. *Blindness and Insight. Essays on the Rhetoric of Contemporary Criticism*, 2. ed. (1971; Minneapolis: U of Minnesota P, 1983) 187-228.

tographs of Gibran, the capacity to subvert or transgress the oppressive notion of symbolic totality. My readings proceed precisely in that direction.

3.3   Transmigrations and Turnovers

"Homeless I am again"[160]

These words of Khalid are not spoken in New York City but in his native village of Baalbek. They are enunciated shortly after he has rejoined what he, when still in the American prison, had envisioned as his people. Khalid is banished from family and home and feels deprived again of any sense of belonging. The declamation of exilic sorrow, equal measures desperate and agitated, is remembered by his friend and fellow-remigrant, Shakib, with tears in his eyes.[161] However, this declaration does not at all mark the end of the anti-hero's cross-cultural identity struggle. Instead of indicating the spiritual resolution of the painful migratory path, accommodating himself within some eternal state of transcendental homelessness, Khalid's words mark the beginning of another (pan- or trans-Arab rather than intercultural) voyage.

For my understanding of this novel and later Anglophone Arab representations, it is crucial to see that Khalid's feeling of extraterritoriality,[162] the strange impression of always being somehow disconnected from the notion of being firmly *here*, is never overcome. He is marginalized in the US; Khalid, like so many characters of Anglophone Arab narratives after him, is forced to feel like an eternal stranger and a problem in the Western metropole. He also repeatedly finds himself in the outsider's position after his return to the Arab world. Ironically, like many other characters in contemporary literary narratives, he feels "like a tourist in a bizarre land"[163] in his natural home. Sometimes unable and often unwilling to place himself firmly within competing local identity constructs of mutually excluding cultures, Khalid's self-conscious attempts at self-determination and his anticipation of a renewed collective self-identification do not easily fit into static paradigms of belonging, either *over there* or *over here*.

Stressing *The Book of Khalid*'s pioneering role in the formation of a particular Arab variety of ethnic or minority literatures, critics working in the field of Arab American studies tend to forget the fictional setting of Khalid's sad exilic enunciation. Reading the novel primarily as a response to Rihani's American experience,

---

160   Rihani, *The Book of Khalid* 141.
161   Rihani, *The Book of Khalid* 141.
162   On the notion of extraterritoriality, see Georg Steiner, *Extraterritorial: Papers on Literature and the Language Revolution* (1972; New York: Atheneum, 1976).
163   Rabih Alameddine, *The Hakawati* (New York: Knopf, 2008) 7.

they equally ignore the geographical place of the author's fixed residence at the time of *The Book of Khalid*'s composition:[164] It is a biographical fact that the man who is seen as the pioneer of Arab American literature par excellence gave birth to Khalid between 1905 and 1910 in Freike, Lebanon.[165] Such tendentious forgetfulness or ignorance is quite telling regarding these scholars' own disciplinary location. It is particularly significant with a view to the academic field's institutionalized taxonomic practice. Reading Rihani's novel as an Arab-American immigrant narrative, while turning away from its obvious re- or transmigrant contiguities, seems to be a direct response to the inherent interpretive postulates of national classifications. At the same time, such a reading risks circumventing or overseeing the complex nexus between failed assimilation, diasporic cultural politics, and the political history of the Middle East. First, I'd like to address this latter aspect before following the fictional remigrant's inner-Arab travails.

Khalid's painful spasms in the American prison inaugurate a transformative process over the course of which the Arab immigrant's rioting visions are turned into the doubtful certainty of being chosen to liberate the Arab world qua revolutionary prophecy. This desire to return to and politically transform his society of descent is by no way the consequence of a natural and thus inevitable re-filiation. It first and foremost results from the contradictory experiences of immigration: experiences of humiliation and benefit, of learning and unlearning, of love and hate. America is described by Khalid as his "greatest enemy and benefactor in the whole world." The host country is cursed as a "dumb-hearted mother [...] in whose iron loins" the proto-revolutionary remigrant has been created: "Was not Khalid [...] born in the cellar? Down there in the very loins of New York?"[166] Before leaving the US, Khalid imagines himself as the misunderstood spiritual child of a surrogate culture that unfairly denounces her immigrant children as monstrous scandals.

Presumably relieved from the pain caused by his often contradictory dogmatisms and continuous shifts between radical rationality, sexual desire, immanent

---

164   For examples of this tendency, see Hassan, *Immigrant Narratives: Orientalism and Cultural Translation in Arab American and Arab British Literature* 38-58; Evelyn Shakir, "Coming of Age: Arab American Literature," *Ethnic Forum: Journal of Ethnic Studies and Ethnic Bibliography* 13.2/14.1 (1993–94): 65-67; Nash, "Beyond Orientalism: Khalid, the Secular City and the Transcultural Self," 63-81; Layla Al Maleh, "Anglophone Arab Literature: An Overview," *Arab Voices in Diaspora: Critical Perspectives on Anglophone Arab Literature*, ed. Layla Al Maleh (Amsterdam: Rodopi, 2009) 2-3; Salah Hassan and Marcy Knopf-Newman, Introduction, *MELUS* 31.4 (2006): 6; Majaj, "Arab-American Literature: Origins and Developments," 62-63.

165   Funk and Sitka, "Timetable of Events in Ameen F. Rihani's Life and in the World," 155. See also Fine, "Afterword" 319. Although Todd Fine does neither ignore the novel's technical genesis in Lebanon nor its distinctive inner-Arab plot, he firmly places *The Book of Khalid* on the virtual bookshelf of Arab American literature. Fine, "Afterword" 317.

166   Rihani, *The Book of Khalid* 123-24.

morality, and mystical spirituality, Khalid chooses, for the first time since he entered New York, to speak for those people with whom he has often been identified against his will. The immigrant's involuntary experience of being perceived (or even of perceiving himself) through an Orientalist lens and of being discriminated against in the Western metropolis is gradually turned into a diasporic vision of political change within the Middle East. Khalid's spiritual strivings of self-revelation and his incessant social self-questioning in reaction to mainstream American anti-Arab racial prejudice are first raised individually and then directed at a common goal whose geographic stage happens to lie outside the US.

It seems that the Arab American immigrant's particular experience of the "color-line"[167] and his re-doubled comprehension of the multiple moral contradictions resulting from this line's inherent deprivations allow a deeper understanding of the modern world that has a decisively "revolutionary potential."[168] I am not saying that Khalid's American experience of alienation is exactly the alienation that many African Americans experienced at the dawn of the 20th century. The latter's experience of slavery forms a unique historical pretext which cannot be compared to that of Arabs in relation to the West. I do, however, believe that the very discriminatory conditions that forced African Americans to reconcile the split visions of their selves in what W. E. B. Du Bois has coined "double consciousness"[169] determine turn-of-the-century Arab American everyday lives as well. At this point, one should keep in mind that, for Du Bois, the question of racism was never solely a matter of racial prejudice against Americans of African descent, nor was his criticism restricted to the innermost American conditions. The implicit internationalist and anti-imperialist critique found in The Souls was directed against inequity, exploitation, and domination in the global relation "of the darker to the lighter races of men."[170] Therefore, the book's emancipatory claim of socioeconomic participation, of sharing the opportunities of modern civilization, and of " be[ing] a co-worker in the kingdom of culture"[171] on the basis of equality and justice was a universal one. It was a claim that could be shared by other discriminated communities of color within the US and by the colonized people of the global South. By the early 20th century, Du Bois's essays had appeared in many of the prominent popular periodicals of the time. The Souls of Black Folk was first published in 1903, only seven years before The Book of Khalid. Although both texts seemingly draw on similar American transcendentalist and European

---

167   Du Bois, The Souls of Black Folk 3.
168   Thomas C. Holt, "The Political Uses of Alienation: W.E.B. Du Bois on Politics, Race, and Culture, 1903–1940," American Quarterly 42.2 (1990): 306.
169   Du Bois, The Souls of Black Folk 8.
170   Du Bois, The Souls of Black Folk 15.
171   Du Bois, The Souls of Black Folk 9.

romantic sources,[172] there is no indication of any direct reception by Rihani of Du Bois's work.

Given Arab Americans' imagined whiteness at that time and with regard to the long history of Arab slave trade and anti-black racism within the Arab world,[173] it is rather questionable that Rihani could easily identify his own immigrant community's sociopolitical struggle or the global positionality of Arabs, for that matter, with the situation of African Americans in the United States. It would be reserved for a later generation of Anglophone Arab intellectuals to express political solidarity with Africans and Black minorities living in the West or even to articulate a Black-Arab identity.[174] One would need a separate study to evaluate in detail possible traces and frictions between Anglophone Arab discourse and the African American sociologist's classic study of race and culture, his political commentary, or his civil rights activism.

It might not be legitimate to link the literary character Khalid's rioting struggle for "the higher Superman"[175] neatly to the unrelenting forceful quest of *The Souls* for "a better and truer self."[176] Whereas the former is presented as the vision of a spiritual merging of Asian, European, and American qualities (thus implicitly excluding African components), the latter longs to attain an African American identity beyond the discriminatory veil that until then separated the two selves of black men living in the US. However, it seems at least justifiable to argue that both texts share a particular concern with the "strange experience" of being a problem in the eyes of dominant white Americans.[177] Both narratives stress the moral inconsistency and limited knowledge resulting from the bonds of cross-cultural arrogance and racial

---

172   On Du Bois's adoption of American transcendentalist terminologies and his use of vocabulary derived from German Romantic thinkers, see Shamoon Zamir, *Dark Voices: W.E.B. Du Bois and American Thought, 1888–1903* (Chicago: U of Chicago P, 1995) and David Levering Lewis, *W. E. B. Du Bois: Biography of a Race, 1868–1919* (New York: Holt, 1993) 305-306.

173   Trans-Saharan slave trade and racism in the Arab World both pre-date and post-date the trans-Atlantic slave trade. Scholars estimate that close to 18 million people were enslaved by Arabs between 800 and 1900. For the competing scholarly positions within the highly controversial debate, see Murray Gordon, *Slavery in the Arab World* (New York: New Amsterdam, 1989); Bernard Lewis, *Race and Slavery in the Middle East: An Historical Enquiry* (New York: Oxford UP, 1990) and Shaun Elizabeth Marmon, ed., *Slavery in the Islamic Middle East* (Princeton: Wiener, 1999). For a good overview on this still virulent issue, see 'Alik Shahadah, "The History of Arab Slavery in Africa" *Arab Slave Trade* (2002–2005), 27 Oct. 2014 <http://www.arabslavetrade.com#convert> and the website of *African Holocaust*, a non-profit civil society dedicated to the progressive study of African history and culture <http://www.africanholocaust.net/>.

174   See, for example, Suheir Hammad, *Born Palestinian, Born Black* (New York: Harlem River P, 1996).

175   Rihani, *The Book of Khalid* 110.

176   Du Bois, *The Souls of Black Folk* 9.

177   Du Bois, *The Souls of Black Folk* 7.

prejudice. Like Du Bois with his work, Khalid turns the involuntary *gift* of knowing others' discriminatory perception of himself into a quasi-transcendental "second-sight"[178]—a double vision that can first be transformed into a powerful narrative of social significance and then function as a resistive tool for revolutionary action.

A similar transformative dynamic is at work in the transnational discourse of early Arab American writers, although to different measures and on a larger geo-graphical scale. Khalid's fictional path of reverse-migration in many ways mirrors the historical role of Levantine diaspora intellectuals within the increasingly politi-cized *Nahda*-movement of the late 19th and early 20th centuries. In particular, it re-flects their ambivalent contribution to the rise of what is variously called Arabism, secular Arab nationalism, or Pan-Arabism.[179] Without uncritically affirming those conventional views of Arab nationalism, which identify Christian Lebanese intellec-tuals as the main social actors of the formative phases in the political history of the modern Middle East, and thus underestimating the importance of other regional contexts, such as the impact of Islamic modernist thinkers and movements,[180] one can argue that Arab nationalism was a local response to the process of the grad-ual incorporation of the Middle East into the colonialist-capitalist world system, a process that was effected by reciprocal external influences related to the glob-alizing idea of the nation-state. Like other nationalist discourses, it represented both a revival of heritage and old loyalties as well as the imaginative fabrication of new uniting myths and traditions appropriate for the political mobilization of group-solidarity.[181] In both pedagogical and performative procedures of narrating the modern Arab nation,[182] the spheres of language and literature were of particu-lar importance. Hence, one cannot be surprised that several writers of the *Mahjar* participated in the construction of Arab nationness. Aside from the various regional points of the Arab nationalist movement's emergence, the transnational discursive

---

178   Du Bois, *The Souls of Black Folk* 8.

179   For a general overview of this complex, often partisan, and highly controversial scholarly de-bate on Arab nationalism from its origins in the 19th century to the present, see Rashid Kha-lidi, "Arab Nationalism: Historical Problems of Literature," *The American Historical Review* 96.5 (1991): 1363-73 and Adeed Dawisha, *Arab Nationalism in the Twentieth Century: From Triumph to Despair* (Princeton: Princeton UP, 2003).

180   For a critique of this view, see C. Ernest Dawn, "The Origins of Arab Nationalism," *The Origins of Arab Nationalism*, eds. Rashid Khalidi, Lisa Anderson, Muhammad Muslih, and Reeva S. Simon (New York: Columbia UP, 1991) 11.

181   Here I refer to the pattern described by Eric Hobsbawm and Benedict Anderson, with a fo-cus on the birth of the Western nation. See Eric J. Hobsbawm, *Nations and Nationalism since 1780: Programme, Myth, and Reality* (Cambridge: Cambridge UP, 1990) and Benedict Anderson, *Imagined Communities: Reflections on the Origins of Nationalism* (London, New York: Verso, 1991).

182   On the constitutive tension between the pedagogical and the performative in the narrative construction of nationness, see Homi K. Bhabha, "DissemiNation," *The Location of Culture* (Lon-don, New York: Routledge, 1994) 146-50.

space created by the Arab periodical press, produced in São Paulo, Buenos Aires, or New York and circulated across both the Americas and the Middle East, significantly contributed to the nurturing of new patriotic visions of a shared Arab future. This trans-American and trans-Atlantic dissemination of open letters, political essays, and books in Arabic, English, Portuguese, and Spanish not only fostered Arab nationalist networks across the diasporas but also secured increasing influence on the Syrian press, thus gaining impact on virulent local debates within the Middle East on what it meant to be Syrian, Lebanese or Arab. Many important diasporic publishing houses, literary societies, and fraternities offered a platform for the formation of political committees and parties. Historians are just beginning to challenge the traditional focus on the sociopolitical geography of the Middle East and the one-sided concern with direct influences from Europe by exploring transnational modes of communication and the role of diasporic media within the cultural politics of early-20th-century Arab nationalism.[183]

Reading Rihani's *The Book of Khalid* can help to re-construct such transnationally expanded interpretive geography for the study of diasporic discourses in relation to Middle Eastern cultural politics. Given the continuing exchange between Arab intellectuals and activists in the diaspora and their colleagues living in the Middle East, the relevance of a decentered relational approach necessarily goes beyond the question of early-20th-century nationalisms. Looking at today's growing number of transmigrant cultural agents who divide their time and work between more than one location and who can no longer be identified in terms of clear-cut group-belonging or place of residence, the study of Arab cultural politics is maybe more than ever in need of diasporic readings (literary and non-literary alike) which transgress the learned ethnic or nation-state analytical framework and which are willing to give up the firmly localized focus on unidirectional transfers and influences in favor of tracing multidirectional cultural dynamics. Anglophone Arab resemblings such as the fictional narrative of Khalid's travails are creative invitations for the study of Arab-Western correlations and these correlations' contested mediations beyond both the ideologies of representational othering and the epistemological consistency of the critique of Orientalism and Occidentalism.

Although Rihani is rarely included in scholarly discussions on the development of Arab nationalist or pan-Arab thought,[184] the author of *The Book of Khalid* was directly involved in the expanding struggle within the Middle East for Arab independence from both the Ottoman Empire and European colonialism from 1909

---

183   See Fahrenthold, "Transnational Modes and Media: The Syrian Press in the *Mahjar* and Emigrant Activism during World War I," 30-54.

184   In Albert Hourani's classic *Arabic Thought in the Liberal Age* (1962), Rihani is completely ignored. Hisham Sharabi mentions him briefly in his *Arab Intellectuals and the West: The Formative Years, 1875–1914* (Baltimore: Johns Hopkins P, 1970) 118-19.

onwards. At least since his first published nonfictional writing in Arabic on "The moral revolution"[185] as the necessary precondition for effective political change, he successively advanced to work as a political activist on both sides of the "Arab/Muslim Atlantic."[186] This publication actually coincided with the inception of the Syrian reform movement which had close ties to the diaspora. It also coincided with the emergence of the *Hizb al-Ittihad al-Lubnani* [Party of the Lebanese Federation], a rather syndicate-like committee that chiefly represented an urban professional class in the diaspora. By 1912, the committee already had a branch operating in New York. Na'um Mukarzil—like Rihani, born in Freike, Lebanon—was the owner of Little Syria's most successful Arabic language dailies, such as *Al-Huda* (Guidance) or *Al-'Alam al-Jadid* (The New World), and served as *Ittihad al-Lubnani*'s closest Arab American partner.[187] Rihani began writing for *Al-Huda* in 1899.[188] In 1911, Mukarzil founded the *Jama'iyya al-Nahda al-Lubaniyya* (Society of the Lebanese Renaissance) in New York to champion Lebanese independence from the Ottoman Empire. In late 1916, Rihani would form a new coalition together with Kahlil Gibran and Ayyub Tabet to counter Mukarzil's long-standing support of an alliance with France. The *Lajna Tahrir Surriya wa-l-Lubnan* (Committee for the Liberation of Syria and Lebanon) instead championed an independent greater Arab federation.[189] It was only during World War I that Rihani's Arab nationalist thinking developed from the support of partial autonomy to an inert call for independence to, finally, a full-fledged revolutionary support of military revolt. While the revolt against the Ottoman Empire was often proclaimed in the name of Islam, his Arabism stressed a secular national rather than a religious identity.[190]

At the time of writing *The Book of Khalid*, Rihani had multiple first-hand experiences of reverse migrations to and extended stays in the country of his birth. Although he spent the 1890s and 1910s predominantly in New York City and alternated between the US and the Lebanese mountains during the 1920s and 1930s,

---

185   This is the English translation of what, according to Nijmeh Hajjar, was Rihani's first Arabic language article: "Al-Thawra al-Khuluqiya" (1909), see Nijmeh Hajjar, "Ameen Rihani's Humanist Vision of Arab Nationalism," *Ameen Rihani: Bridging East and West: A Pioneering Call for Arab-American Understanding* 134-47, 145n19.

186   The notion of an Arab/Muslim Atlantic is taken from Ella Shohat's discussion of a multiply raced Atlantic of multidirectional routes of Orientalist and Occidentalist ideas, see Shohat, "The Sephardi-Moorish Atlantic: Between Orientalism and Occidentalism," 50-55, here 55. On Rihani's transatlantic political activism, see Hajjar, *The Politics and Poetics of Ameen Rihani* 43-68.

187   Fahrenthold, "Transnational Modes and Media: The Syrian Press in the *Mahjar* and Emigrant Activism during World War I," 33-36.

188   Funk and Sitka, "Timetable of Events in Ameen F. Rihani's Life and in the World," 154.

189   Fahrenthold, "Transnational Modes and Media: The Syrian Press in the *Mahjar* and Emigrant Activism during World War I," 36-37.

190   Hajjar, *The Politics and Poetics of Ameen Rihani* 120-231 and 245.

the man who gained American citizenship in 1901 in fact spent most of his lifetime in the Arab world. Rihani returned to Lebanon for the first time between 1897
and 1899 to teach English at a Maronite school and to undertake a re-education
in classical Arabic. *The Book of Khalid* was written during a five-year sojourn at the
family home in Freike between 1905 and 1910, interrupted by at least two extended
visits to Egypt.[191] These were extremely turbulent times in this part of the world,
with the so-called Young Turk Revolution in 1908 providing a short moment of
hope followed by an enduring delusion among reformers in the Arab provinces of
the Ottoman Empire. The young Arab American remigrant participated in the increasing local protests against the declining Turkish-Islamic Empire and wrote an
impressive number of political and philosophical essays and speeches in Arabic,
later collected and published as the *Ar-Rihaniyaat*. Although Rihani was known as
a public critic of Christian dogmatism, and although he accepted the special place
that Islam would have in the cultural life of the future Arab nation, his secular
notion of Arabism was that of a Maronite and of man of letters who had spent a
good part of his life abroad in the West. His understanding of what it meant to be
an Arab in the increasingly globalizing modern world could, of course, easily clash
with local conceptions of national belonging and independence, particularly with
Lebanese-Christian and Islamic modernist ideologies, both in socio-political and
materialistic-economic regards as well as in terms of spirituality and morality.[192]
As an auto-fictional narrative, *The Book of Khalid* seems to resonate with some of
these local clashes. As a conflictual imaginary of Anglophone Arab transmigrancy,
however, it anticipates a much broader spectrum of predetermined frictions and
unpredictable breaking points, of sudden raptures, visions of radical renewal, and
incomplete turnovers.

Khalid leaves America and returns to Lebanon together with Shakib. The irri-
tation of the Western reader's preconceived notions resulting from this narrative
shift is directly anticipated by the editor-narrator. Without further elaborating on
the altered narrative setting's destabilizing effects regarding our learned reading
positionalities and spatial knowledge, s/he implicitly warns her or his Anglophone
audience of becoming religated readers, at least regarding their culturally predetermined reading competence: "Our readers, though we do not think they are sorry
for having come out with us so far, are at liberty either to continue with us, or say
good-bye."[193]

We have no real choice, of course. A decentered relational reading of *The Book
of Khalid*, or of any other Anglophone Arab representation, for that matter, does
not allow so premature a farewell. It necessitates the obvious: to transgress one's

191   Funk and Sitka, "Timetable of Events in Ameen F. Rihani's Life and in the World," 53-62.
192   Dawn, "The Origins of Arab Nationalism," 11.
193   Rihani, *The Book of Khalid* 134.

apodictic certainty of contextual familiarity and to join those portions of the novel which are set in a rather uncanny *over there*. I will elaborate on the ambivalent shift of narrative authority and power in favor of the editor-narrator, partly resulting from the spatial alteration of the story's fictional landscape, at a later point in my analysis. For the time being, I want to focus on the content, contexts, intertexts, and anticipations of the respective novelistic part.

This part is by far the longest of *The Book of Khalid*, and it tells significantly more than a simple story of an Americanized Arab's final coming-home. According to the editor-narrator, it is actually "the more interesting portion"[194] of the novel. It is, therefore, misleading to argue, as Geoffrey Nash does, that the novel "ends within a Syro-Lebanese setting."[195] To describe the substantial section of 177 pages as an ending and to thus put it on the same structural level as the nine-page beginning section with an equally Syro-Lebanese setting[196] makes the New York immigrant episode of just 100 pages appear as the novel's proper main part.[197] Such tendentious hierarchical valuation of the different sections implicitly adheres to a principally US-centric divide between center and periphery that is radically questioned by this novel's constitutive narrative strategies of spatial transgression. In addition, such reading marginalizes those lines of action set in other, non-Syro-Lebanese narrative spaces.[198] While it is true that a significant part of *The Book of Khalid* is set in the US, this novel has clearly more to offer than an Arab-American immigrant narrative. In addition to providing an account of the main protagonist's failed attempt to re-invent himself in the American socio-cultural environment, it tells a story of emigration from and re-migration to Lebanon and accounts for subsequent migrations within the so-called Arab world. By doing so, it touches the core of 20th- and 21st-century Anglophone Arab narratives of transmigration.

Khalid and his fellow-remigrant, Shakib, "silently steal away"[199] from a country that was supposed to make them "forget their native land."[200] The reader, willing to join them, might expects that Khalid's return to Lebanon naturally and necessarily leads to a decrease in cross-civilizational conflicts. But ideological collisions, social frictions, and other conflictual correlations in fact rather increase with Khalid's

---

194   Rihani, *The Book of Khalid* 134.
195   Nash, *The Anglo-Arab Encounter* 46.
196   Nash, *The Anglo-Arab Encounter* 46.
197   My page count refers to Todd Fine's 2012 edition.
198   See A. A. Rihani, "The Book of Khalid and The Prophet: Similar Universal Concerns with Different Perspectives: A Comparative Study," 39. Referring to the first three chapters, set in Baalbek and Damascus, as the novel's main chapters of Arab national concern, A. A. Rihani strangely excludes the following chapters of explicit Arab setting. Here the critic's Lebanese self-identification and related interpretive positionality obviously leads to a rather narrow focus for his analysis of Khalid's political self-identification.
199   Rihani, *The Book of Khalid* 132.
200   Rihani, *The Book of Khalid* 121.

remigration to the Arab "homeland." The returnee feels obliged to introduce to his people more than those "three prominent features of Civilization" that remigrants have until then brought to their country: "namely, a little wealth, a few modern ideas, and many strange diseases."[201] Back in Baalbek, Khalid, transformed by his experience of migration and equipped with even greater transformative ambitions, renounces all local filiative relations and religious authorities:

> I hate Familism, which is the curse of the human race. And I hate this spiritual Fatherhood when it puts on the garb of a priest, the three-cornered hat of a Jesuit, the hood of a monk, the gaberdine of a rabbi, or the jubbah of a sheikh.[202]

Denounced by Jesuits to the Ottoman government as an anarchist and expelled from the town due to a blasphemous pamphlet against the church, Khalid's long-desired reunification with his cousin, Najma, seems to be utterly impossible. Their marriage is called off; Najma is first placed in bonds and then wedded against her will to a local nobleman. The tragic-romantic episode might echo Rihani's own excommunication from the Maronite church in 1903 as a consequence of his public critique of its religious dogmatism.[203] On the level of the narrative plot, however, it inaugurates Khalid's temporary disappearance within "The Kaaba of Solitude."[204] He retreats to a hermit's place in the beautiful forests of the Lebanese mountains—"this grand Mosque of Nature"[205]—to contemplate Whitman, Emerson, and Thoreau, the shortcomings of scientific naturalism, and the primacy of social alliance. Khalid's lonely search for a spiritually grounded social harmony beyond the diacritical signs of historically generated and institutionalized religious dissonance leads directly to an ecstatic disentanglement or multiplication of his self that exceeds his New York prophecy. Questioning the established "logic about the I and the not-I,"[206] he shifts the focus from the question of intrinsic honesty and authenticity in the individual articulation of self-identity to the practical need of the innovative mixture and social mediation of this self's various contingents. The matured prophet is not afraid of possible frictions between his Arab and non-Arab sources of selving. Nor does he fear the conflicts resulting from his new truism's diverse spiritual and materialistic components:

> I have often worked and slept in opposing camps. So, do not expect from me anything like the consistency with which the majority of mankind solder and

---

201   Rihani, *The Book of Khalid* 131.
202   Rihani, *The Book of Khalid* 138.
203   See Hassan, *Immigrant Narratives: Orientalism and Cultural Translation in Arab American and Arab British Literature* 40 and Hassan, "The Rise of the Arab American Novel: Ameen Rihani's The Book of Khalid," 41.
204   That is the title of the novel's chapter VIII, *The Book of Khalid* 171-80.
205   Rihani, *The Book of Khalid* 179.
206   Rihani, *The Book of Khalid* 210.

shape their life. Deep thought seems often, if not always, inconsistent at the first blush. The intensity and passiveness of the spirit are as natural in their attraction and repulsion as the elements, whose harmony is only patent on the surface. Consistency is superficial, narrow, one-sided.[207]

While Khalid's vision does not promise the equilibrium of any transcultural total-ity, the political liberation from imperial occupation and sectarian repression that it foresees nevertheless supposes a new universal transcendental spirit to come. He knows that the road to "freedom, faith, hope, health, power, and joy" will be inevitably and "always dominated by the instinct of self-interest." But he has the equally strong belief that the days of a narrow-minded "body-politic"[208] are over. It is against this rather disembodied notion of identity politics that one needs to understand Khalid's unabashed struggle for change within himself and within the Arab world. He is not afraid of "falling on either side of the fence [that divides East and West], so he knows what lies behind."[209] His revolutionary "rhapsodies"[210] of Arab political unity through the identification of West-Eastern inconsistencies are clearly loaded with motives of martyrdom. At times, they are explicitly suicidal: "for both [Orient and Occident] I shall work and suffer and die."[211] His suffering al-most appears like a universal humanitarian cause. Khalid sees himself as taking up humanity's historical role to imagine a global politics of the future beyond narrow materialist egoisms. Looking at this discourse from a contemporary perspective of a militant Islamist language of self-sacrifice, one cannot but see Khalid as a hy-per-moral *terrorist in search of humanity*.[212] His heroic action has no moral center. Aimed at the liberation of the Arab world, it takes the whole planet as an arena of inspiration. His universalist discourse sometimes almost seems like a parody of those interventionist humanitarian actions which were ideologically framed by the European promotion of human rights to justify colonialism as a civilizing project.

Armed with the notion of a strategically re-composed ego and a proto-perfor-mative program of identity politics, which does not shy away from inconsisten-cies and inner contradictions, Khalid then sets out to further his moral revolution to the world of power and politics. What was inaugurated in New York City by

---

207   Rihani, *The Book of Khalid* 221.
208   Rihani, *The Book of Khalid* 225.
209   Rihani, *The Book of Khalid* 225.
210   Rihani, *The Book of Khalid* 225.
211   Rihani, *The Book of Khalid* 226.
212   Faisal Devji, *The Terrorist in Search of Humanity: Militant Islam and Global Politics* (London: Hurst, 2008). Khalid's discourse shares several characteristics with the suicidal discourse of contem-porary militant Islamist, as analyzed by Devji, such as trans- and supranational orientation, a lack of center, an environmentalist metaphoric, the transcendental identification with the suffering of others, and a heroic vision of self-sacrifice as humanitarian acts.

cross-cultural self-education, the experience of racist discrimination and Orientalist misrepresentation, as well as by the plural executions of social, sexual, and moral transgressions, and what brought him back into temporary exilic isolation in the Lebanese mountains, now decisively turns from spiritual "revolutions within" to revolutionary agitation "without."[213]

Khalid's new worldly journey first brings him to Beirut, where he starts lecturing and writing manifestos on spiritual and moral freedom. He then travels to the principle cities of Syria. The highly controversial itinerant preacher of Arab national emancipation finally arrives in Damascus to give a speech in the city's Great Mosque. "Khalid's name, and Khalidism, and Khalid scandals"[214] are by then well known throughout the region. He is hailed by some as the real emancipator, true builder, and future leader "of a great Asiatic empire" and assailed by others as an instrument in the hands of European colonial powers and American speculators "who would build sky-scrapers on the ruins of our mosques."[215] In the meantime, Khalid falls in love with "a certain American lady, a Mrs. Goodfree, or Gotfry,"[216] who has adopted the Arabic name Jamilah. She is a wealthy votary of Baha'ism, who goes every year on a pilgrimage to the modern religion's spiritual center in Haifa, Palestine. The biting comments of the Egyptian press on the political prophet's cross-cultural liaison are directed at both the non-Arab woman as a representative of foreign interests and the successively internationalizing Baha'ist movement's cosmopolitan assimilation of the three monotheistic religions' eschatologies:[217] "Our new Muhdi has added to his hareem an American beauty with an Oriental leg."[218]

While Khalid's conception of political revolution does incorporate the legacy of Western scientific modernity and democracy, he decisively emancipates himself from these models' exclusive claims of authority: "For the world is not Europe, and the final decision on Who Is and What Is To Rule, was not delivered by the French Revolution."[219] He warns Arabs to simply imitate European instant knowledges that have long been discarded by European critics without drawing on their

---

213 "Revolutions within and without" is the title of the novel's Chapter VI. Rihani, *The Book of Khalid* 262-71.

214 Rihani, *The Book of Khalid* 273.

215 Rihani, *The Book of Khalid* 274.

216 Rihani, *The Book of Khalid* 259.

217 The Baha'ist governing body sat and still sits in the city of Haifa, then located in an Ottoman province, today in Israel. On this modern monotheistic religion, which was founded in the 19th century in Persia to emphasize the spiritual unity of all humanity and has since the early 20th century gained an increased footing in Europe and the US, particularly on its relation to the dynamics of cultural globalization, see Christopher Buck, "The Eschatology of Globalization: The Multiple Messiahship of *Bahā'u'llāh* Revisited," *Studies in Modern Religions, Religious Movements and the Bābī-Bahāʾī Faiths* (Leiden: Brill, 2004) 143-78.

218 Rihani, *The Book of Khalid* 274.

219 Rihani, *The Book of Khalid* 262.

own culture's inherent spiritual virtues. His critique of the old European colonial powers, whose ambitions in the region had become obvious, sometimes evokes a more positive role for the American model of hyper-modernity. But the core source of Khalid's heroic dream of an Arab Empire that stands "even higher than the Americans and the Europeans"[220] is a blatantly declaimed Nietzschean "will-power"[221] to search for and rediscover Arab culture's own spiritual and hence superior inherent modernity. In the face of missing transformations in the Syrian provinces of the Ottoman empire after the turn-over by the Young Turks, the spiritual revolutionary, with the intent of political change, strategically bets on the transformative capacity of an alliance between "American arms and an up-to-date Korân."[222]

This strategy, however, quickly turns out to be a fatal mistake. Khalid's speech at the crowded Great Mosque of Damascus in the presence of secular nationalists and political Islamists of various sectarian filiations ends up in a violent riot, in the course of which the naïvely radical speaker is almost killed. Although his allegorical denouncement of the West's one-sided utilitarian spirit and decadent materialism is enthusiastically responded to by the audience, the vision of a reformed Islam to be modeled on the example of Saudi Wahhabism instead of popular anti-colonial Islamic modernists like Jamal ad-Din al-Afghani[223] or Muhammad Abduh[224] leads directly into tumultuously erupting accusations of infidelity: "Reactionist! Infidel! Innovator! Wahhabi! Slay him! Kill him!"[225] Khalid's spontaneous announcement of the "beginning of Arabia's spring"[226] in reaction to the impressive assembly of murmuring men with red fezes and green and white turbans, suggesting the image of "a verdant field overgrown with daisies and poppies,"[227] must be postponed. With a "stiletto-thrust in the back and a slash in the forehead,"[228] and with the help of Shakib and the American-Baha'i beauty, he manages to escape to Baalbek.

Excommunicated again, but still dreaming of the Arab awakening and not giving up "ejaculat[ing] somewhat of martyrdom,"[229] Khalid promptly seeks asylum in Egypt. Mrs. Gotfrey, Shakib, and the seriously sick Najma, who has been in the meantime abandoned by her husband and has given birth to little Najib, join him.

---

220 Rihani, *The Book of Khalid* 265.
221 Rihani, *The Book of Khalid* 265.
222 Rihani, *The Book of Khalid* 276.
223 See Nikki R. Keddie, ed., *An Islamic Response to Imperialism: Political and Religious Writings of Jamal al-Din al-Afghani*, new ed. (1968; Berkeley: U of California P, 1983).
224 Malcolm H. Kerr, *Islamic Reform: The Political and Legal Theories of Muhammad 'Abduh and Rashīd Ridā* (Berkeley: U of California P, 1966).
225 Rihani, *The Book of Khalid* 292.
226 Rihani, *The Book of Khalid* 287.
227 Rihani, *The Book of Khalid* 287.
228 Rihani, *The Book of Khalid* 292.
229 Rihani, *The Book of Khalid* 296.

The final flight brings them to the Libyan desert near Cairo. The American lover stays in a hotel. The four intra-Arab refugees live in Bedouin tents.

The remaining part of the novel is not easy to grasp interpretively. Far from the world of power and politics, Khalid for the first time seems to be "perfectly happy."[230] Soon after Shakib leaves the camp to start a career as a "poet laureate,"[231] a hired pen in Cairo, little Najib suffers from unexplainable convulsions. When the child is almost completely paralyzed, Khalid decides to consult a man known as "the great English physician."[232] The "great guesswork Celebrity"[233] surgeon opens the boy's skull and "finally holds the instrument up to his assistants to show them that there is—no pus!"[234] Within only three days, Najib, Khalid's spiritual son and the main source of his newly discovered deeper understanding of purest joy, dies under the influence of analgesics. Najma and Khalid bury him in the desert. Then Khalid again disappears like a hidden Shiite Mahdi. The reader cannot know if he has simply gone deeper into the desert or if he has entered another spiritual dimension from which he will reemerge with new visions of even deeper truths. The transmigrant narrative and the meaning of its Arab title character's name, Khalid (the immortal), have thus come full circle.

Najib's death and Khalid's disappearance mark at least a temporary end of the prophet-turned-man's tragically failed attempts to liberate the Arab world spiritually and politically. Khalid's revolutionary vison would rarely be reciprocated within the various Arab nationalist and pan-Arab movements that, after the Ottoman defeat and the end of the Second World War II, became the overwhelmingly dominant movements in the Middle East.[235] He (and maybe Rihani too) had underestimated the intensified colonial aspirations of European powers in the region. Khalid could neither foresee the altered geopolitical framework after the implementation of the 1916 Sykes-Picot Agreement between Great Britain and France nor could he anticipate the effects of the 1917 Balfour Declaration, which paved the way for the establishment of a Jewish state in Palestine in 1948. The hope that the US would play a more positive and less imperialistic role in the region would turn out to be a fatal error after World War II. The national liberation struggles, military coups, and revolutions, which during the 1950s and 1960s changed the political power-configurations within the region and which, in various ways and to different degrees, ideologically drew on a shared language, a common history and religious-cultural identity, and political solidarity between the Arab people, do hardly fit in

---

230 Rihani, *The Book of Khalid* 304.
231 Rihani, *The Book of Khalid* 311.
232 Rihani, *The Book of Khalid* 313.
233 Rihani, *The Book of Khalid* 313.
234 Rihani, *The Book of Khalid* 314.
235 See C. Ernest Dawn, "The Formation of Pan-Arab Ideology in the Interwar Years," *International Journal of Middle East Studies* 20.1 (1988): 67-91.

with Khalid's both ambiguous as well as diffuse program toward the liberation of a territorially and politically integrated pan-Arab homeland. His notion of a cross-culturally generated transcultural spirituality of universal humanity cannot easily be integrated into a programmatic theory of political action. Finally, Khalid's diaspora-inspired elitist discourse of pan-Arab identity highlights the importance of political choice and voluntary aspiration rather than a return to some sort of natural unity of belonging[236] that could serve as a very powerful idea for the ideological mobilization of large masses.

It is maybe first and foremost this non-essentialist notion of Arabness, derived from the diasporic concept of figurative Arab-ness, that *The Book of Khalid* shares with many of the more recent Anglophone Arab representations that my study explores. It is both a document of the early transnational cultural politics of the Arab American diaspora in the US and the Middle East and a fictional narrative that anticipates the unhoused re-coding of (Arab) identities in 20th- and 21st-century Anglophone Arab transmigrant writing. If it is true that some *Mahjar* writers, against the background of their social and intellectual lives within the American nation-space, opted for participating in the Arab nationalist movement by narratively turning the émigré experience of cultural difference and their renewed notion of Arab identity resulting from that experience from the American context to the Middle East, *The Book of Khalid* is a complex and contradictory expression of such an Arab nationalist endeavor. This narrative does not simply try to creatively turn the very boundaries of belonging, which within the Western metropolis discriminated and excluded Arabs like the fictional character of Khalid, into an inclusive sign of Middle Eastern solidarity or trans-Arab shared identity, but it also demonstrates the many obstacles and pitfalls of such a large-scale project of political prophecy, both at home as well as across continents. This is why it cannot possibly be exhaustively grasped as an American ethnic novel or an Arab-American immigrant narrative.

The Book of Khalid is not only an important intertext for our understanding of an Anglophone Arab politics of representation that aims at countering the long-standing consistency of Orientalist misrepresentations and discriminatory practices or at debunking the internal paradoxes of Western secular modernity from within the West. In addition, it provides a helpful interpretive matrix to visit works that are concerned with new ways of articulating forgotten, marginalized, or intentionally excluded local Middle Eastern experiences of the global present to an international English-speaking audience. Most of my readings actually revolve around such works. Almost all of them are to an extent influenced by the material and/or discursive exchange between the Arab diaspora and the Arab Middle East. They are often triggered by personal experiences of continuing transmigrations between

---

236   See also, on Rihani's Arab nationalism of Arabness by choice: Hajjar, "Ameen Rihani's Humanist Vision of Arab Nationalism," 139.

disparate geographic locations. In some cases, they are produced by writers, artists, and activists who are physically placed within the Middle East. The role of Anglophone Arab cultural representations is of particular relevance within Palestinian debates and practices of cultural resistance against occupation.

While some critics, like Todd Fine, stress the 20th-century novel's transhistorical value to the political present of the early 21st century by re-coining the so-called Arab spring events of 2011 "The Khalid Revolution,"[237] I cannot see the plausibility of such a connection. Although the transregionally expanding chain of revolts, somehow overhastily code-named the Arab Spring, was co-inspired by diasporic Arab discourses, fictional and non-fictional ones alike, it seems misleading to retrospectively explain "Rihani's brand of Arab nationalism," represented in the literary character of Khalid, as the intellectual seed for this very revolt. Only someone who overemphasizes the movements' general cosmopolitan and strategic universal humanitarianism or the partial American orientation of the open-ended set of emancipatory uprisings against domestic tyranny and foreign domination inaugurated in Tunisia and Egypt can seriously assert that "every Arab youth [...] has become a Khalid."[238] Such ahistorical comparison implicitly affirms the dominant view of the Arab world's intrinsic belatedness in terms of sociopolitical developments. With a view to the explicit post-ideological approach of the movement's early activists and their innovative strategy to subvert the learned nationalist aesthetics and ethics of ideological utopianism such as Arabism, Arab nationalism, or pan-Arabism, it is almost insulting. In addition, any connection drawn between Khalid's spiritually inspired imagination of an US-sponsored Arabian spring to the Arab emancipatory struggles of 2011 negates the decisively local worldliness of these avant-garde strategies. Although most of these civil rights movements were based on the internationally codified ideas of human rights and democratic participation, they distanced themselves from all kinds of exhausted universalisms, religious and secular alike. Most importantly, the recent nonviolent, at least in its early phase, Arab emancipatory struggle carried a post-postcolonial aesthetics and ethics of resistance that cannot be arrested within the logics of Orientalism and Occiden-

---

237   Todd Fine, "'The Beginning of Arabia's Spring': The Khalid Revolution," *Middle East Institute Viewpoints: Revolution and Political Transformation in the Middle East*. Outcomes and Prospects, Vol. III (Washington: The Middle East Institute, 2011) 20-25, <http://www.mei.edu/sites/default/files/publications/RevolutionVol.III_.pdf>.

238   Fine, "'The Beginning of Arabia's Spring': The Khalid Revolution," 24. For the selective polemical assertion of a connection between the novel and the popular uprisings of 2011, see also Jane O'Brien, "Century-old Book of Khalid sheds light on Arab unrest," *BBC News Online – Middle East* 9 Apr. 2011, 4 June 2015 <http://www.bbc.com/news/world-middle-east-13017564>.

talism:[239] an aesthetics and ethics that Rihani did not manage to, and probably did not even intend to, fully escape from.

Khalid's vision of democratic transformation toward freedom, justice, and economic prosperity within the Arab world through the merging of the West's capitalist spirit with Oriental spirituality did not come true—either through the Arab nationalist revolutions of the 20th century or as a result of the most recent Arab revolutions. If the synthesis of American entrepreneurship and reformed Arab-Islamic orthodoxy has ever been achieved at all, it seems to have lost the democratic components of freedom and justice envisioned by Khalid on the way to its doctrinal establishment as modern nation-states. A paradigmatic example of such a pseudo-spiritual political order would probably be the Wahhabi o(i)ligarchy of the Saudi Kingdom, whose oppressive power-mix of neo-puritanical Islamic discipline and ruthless economic exploitation of local resources has been so powerfully depicted in ʿAbd el-Rahman Munif's literary writings. Departing from this hypothesis and arguing further that Khalid's vision of Arab modernity could also be related to the so-called Islamic State's contemporary strategy of using "American arms and an up-to-date Korân"[240] to gain control over the region's resources would probably go too far. It would at least demand a relational stretching or even theological and ideological re-definition of the concepts of global contemporaneousness and local up-to-date-ness: a task that cannot be fulfilled properly at this point.

3.4   Quixotic Entanglements and Disruptive Translations

"The Oriental, when he tells the truth, is seldom believed. The Occidental, when he tells a lie, is seldom doubted."[241]

Up to this point, my discussion has basically revolved around the things told, evoked, or anticipated in the *The Book of Khalid*. The focus on what is signified by the literary narrative in terms of topicality, eventuality, and context largely excluded the question of the novel's narrative discourse—its particular signifying structure, or what Gérard Genette called "the narrative game."[242] I will now shift my attention to that very game.

---

239   On this particular aspect of the uprisings, see Hamid Dabashi, *The Arab Spring. The End of Postcolonialism* (London: Zed Books, 2012).

240   Rihani, *The Book of Khalid* 276.

241   Ameen Rihani, "The Lying Oriental," *The Path of Vision: Pocket Essays of East and West*, by Ameen Rihani (New York: White & CO, 1921) 191.

242   Gérard Genette, *Narrative Discourse: An Essay in Method*, trans. Jane E. Lewin (Ithaca, New York: Cornell UP, 1980) 34. First published in French in 1972 as *Discours du récit*.

The internal organization of the first Anglophone Arab novel's narrative playing field is a highly complex one and demands closer investigation. Such investigation, in turn, invites more general narratological and metafictional reflections on the almost inevitable tension between representational reliability and strategic inaccuracy in cross-cultural representations within and in-between the Middle East and the West. The question of narrative structures is thus directly related to the *dialogics* of authorship, narrative authority, readership pre-disposition, and strategic (mis-)translation at work in Anglophone Arab discourses of critical correlation. Although I find Genette's approach indispensable for the analysis of any given text's narrative structure or the extrapolation of the information it delivers, in order to explore the metafictional implications of Anglophone Arab representations, one needs to pay particular attention to these representations' constitutive transgressions between the fictional diegesis and the pseudo-mimetic claims of narrative patronage that are impossible to grasp in a strictly structuralist analysis.

Focusing on Miguel de Cervantes's *Don Quixote* as an important intertext for the narrative mode employed in *The Book of Khalid*, I include an early modern classic that not only represents a visionary mode of telling lies in order to tell the truth but also is the Andalusian mother of the modern novel. By relating contemporary Anglophone Arab narrative discourse to a Spanish work of partial Arab genesis that, during its long history of reception, never ceased to inspire writers, poets, composers, visual artists, and filmmakers all over the world, I place my discussion of what might be called Anglophone Arab meta-narratology in a translocal literary sphere that cannot be firmly assigned to either the West or the Middle East. It is, in fact, one of my arguments that the narrative and performative strategies at work in Anglophone Arab writings go beyond both the questioning of the factual accuracy of Western truth claims and the stretching of Arab truths. Due to their dialogic determinacy and cross-cultural directionality, they often narrate, speak, and act under the metaphorical or real surveillance of the dominant Western narrative mode. When an Anglophone Arab narrator "recounts facts which [s/]he knows perfectly well" for a Western audience, s/he partially produces "a sign of the [Westerner's skeptical] reading act."[243]

The performative evidence of these works' trustworthiness thus not only lies in their creative search for alternative documents and figments but also results from their strategic invention of modes of telling meaningful stories which anticipate and yet manage to escape the Western reader's overhasty "answering word."[244] Al-

243 See Roland Barthes and Lionel Duisit, "An Introduction to the Structural Analysis of Narrative," *New Literary History* 6.2 (1975): 260.

244 See Mikhail M. Bakhtin, "Discourse in the Novel," *The Dialogic Imagination: Four Essays*, by M. M. Bakhtin, ed. Michael Holquist, trans. Caryl Emerson and Michael Holquist (Austin: U of Texas P, 1981) 280.

though these stories try to surpass or subvert the doubtful veracity of hegemonic Western narratives and to erode these narratives' main referential systems, they can have truth effects in the world. Consequently, the following section is first and foremost interested in modalities of the narrative production of a meaning that intentionally refuses to be fully translated and thus cannot be grasped as the inter-cultural translation of Arab truth. I will focus in particular on this willful untrans-latability of Anglophone Arab texts, their strategic resistance to being assimilated within normative Western notions of intersubjectivity or intercultural accuracy, as well as their refusal to be harmonized with the moral authority of exceptional Western reliability. It is Anglophone Arab articulations' capacity to turn their dis-cursively inscribed and, therefore, inescapable cross-cultural unreliability into a self-confident narrative weapon of critical validity across the formerly separated representational spheres upon which my readings rely.

In order to structurally examine a literary representation's levels of narration, one has to first distinguish between its narrative voices and source materials. In *The Book of Khalid*, there are at least three main narrative voices involved: those of the editor-narrator, Khalid, and Shakib. The anonymous first-person narrator in-troduces her-/himself as an editor and transcriber who combines all the qualities of an investigative researcher, an expert of the social history of Arab-Western encoun-ters, and a literary and cultural critic. S/he presents the English text as an anno-tated montage based on selective translations of the Arabic manuscript of Khalid's spiritual auto-narration and the French *histoire intime* written by Shakib. The novel begins with an editorial introduction on the discovery of Khalid's manuscript and its function within the narrated story. The opening section's title, "Al-Fatihah,"[245] refers to the opening Quranic surah with the same name and thus seems to some-how act as a substitute for the classical religious inauguration of any text written by a believing Arab Muslim: Bism allah ar-rahman al-rahim [In the name of Allah, the gracious, the merciful]. But the title choice rather hints at a quite secular reve-lation: the narrator's archival searching and finding of a hitherto forgotten pseudo-prophetic book in Egypt's royal library at the beginning of the 20th century. The in-augural narrative moment of proto-literary divination presents an editor-narrator who is both the privileged receiver of what is revealed and the secondary messenger of the disclosed text:

> In the Khedivial Library of Cairo, among the Papyri of the Scribe of Amen-Ra and the beautifully illuminated copies of the Korân, the modern Arabic Manuscript which forms the subject of this Book, was found. [...] and after examining it, we

---

245   Rihani, *The Book of Khalid* 3.

hired an amanuensis to make a copy for us. Which copy we subsequently used as the warp of our material; the woof we shall speak of in the following chapter.[246]

The Khedivial Library Manuscript has a double function within the general narrative order. On the one hand, it is presented as the original source or main medium of the narrative. On the other hand, it is just one diegetic element among many other elements of the novel's plot. The narrator of *The Book of Khalid* does not allow Khalid's story to tell itself. It is "woof" and "warp,"[247] it forms the basic raw material for her or his narrative weaving, but it is by no means identical with the literary fabric presented to the reader. We are informed that what was supposedly the Arab American transmigrant's authentic auto-narrative is copied by a hired amanuensis. Although the exact measure of loss of information resulting from this early transcription remains unclear to the reader, the transcoding act represents the first entropy of Khalid's self-representational data. Some original data is always lost in the process of making a copy. This principal dynamic of what can be considered a form of textual generation loss—the reduction of resolution and the loss of information in the process of transmission and abstraction—is symbolically reciprocated by the editor-narrator's gradually progressing abbreviation of the source text. The source text introduced as the Khedivial Library Manuscript soon gets abbreviated as "Khedivial Library MS" and is finally reduced to "K. L. MS."[248] The narrator's raw material is not as raw as s/he claims. Her or his narrative act rather multiplies the generational losses by producing selective translations and making rough abstractions of the copy.

What must be considered a loss with a view to Khalid's agency of narrating his real self marks the gain of influence and narrative authority from the perspective of the editor-narrator. Although the novel's title, *The Book of Khalid*, suggests that the eponymous anti-hero's point of view governs the narrative, the editor-narrator's frantic appeal and direct address to the reader repeatedly remind us that it is s/he who produces meaning by undermining her or his characters' authority and their narratives' reliability with a view to the Western reader's perceptions and generic conventions. Already on the first pages, the eponymous hero's neo-Byronic autofiction is devalued for not having studied the self-reflexive method and necessary narrative techniques of the memoir genre: "It is to be regretted, however, that he has not mastered the most subtle of arts, the art of writing about one's self."[249] The normative reference operationalized by the editor-narrator is defined by the exalted autobiographical writings of the Western canon: "Gibbon [...] Rousseau [...]

---

246   Rihani, *The Book of Khalid* 3.
247   Rihani, *The Book of Khalid* 3.
248   Rihani, *The Book of Khalid* 12-13.
249   Rihani, *The Book of Khalid* 12.

Spencer."[250] Here, the editor-narrator is mimicking and maybe also mocking the Orientalist imputation that there is something intrinsic to Arab culture and the Arab psyche which precludes proper literary self-reflection of autonomous individuality corresponding to Western autobiographical writing.[251] Unlike Khalid, s/he claims to know the legible narrative aesthetic for addressing an enlightened English-speaking readership that believes in the fiction of the self.[252] Unlike the author of the K. L. MS., who does not care for any Western masters' example or the poetic standards of classic Arabic literature when narratively setting fire to New York or flirting with the Arab nationalists' visions, the editor-narrator "must keep the [Western] reader in mind."[253]

If one understands autobiography as a trope of reading or the autobiographical as an inescapable allegory of literary interpretation, then *The Book of Khalid* is the editor-narrator's text of selving rather than a generic auto-fiction written by Rihani.[254] The novel is not Khalid's book; it is not the *Kitab Khalid* [The Book of Khalid] which the editor claims to have discovered in a Cairo library. Nevertheless, the calligraphic cover of the Arabic manuscript with Khalid's name (fig. 7) is reproduced on the novel's cover side by side with the English title. The title is thus fraught with an ambivalent double meaning: Khalid is and is not the person whose name is on the English book cover. If we consider in addition that the reader cannot assume the editor-narrator to be the historical person of Ameen Rihani mentioned as the novel's author, the title advances to a supreme emblem of the literary representation's metafictional contiguities.

Against the background of the dominant *Nahda* debate during what is usually thought of as the Arabic novel's formative period, the editor-narrator's claim of exemplarily unlocking an archive of forgotten or marginalized modern Arabic texts and making these texts accessible to the English-speaking world through the appropriation of the Western mode of emplotment is full of ironic ambivalences. It not only emphasizes the existence of mutually foreclosed literary archives within the Middle East and the West but at the same time reciprocates the notion of the beginning of Arab literary modernity as the merely defective imitation of Western models. The found manuscript can be seen as one of thousands of dusty documents

---

250   Rihani, *The Book of Khalid* 12.

251   For this by now long-revised Orientalist philologist position, see Gustav E. von Grunebaum, "Literature in the Context of Islamic Civilization," *Oriens* 20 (1967): 1-14. Cf. Dwight F. Reynolds, ed., *Interpreting the Self. Autobiography in the Arab Literary Tradition* (Berkeley: U of California P, 2001).

252   See Michael Sprinker, "Fictions of the Self: The End of Autobiography," *Autobiography: Essays Theoretical and Critical*, ed. James Olney (Princeton: Princeton UP, 1980) 321-42.

253   Rihani, *The Book of Khalid* 12.

254   See Paul de Man, "Autobiography as De-facement," *Modern Language Notes* 94.5. (1979): 919-30.

of non-canonized late-19th- and early-20th-century popular fiction stored in Middle Eastern libraries and archives to this day. It seems to fictionally represent those un-read and unstudied books which, although they mirror the complex transnational social and cultural dynamic of their time, are still academically excluded by most scholars of the modern Arabic novel due to their hybrid narrative style.[255]

Stressing the inescapability of raiding the O/other's literary syntax and nar-rative mode in any cross-cultural translational endeavor, *The Book of Khalid* carries the very argument of plagiarism ad absurdum. As a transnational fiction, it sub-verts the culturalist assumption of originality and teleological itinerary which was prevailing among turn-of-the century Arab nationalists and Western Orientalists alike. The editor-narrator presents her or his reverse translation of a discovered Arabic story of emigration and re-migration as a work of novelistic fiction in its own right "outside of the teleology that leads from a vague origin in nineteenth century Europe to local realism and its avatars."[256] Her or his generically hybrid narrative shows persistent resonances to both the historical tension among Arab intellectuals of the time between what was seen as "high" classicist-nationalist and "low" popular culture and the increasingly challenged Eurocentric binary of Middle Eastern traditionalism versus Western modernism. There is no definite (af)filiation to either of the intertwined debates. Although the editor-narrator pretends to have adapted strictly Western modes of narration to present to the English-reading au-dience the formally insufficiently modulated traditional life story of an Arab hero, her or his aesthetic vocation of juxtaposing Khalid's discourse to her or his own superior one leads to unique narrative gestures of Anglophone Arab self-empow-erment as correlational subjectification.

The extradiegetic-homodiegetic editing voice repeatedly leaves the in-tradiegetic level on which her or his edited product is presented to establish a narrative level that exhibits the editing act itself in virtual dialogue with the metadiegetic Arabic material. While s/he can be clearly identified as a fictional researcher-editor character who appears on the novel's frame-story's intradiegetic level in her or his search for Khalid's true (his-)story, the narrator's semi-scholarly selecting and critically commentating voice constantly penetrates her or his hero's discourses. That the editor-narrator even meets one of her or his metadiegetic

---

255 On this understudied corpus of popular literature, see Selim, "The *Nahda*, Popular Fiction and the Politics of Translation," 71-89. One of such long-neglected important books, Khalil al Khuri's *Wayy idhan lastu bi Afranji* [Alas, then I am not a Foreigner] dates to 1859. The manuscript was rediscovered in a rare books collection held by the American University of Beirut and was reissued by the Egyptian state press (Cairo: Maktab al-Majlis al-'Ala lil Thaqafa, 2007) as the first Arabic novel. Set in Aleppo, it tells the story of a Westernized Arab merchant's cross-cultural encounters. See Johnson, "Importing the novel: Arabic literature's forgotten foreign objects," n. pag.

256 Selim, "The *Nahda*, Popular Fiction and the Politics of Translation," 76.

characters further complicates the novel's narrative structure. Uncertain regarding Khalid's historical existence and his autobiography's reliability, s/he initially sets out to search for biographical traces and contemporary witnesses of the literary character's very existence. With the help of a Cairo sand-diviner and thanks to the mocking hints of hashish-smoking and laughing intellectuals, s/he finds Shakib at a colonial luxury hotel near the pyramids:

> In the grill-room of the Mena House we meet the poet Shakib, who was then drawing his inspiration from a glass of whiskey and soda. Nay, he was drowning his sorrows therein, for his Master, alas! has mysteriously disappeared.[257]

When the narrator informs Shakib about her or his ambitious editorial project, the former-companion-turned-poet of the would-be-novel's main character shows himself overjoyed with the idea of making Khalid known to the world. He immediately offers his just finished *histoire intime* to be used to that end. Khalid's fellow-traveler's manuscript is to help the editor-narrator and her or his future Western readers to better understand his master's life and visions. It promises and is initially expected to metaphorically provide the narrative underwear and contextual chemise for the main hero's self-narrated outline: "'That will give you *les dessous de cartes* of his character.' '*Les dessons*'—and the Poet who intersperses his Arabic with fancy French, explains.—'The lining, the ligaments.'—'Ah, that is exactly what we want.'"[258]

The editor agrees to explicitly mention Shakib in the book—"For after all, what's in a name?"—as to then set out to incorporate the information offered in the French text. The informant is assumingly acknowledged as the author of the second intermediary narrative, as the novel's secondary co-author. But the personal historiography is only brought to the first narrative level before it is taken charge of by the editor-narrator. S/he hires "a few boys to read it [...] and mark out the passages which please them most. This will be just what an editor wants."[259] We do not learn whether the editor does her or his own translations of the sections selected by the unnamed boys. What we are instead informed about is that Shakib's journal can only partially compensate for his friend's auto-text's stylistic deficits, as he finds "no exaggeration in Khalid's words."[260] In his journal, Shakib repeatedly admits that he considers it inappropriate "to incriminate his illustrious Master."[261] His intimate historiography of Khalid's life comes close to a one-sided affirmative hagiography and is thus insufficiently appropriate for the ambitious narrative project. The editor shows little respect for Shakib and his narrative authority. S/he

---

257   Rihani, *The Book of Khalid* 15.
258   Rihani, *The Book of Khalid* 17.
259   Rihani, *The Book of Khalid* 17.
260   Rihani, *The Book of Khalid* 16.
261   Rihani, *The Book of Khalid* 42.

suspects him of the chicanery of intentionally shifting narrative responsibility to her/himself. Consequently s/he calls him "our Scribe"[262] instead of by his name, as promised.

It is the narrator's editing devices which provide the decisive correctives. S/he defines the organizational frame for the reader's production of narrative meaning in *The Book of Khalid*. S/he selects and reassembles narrative fragments, splits up lines of events, re-orders voices, and combines story segments. Her or his literary montage dictates the reader's angles and perspectives. It is s/he who explains to the English-speaking audience how to translate Arabic terms and phrases or how to understand internal Arab sociohistorical conditions and the Arab hero's states of mind. The stylistic autonomy of the character's self-narrations is constantly undermined through her or his commentating and correcting presence. In these moments, s/he is clearly more than an editor and a translator. Her or his narrative act openly manipulates and censors the textual material produced by Khalid and Shakib. The editor-narrator leaves her or his traces in the narrative discourse, and s/he does so deliberately. At times, her or his ironically biting pathos of narrative authority and overexposure of absolute truth-claims even outstrip those of Khalid. In these moments, the editor-narrator is the true hero of *The Book of Khalid*, and Khalid's (hi-)story is her or his narration, her or his historiography.

The novel's particular metafictional dialectic results from the constant blurring of the editor-narrator-critic's level of narration and the metadiegetic level established by Khalid's and Shakib's narratives. Since these dynamics are significantly framed and determined by the anticipation of a general Western text, the queering of narrative levels implicitly carries signs of the Anglophone audience's reading act that happens or is expected to happen at the same time inside and outside the diegetic level. Such blurring of the line between the intradiegetic and extradiegetic level cannot be exhaustively explained in structuralist terms. In a certain sense, the narrative strategy invites the Western reader to read the narrative of his own reading quasi ex negativo and thus discover the limits of comprehension in this very reading act. But it first and foremost affirms the Anglophone Arab narrator's authority and stresses her or his representational power: the power to control which truth gets transferred to the English audience. Although the novel's editor-narrator, in many ways, is what s/he accuses the authors of her or his source texts to be, namely a "poor third-hand caterer"[263] of derivate information, s/he triumphs over both her or his auto-narrators and her or his anticipated readers.

Let me explain the particular technique that leads to this triumph in more detail: After the story of how Khalid and Shakib "were smuggled out of their country" is told, the editor-narrator traces how the two young Arabs "smuggled themselves

---

262 Rihani, *The Book of Khalid* 42.
263 Rihani, *The Book of Khalid* 211.

into the city of New York."[264] The reader learns that Khalid, at the time of his arrival in the US, suffered from a serious case of trachoma. As a consequence, he is first detained in a hospital of the immigration board and then threatened to be deported back to Lebanon. Thanks to an intrigue of bribery by Shakib, however, he manages to escape, and the two start their peddler business with the faked contraband of imaginary Holy Land relics. It is at this point of the narrative that the editor-narrator first discloses her or his Arab identity without providing any further autobiographical detail. S/he does so while stressing the importance of the trope of smuggling in the context of Anglophone Arab literary migrations without explaining the Arabic etymology of this very metaphorical hint. The editor-narrator's self-justification deliberately sidesteps the explanation of the metaphorical meaning and discursive implications of the Arabic term through the evasion maneuver of drawing on her or his alterity instead of on cross-lingual translation. By doing so, s/he acts as a narrative smuggler in her or his own right:

> (we beg the critic's pardon; for, being foreigners ourselves, we ought to be permitted to stretch this term, smuggle, to cover an Arabic metaphor, or to smuggle into it a foreign meaning), these two Syrians, we say, became, in their capacity of merchants, smugglers of the most ingenious and most evasive type.[265]

The evoked, yet hidden, Arabic metaphor openly clashes with the anticipated reader's monolingualism. One could, in fact, argue that the Arab editor-narrator's Anglophone narrative act willingly clashes with an unconditional ethics of direct translation. Circumnavigating the terrain of linguistic diversity and avoiding a crude transcultural recoding (or what Gayatri Chakravorty Spivak calls "transcoding"[266]), s/he does not want to be accountable for writing/translating any presupposed original meaning. If we leave aside her or his strategic reluctance for a moment, we can try to differentiate—because to theorize the pitfalls of cross-cultural translation, one needs to somehow think linguistic difference—what the respective section could transpose to a non-implied or additionally implied reader: The Arabic term *tahrib* [smuggling] is derived from the verbal form *haraba* [to escape or flee, or to desert]. The transitive verb *harraba* can be translated as both "to break free" or "free someone" and "to smuggle [something]." Hence, the *muharrib* is at the same time a refugee or emigrant as well as a smuggler. The half-covered etymological hint stresses that it is not only migrants and non-human smuggled goods that are carried from one place to another. It sensitizes the reader for the narrative *carrying across* involved in any translational or metaphorical transferring of meaning. Forcing the reader to reconsider what is really indicated by the English

264   Rihani, *The Book of Khalid* 42.
265   Rihani, *The Book of Khalid* 42.
266   Spivak, "Translation as Culture," 244.

notions of translation (deriving from the Latin *translatio*) and metaphor (from the Greek μεταφορά), the editor-narrator's hint reminds us of the impossibility of taking any truth translated in Anglophone Arab cultural migrations in a non-metaphorical sense. When the Arab migrant-translator carries herself or himself across, if s/he wants to escape the inevitable violence of total assimilation, s/he must prevent the Western audience from having a direct grasp of her or his truths. S/he must expand the parameters of the real and transfer content in the sense of a strategic act of ποίησις rather than mimetic (self-)representation.[267]

Such a doubled metaphor of translation—as an emancipative migratory act of smuggling ex-centric meaning by smuggling oneself into a given normative cultural setting while resisting being consumed in direct translations is at work in many anticolonial, decolonial, and postcolonial representations. Writers and critics like Assia Djebar, Abdelkébir Khatibi, Édouard Glissant, or Ngũgĩ wa Thiong'o have each demonstrated, in her and his own way, how strategic translation, selective translation, or even non-translation can become a form of resistive identification under the historical condition of (post-)coloniality. Whereas Ngũgĩ's nativist identity politics of literary language lament the (neo-)colonial hegemony of the (former) colonizer's language in African literature as an extension of socio-economic discipline into the linguistic spheres of "mental control"[268] and therefore see in the use of one's native language a necessary tool of self-definition and mental decolonization, Djebar, Glissant, and Khatibi rather take a poststructuralist approach of doubled or bidirectional decolonization through the redeployment of linguistic differences as translational interference and irreducible relational "opacity"[269] in their respective use of the French "stepmother tongue."[270] Where Ngũgĩ counters what he, in his 2010 Wellek Library Lectures on *Globalectics*, calls "an aristocracy of languages"[271] by reversing colonial-racist hierarchies and dedicating himself to the assumed essential clarity of his community's internal communication, the Francophone Arab and Francophone Caribbean intellectuals see the cross-linguistic translational literary text as a vehicle for the strategic multiplication of non-transparency and ambiguity. Glissant, in his *Poetics of Relation*, insists on the Caribbean writer's "right to opacity" as a logical aesthetic extrapolation of her or his ethical "right to difference."[272] In *La*

---

267   Spivak, "Translating into English," 256-74, here 265.

268   Ngũgĩ wa Thiong'o, *Decolonizing the Mind: The Politics of Language in African Literature* (1986; Oxford: James Currey; Nairobi: EAEP; Portsmouth, NH: Heinemann, 2005) 16.

269   Glissant, *Poetics of Relation* 186, see also 189-94.

270   Assia Djebar, *Fantasia: An Algerian Cavalcade*, trans. Dorothy S. Blair (Portsmouth, NH: Heinemann, 1993) 214. See also Soheila Ghaussy, "A Stepmother Tongue: 'Feminine Writing' in Assia Djebar's *Fantasia: An Algerian Cavalcade*," *World Literature Today* 68.3 (1994): 457-62.

271   Ngũgĩ wa Thiong'o, *Globalectics: Theory and the Politics of Knowing* (2012; New York: Columbia UP, 2014) 60-61.

272   Glissant, *Poetics of Relation* 190.

langue de l'autre, Khatibi similarly reclaims the exercise of intentional unreadability as a technique that writing fiction in between two idioms affords.[273] Finally, Djebar, while clearly identifying French *écriture* with male repression (Arab and colonial alike), paradoxically uses "the language of the former conqueror"[274] to express her alienated and gendered experiences as an Algerian woman. On the one hand, she constantly questions the French language as an adequate idiom for conveying her Arabic memories of racist and sexist subjugation. On the other hand, Djebar's narrative practice of equally "disruptive" and "extended translation"[275] turns the doubly paternal language into a self-empowering instrument of queering dominant male French *his-story* with *her stories*.

Many of the Anglophone Arab representations with which I am concerned in the course of this study pursue a similar strategy as do the works of Djebar, Glissant and Khatibi. They re-write Arab experience in a language that defines them as Other without claiming to represent the truth of that experience. They perform selectively extended translations of Arab-ness to make themselves heard without promising to transparently mirror any real presence. If they conceal an essential truth claim, it is not simply transferred to the reader. To effectively *smuggle* their message into the dominant Anglophone discourse while *escaping* from the threat of disciplined integration, these travelling narratives repeatedly *desert* any normative mode of telling truth and *take refuge* in false translations. In these moments, their transgressive poetics of *breaking free* is one of *real doing* rather than of representing the real. Moreover, when reading Anglophone Arab texts, one should not lament the irreducible opacity of the text but rather ask how this lack of transparency relates to the always evolving intentional opacity of the author or to our own discursive closeness as readers. Cross-cultural translation in Anglophone Arab fiction does not necessarily attempt to provide a transparent passage between a conflictual source text and the comfortably placed Western reader. The use of the English "vehicular language" does not indicate the attempt to give transparency to any "vernacular"[276] Arab texts. In my view, the Anglophone Arab text's opacities do not primarily result from linguistic difference, the Western reader's lack of cross-lingual competence, or conversely interlexicality; rather, they must be understood as poetic expressions irrespective of the problem of lingual separateness. They reciprocate a relational discursive formation that is all too often overwhelmed by politics of arrogant separation and representational alterity. One, therefore, cannot exhaustively

---

273   Abdelkébir Khatibi, *La langue de l'autre* (New York : Les Mains Secrètes, 1999). See also David Fieni, "The Language of the Other: Testimonial Exercises," [Excerpt from the introduction to Khatibi's *La langue de l'autre*], trans. Catherine Porter, *PMLA* 125.4 (2010): 1002-04.

274   Djebar, *Fantasia: An Algerian Cavalcade* 181.

275   Ghaussy, "A Stepmother Tongue: 'Feminine Writing' in Assia Djebar's *Fantasia: An Algerian Cavalcade*," 460.

276   Glissant, *Poetics of Relation* 116.

interpret the translational role that Anglophone Arab representations play in cross-cultural communication by simply stressing their functional capacity to correct the dominant Western obliteration of their true "source culture" without at the same time addressing the strategic use of untranslatability or of what is intentionally not translated for "the smuggling of foreign goods"[277] into whichever target culture.

It is certainly true that many Anglophone Arab writers, as "cultural translators and members of an embattled minority," are forced to place their works within a discursive spectrum defined by the poles of assimilationist self-domestication and corrective foreignization of the dominant modes of alterity, as Waïl Hassan argues in his 2011 study of Arab immigrant narratives.[278] However, as the Libyan American translator and poet Khaled Mattawa explains, using the anecdote of his own translational endeavors during an interview with a consular official at the American embassy in Athens in the course of his family's visa application, Anglophone Arabs sometimes have to lie in translation if they attempt "to make the powerful less powerful, and the powerless less powerless." Against the background of his own experiences as a refugee, Mattawa stresses that the translation of Arab lives into the English language "does not take place [in a politically neutral] cultural détente" and that therefore "generosity" of truths or "solicitude" regarding one's own sincerity are not always "viable way[s] to cross distances."[279] Ameen Rihani makes a similar argument in one of his short *Pocket Essays for East and West* entitled "The Lying Oriental."[280] More than 90 years before Mattawa questions the value of unconditional translational honesty for the purpose of migratory cross-overs, Rihani warns Arabs of "naive truthfulness"[281] and encourages them toward the instrumental use of creatively crafted truth in relation to the West:

> Honesty itself ceases to be a virtue when it is made a means to an ignoble end. And the Oriental, whose craftiness is often practised in self-defense, negatively, seldom regards it as a positive method, a material virtue, an instrument of success.[282]

---

277   Khaled Mattawa, "Identity, Power, and a Prayer to Our Lady of Repatriation: On Translating and Writing Poetry," *Kenyon Review Online* (Fall 2014): n. pag., 13 Mar. 2015 <http://www.kenyonreview.org/kr-online-issue/2014-fall/selections/khaled-mattawa-essay-1-656342/>.

278   Hassan, *Immigrant Narratives: Orientalism and Cultural Translation in Arab American and Arab British Literature* 37, see in particular 28-37. Hassan's translational argument specifically draws on Antoine Berman, *The Experience of the Foreign: Culture and Translation in Romantic Germany*, trans. S. Heyvaert (Albany: SUNY Press, 1992) and on Lawrence Venuti, *Scandals of Translation: Towards an Ethics of Difference* (London: Routledge, 1998).

279   Mattawa, "Identity, Power, and a Prayer to Our Lady of Repatriation: On Translating and Writing Poetry," n. pag.

280   Rihani, "The Lying Oriental," 189-95.

281   Rihani, "The Lying Oriental," 191.

282   Rihani, "The Lying Oriental," 192.

Particularly in the context of international politics and merchandise, the author of *The Book of Khalid* recommends adapting Bismarck's negotiation strategy of "lapsing periodically into truth."[283] Rihani stresses the moral relevance of intention and motive rather than factuality when choosing a particular communicative method or direction. He closes his English-language essay with an anecdote that allegorically explains "Oriental lying" as a strategically justifiable and sophisticated way of countering Western lies, if not a legitimate one. Since this, to my knowledge, is the earliest Anglophone Arab articulation of the notion of cross-cultural counter-lying, I quote the respective section in full length:

> Once in Damascus I saw a merchant selling some ancient coins, which were probably made in Germany. Their patina seemed authentic and real. They even smelled of the earth. But the merchant sorted them out into two lots, carefully sifting and examining, and finally said, these are false, my Lord, these are genuine. And he swore by Allah and the Prophet that he was speaking the truth. Which was quite unexpected by the tourist, who was much impressed. He was in fact taken in. For by admitting that some of the coins were not genuine, the wily shop-keeper was able to sell to mylord some of the others, which were equally false. I spoke with him afterwards and he admitted to me—told me the other half of the truth—that the European who sold him the antiquified coins taught him also the trick. [284]

When reading Anglophone representations from a relationally extended translational perspective, we should remember Rihani's anecdotal justification for the countering of Western half-truths with the narrative insertion of partial Arab truths. What if, in the case of these representations, the first stage of translation is not "initiative trust" in "the coherence of the world,"[285] as George Steiner puts it in his seminal work of translation theory, *After Babel*, but rather a learned distrust regarding the capacity of the Western semantic system to permit entrance to a non-Western meaning that is perceived as antithetical and intrinsically mendacious? What if we have not left Babel behind us yet? Could it be that the producer of Anglophone Arab works sometimes cannot get it right in his own transgressive interest without intentionally getting it wrong for the Western receiver? Is it possible to modify Walter Benjamin's important definition of "The Task of the Translator"[286] to interpretively include translational violations that go beyond extending

---

283 Rihani, "The Lying Oriental," 192.
284 Rihani, "The Lying Oriental," 195.
285 George Steiner, *After Babel: Aspects of Language and Translation*, 3. ed. (Oxford: Oxford UP, 1998) 312.
286 Walter Benjamin, "The Task of the Translator," *Selected Writings Vol. 1, 1913-1926*, eds. Marcus Bullock and Michael W. Jennings (1996; Cambridge: The Belknap P of Harvard UP, 2002) 253-63.

the parameters of one's own language as part of a general universalist longing for transcultural linguistic "kinship"[287] and "complementation"?[288] Benjamin assesses "any translation[s] that intend[ ] a transmitting function [...] as bad translations" because they cannot transmit anything but "inessential content."[289] Instead, he sees in proper translation a cultural practice that is "midway between poetry and theory" and that aims at "something other than reproduction of meaning."[290] His supplementary understanding of the translator's task stresses the linguistic voicing of an original work of art's true "*intentio*"[291] in a principally harmonic translational act. But what if one radicalizes Benjamin's advice to transgress the barriers of one's native linguistic system by extending this transgressive advice to the ethical paradigms of intercultural communication? Can we then imagine new ways of being fellow humans in an era of impossible direct (self-)translations? How can one interpretively grasp Anglophone Arab representations in which no original is transplanted but in which the notion of cross-cultural translation itself gets radically questioned and displaced? How does one make sense of partial translational endeavors, inventive pseudo-transfers, strategic opacities, or faked transmittings which, although they consider the discursive disposition which regulates the communicative relation between sender and receiver, neither aim at doing justice to any original Arab source nor intend to serve the Western reader's neo-ethnographic desire for prefigured Arab truth? What, in other words, if we are dealing with translations of Arab-ness that are meant for "readers" who do not want to understand, so that strategic untranslatability and not "translatability is an essential quality"[292] of their narrative transposing? If it is true, as Benjamin argues, that the "language of truth [...] is concealed in concentrated fashion in translation,"[293] what is the language spoken by those Anglophone Arab representations that turn the drama of mendacious cross-cultural "symbolizing into the symbolized itself?"[294] These questions and related cognitive interests guide my following discussion.

Cultural representations like *The Book of Khalid* not only metafictionally reflect the Western discourse of alterity as one important condition of Anglophone Arab narrative selving but, in addition, directly project this shadow-text formed by the conditions of external communication onto the narrative level of internal communication. By doing so, they transgress both the functional difference between au-

---

287   Benjamin, "The Task of the Translator," 255.
288   Benjamin, "The Task of the Translator," 260.
289   Benjamin, "The Task of the Translator," 253.
290   Benjamin, "The Task of the Translator," 259.
291   Benjamin, "The Task of the Translator," 260.
292   Benjamin, "The Task of the Translator," 254.
293   Benjamin, "The Task of the Translator," 259.
294   Benjamin, "The Task of the Translator," 261.

thor and reader and the structural differentiation between the implied reader and the worldly (empirical) receiver of the literary text. The effect of this narrative technique, equally strange and estranging, is reminiscent of what Jorge Luis Borges has demonstrated with his short story "Pierre Menard: Author of the Quixote": "truth [...] is not 'what happened'; it is what we *believe* happened."[295] Consequently, the real author of a story "is not only he who tells it, but at times even more, he who hears it."[296]

Given *The Book of Khalid*'s multiplicity of extra- and intradiegetic narrative voices and competing authorship claims as well as the editor-hero's power to selectively narrate, the Western readers' co-authoring function is in fact quite ambivalent. On the one hand, they are offered a certain privilege regarding the knowledge of discursively prefigured limits of the narrative's evidence. On the other hand, they are constantly reminded that very little is certain and that much was lost during the Arab narrator's rigorous editing work. What the Western reader is allowed access to is basically a selectively translated and highly abstracted world of shifting individual accounts of appearances that cannot easily be evaluated, either as facts or illusions. By making up a story that makes us believe that these events might have truly happened while not entirely letting us accept that something else possibly did not happen, the Anglophone Arab narrator invites us to discover the limits of our own perceptive power in the making of cross-cultural meaning. S/he presents herself or himself as a very ambivalent quasi-character of contradictory functions. On the one hand, s/he has no other rights to the story than those of the reader and translator of two transmigrant Arab texts. The novel's kernel sections are ascribed to the authors Khalid and Shakib; s/he rarely pretends to know anything for sure and consequently cannot be made responsible for the tales of others. On the other hand, s/he exercises her or his irresponsible game of translation as the abstraction, recoding, falsification, invention, and distortion of narrative Arab-ness with blatant authorial authority. The narrative celebration of her or his creatively distorted reading obviously overdoes and thus exhibits its own literary hoax. The excess of the disavowed invention of stories ascribed to others sometimes almost borders on its own parody.

Drawing on Jorge Luis Borges's self-ironic preface to his *Universal History of Infamy*, one could say that the editor-narrator in *The Book of Khalid* constantly reminds us "that good readers are even blacker and rarer swans than good writers."[297] The novel is thus an important reminder for the potential good reader of Anglophone

---

295   Jorge Luis Borges, "Pierre Menard: Author of the Quixote," *Collected Fictions*, by Jorge Luis Borges, trans. Andrew Hurley (New York: Penguin, 1998) 94.

296   Genette, *Narrative Discourse* 262.

297   Jorge Luis Borges, Preface to the First Edition [1935], *A Universal History of Infamy* (1972; New York: Penguin, 1987) 15.

Arab representations that her or his exercise of reading must involve a constant re-thinking of her or his own reading act in relation to the question of authorship and narrative authority. It goes without saying that such responsive transgression of the reading-writing binary necessarily involves self-critically transgressing the differentiation between the poetics of an individual work, the theoretical implications of its metafictional dialectics, and the ethical insights offered in that work in equal measure.

3.4.1 Cervantes's Fictional Flight, the Moorish Unconscious, and Reversed Plagiarism

The *Book of Khalid* offers numerous intra- and intertextual hints for the endeavor of transgressive Anglophone Arab readings. Khalid neither firmly believes in the scandalous truth that he claims to be—"Better keep away from the truth, O Khalid," he says to himself, "better remain a stranger to it all thy life"[298]—nor does the narrator see his discourse of "editorialship" itself "bound [...] to maintain in any degree the algidity and indifference of our confrères' sublime attitude."[299] The editor-narrator is not afraid of misrepresenting her or his two heroes. Calling Shakib and Khalid her or his "gewgaws,"[300] s/he clearly indicates their subordinated function as mere playthings for her or his narrative game. The non-conclusive reconciliation of the secondary-author-heroes' claimed facts and her or his own editorial truths sometimes leads to open complaints regarding the found text's literariness and consequently to their rigorous suppression: "Too tragic, too much like fiction it sounds, that here abruptly we must end this Chapter."[301] At other occasions, Khalid, irrespective of all stated aesthetic deficits and uncovered lies of his manuscript, functions as a foil to the editor's own narrative veracity: "he is genuine, and oft-times amusingly truthful."[302] The ambiguities resulting from an editor-narrative voice, which turns the editor into both the protagonist of *The Book of Khalid* as well as the reader of Khalid's book, culminate into absurd tragedy when Khalid's hopeless battle for spiritual freedom and sociopolitical justice almost leads to his martyrdom in the Great Mosque of Damascus. At this point of the narrative, Khalid's fight against internal and external enemies of the diegetic world has repeatedly presented itself as the naïvely idealistic battling of an imaginary enemy, namely the editor-narrator's notion of reality. Shakib's almost unconditional loyalty has by then already turned Khalid into a tragically unrecognized prophet-knight-errant and lets Shakib appear to be a foolish companion, worshipping his downright-mad master.

---

298   Rihani, *The Book of Khalid* 68.
299   Rihani, *The Book of Khalid* 68.
300   Rihani, *The Book of Khalid* 69.
301   Rihani, *The Book of Khalid* 170.
302   Rihani, *The Book of Khalid* 182.

Thus, one cannot be surprised to find the editor-narrator anticipating the readers' quixotic associations.

> In this grievous state, somewhat like Don Quixote after the Battle of the Mill, our Khalid enters Baalbek. If the reader likes the comparison between the two Knights at this juncture, he must work it out for himself. We cannot be so uncharitable as that; especially that our Knight is a compatriot, and is now, after our weary journeying together, become our friend.—Our poor grievous friend who must submit again to the surgeon's knife.[303]

The editor's narrative preemption of the reader's intertextual comparison of *The Book of Khalid* with Miguel de Cervantes's arch-novel is not elaborated further. S/he explains her or his reluctance to offer such an elaboration with the shared national filiation and close ties of friendship between narrator and hero. The simultaneous avowal and disavowal of the novel's quixotic entanglements has metafictional implications that go far beyond the spheres of narratology and intertextuality. The implications of the short intradiegetic gesture even transgress the individual reading of the text in which it flourishes.

In this respect, I do not wait to receive the editor-narrator's official invitation for the comparative use of *Don Quixote*.[304] The Spanish classic from 1605/15 in fact forms a constant matrix or virtual parallel reading for my interpretive attempts to theoretically grasp relational narratives of Arab-Western encounters. For the purpose of my study, the *Quixote* is an intertext of basic relevance. It cannot only be seen as an overall early modern antecedent to contemporary postcolonial writings;[305] it also quite concretely anticipates many of the narratological, translational, and poetical-ethical questions already discussed in the previous sub-chapter and might conceal even more critical hints for our understanding of Anglophone Arab representations. In this regard, it is less important to see the obvious: that *The Book of Khalid* is a quixotic novel, that its narrative structure is patterned after Cervantes's model of retelling a story revealed as someone else's work, or that Khalid and Shakib bear several similarities to Don Quixote and Sancho Panza. As Lionel Trilling already proposed in 1950, such ascertainment of thematic and structural variation would actually be true for almost all prose fiction that came after

---

303   Rihani, *The Book of Khalid* 297.
304   Miguel de Cervantes Saavedra, *Don Quixote de la Mancha*, ed. E. C. Riley, trans. Charles Jarvis (Oxford: Oxford UP, 1992). This translation was first published in 1742.
305   William Childers, *Transnational Cervantes* (Toronto: U of Toronto P, 2006) 44-80.

Don Quixote.[306] This certainly applies to Voltaire's *Candide, ou l'optimisme* (1759)[307] and Thomas Carlyle's *Sartor Resartus* (1833–34). According to Waïl Hassan, the two latter texts can just as well be read as "antecedent examples"[308] for Rihani's literary project.

For the purpose of my discussion, I prefer to focus on *Don Quixote*. It is crucial to remember that the early-17th-century story of the (mis-)adventures of an Andalusian *hidalgo* who seeks to re-establish the traditions of knight errantry was originally written in Arabic, or rather, that the editor-narrator (the author Cervantes?) claims that this story was transferred from an assumingly unreliable Moorish source text. For Jorge Luis Borges, the *Quixote*'s "Partial Magic" of juxtaposing "a real prosaic world to an imaginary poetic world"[309] first and foremost derives from precisely this narrative device:

> It is also surprising to learn, at the beginning of the ninth chapter, that the entire novel has been translated from the Arabic and that Cervantes acquired the manuscript in the marketplace of Toledo and had it translated by a *morisco* whom he lodged in his house for more than a month and a half while the job was being finished.[310]

Although we can never be sure of possible additional layers of narration, perhaps a "segundo autor" as the final editor or even "a more obscure ultimate author,"[311] Cervantes's narrative follows a relatively strict tri-level author-translator-editor pattern. Accordingly, it is the Moorish historian and Muslim philosopher Cide Hamete Benengeli who has recorded the events in the lives of the two anti-heroes, Don Quixote and Sancho Panza. The Spanish version is edited by Cervantes. The unnamed *morisco* (a forced Christian convert from Islam) who translated the Arabic manuscript is never clearly identified. The editor's narrative shows a strange double-treatment of his Arab source text. He echoes Cide Hamete Benengeli even as he questions the historian's reliability and openly suppresses his voice. What foremost undercuts Benengeli's authority seems to be his Arab descent. He is a Moor

---

306 Lionel Trilling, *The Liberal Imagination: Essays on Literature and Society* (New York: Viking P, 1950) 207-209. For the field of British literature, see, for instance, J. A. G. Ardila, ed., *The Cervantean Heritage: Reception and Influence of Cervantes in Britain* (London: LEGENDA, Mod. Humanities Research Assn. and Maney Pub., 2009).

307 *Candide* was published under the pseudonym Docteur Ralph.

308 Hassan, *Immigrant Narratives: Orientalism and Cultural Translation in Arab American and Arab British Literature* 49.

309 Jorge Luis Borges, "Partial Magic in the Quixote," *Labyrinth: Selected Stories & Other Writings*, by Jorge Luis Borges, eds. Donald A. Yates and James E. Irby (New York: New Directions, 1964) 193.

310 Borges, "Partial Magic in the Quixote," 194.

311 Howard Mancing, "Cide Hamete Benengeli vs. Miguel de Cervantes: The Metafictional Dialectic of Don Quijote," *Cervantes: Bulletin of the Cervantes Society of America*. 1.1-2 (1981): 64.

and is therefore seen as a quasi-congenital liar. According to the editor-narrator, Arabs are "all imposters, liars and visionaries."[312] Calling Benengeli "a lying dog of a Moor," the editor-narrator's racist discrimination goes significantly beyond subtle objections related to the play of competing narrative levels.[313] He gradually reduces the stature of the Arab source narrator and alienates the reader from him. Openly ridiculing him, the editor not only makes the Moor an object of the reader's laughter, thus almost replacing the mad knight errant, Don Quixote, as the main source of comic antics, but at the same time underscores his own reliability.

The metafictional effect of this inversing narrative strategy is of direct consequence for the reader. S/he is turned into the final target of the literary work's extradiegetic laughter: that is, her or his own laughter. In all this, the *morisco* translator is almost neutralized. Although the Spanish editor can never be sure about the accuracy of his cross-linguistic transferring, and though the *morisco* omits some of the historian's lengthy descriptions, his translation is presented as presumably accurate. Lodged (or locked) in the cloister of a church, he represents an important yet subjugated narrative link between *original* author and authorial editor. For my reading of *The Book of Khalid* and, respectively, Anglophone Arab representations, the convert's mediating function is of particular importance. It is significant that the Anglophone Arab editor-narrator does her or his own translations of Arab texts. S/he often does so in suspicious mind. But due to the shared anticipation of not being believed by the Western audience, there remains a certain alliance. Even if s/he knows that s/he has to strategically disrupt her or his translational mediation of Arabness to the point of lying, s/he will therefore regularly pretend to tell the whole truth, and nothing but the truth.

While Borges stresses the magical effects of the *Quixote*'s inversion of readership and authorship—in particular, the reader's becoming aware of her or his own semi-fictitious positionality as co-writer of a fictional work that is not really written by the man whose name is on the book's cover—the Lebanese writer and critic, Elias Khoury, in turn uses the Argentinian intellectual's surprise as a point of departure to raise the issue of correlational identification in contemporary Arab cultural discourse. In his 2003 essay, "Reading Arabic,"[314] he, like Borges, is less interested in notions of authenticity or the truthfulness in the claim of translation than in the implications of this claim's full-throated enunciation. Khoury's allusion to Cervantes's playful account of cross-cultural translation is to undermine

---

312   Cervantes, *Don Quixote de la Mancha* 484.
313   Cf. Mancing, "Cide Hamete Benengeli vs. Miguel de Cervantes : The Metafictional Dialectic of Don Quijote," 66.
314   Elias Khoury, "Reading Arabic," *DisOrientation: Contemporary Arab Artists from the Middle East* (Berlin: Haus der Kulturen der Welt, 2003) 10–13.

the all too often overstated and misleading question of authenticity or cultural origin in debates revolving around global cultural production. He instead suggests an
understanding of literary and artistic creativity, or critical reading for that matter,
which acknowledges contemporary Arab writers' and artists' capacity for narrative,
audio-visual, or performative identifications that express the encounter with the
West while blurring those boundaries that for too long discursively regulated the
representation of this very encounter. According to Khoury, such self-questioning
literary, artistic, and/or critical text "emerges where the author, [the literary writer,
the artist, or the critic] migrates along with his text"[315] and transcends the ethno-
cultural fragmentation of creative expression and interpretation alike. It ultimately
presumes a translational mode of relation that does not primarily care for originality and that is not afraid of the dynamics of what the Arab critic calls "reversed
plagiarism."[316] Expressing and at the same time criticizing, from within such fictocritical texts, the structural limitations of its own cross-cultural endeavor, performative acts, sounds, or images can become the bases of future socio-political
encounters in which the critique of "pre-packed ideas"[317] is institutionally turned
into new forms of coexistence. Khoury describes this capability of writing and reading Arabic today as the "potential for identification through correlation."[318] It is this
potential that my readings of Anglophone Arab representations want to flagrantly
max out without irreverently exploiting it.

Neither Khoury nor Borges are concerned with the historical context of Cervantes's work. Their shared focus on the magic encounter between the real and
the imagined in literary communication can give us a hint regarding the importance of the reception and transformation of magical (realist) modes of representation within Anglophone Arab discourses. I will touch upon the divergent fantastic
strategies of destabilizing the static Western paradigms of identity, reality, or history by telling *Lies that Tell the Truth*[319] in the course of other readings. At this point,
however, I want to revisit the specific socio-historical conditions of the *Quixote*'s
emergence and, in particular, the historicity of the novel's imaginative Arab intertext. I thus wish to direct my and your attention to a chronotopic frame that
regularly interferes with Anglophone Arab memories and narratives; one that can
be grasped as both a cognitive and psychological concept as well as a political vision and a narrative feature. *The Book of Khalid* refers to this temporal and spatial
setting only in passing when comparatively explaining the great expectations and
even greater disappointments related to Arab-American immigrations:

---

315 Khoury, "Reading Arabic," 13.
316 Khoury, "Reading Arabic," 10, 13.
317 Khoury, "Reading Arabic," 13.
318 Khoury, "Reading Arabic," 12.
319 Anne C. Hegerfeldt, *Lies that Tell the Truth: Magical Realism Seen through Contemporary Fiction
     from Britain* (Amsterdam: Rodopi, 2005).

> What the Arabs always said of Andalusia, Khalid and Shakib said once of America: a most beautiful country with one single vice—it makes foreigners forget their native land. But now they are both suffering from nostalgia, and America, therefore, is without a single vice.[320]

Don Quixote as a structural intertext at work in *The Book of Khalid* conceals quite a different aspect of Arab Andalusian memories. It sheds oblique light on a violent era in which Spain's Muslim culture came to a forcible end. Whether the historian Benengeli is a narrative jest or not does not matter here. He is, apparently, just as earnest as Don Quixote, just as peculiar, and just as important as the editor-narrator for understanding what this novel is about. What does matter is that, at the time when Cervantes was writing his proto-novel, an Arabic-speaking Muslim would not have easily been found in a public space like the Toledo marketplace. Jews had already been violently expelled from Al-Andalus during the *Reconquista* of 1492. Books in Arabic had been burned soon after with all the ferocity that the priest applies to Don Quixote's library of chivalric narratives. Muslim converts, like the translator in *Don Quixote*, had been completely expelled from Spain since 1609—just after the first part of Cervantes's novel was published. During the 16th century, forced Arab converts to Christianity lived as Muslims clandestinely, communicating in *aljamiado*—Spanish written in Arabic characters. Within only one century, Andalusia's multiculture of interreligious coexistence and collaboration had degenerated into a vicious cycle of intolerance, violent repression, and Inquisition, until the final expulsion of all Muslims from the Iberian Peninsula in 1614.[321]

Don Quixote is born of memories latent in extinct and condemned Arabic texts. The earliest European novel seems to partly resonate the social dynamics of a time in which Arab-Muslim culture and religion, which had been part of Andalusian life for eight centuries, were forcibly suppressed. It is not only an ironic re-vision of a romance of chivalry; it can also be read as a tale of religious intolerance and ethnic cleansing. In such a reading, Benengeli's manuscript is a ghost story about the Arab memory of a lost world. Its degradation and partial suppression by the editor narratively reciprocates the traumatic Arab-Muslim-Jewish experience of oppression and expulsion. The historical person Cervantes could hardly have wandered around La Mancha without coming upon traces of that trauma. Whether the Spanish writer might have himself come from a family of *conversos*, and thus have been the "victim of a social order in which he belongs to a class that has no func-

---

320   Rihani, *The Book of Khalid* 121.
321   For details on this historical background, see L. P. Harvey, *Muslims in Spain, 1500 to 1614* (Chicago: U of Chicago P, 2005) and L. P. Harvey, *Islamic Spain, 1250 to 1500* (Chicago: U of Chicago P, 1990).

tion,"[322] cannot be answered here. Selectively drawing on Erich Auerbach's socio-psychological interpretation of *Don Quixote*, however, allows to argue that the editor-narrator's disavowing treatment of the Arab historian's truth claims represents "a flight from a situation which [had become] unbearable,"[323] a violent attempt to emancipate.

Of course, Rihani did not want to compose another *Don Quixote*. As I have explained, the similarity between *The Book of Khalid*'s structure of narration and the classic's narrative organization first and foremost concerns the shared use of the found manuscript editor-narrator pattern for the disruptive-translational transgression of the truth/non-truth binary. If the Anglophone Arab novel is a structural plagiarism, it is the plagiarism of a successive literary transcription of an Arabic source narrative; it is an instance of Arab reverse plagiarism rather than plagiarism tout court. And if this reversed inversion of original and translation has an emancipatory objective, it must first be seen in the Arab narrator's flight from the unbearable situation of being translated by Westerners. In the context of my discussion, it is important to note that Rihani's short, direct excursion into the Andalusian chronotope is used for an ironic comment on the Arab American immigrant's forgetfulness and nostalgia.

The theme of Al-Andalus has featured prominently in both the Arabic and the Anglophone Arab novel throughout the 20th century and continues to be creatively extrapolated in narrative fiction.[324] Radwa Ashour's 1994 *Gharnata* [Granada],[325] the saga of an Arab family that remains in Granada after the defeat of the last Muslim dynasty, and Diana Abu-Jaber's *Crescent*,[326] a 2003 post-mythical novel of dislocated Arabness and impossible conviviality, are two recent and particular paradigmatic examples of this equally translinguistic and transnational sub-genre of Arab literature. The Andalusian imaginary does not simply help Arab writers to express their nostalgic desires for an irreversibly lost past but can equally represent a present

---

322 Erich Auerbach, *Mimesis: The Representation of Reality in Western Literature*, trans. Willard R. Trask (Princeton: Princeton UP, 1953) 137.

323 Auerbach, *Mimesis: The Representation of Reality in Western Literature* 137.

324 William Granara, "Nostalgia, Arab Nationalism, and the Andalusian Chronotope in the Evolution of the Modern Arabic Novel," *Journal of Arabic Literature* 36.1 (2005): 57-73.

325 Radwa Ashour, *Gharnata* (Cairo: Dar al-Hilal, 1994). The novel forms the first part of the Granada Trilogy: Radwa Ashour, *Thulathiyat Gharnata* (Beirut: Mu'assasa al-'Arabiya lil-Dirasat wa-n-Nashr, 1998). On the use of the Andalusian chronotope in *Gharnata*, see Granara, "Nostalgia, Arab Nationalism, and the Andalusian Chronotope in the Evolution of the Modern Arabic Novel," 67-71.

326 Diana Abu-Jaber, *Crescent* (New York: Norton, 2003). On the use of the Andalusian chronotope in *Crescent*, see Nouri Gana, "In Search of Andalusia: Reconfiguring Arabness in Diana Abu-Jaber's Crescent," *The Edinburgh Companion to the Arab Novel in English: The Politics of Anglo Arab and Arab American Literature and Culture*, ed. Nouri Gana (Edinburgh: Edinburgh UP, 2013) 198-216.

struggle for better local futures or the impossibility of the return to any geopolitically framed form of clear belonging. As a recurring formal feature of modern novelistic writing, it has a polyvalent, almost encyclopedic function. Due to its past-to-present-to-future temporality and the related expansion or transgression of spatial boundaries, it advances to a dynamic narrative vehicle for crossing over from the historical memory (or amnesia) of Al-Andalus as the lived experience of Arab-Western coexistence and exchange as well as racist discrimination and violent exclusion to today's conditions of tomorrow's cross-cultural relations.[327]

In *The Book of Khalid*, this journey goes significantly beyond the nostalgic idealization of Andalusian beauty and *convivencia*. By juxtaposing the memory of a golden Iberian past with the present suffering of cross-cultural conflicts in America while using a Quixotic narrative pattern, the novel doubles or even triples the trope of Al-Andalus. At the same time, it carries the cross-Atlantic diasporic memory of "The Two 1492s,"[328] long tabooed by Arabs and non-Arabs alike: the temporal coincidence and ideological nexus between the *Reconquista* of the Iberian Peninsula and the *Conquista* of the Americas. As Ella Shohat has argued at various occasions and in different contexts, this nexus refers equally to the dismembered history of both Islamic-Jewish and Arab-Western encounters.[329] Relating the beginning of the modern colonial discourse manifested in the Iberian expansionism to the expulsion of Jews and Muslims from Spain allows the theoretical awareness of early modern European anti-Semitism and Islamophobia as the decisive conceptual framework for the racist colonization of the Americas, Africa, and Asia. Seen through this important relational diasporic lens, one can indeed argue that, by drawing on *Don Quixote* as an intertext, *The Book of Khalid*, like many other more recent Anglophone Arab representations, implicitly recalls "the 'proto-Orientalism' of the Reconquista"[330] to counter the Orientalist discourse of its own present. The Andalusian chronotope then allows the narrative transfer of what Shohat calls "the Moorish unconscious"[331] into the self-conscious contemporary struggle for post-Andalusian conviviality. It establishes a spatio-temporal reference and metafictional frame in

---

327   Granara, "Nostalgia, Arab Nationalism, and the Andalusian Chronotope in the Evolution of the Modern Arabic Novel," 58-60.

328   This is the title of a section of Ella Shohat's essay, "The Sephardi-Moorish Atlantic: Between Orientalism and Occidentalism," 50-55.

329   See Shohat, "The Sephardi-Moorish Atlantic: Between Orientalism and Occidentalism," 42-62 and Ella Shohat, *Taboo Memories, Diasporic Voices* (Durham: Duke UP, 2006) 209-213; Ella Shohat, "Taboo Memories and Diasporic Visions: Columbus, Palestine, and Arab-Jews," *Performing Hybridity*, eds. May Joseph and Jennifer Natalia Fink (Minneapolis: U of Minnesota P, 1999) 131-56.

330   Shohat, "The Sephardi-Moorish Atlantic. Between Orientalism and Occidentalism," 51.

331   Shohat, "The Sephardi-Moorish Atlantic. Between Orientalism and Occidentalism," 54.

which the memory of violent exclusion and loss stands in sharp contrast to the desire for peaceful coexistence across cultural, racial, and religious divides.

In *The Book of Khalid*, the subtle arrangement of the Andalusian theme, together with the novel's disruptive and selective merging of translated auto-narratives and its constant blurring of disparate narrative sequences, leads to a high degree of internal distances, discordances, concurrences, and external interferences. The scholarly obsession with stylistic purity and clear generic filiations is not satisfied. The novel presents itself as a fantastic narrative of entertainment and leisure, a realist transmigrant adventure-story, a piece of political crime fiction, and a spiritual auto-fiction. There are resonances to medieval Arabic narratives, popular epic cycles, and folk tales side by side with traces of European and American classics of modern poetry and fiction and new genres of popular fiction. Partly addressing the crisis of the cosmopolitan Arab subject in transmigration between worlds torn apart by the clash of competing modernities, *The Book of Khalid* is a realist novel. At the same time, it takes the form of a biting social satire, a cosmopolitan thriller, a cross-cultural romance, and an intercultural philosophical melodrama, thereby mutilating or even completely eluding the nationalist-realist conceptualization of narrative subjectification in a clearly fixed time-space configuration. The novel mobilizes familiar and unfamiliar narrative codes and lexical and syntactic canons at such great liberty that it escapes any genuinely comparative morphology.

Like other Anglophone Arab texts, this fictional work constantly reminds us that it exists within a larger cross-cultural and trans-temporal meta-text of symbolic mediations and deviations directly related to the long and rarely peaceful history of Western-Arab encounters. As I have shown in the previous section, the interplay between an individual Anglophone Arab text and such a meta-text, as well as the sometimes subtle effects of dialogic frictions between the two levels, cannot be exhaustively traced in a rarified analysis of the narrators' and heroes' internal narrative discourses. The exploration of cross-cultural communicational structures at work in Anglophone Arab representations needs to combine the structuralist analysis of the individual text (or the individual representation's visual or performative order) with the study of this internal organization's external discursive prefiguration. Such an approach on the one hand considers the presence of Western narrative modes, which have fixed Arabs within a differential network of unequal relations for a long time and which, therefore, still form an important matrix for Arab correlational representations. On the other hand, it is sensitive to the fact that these representations rarely care for the notions of culturally specific literary syntax or narrative genealogies. Whoever sees herself or himself as the intended receiver of an Anglophone Arab narrative should be aware of the ambivalent translocations of assumingly firmly located modes of emplotment or frames of references at work in the respective narrative. Wherever the interpreter is geographically located, s/he is confronted with translation as a deeply ambivalent and often contested activity that goes beyond carrying a meaning that is at home in one language across into another language.

If it is true for any cultural imaginary that a direct non-tropic grasp on events or things is rarely possible, then the reader of Anglophone Arab representation faces a particularly complex and enriching dilemma related to the impossibility of definite tropical filiations, clear-cut semantic itineraries, or stylistic aptitudes. These representations translate without much scruple regarding their own faithfulness into any original cultural text or local truth. They sometimes do so in a literally linguistic and almost physical sense, but their disruptive translations are mostly metaphoric: they *smuggle* meaning from one place to another and thus displace self-totalizing truth claims and related representational modes on all sides. If they tell lies, they do so intentionally, not intrinsically. The strategic decision to lie results instead from the need to counter other hegemonic lies, and it celebrates the empowering will to *lie back*. Such neo-translational smuggling blurs the principally Eurocentric divide between center and periphery and weakens the learned division of *here* and *there* that is confined by the constitutive strategies of othering and selving. Just like Khalid disregards the spatial norms of New York, Baalbek, or Cairo because he either does not know his "right place" or is not willing to take up the social position designated to him, the readers of *The Book of Khalid* are forced to somehow read out of place and hence commit an interpretive transgression. This transgression has not only a spatial dimension related to the entering of an unknown social and cultural geography. The revision of spatially determined value and meaning ultimately gains an epistemological and moral component.[332] As readers, we are often not enough "in-place"[333] to fully grasp the socio-historic evidence and moral consistency of the world that is narrated. There is no easy affective attachment to the narrated cultural space possible. The reader is constantly reminded that s/he cannot place herself or himself in the narrative space without the editor-narrator's agreement. Seen from such a geocritical perspective,[334] Rihani's novel is a very early exponent of Anglophone Arab narratives of spatial and social transgressions within and in-between the Middle East and the West. It anticipates the inherent epistemological and moral transgressivity of many contemporary Anglophone Arab representations. As "spatial trajectories," these representations can cut across what our ideological maps cut up.[335] Allowing its heroes

---

332   On the link between social geography and the humanities and between spatial transgression and moral transgress, see Tim Cresswell, *In Place/Out of Place: Geography, Ideology, and Transgression* (Minneapolis and London: U of Minnesota P, 1996).

333   Tim Cresswell, *Place: A Short Introduction* (Malden, MA: Blackwell 2004) 51.

334   Bertrand Westphal, *Geocriticism: Real and Fictional Spaces*, trans. Robert T. Tally, Jr. (New York: Palgrave Macmillan, 2011) 41-74.

335   Michel de Certeau, *The Practice of Everyday Life*, trans. Steven F. Rendall (Berkeley: U of California P, 1984) 115. Here, I am referring to de Certeau's famous dictum on the particular capacity

and anti-heroes to wander promiscuously amongst a hyperbolic range of locations, these narrative trajectories transgress the West/non-West binary. In their narrative play of abstracted bi-directional adaptations and selective translations, New York or London almost become Beirut, Cairo, or Andalusia and vice versa. It is increasingly difficult to differentiate between what is domestic and what is foreign, what has been imported and what has been exported. Narrative modes and linguistic signifiers associated with certain socio-spatial or ethno-cultural identities give way to a conflictual gesture of horizontal (although not necessarily equal) exchange in which translation no longer means one-sided imitation or adaptation. The genuine forgery of Anglophone Arab representations is regularly committed against narrative morphologies and normative moralities on both sides of the historically generated divide. Due to their willful cross-cultural contaminations, selective translational distortions, and strategic inauthenticities, these representations have unpredictable effects that exceed the institutionalized control of intercultural translation, poetic canonicity, and moral judgment. Thanks to their structural and semantic correlationality, they disrupt both our aesthetic conventions of cultural specificity and ethical norms of universal accountability: "And there thou art left in perpetual confusion and despair. Where wilt thou go? Whom wilt thou follow?"[336]

Khalid might not prove to be chosen, but he is virtually immortal. The immortal, the endless, or the eternal—that is the meaning of his Arabic name. Given the many extreme occasions in which he finds himself and looking at the almost endless chain of humiliations he suffers, one might translate his name as "the unbreakable." Khalid resists forces employed by individual men, he refuses sexual and psychological exploitation, he is not crushed by religious dogmatism, and he stands up against the social violence of systemic degradation. If he is indeed destined to suffer injustice, he is not obliterated by it. Violence comes to seem almost external to Khalid, both as victim and perpetrator. Before his immanent morality, the amoral perpetrator and the naïve victim stand almost equally innocent in the same distress. However, the casual discriminations, willful exclusions, misperceptions, and repeated heaping-up of violent deeds never culminate into incurable bitterness. Although the narrative often has a tone of pain and a coloring of sorrow, the editor-narrator never allows it to drop into lamentation. Justice and equality, which have hardly any place in this story of extremes, still guide the narrative's spirit. It is the ironic magic of *The Book of Khalid* that it lays bare the unhappiness of those suffering from injustice and inequality without dissimulation and disdain. Even the depiction of competing exercises of power usually comes with an utterly moral neutrality that presents itself as naïve innocence. The narrative's many passages

---

of literary fiction as spatial trajectory: "what the map cuts up, the story cuts across," 129. See also 116-30.

336   Rihani, *The Book of Khalid* 5.

have disturbing and dislocating impulses for the reader, but they testify to the narcissistic power of both Khalid and the editor-narrator to self-referentially produce meaning. The reader's alienation thus affirms the connection of both the editor-narrator and the performing anti-hero to the sociocultural spheres that they claim to inhabit without knowing how to comprehend them. The shock of mutual incomprehension is somehow turned into an anti-aesthetic principle which denies itself the illusion of cross-cultural mimetic beauty. Instead, it gives place to narrative discontinuities with the self-asserted universal exceptionality of Western reason. The self-conscious narrative is polyphonic and transgressive without demanding a harmonic resolution. There are possibilities of cross-overs and of testing limits. But these possibilities are not orchestrated by any consistent meta-narrative. *The Book of Khalid* as a piece of Anglophone Arab literary fiction is derived from more than one socio-historical space and is organized in mutual transgression. How could it but place itself within a poetic and ethic non-place off the normative edge?

4. Nocturnal Traces and Voyaging Critique: From Shahrazad to Said

Perhaps there is no narrative that can better accommodate the desire of Western mainstream readers to unveil and penetrate the hidden worlds, bodies, and minds of Arabs than *The Arabian Nights*. If Miguel de Cervantes's *Don Quixote* is the Andalusian mother of the modern European novel, *Alf Layla wa Layla*, known in English as *One Thousand and One Nights* or *The Arabian Nights*, is truly its Arabic grandmother. By 1908, Martha Pike Conant had already dubbed the assemblage of parables, fables, and stories "the fairy godmother of the English novel."[1] Given the enthusiastic exoticism almost intrinsically linked to the long history of selective receptions, tendentious translations, and literary assimilations of the *Nights* in the West, some might be surprised to find its transgeneric mode of spinning stories within stories at work in the formation and transformation of Anglophone Arab representations. Sure, the strategy of firmly inserting Arab representations into the lasting and, by now, transnational narrative tradition running from Antoine Galland's twelve-volume transference, *Les mille et une nuits* (1704–1708), to the latest adaptations by Hollywood and the tourism industry or the net spheres of video and platform games perfectly makes sense for works that are meant to reach a global audience by way of Orientalizing themselves.[2] But the seemingly well-established functional route of self-marketing can hardly be adapted (at least not in an unbroken way) in those representations in which I am predominantly interested here: representations that, although they do not necessarily explicitly counter dominant perceptions of Arabs, often desperately struggle to emancipate themselves from the globalized Orientalist archive and its truth effects. However, if we consider not only the *Nights*'s almost unrivaled place in what we are used to calling world literature but also keep in mind this work's profound influence on the global production of Orientalist theater, opera, music, painting, architecture, and popular

---

1   Martha Pike Conant, *The Oriental Tale in England in the Eighteenth Century* (New York: Columbia UP, 1908) 243.
2   See Edward W. Said, *Orientalism*, 4th ed. (1978; London, New York: Penguin, 1995) 325.

culture, and if we, in addition, allow ourselves to recognize the obvious—that Anglophone Arab representations are products of our increasingly globalized world and that their genesis consequently takes place within that world—then it might be less astonishing to discover traces of the nocturnal narration in Anglophone Arab representations.

The Book of Khalid can only partially anticipate this development, which occurred in the second half of the 20th century. Its eponymous hero is particularly successful in marketing his exotic attraction to American women. We learn that he does so "with all the rude simplicity and frankness of the Arabian Nights."[3] Elsewhere, the narrator compares certain adventures depicted in the Khedivial manuscript with those incidental stories "which Shahrazad might have added to her famous Nights."[4] Due to the focus of these depictions on negligible details and their ethical marginality, they are, however, quickly deemed not worthy of being transcribed and included in the novel. Although Rihani wrote a short study on *The Lore of the Arabian Nights* between 1928 and 1930, this text was not published during his lifetime.[5] Basically concerned with demonstrating the quintessentially Arab origin of the famous tales and tracing the history of their various European translations, his enthusiastic espousal of the passionate traditional Arab storyteller's natural sensuality and her capability of producing great works of imagination is almost a reversed caricature of the early 20th-century rejection of the *Nights* as popular entertainment outside the domains of both Arab *Adab* [high literature] and European *belles lettres*.[6] The study certainly does not recommend the appropriation of the famous tales or the narrative mode employed in them in modern fictional writing. In fact, *The Book of Khalid*'s relation to the *Nights* is likewise imbued with this contradiction. On the one hand, the earliest Anglophone Arab novel offers little evidence for any importance that *The Arabian Nights* might have for the transgeneric deviation of Anglophone Arab poetics; if the editor-narrator comes across any such nocturnal presence in her or his source material, s/he explicitly rejects their entry into her or his narration. However, the novel shows clear affinities with the basic motifs and general features of Shahrazad's narration, such as the relationship between enframed stories and frame story, the use of the runaway-return scheme, the coexistence of a variety of narrative styles, and the hyperbole of cross-cultural estrangement and ironic bricolage. This contradiction might be explained by arguing that the influence of the *Nights* has been so pervasive in the global literary production of the last three centuries, perhaps only second to the Bible, that it is difficult

---

3   Rihani, *The Book of Khalid* 84.
4   Rihani, *The Book of Khalid* 97.
5   This study was published in 2002: Ameen Rihani, *The Lore of the Arabian Nights* (Washington, DC: Platform International P, 2002).
6   Muhsin Al-Musawi, *The Postcolonial Arabic Novel: Debating Ambivalence* (Leiden: Brill, 2003) 76-80.

to find any writer who has completely abstained from at least unintentionally alluding to it. I do, however, believe that *The Book of Khalid*'s incoherent stance over Shahrazad's narrative, at the same time strictly excluded and bashfully present, is indicative of a much deeper grounded uncertainty regarding the popular medieval tales' recognition among contemporary readers.

Such uncertainty is no longer seen as an obstacle by contemporary Anglophone Arab writers. The *Nights* have long made their way into those cultural representations in which I am primarily interested here. Yet, the ambivalences involved in this process of varying appropriations have by no means been resolved. On the contrary, they have been strategically multiplied and thus turned into a powerful metafictional weapon that goes beyond sole aesthetic preoccupations. In some cases, this regaining of Shahrazad as a narrative guide for resisting (neo-)patriarchy and countering hegemony is openly performed. In other cases, the recourse to the *Nights* rather takes the form of an oblique allegory. While many Anglophone Arab revisionist readings show the tendency to see Shahrazad as the prototypical feminist, the reclamation of her anti-hierarchical narrative technique and generic crossing is not at all restricted to female writers. At the same time, sustained creative engagement with the *Nights* paved the way for new directions in the spheres of socio-cultural criticism and political activism. All these developments ask the contemporary reader of Anglophone Arab representations to take into consideration the multiple and often contradictory nocturnal affiliations that inform these representations.

In order to seriously trace such affiliations, one would first have to revisit *The Arabian Nights*'s transcultural genesis in various oral traditions. One could then have a closer look at the dialectics between the tales' early textual codification and devaluation in Arabic literature and their continuing reception in Western translations and adaptations. Only on the basis of the profound knowledge of this complicated cross-cultural exchange can one understand the ambivalent role that the *Nights* played in the growth of modern Arabic fiction in general and the postcolonial Arabic novel in particular. And it is from these more recent developments that one can finally try to understand Anglophone Arab writers' and artists' increasing interest in and appropriation of the *One Thousand and One Nights*. Yet it goes without saying that the task of such exhaustive cross-cultural mapping of the composite genesis of contemporary Anglophone Arab nocturnal works lies decisively beyond the scope of this chapter.[7]

---

7   For overviews, see Robert Irwin, *The Arabian Nights: A Companion* (London: Allen Lane; New York: Penguin, 1994); Ulrich Marzolph and Richard van Leeuwen, eds., *The Arabian Nights Encyclopedia* (Santa Barbara: ABC-Clio, 2004); Ulrich Marzolph, ed., *The Arabian Nights Reader* (Detroit: Wayne State UP, 2006); Ulrich Marzolph, ed., *The Arabian Nights in Transnational Perspective* (Detroit: Wayne State UP, 2007).

I will therefore restrict myself to giving a basic outline of those key migrations and transmigrations which have transposed the fictional voyages of the *Nights* into Anglophone Arab representations. I am less interested in answering questions of origins, influences, or directions of reception than in the function of the *Nights* as an intertext and of nocturnal poetics as a critical tool. My relational discussion will sometimes have to go beyond the Arabic-Western-Anglophone Arab nexus to include other postcolonial discourses which have turned the model provided by the arch-Oriental(ist) classic into a unique magical realist, science fiction, or feminist mode of telling stories and which, in turn, have influenced Anglophone Arab discourse. Using the Shahrazadian narrative as a paradigmatic intertextual point of departure, I will, in addition, introduce other intertexts and discursive affinities. These cursory and highly selective references include Anglophone Arab and Arabic texts as well as non-Anglophone non-Arabic discourses. Blurring the boundaries between the spheres of creative writing and criticism, I will finally consult Edward Said's cultural critique as an Anglophone Arab (studies) text. This revisiting will also allow me to address further critical precursors of particular importance and theoretical positions informing the production of Anglophone Arab representations as well as to clarify the role of Said's work in my own project.

Despite international scholarly efforts to track the *Nights*'s transcultural origins, internal Arabic transformations, cross-cultural receptions, and global mutations, many details of this influential text's early genesis are still unclear. The narrative, the earliest extant fragment of which dates from the 9th century and the oldest extended manuscript version, used by Galland for his early 18th century translation, of which dates from the 14th century, is by definition a multiplicity of texts, translations, rearrangements, variations, and editions. There is no point zero clearly located in a specific historical era and geographical space. Scholars can neither agree on an original text that burgeoned into later variants nor pinpoint an individual author or editor who can claim authority over this narrative.[8] What we know is that the *Nights* were probably inspired by the Indian classic, *Panchatantra*, and the Persian *HazarAfsan* as well as perhaps by Babylonian and Greek narrative traditions and other royal chronologies. We know that these stories were preserved and supplemented by Arabs in the Middle Ages and that, beginning in the 18th century, they were translated into European and other languages. Therefore, I do strongly agree with Ferial Ghazoul, who argues in her seminal 1996 study *Nocturnal Poetics* that the Orientalist experts' obsessions with this narrative's origins "are exercises in guesswork and are hardly convincing or relevant"[9] for grasping the contemporary global significance of the *Nights* in comparative perspective. Given the tales' uncertain

8   Ferial J. Ghazoul, *Nocturnal Poetics: The Arabian Nights in Contemporary Context* (Cairo: American U in Cairo P, 1996) 2-5.
9   Ghazoul, *Nocturnal Poetics: The Arabian Nights in Contemporary Context* 12.

origin, unfixable textuality, and inescapable incompleteness, identifying the first Cairo edition from 1835, commonly known as the Bulaq edition, as the most "complete" Arabic version or deliberating whether Edward William Lane's uninspired expurgation from 1838/40[10] or Richard Burton's 1885 unabridged English transference of the second Calcutta edition (1839-1842)[11] is closer to the Arabic original in many ways ridicules the notions of the *Nights*'s completeness and authenticity or at least equips both notions with a certain irony.[12] The *Nights* simply resist canonization.

In cross-cultural perspective, the perhaps even greater irony results from the fact that the belated recognition of the tales in their own right among Arab scholars and literati was to a large extent a reaction to the vogue of the *Nights* in the West, in particular to 19th century European Orientalist interests in the tales.[13] This controversial process of re-appropriation and rehabilitation of a narrative corpus that the elite had until then associated with popular street storytellers and coffeehouse entertainment was decisively triggered by the Nahda discourses of the late 19th century and the reception of Western (mis-)representations of the Arab world. But it was only with the change in outlook towards the novel as a literary genre during the 20th century that attention was drawn to the long-depreciated tales as worth reading and studying by themselves as well as for the purpose of encouraging contemporary fictional writing in Arabic.[14] The pressure of novelistic selving by mirroring the Western image of modernity, in other words, had a part in leading to the discovery of the broken mirror of the Arab self in the West's obsession with the *Nights*.[15] As Maher Jarrar argues, contemporary Arabic novelists "draw on the *Nights* both from within [...] and from without."[16] The same is largely true for the relation between contemporary Anglophone Arab representations and the Arabic tales. In fact, I argue that the reception of the *Nights* in Anglophone Arab literature and arts is directly related to its reception within the postcolonial Arabic novel. The particular Anglophone Arab configuration further complicates the differentiation

---

10   Edward William Lane, *The Thousand and One Nights*, ed. Edward Stanley Poole (London: Bickers, 1877), first published in three volumes between 1838 and 1840.

11   Richard Burton, *The Book of Thousand and One Nights* (London: Burton Club, 1885-1888); Richard Burton, *Supplemental Nights to the Book of the Thousand Nights and a Night, with Notes Anthropological and Explanatory* (London: Burton Club, 1886).

12   Ghazoul, *Nocturnal Poetics: The Arabian Nights in Contemporary Context* 3.

13   Muhsin al-Musawi, *Scheherazade in England: A Study of Nineteenth-Century English Criticism of the Arabian Nights* (Washington: Three Continents P, 1981).

14   Al-Musawi, *The Postcolonial Arabic Novel: Debating Ambivalence* 76-94.

15   Elias Khoury, "Ar-riwaya wa miraya al-waqi' al-maksur," [The novel and the broken mirror of reality], *Al-Mulhaq ath-Thaqafi* 25.05.1996, 18-19 and 01.06.1996, 18-19.

16   Maher Jarrar, "The Arabian Nights and the Contemporary Arabic Novel," *The Arabian Nights in Historical Context: Between East and West*, eds. Saree Makdisi and Felicity Nussbaum (Oxford: Oxford UP, 2008) 299.

between inside and outside. However, the general ambiguity involved in using a re-imported text as a local and essentially Arabic intertext remains. The directly related anxiety of Western Orientalist (and hence uncanny) influence[17] might explain the occasional recourse into exaggerated nativist reclamations of the *Nights*. But such anxiety can equally be seen as a source for the particular bidirectional metafictional richness of Anglophone Arab writings in the wake of Shahrazad. In other words, although the Shahrazadian text returned to Arabic literature as a European export from the colonial center and from there entered Anglophone Arab representations, it was successively reclaimed as part of a long-neglected Arab heritage of resisting centric narratives and hegemonic discourses of all kinds.[18] In such relational nocturnal view, local monarchies, dictatorships, or pseudo-democratic cleptocracies and Western (neo-)colonial powers can be seen as historical duplicates of the *Nights*'s fictional character, King Shahrayar. Whereas authoritarian and imperial discourses are placed in a transcultural genealogy of violent repression, illegitimate authority, and unjust patriarchy, the trope of Shahrazad instead stands for the subaltern project of narrative resistance and emancipation: "Global powers can assume some unredeemed Shahrayar's role, so can dictators and neopatriarchs, to enforce presence and control, whereas the Scheherazades are the defiant communities and individuals who fight for a place of their own."[19]

At this point, it seems advisable to stress that nocturnal representations, Arabic and Anglophone Arab alike, do not necessarily draw on the many fantastic qualities of *The Arabian Nights*'s individual stories, which paved the way for their early European career during the 18th and 19th centuries. In fact, it is rarely the blatant reference to jinnis, animals or plants speaking like humans, human beings with supernatural powers, sexualized romances of enslavement, flying horses and magic carpets, subterranean worlds, or enchanted urban spaces that indicate a narrative's nocturnal traces. The representations with which I am here concerned reciprocate, in the majority of cases, the frame story's general subaltern drive to counter tyranny and hegemony, to appropriate its open character of permitting and perpetuating oppressed voices, and to adapt its anti-authoritarian emancipatory capacity. As Ferial Ghazoul demonstrates, the narrative significance of the *Nights* derives from an indispensable frame story which, set in abstract time, encloses and connects all other stories and stories told within these stories. Consisting of four narrative blocks, it accounts for the conditions of the act of storytelling—for Shahrazad sitting "on her very deathbed narrating stories."[20]

---

17   Cf. Harald Bloom, *The Anxiety of Influence: A Theory of Poetry* (Oxford: Oxford UP, 1973).

18   Al-Musawi, *The Postcolonial Arabic Novel: Debating Ambivalence* 71-115.

19   Al-Musawi, *The Postcolonial Arabic Novel: Debating Ambivalence* 74.

20   Ghazoul, *Nocturnal Poetics: The Arabian Nights in Contemporary Context* 35.

For the purpose of my argument, I will focus here on the two main narrative blocks of the frame story. In the first, the monarch, Shahrayar, witnesses his wife copulating with a black slave and kills them both. As a consequence, he decides to marry a virgin every night, only to kill her in the morning. After three years, it becomes increasingly difficult for the king's minister to find potential brides. When the latter's elder daughter, Shahrazad, offers to marry the king and thus save the lives of innocent fellow women, she is taken to the royal palace. After sexual intercourse, Shahrazad asks the monarch for permission to relate some tales. He allows it, and with this, the first narrative block is fused with the second: Shahrazad continues to tell stories all night until dawn. The royal listener, anxious to hear more, postpones her sentence night after night. On the thousand-and-first night, Shahrayar frees Shahrazad from the threat of beheading. They live happily ever after until they are parted by death.

The particular dialectic of this enframing narrative has narratological and metafictional dimensions in equal measure. It is not only a narrative about the conditions and effects of narration but also a meta-discourse about the relation of power and narrative. Although Shahrazad seems to submit to the king's authority,[21] she resists his truth-regime and effectively subverts his will to kill her. While she is decisively not *Speaking Truth to Power*,[22] to use a phrase coined in reference to an Anglophone Arab critic whose work will be discussed in the following subchapter,[23] Shahrazad narrates to the very power that Shahrayar represents. Telling him stories without letting him know her true intention, she puts off the moment of death and manages to save her own and other women's lives. Shahrazad narratively re-invents herself as an agent and thus changes the rules set by the man in power who perceives her as the passive object of his sexual/murderous aggression: "The phallic pleasure is turned into a discursive pleasure."[24] Storytelling, and not truth-speaking, thus almost becomes a form of political action, of non-violent resistance, and subversion. It is the narrative performance of the resistant capacity of narrating within and against the discourse of patriarchal power as well as the storytelling heroine's unrelenting struggle against the deadly silencing of herself and other marginalized voices that marks the Shahrazadian text as an emancipatory intertext.[25]

Of course, the relationship between the enframed and the enframing parts, the ways in which divergent narrative genres are mocked, and the intensity in which

---

21   Cf. Jarrar, "The Arabian Nights and the Contemporary Arabic Novel," 303.
22   Here I am referring to Paul A. Bové, *Edward Said and the Work of the Critic: Speaking Truth to Power* (Durham: Duke UP, 2000).
23   See my sub-chapter on Edward Said's importance for Anglophone Arab representations and Anglophone Arab studies, 4.2. of this study.
24   Ghazoul, *Nocturnal Poetics: The Arabian Nights in Contemporary Context* 95.
25   Ghazoul, *Nocturnal Poetics: The Arabian Nights in Contemporary Context* 35.

narrative voices are multiplied and sub-stories are perpetuated can vary in nocturnal works, depending on the specific topical focus, historical and sociopolitical context, or intradiegetic dynamics. However, it seems to be foremost the metafictional implications and counter-narrative qualities of the narrative frame pattern that characterize the trope of Shahrazad as a counter-discursive trope in Anglophone Arab representations. Anglophone Arab writers and artists find in the *Arabian Nights* a particularly engendering matrix for their own undertakings of creating "an-other poetics" that is translocated across and in-between Western and Arab discourses.[26] I believe it is not least the marvelous collection's nomadic quality and cultural impurity, its non-canonicity, and its stylistic liberty to include diverse narratives from discrepant historical and cultural contexts that make this work so appealing for Anglophone Arab intellectuals. Although, or maybe precisely because, the *Nights* have long been assimilated into Western and Arab mass culture and literature, its "otherness"[27] in relation to both discursive situations remains. Therefore, whoever wants to claim the *Nights* as a representation of authentic Arabness has to rethink the tales' ambivalent function within the colonial and postcolonial discourse of alterity and misrepresentation. It is this implicitly canonized (and, therefore, necessarily ambivalent) otherness of the nocturnal classic "strangely fraught with a mixture of need and rejection"[28] that makes it so important as an intertext for contemporary Anglophone Arab narrative, audio-visual, and performative attempts to uncover dominant structures, to articulate what has not been articulated, and to show what has been hidden.

I am not saying that Anglophone Arab representations are literary children or direct reverberations of the Shahrazadian text in the sense that they that can be firmly placed into a causal nexus of origin-influence legacy. It is rather my argument that the *Nights*, as an intertext in Anglophone Arab representations, is equipped with a particular, complex, and often contradictory cross-cultural meaning. This ambivalence partially results from the many discrepant ideological and translational contexts into which the fantastic Arabic tales, enframed by Shahrazad's storytelling were historically placed. Although the *Nights*, a work of transcultural genesis, travelled and transgressed many boundaries in the course of its global reception, it constantly functioned as a carrier of Orientalist constructions of difference.

Whereas its significance for the internal transformation of the postcolonial Arabic novel or South American magical realist writing seems to be undisputed, and whereas Shahrazad has been widely acknowledged as a salient marker of Arab fe-

---

26   Ghazoul, *Nocturnal Poetics: The Arabian Nights in Contemporary Context* 152.
27   Ghazoul, *Nocturnal Poetics: The Arabian Nights in Contemporary Context* 152.
28   Al-Musawi, *The Postcolonial Arabic Novel: Debating Ambivalence* 77.

male and diasporic Arab feminist discourses,[29] it proves extremely difficult to determine the place and function of the *Nights* within contemporary articulations of Anglophone Arab encounters. If, for instance, Pauline Kaldas and Khaled Mattawa entitle their 2004 anthology of Arab American short stories *Dinarzad's Children* to representationally frame such diverse writers as Mohja Khaf, Rabih Alameddine, Rawi Hage, Laila Halaby, Diana Abu-Jaber, Joseph Geha, Yussef El Guindi, or Evelyn Shakir, the filiative gesture towards Shahrazad's sister signifies hardly more than a rather diffuse identiterian claim of cultural ancestry or the use of the legendary tales and their allusions to Oriental narrative passion for the purpose of self-branding.[30] In order to grasp what nocturnal Anglophone Arab writing can mean beyond the use of the classic's image as a sign of inherited or chosen Arabness and the specific feminist appropriations of its anti-patriarchal contiguities and anti-sexist poetics, one will have to turn to those literary works of the 20th and 21st centuries which carried the nocturnal mode of narrating across temporal, spatial, and linguistic boundaries. These narratives must have had an impact on Anglophone Arab arts and literatures: perhaps a more enduring one than the marvelously traveling story-machine variously known as *Alf Layla wa Layla, One Thousand and One Nights*, or *The Arabian Nights*. They can, therefore, be seen as intertexts of Anglophone Arab representations in their own right.

I can only mention here some of what I perceive as the most significant and influential exponents of this equally transgeneric and transnational type. With a view to modern Arabic writing, I would like to focus on the so-called post-Mahfouzian novel, a generic term coined by Edward Said.[31] Not solely due to its relative contemporaneity, this more recent prose fiction seems to have the most immediate impact on Anglophone Arab representations. Its exemplary value for Anglophone Arab nocturnal writing probably also relates to the fact that these writings are almost consistently (if not always immediately) available in English translation.

Naguib Mahfouz's own recreation of the *Nights* in his 1978 *Layali alf Layla* [*Arabian Nights and Days*][32] is an early key work at the crossroads of this development. Although the novel's contemporaneous regrouping of the *Nights*'s sociopolitical

---

29   On the importance of the *Nights* in Arab and Anglophone Arab women's writings and feminist discourses, see Fedwa Malti-Douglas, "Shahrazād Feminist," *The Thousand and One Nights in Arabic Literature and Society*, eds. Richard G. Hovannisian and Georges Sabagh (Cambridge: Cambridge UP, 1997) 40-55 and Susan Muaddi Darraj, ed., *Scheherazade's Legacy: Arab and Arab American Woman on Writing* (Westport, CT: Praeger, 2004).

30   Pauline Kaldas and Khaled Mattawa, eds., *Dinarzad's Children: An Anthology of Contemporary Arab American Fiction*, 2nd ed. (2004; Fayetteville: U of Arkansas P, 2009) xv-xx.

31   Edward Said, "After Mahfouz," *Reflections on Exile and Other Essays* (2000; Cambridge: Harvard UP, 2001) 317-26.

32   Najib Mahfouz, *Layali alf Layla* (Cairo: Maktab Misr, 1978); English translation: *Arabian Nights and Days*, trans. Denys Johnson-Davis (New York: Doubleday, 1994).

morals is not confined to the framing tale, it celebrates Shahrazad's regaining of control of authority in a way that stresses the political instrumentality of the fantastic and "story telling as a way to justify action."[33] As a political allegory written against the backdrop of Anwar as-Sadat's neo-liberal open-door policy of economic privatization and the rise of militant Islam in Egypt, the novel represents a fictional exercise in the cultural politics of novelistic writing. Influenced by the ethics and aesthetics of Islamic mysticism, it mixes political concerns with metaphysical speculations on the relation of spiritual power and worldly power. While Shahrazad's Sufi sheikh guide represents the mystic counter-vigor to the ruler's repressive force on the level of the frame story, the enframed stories say obliquely what could not be said directly in an Egyptian novel of that time. *Layali alf Layla* thus mixes the critique of the real with supernatural narrative devices.[34]

However, it was not Mahfouz's re-creation of the *Nights* but the Palestinian Emile Habibi's *Al-Mutasha'il: al-waqa'i' al-ghariba fi ikhtifa' sa'id abi al-nahs al-mutasha'il (The Secret Life of Saeed, the Ill-Fated Pessoptimist)*[35] that set the tone for what I, for the purpose of this study, call the postcolonial nocturnal novel in Arabic. First published in the daily *Al-Jadid* in Haifa, Israel between 1972 and 1974, it is widely considered a breakthrough in post-Mahfouzian writing. The pessoptimist Saeed is a Palestinian inmate of a psychiatric clinic in Israel who pretends to have found refuge with extraterrestrial friends. He reports on his pre-exilic hopeless situation as a stranger in his own land through a series of letters. The tragic and consistently ironic life story of the Kafkaesque anti-hero represents the collective Palestinian experience of "deterritorialization."[36] Drawing on the Shahrazadian narrative structure of circularity and repetition, it allegorically describes the invisible condition of those who remained in the newly founded Jewish state after 1948 to become a despised and disenfranchised minority of second-class citizens. By inaugurating an anonymous redactor who finally reveals himself as the overt narrator of the frame story, the novel reflects the lived experience and surrealistic perception of Palestinian Israelis who, in order to stay in what is the right and the wrong place, cannot but jam together realistic pessimism with an narrative optimism that is close to madness.

---

33   Al-Musawi, *The Postcolonial Arabic Novel: Debating Ambivalence* 386. See, on Mahfouz' *Layali alf Layla* 375-87.

34   Ghazoul, *Nocturnal Poetics: The Arabian Nights in Contemporary Context* 134-54.

35   Emile Habibi, *Al-Mutasha'il: al-waqa'i' al-ghariba fi ikhtifa' sa'id abi al-nahs al-mutasha'il* (Beirut: Dar Ibn Khaldun, 1989). English translation: *The Secret Life of Saeed, the Ill-Fated Pessoptimist: A Palestinian Who Became a Citizen of Israel*, trans. Salma K. Jayyusi and Trevor Le Gassick (New York: Vantage P, 1982).

36   Maher Jarrar, "A Narration of 'Deterritorialization': Imīl Habībī's The Pessoptimist," *Middle Eastern Literatures* 5.1 (2002): 15-28.

Since the late 1970s, several post-Mahfouzian nocturnal novels have appeared in Arabic. Among these novels are the diverse works of such eminent literary figures as the Egyptian feminist writer, Nawal El Saadawi,[37] her equally influential compatriot, Edwar al-Kharrat,[38] the Lebanese Rashid al-Daif,[39] or, of the exilic literati of the region par excellence, 'Abd al-Rahman Munif. I have discussed Munif's 1977 novel, *An-Nihayat (Endings)*, in my beginning chapter. The attentive reader will remember the remarkable night of collective mourning after the death of 'Assaf, the eccentric outsider and solitary hunter, which marks the beginning of the narration's second part. Here the author draws on the narrating-against-death matrix of the Shahrazadian model. During that night, the almost-endless perpetuation of anonymous stories successively leads to the emancipation of the enframed narratives from the frame story's account of what happened. The intradiegetic listeners, and with them the readers, are immersed in a narrative conglomerate of a particularly empowering quality that finally culminates in the anticipation of extradiegetic resistive action. Similarly, Munif's five-volume work, *Mudun al-Milh (Cities of Salt)*, despite the presence of an assumingly omniscient narrator, employs the principle of weaving stories, one inside one another, and thus allows the inauguration of other uncontrollable narrative voices.

Perhaps the most significant living proponent of contemporary nocturnal writing in Arabic is Elias Khoury. In my view, his fictional work not only functions as a particularly important intertext for our understanding of today's Anglophone Arab representations but also forms a constant source of inspiration for several of

---

37   One of El Saadawi's paradigmatic feminist nocturnal novels is Nawal El Saadawi, *Suqut al-Imam* (Cairo: Dar al-Mustaqbal al-'Arabi, 1987) English translation: *The Fall of the Imam*, trans. Sherif Hetata (London: Methuen, 1988). See also Al-Musawi, *The Postcolonial Arab Novel* 101-108.

38   Edwar al-Kharrat, *Rama wa-l-tinnin* (first published in a limited edition in 1979 in Cairo). English translation: *Rama and the Dragon*, trans. Ferial Ghazoul and John Verlenden (Cairo: The American U in Cairo P, 2002) and Edwar al-Kharrat, *Tarubuha Za'faran* (Beirut: Dar al-Adab, 1985). English translation: *City of Saffron*, trans. Frances Liardet (London: Quartet, 1989). In *Rama wa-l-tinnin*, both the narrator and the implied narrator perceive themselves and mutually allude to each other as Shahrazad. *Tarubuha Za'faran* uses the *Nights*'s model of circularity to present the experience of narrative recollection as a decentered mosaic of motifs and images that defy any rule of linear composition. See also Jarrar, "The Arabian Nights and the Contemporary Arabic Novel," 312-13 and Al-Musawi, *The Postcolonial Arabic Novel: Debating Ambivalence* 109 and 250-51.

39   See, for instance, Rashid al-Daif, *Tistifil Meryl Streep* (Beirut: Riad al-Rayyes, 2001); English translation: *Who is Afraid of Meryl Streep?* Trans. Paula Haydar and Nadine Sinno (Austin: U of Texas P, 2014). This novel's fragmentary application of the *Nights*'s frame story alludes to Shahrayar's aggressive voyeurism in order to amplify the main character's sexual obsession with the visual. See also Jarrar, "*The Arabian Nights* and the Contemporary Arabic Novel," 312.

these representations. This assumed influence transgresses the spheres of litera-ture. As a public intellectual, Khoury plays a major role in the cultural scene of the Arab Mashreq and beyond. His twelve novels have been translated into numerous languages; almost all are available in English. In addition, he is well known as a literary critic, playwright, curator, and as a cultural activist who served as a direc-tor at the Theatre of Beirut and co-director of the *Ayloul* Festival of Modern Arts in Beirut. In his native Beirut, he served as director and editor-in-chief of *Mulhaq*, the weekly literary supplement of the local daily, *An-Nahar*. His academic career includes his work as visiting professor and research fellow at the Lebanese Univer-sity, the American University of Beirut, Columbia University, Wissenschaftskolleg zu Berlin, and New York University. In 2001, Khoury was appointed Global Distin-guished Professor of Middle Eastern and Islamic Studies at NYU. In addition, the internationally renowned intellectual regularly attends readings, academic confer-ences, and other public events all over the world. Already between the late 1970s and the mid-1990s, Khoury established a radically decentered novelistic mode of telling stories while speculating on histories with his novels *Al-jabal as-saghir* (*Lit-tle Mountain*),[40] *Rihlat Ghandi as-saghir* (*The Journey of Little Gandhi*),[41] *Mamlakat al-ghuraba'* (*Kingdom of Strangers*),[42] and *Majma' al-asrar* [Junction of Secrets].[43] In dif-ferent ways, these narratives almost perpetuate themselves. The reader is merged into countless stories told by characters whose truthfulness cannot be guaranteed by an omniscient narrator. Historical events are presented in different versions, with competing beginnings and, at best, temporary endings. Each story reveals its own and other stories' factual inconsistencies. Due to their fragmentary and poly-phonic modality, these narratives constantly struggle with the challenge of differ-entiating between "Where is the story? And where is the truth?" without providing a final resolution.[44] Like his literary representations, Khoury's criticism is concerned with the fictional nature of historiography just as much as with the role of liter-ature as a practice of counter-memory. A collection of critical essays published in 1982 is almost exclusively devoted to the contemporary necessity and conditions of (im-)possibility of narratively regaining what he calls *The Lost Memory*.[45]

---

40   Elias Khoury, *Al-jabal as-saghir* (Beirut: Mu'assasat al-Abhath al-Arabiya, 1977). English trans-lation: *Little Mountain*, trans. Maia Tabet (Manchester: Carcanet P, 1989).

41   Elias Khoury, *Rihlat Ghandi as-saghir* (Beirut: Dar al-Adab, 1989) English Translation: *The Jour-ney of Little Ghandi*, trans. Paula Haydar (Minneapolis: U of Minnesota P, 1994).

42   Elias Khoury, *Mamlakat al-ghuraba'* (Beirut: Dar al-Adab, 1993). English translation: *The King-dom of Strangers*, trans. Paula Haydar (Fayetteville: U of Arkansas P, 1996).

43   Elias Khoury, *Majma' al-asrar* [Junction of Secrets] (Beirut: Dar al-Adab, 1994).

44   Khoury, *Majma' al-asrar* 151.

45   Elias Khoury, *Al-dhakira al-mafquda: dirasat naqdiya* [The lost memory: critical studies] (Beirut: Mu'assasat al-Abhath al-Arabiya, 1989). On Khoury's novelistic and critical work, see also Sonja Mejcher-Atassi, "On the Necessity of Writing the Present: Elias Khoury and the 'Birth

In the context of Anglophone Arab representations, the poly-vocal recollection and narrative reassembling of exilic Palestinian memories of displacement and refugeeship in Khoury's 1998 anti-heroic epic, *Bab ash-Shams (Gate of the Sun)*,[46] represent the by far most elaborate piece of nocturnal fiction in Arabic. Here, he not only employs the act of narrating as a particularly powerful practice of delaying death and fighting forgetfulness but, at the same time, uses this act's inherent ideological pitfalls, multiple gaps, and absences to open up a metafictional, almost metahistorical, space for a reflection on the imaginative limits of telling marginalized (hi-)stories and for the strategic insertion of counter-memories. The frame narrative is set in the makeshift hospital of a refugee camp on the outskirts of Beirut. Yunis, a well-known Palestinian freedom fighter who once made his people believe "that the road to the villages of Galilee was open,"[47] is in a coma. He is nursed by his adoptive son, Dr. Khaleel, a man who has no real medical qualification but possesses remarkable skills of storytelling. The quasi-Shahrazadian narrator tries to heal the dying embodiment of armed resistance by telling him his own heroic role in the Palestinians' struggle for justice: "HEY, YOU! How am I supposed to talk to you, or with you or about you? Should I tell you stories you already know, or be silent and let you go wherever it is you go?"[48] Yet Khaleel realizes from the very beginning that he does not know any factual event well enough to re-narrate it, that he can no longer rely on the stories that have been told, and that he consequently has to question his self-chosen mission of narrating legendary tales of national resistance: "Do you think of yourself as the hero in a love story? Why have you forgotten your other heroic roles? Or maybe they weren't so heroic."[49]

Khaleel's discourse constantly shifts between a virtual dialogue with the non-responsive Yunis, the symbolic representative of the heroic narrative whose disintegration he refuses to admit, and the many micro-stories of other Palestinian lives not yet told. It seems that only the father figure's approaching death allows these other stories to incessantly find their way into the enlarging fissures and gaps of the filial grand-narrative. The novel draws partly on dozens of interviews that Khoury conducted with Palestinians living in Lebanese, Syrian, and Jordanian refugee camps in preparation for his novelistic endeavor. These uprooted people are the true storytellers of *Bab ash-Shams*. The simultaneous narration within and against one unitary version of memory not only leads to the intradiegetic multiplication of narrative voices of extradiegetic origin but also implies the radical

---

of the Novel' in Lebanon," *Arabic Literature: Postmodern Perspectives*, eds. Angelika Neuwirth, Andreas Pflitsch, and Barbara Winckler (London: Saqi, 2010) 87-96.

46   Elias Khoury, *Bab ash-shams* (Beirut: Dar al-Adab, 1998). English translation: *Gate of the Sun*, trans. Humphry Davis (2005; London: Vintage, 2006).

47   Khoury, *Gate of the Sun* 14.

48   Khoury, *Gate of the Sun* 7.

49   Khoury, *Gate of the Sun* 24.

self-questioning of Khaleel's (and the novel's) narrative intention: "I say I want one thing, but I want thousands of things. I lie, God take pity on you, on me and on your poor mother."[50] The reference to *One Thousand and One Nights* is obvious. Thanks to the step-son's ceaseless nursing efforts, Yunis survives for more than seven months before finally taking the shape of a baby. The Shahrazadian pseudo-doctor waits for his parental patient's re-birth: "Now we're at the beginning, as you asked, and you have to go through all the torments of childhood. Come on, let's begin."[51] However, the magical therapy of rousing the ideological and spiritual father with his words has no success. The former hero does not stand up again: maybe because he cannot, maybe because he does not like the stories that have been told. The cyclical mode of narration reaches its metafictional peak with Yunis's death. His physical end marks the beginning of a new relation between the novelistic text and the reader. Now the latter cannot but accept his position as the primary addressee: "Would you like to hear a new story that its narrator and hero doesn't believe? We'd decided to stop telling such stories. We'd decided we wanted stories as real as the truth."[52]

While the novel's end anticipates a new communicative set-off beyond the in-consistencies of hegemonic truth claims within communities and between collective formations of belonging, the actual novel opens with a narrator who does not know the truth anymore and, therefore, sets out to tell a tale of infantile innocence: "Once upon a time there was a baby." The opening line, *kana ya ma kana* (literally "it was or it wasn't;" figuratively not quite "once upon a time"), can be easily identified as the classical Arabic inauguration of any oral folk tale, such as the *Arabian Nights*. For the insecure narrator, however, it triggers much more: His own tale's beginning line provokes a self-critical reflection on the relation between historical events and narrative emplotment and finally results in Khaleel starting the story with its end-ing—that is, with the stroke which has caused Yunis's coma. For the purpose of my study, his short excursion into the narrative ethics of premodern Arabic sto-rytelling almost paradigmatically grasps a nocturnal poetics that promotes a non-hierarchic adjustment of meaning between lived lives and told stories:

> In the beginning they didn't say, "Once upon a time;" they said something else. In the beginning they said, "Once upon a time, there was—or there wasn't." Do you know why they said that? When I first read this expression in a book about ancient Arabic literature, it took me by surprise. Because, in the beginning, they didn't lie. They didn't know anything, but they didn't lie. They left things vague, preferring to use that "or" which makes things that were as though they weren't, and things that weren't as though they were. That way the story is put on the

---

50   Khoury, *Gate of the Sun* 7.
51   Khoury, *Gate of the Sun* 425.
52   Khoury, *Gate of the Sun* 492.

same footing as life, because a story is a life that didn't happen, and a life is a story that didn't get told.[53]

Khoury's *Gate of the Sun* does not negate the difference between narrative and life or reality and fiction. It rather stresses the often painfully learned insight that so-called matters of fact of real lives do not always speak for themselves but must be acted out in a narrative of their own to be recognized in and by the world. It is not only in this regard that the novel's title clearly refers to Ghassan Kanafani's classic of resistance literature, *Rijal fil-shams* (*Men in the Sun*),[54] a 1972 short story which gives voice to three illegal Palestinian migrants as the narrators of their own tragic deaths during a failed passage inside the empty water tank of a truck on the Iraq/Kuwait border. Due to its allegorical quality, the narrative of human trafficking and silent suffocation suggests "a call for purposeful [narrative] resistance that brings life into death."[55]

The importance of Arabic writings like *The Pessoptimist*, *Gate of the Sun*, or *Men in the Sun* as intertexts for Anglophone Arab representations and, in particular, Anglophone Palestinian representations should not be underestimated. But they are not the only possible points of departure for reconstructing transtextual chains of relation. With a view to the broader discursive field's nocturnal traces, it is natural to consider detours of reception and loop ways of influences that do not necessarily lead directly from the medieval Arabic heritage of telling stories to Anglophone Arab representations. In this context, it is noteworthy that South American literature always had and still has a profound impact on both the contemporary Arabic novel and Anglophone Arab writings. This is particularly true for the works of those South American writers who themselves appropriated the *Arabian Nights*.[56]

Over the course of this and the previous chapter, I have repeatedly referred to Jorge Luis Borges. Not only does he, as a literary critic, attribute the genesis of the Romantic movement to Galland's translation of the *Nights*, he also uses the tales as a pretext for poetological speculations on the relation between reality, imagination, and lingual representation. In fact, Borges's own fictional oeuvre—at least from the mid-1930s onward—can be seen as the product of a continued literary intercourse with the Shahrazadian narrative. This exchange goes significantly beyond the adaptation and extension of certain themes, motifs, or stylistic devices. Beginning with two short stories explicitly ascribed to the *Nights* and published in

53   Khoury, *Gate of the Sun* 25-26.
54   Ghassan Kanafani, *Rijal fi-shams* (Beirut: Dar at-Tali'ah, 1972). English translation: *Men in the Sun, and other Palestinian Stories*, trans. Hilary Kilpatrick (London: Heinemann, 1978).
55   Al-Musawi, *The Postcolonial Arabic Novel: Debating Ambivalence* 123.
56   Jarrar, "The Arabian Nights and the Contemporary Arabic Novel," 312.

his *Universal History of Infamy* [57] and the famous ironic essay on "The Translators of the *1001 Nights*,"[58] the Borgesian corpus regularly presents itself as an equally intimate and ironic re-articulation of the Arabic classic and its fictocritical spirit.[59] The tales and their curious mistranslations function as a template for Borges's own infinite textuality of (re-)reading and (re-)writing, questioning claims of originality and authorship, and framing translation as a polemical tool of creation.[60] His frequent references to the *Nights* show that his poetic anti-theory of translation does not only acknowledge the translational act's generally intricate relation with the process of literary production but also stresses the unavoidability of mistranslation and censorship in cross-cultural exchange.[61] Borges's post-romantic praise of "creative mistranslation"[62] in many ways anticipates the creative commission and critical juxtaposing of the deforming mirrors of alterity at work in contemporary Anglophone Arab representations.

Similarly, the Colombian novelist, screenwriter, and journalist, Gabriel García Márquez, "dared to think that the marvels recounted by Scheherazade really happened in the daily life of her time, and stopped happening because the incredulity and realistic cowardice of subsequent generations."[63] His 1967 masterpiece, *One Hundred Years of Solitude*,[64] is one of the best known examples of the magical mode of novelistic writing. The narrative emancipates itself from the strictly realist paradigm in order to reconstruct the lost memory of South America's violent history, the (post-)trauma of the (continuing) *conquista*, and the failed dream of living a reality that is constantly "slipping away."[65] The magical, or rather the myth-

---

57   Jorge Luis Borges, "The Chamber of Statues," *The Universal History of Infamy*, by J. L. Borges, trans. Norman Thomas di Giovanni (London: Penguin, 1975) 107-10, and "Tale of the Two Dreamers," 111-13.

58   Jorge Luis Borges, "The Translators of *The Thousand and One Nights*," *The Total Library: Non-Fiction 1922-1986*, by Jorge Luis Borges, ed. Eliot Weinberger, trans. Esther Allen, Suzanne Jill Levine, and Eliot Weinberger (London: Penguin, 1999) 92-109.

59   Ghazoul, *Nocturnal Poetics: The Arabian Nights in Contemporary Context* 121-31.

60   For a paradigmatic example, see Jorge Luis Borges, "The Thousand and One Nights," trans. Eliot Weinberger, *The Georgian Review* (Fall 1984): 564-74.

61   On the importance of (mis-)translation in Borges's work, see Dominique Jullien, "In Praise of Mistranslation: The Melancholy Cosmopolitanism of Jorge Luis Borges," *Borges in the 21st Century*, spec. issue of *Romanic Review* 98.2-3 (2007): 205-24 and Efraín Kristal, *Invisible Work: Borges and Translation* (Nashville: Vanderbilt UP, 2002).

62   Jorge Luis Borges, "The Translators of the *1001 Nights*," *Borges: A Reader. A Selection from the Writings of Jorge Luis Borges*, eds. Emir Rodríguez Monegal and Alastair Reid (New York: Dutton, 1981) 84.

63   Gabriel García Márquez, *Living to Tell a Tale*, trans. Edith Grossman (New York: Knopf, 2003) 219.

64   Gabriel García Márquez, *One Hundred Years of Solitude*, trans. Gregory Rabassa (1970; London: Penguin, 2014).

65   Gabriel García Márquez, *One Hundred Years of Solitude* 46.

ical, in *One Hundred Years of Solitude* has a particular capacity to preserve a historical experience that is often idealistically discriminated as illusionary. The novel tries to capture what cannot be fully captured in rationalized versions of truths and thus develops a paradigmatic model for working narratively through the trauma of imperialism.[66] Of course, the emancipatory motive of relieving traumatized victims of colonial-racist violence from the status of passive witnesses to their own violation and turning unbearable memories into visions of alternative futures is not unique to the writings of García Márquez. But his profound influence on global literary production and postcolonial writing in English is undisputed.[67] How could it not have influenced Anglophone Arab writing?

Salman Rushdie's 1980 novel, *Midnight's Children*,[68] is another case in point for the widely ramified voyage of the Shahrazadian trope and her nocturnal mode of stretching the truth. With this narrative, Rushdie inaugurates a long chain of writings with fractal nocturnal imaginaries, of which *Two Years Eight Months and Twenty-Eight Nights*[69] presents perhaps the most obvious allusion to the *Nights*. Although the time span in the 2015 novel's title may add up to 1,001 nights, the auto-mythical science fiction narrative identifies with the medieval Andalusian polymath, Ibn Rushd (Averroes), whose controversial Aristotelian theology put his life in danger, rather than with Shahrazad's successful survival strategy of telling stories. In *Midnight's Children*, the proudly unreliable narrator-hero, Saleem Sinai, informs the reader that he was born on August 15, 1947 "[o]n the stroke of midnight, as a matter of fact,"[70] the night of India's arrival at independence. While he introduces himself as an individual "handcuffed to history"[71] and thus as the involuntary metonymic personification of the nation's modern travails, he consistently resists representational accuracy. Instead, Saleem functions as a narrative vehicle to place the reader into a highly fragmented conglomerate of intertwined reports, memories, tales, rumors, miracles, elisions, additions, and outright inventions. In the context of my study, it is not only important to note that all these stories and sub-stories claim equal historical evidence but also that they assert to be intertextually tracing the sources' fantastic power of telepathically communicating India's trans-individual

---

66   See Eugene L. Arva, *The Traumatic Imagination: Histories of Violence in Magical Realist Fiction* (Amherst: Cambria P, 2011) 173-96.

67   See Michael Bell, "García Márquez, Magical Realism and World Literature," *The Cambridge Companion to Gabriel García Márquez*, ed. Philip Swanson (Cambridge: Cambridge UP, 2010) 179-195 and Pramod K. Nayar, *Postcolonial Literature: An Introduction* (Delhi: Pearson Longman, 2008) 13.

68   Salman Rushdie, *Midnight's Children* (1981; New York: Penguin, 1991).

69   Salman Rushdie, *Two Years Eight Months and Twenty-Eight Nights* (New York: Penguin Random House, 2015).

70   Rushdie, *Midnight's Children* 3.

71   Rushdie, *Midnight's Children* 3.

experiences. In a direct address to the reader, the narrator explains that he is just one of many magically powerful midnight children.

> Understand what I'm saying: during the first hour of August 15th, 1947—between midnight and one a.m.—no less than one thousand and one children were born within the frontiers of the infant sovereign state of India. In itself, that is not an unusual fact (although the resonances of the number are strangely literary) [...].[72]

The numerical code used in this pseudo-didactical elaboration merges a hyperbolic reference to the infinite narrative of the *Nights* with a specific symbolic hint to the country's post-independence politics. Within ten years, 420 of the children die. Alluding to Shahrazad's 1,001 tales, while narratively subtracting the statistical death rate, reduces the group of worldly survivors to 581, which is exactly the number of members of India's parliament.[73] The merging of the fantastic and the real in *Midnight's Children* is not an aesthetic exercise for the sake of stylistic innovation; it aims at narratively questioning the oppressive fiction of unitary truth. A similar aim guides many Anglophone Arab works.

4.1   Lies, Counter-Lies, and Self-Made Lies

> "To those who see with one eye, speak with one tongue, and see things as either black or white, either Eastern or Western."[74]

By now it should be clear that, even if we take the *Arabian Nights* as the original *root* for the nocturnal traces in contemporary Anglophone Arab representations, it is virtually impossible to differentiate exactly between the various *routes* of reception and re-reception that these representations have taken. Moreover, there are many additional pre- and intertexts at work in the discourse, which I will explore in the following. These texts do not necessarily offer themselves to be easily grasped with the trope of the *Nights* or to be directly related to the transtextual voyages of one of the Arabic classic's narrative modes.

Let me continue my cursory journey into what I perceive as important intertexts by giving two particularly significant examples of these other points of departures. Re-visiting Jabra Ibrahim Jabra's 1960 Anglophone novel, *Hunters in a Narrow*

---

72   Rushdie, *Midnight's Children* 224.
73   See Arva, *The Traumatic Imagination: Histories of Violence in Magical Realist Fiction* 209-10.
74   Tayeb Salih, *Season of Migration to the North*, trans. Denys Johnson-Davies (1969; London: Heinemann, 2010) 150-51.

Street,[75] and re-reading Tayeb Salih's *Mawsim al-hijra ila-sh-shamal*[76] as a 1966 Arabic text in English translation will forge supplementary links to expected and less expected discursive affinities for the reading of Anglophone Arab works and thus contribute to the further diversification of my discussion.

Hunters in a Narrow Street belongs to a corpus of early Anglophone Arab writings produced within the Arab world. Due to its place among just a few scattered Arab writings in English from the 1960s, the question of the novel's literary affiliations cannot be easily answered. In my view, it cannot be resolved by emphasizing its "dual nationality."[77] If there is any dual national affiliation to speak of, it would be a Palestinian-Iraqi one rather than an Arabic-English one. Educated in Jerusalem and at Cambridge University in England, the Palestinian exile Jabra was a renowned novelist, poet, playwright, literary and art critic, and translator. Until his death in 1994, he spent most of his professional life in Iraq. As a founding member of the Baghdad Modern Art Group, he was closely associated with the Iraqi modernist movement of the 1950s and 1960s. His criticism contributed significantly to the introduction of new experimental forms of painting and sculpturing to the growing educated, urban middle-class of the region. Like the movement's most prominent representative, Jewad Salim, Jabra argued for an explicitly avantgardist Arab heritage art, or *"turath*[heritage]-as-art,"[78] that synthesized the search for distinctively local forms of artistic expression with a clear commitment to the universal aesthetics of modernism.[79] Similarly, he saw Arab literary production as an inevitably interpoetic project,[80] both arising from a particular literary tradition while at the same time being intrinsically tied to and participating in other, non-Arab literary legacies such as the Western one. As Jabra has put it in 1971:

> If all the arts of an epoch are inter-related, the arts of all epochs are inter-related too. Change, in the final analysis, is an extension of creativity, a battle against

---

75   Jabra Ibrahim Jabra, *Hunters in a Narrow Street* (1960; Boulder: Three Continents, 1996).

76   Tayeb Salih, *Mawsim al-hijra ila-sh-shamal* (1966; Beirut: Dar al-Auwdah, 1967).

77   See Hilary Kilpatrick, "Arab Fiction in English: A Case of Dual Nationality," *New Comparison* 13 (1992): 54. See also Nouri Gana, "The Intellectual History and Contemporary Significance of the Arab Novel in English," Introduction, *The Edinburgh Companion to the Arab Novel in English: The Politics of Anglo Arab and Arab American Literature and Culture*, ed. Nouri Gana (Edinburgh: Edinburgh UP, 2013) 9-11.

78   Samir al-Khalil [Kanan Makiya], *The Monument: Art, Vulgarity, and Responsibility in Iraq* (London: André Deutsch, 1991) 78.

79   Nathaniel Greenberg, "Political Modernism, Jabra, and the Baghdad Modern Art Group," *CLCWeb: Comparative Literature and Culture* 12.2 (2010): 1-11, 24 Mar. 2012 <http://docs.lib.purdue.edu/clcweb/vol12/iss2/13>.

80   On the notion of interpoetics, see Jabra Ibrahim Jabra, "On Interpoetics," Interview with Najman Yasin, *The View from Within: Writers and Critics on Contemporary Arab Literature*, eds. Ferial Ghazoul and Barbara Harlow (Cairo: The American U in Cairo P, 1994) 207-12.

impoverishment—not only for one part of the world, but for the whole community of man. For the arts of all nations are equally inter-related. Thus Arab writers in their intellectual communion with the West have sought not only to take but also to give: theirs has been an endeavour to contribute to those very ideas that make up the spiritual and mental climate of this century. Many of them, whether poets, novelists, or dramatists, have even written in the languages of the West. Without forfeiting their own legacy, they are here to participate in the pool of all legacies: the civilization of today.[81]

Hunters in a Narrow Street must be read against this background. Jabra's second novel remains his only fictional work originally written in English. The story is set in pre-revolutionary Baghdad of the late 1940s and early 1950s, a city for which "[i]t's all very well for [Western, basically British and American] foreigners, who live off the fat of our land unbothered by our problems, to say it's a wonderful place,"[82] as one of the main protagonists puts it. The obviously auto-fictional narrator, Jameel Farran, is a Palestinian refugee, a college teacher, and a poet who spends most of his free time with his friends, Adnan and Husain. Desperately longing for a successful upheaval against the British-supported puppet-monarchy, the young men discuss the role of Arab cultural heritage in Western-style modernity, lament the absence of private freedom and the religious taboos regulating the social relations between the sexes, and participate in revolutionary cultural politics. In many of their meetings in the streets of Baghdad or at public places, such as bars and cafes on the banks of the Tigris River, they are joined by Brian Flint, "a fair-haired, blue-eyed foreigner" whom Jameel and Adnan first get to know during an obviously homoerotic encounter in a public bath. [83] Flint pretends to be an Oxford graduate of Oriental studies who traveled to Iraq to improve his Arabic. The three friends suspect the Englishman of working for the British intelligence and/or the Western oil industry: "*Your* interest in us is because of oil,"[84] Adnan accuses him. Although a certain suspicion remains, they want him "to know Baghdad from within."[85] The slightly naïve foreigner (and with him, the curious reader) is taken to the narrow streets of the rapidly modernizing city to see for himself (for themselves) how the secular Arab men's daily lives are caught in an overlapping web of local and global power-politics of oppression. Their condition is described as that of a "double servitude: to evil masters from without, and to diseased powers from within. And both closely

---

81   Jabra Ibrahim Jabra, "Modern Arab Literature and the West," *Journal of Arab Literature* 2 (1971): 91.

82   Jabra, *Hunters in a Narrow Street* 209.

83   Jabra, *Hunters in a Narrow Street* 36.

84   Jabra, *Hunters in a Narrow Street* 59.

85   Jabra, *Hunters in a Narrow Street* 58.

related."[86] Flint, seemingly ignorant but always well informed, turns out "to love everything he saw, even the dirt of Rashid Street. 'At least,' he said, commenting on it, 'it's authentic'."[87] The outsider's exoticist gaze is countered with Jameel's street-level depiction of the city's tough social reality and his friends' private reports or journal entries. Jameel, a private English tutor, falls in love with the daughter of a notable, Sulafa, who desperately wants to read *The Oxford Companion to English Literature* and badly needs a gun to kill either herself or the man her father wants to marry her against her will.[88] Sulafa's corrupt uncle threatens to throw Jameel out of the country if he does not give up loving her, and the two have to wait, meet in secret, and nearly go mad. Adnan kills Sulafa's father for other, rather ideological, reasons. He and Hussain are temporarily imprisoned due to their participation in student protests. While Flint, "in the meantime, becoming proficient in Arabic was learning to play the *mutbidge*, that very Arab twincane instrument",[89] the local Arab men "impaled themselves on rows of political and social swords".[90]

Scholars of Arabic literature have placed *Hunters in a Narrow Street* within a broader tendency of experimental novelistic writing in Arabic of that time. On the one hand, they see the novel as influenced by the free verse form of so-called Tammuz poetry, a contemporary mythopoetic movement that emancipated itself from any codified bonds of classical Arabic poetry.[91] On the other hand, they stress Jabra's appropriation of traditional oral narrative traditions, specifically of the *Nights*.[92] There might be some mythical motives at work in the novel, and one can surely attest a certain fragmentation of multi-layered narrative voices that reminds of Shahrazad's perpetual mode of telling stories within stories. However, in the context of my study, I tend to stress quite different aspects: the novel's clear political commitment to revolutionary politics, its deep concern with the spatial dynamics and the "new [social] kineticism"[93] of the urban setting, the almost existentialist juxtaposition of outward appearance and immanent experience, as well as the explicit anticipation of a non-Arab Western audience. In my view, this novel can be grasped as an early expression of political Arab modernism in cross-cultural translation, as an Anglophone Arab narrative that, in many ways, anticipates the so-called *adab al-multazim* [literature of commitment] of the 1960s. The *Iltizam* [commitment; literarily: responsibility] debate was significantly inspired by Jean-Paul

---

86   Jabra, *Hunters in a Narrow Street* 60.
87   Jabra, *Hunters in a Narrow Street* 41.
88   Jabra, *Hunters in a Narrow Street* 153-55.
89   Jabra, *Hunters in a Narrow Street* 226.
90   Jabra, *Hunters in a Narrow Street* 232.
91   Kilpatrick, "Arab Fiction in English: A Case of Dual Nationality," 46-55.
92   Allen, *The Arabic Novel. An Historical and Critical Introduction* 16.
93   Greenberg, "Political Modernism, Jabra, and the Baghdad Modern Art Group," 2.

Sartre's notion of *littérature engagée* [committed writing][94] and Albert Camus's existentialist body of work.[95] Following Sartre's example, *Hunters in a Narrow Street* engages in writing as willful political act rather than literary representation for literary craft's sake. What makes it so unique is its simultaneous commitment to local change and the explicitly interpoetic sense of its representational obligation toward an English-speaking audience. Although the notion of *Iltizam* began to disintegrate, along with the ideologies of pan-Arabism or Arab socialisms, after the Arab defeat in the June War of 1967, giving way successively to other concepts of cultural commitment and resistance, Jabra's understanding of cross-cultural representation as a tool of local social change that involves the strategic obligation to address a global audience is still an important incitement for Anglophone Arab writers and artists working within the Middle East. From a relational studies point of view, *Hunters*, like many Anglophone Arab articulations after it, represents a work of self-translation that mediates a local discourse across linguistic divides. When, in 1974, the novel was translated into Arabic, partly by Jabra himself, it became a vehicle of double mediation that transferred a pro-revolutionary English text across a temporal gap into a post-revolutionary Arab discourse.[96]

It is difficult to specify the exact measure of Jabra's impact on contemporary Anglophone Arab representations. Unlike other authors of the Arab literary landscape of the 1960s who completed only a single work in English, such as Waguih Ghali (*Beer in the Snooker Club*)[97] or Isaak Diqs (*A Bedouin Boyhood*),[98] Jabra wrote *Hunters in a Narrow Street* in his early years as an intellectual, after which he went on to influence critical debates and cultural practices in the Arabic speaking world throughout the twentieth century.[99]

Diqs's nostalgic childhood narrative is his only piece of prose writing. The autonarrator looks back on his formative years among Bedouin tribesmen at the edge of the Negev desert from his adult position in the Jordan Ministry of Agriculture. The narrative draws on Arabic oral traditions to serve Western readership expectations while rather subliminally recounting the catastrophe that the 1948 war and the cre-

94   On Jean Paul Sartre's 1945 introductory statement to *Les Temps modernes*, devoted to littérature engagée, see Steven Unger, "1945, 15 October: Rebellion or Revolution?" *A New History of French Literature*, ed. Denis Hollier (1989; Cambridge, MA: Harvard UP, 2001) 972-77.

95   On the Arab *Iltizam* debate, see Verena Klemm, *Literarisches Engagement im Nahen Osten: Konzepte und Debatten* (Würzburg: Ergon, 1998).

96   See Jabra Ibrahim Jabra, *Sayyadun fi shari' dhayyiq*, trans. Mohammad Asfour and Jabra Ibrahim Jabra (Beirut: Dar al-Adab, 1974). On this translation, see Nibras A. M. Al-Omar, "The Self-Translator as Cultural Mediator: In Memory of Jabra Ibrahim Jabra," *Asian Social Science* 8.13 (2011): 211-19.

97   Waguih Ghali, *Beer in the Snooker Club* (London: André Deutsch, 1964).

98   Isaak Diqs, *A Bedouin Boyhood* (London: Allen and Unwin, 1967).

99   Cf. Nash, *The Anglo-Arab Encounter* 48-50.

ation of the state of Israel meant for those who were dispersed, impoverished, and condemned to live as refugees.

Written while the author was in exile in Finland and Germany, Waguih Ghali's *Beer in the Snooker Club* is known as the first Egyptian novel in English. Long neglected by Western and Arab critics alike, the story is set in Cairo's cosmopolitan milieu of the 1950s. The novel has only recently been translated into Arabic.[100] Constantly shifting between subversive humor and disillusioned sarcasm, the story of the Coptic Ram, Edna, his Jewish lover and mentor, and the over-Anglicized Font takes up the perspective of those Westernized urban minorities and foreign non-citizens who were forced to leave Egypt after the 1956 Suez conflict. Ghali himself left Egypt in the late 1950s. *Beer in the Snooker Club* remained his only novel and, to my knowledge, had no traceable influence on Anglophone Arab writing. Considering the renewed interest in the book in Egypt, this literary sublimation of the inebriated dream of gambling with one's identity and the bitter irony of impossible secular affiliations in the age of ideological polarization definitely deserves further investigation.[101]

Jabra continued to write fiction, poetry, and art criticism after he published *Hunters in a Narrow Street*. His 1978 novel, *Al-bahth 'an Walid Mas'ud* (translated in 2000 as *In Search of Walid Masoud*),[102] and the 1982 experimental work, *'Alam bi-la khara'it* [World without Maps],[103] co-authored with 'Abd al-Rahman Munif, had a strong impact on Arabic and Anglophone Arab cultural practice.[104] The collaborative project has been described by Muhsin al-Musawi as "a novel on the art of the novel."[105] In relational perspective, the meta-novelistic undertaking represents an excess of cross-cultural intertextuality, with allusions ranging from the Abbasid poet, Al-Mutanabbi, to the Romantic English poet, John Keats, that does not stop at the imaginative boundaries of ethnic or national literatures.

---

100   There are two translations available: Waguih Ghali, *Bira fi nadi al-bilyardu* (translation of *Beer in the Snooker Club*, 1964), trans. Mahir Shafiq Farid and Hana' Nasir (Cairo: Dar al-'Alam al-Thalith, 2006) and Waguih Ghali, *Bira fi nadi al-bilyardu* (translation of *Beer in the Snooker Club*, 1964), trans. Iman Mersal and Reem al-Rayyes (Cairo: Dar ash-Shuruq, 2013).

101   Cf. Deborah A. Starr, "Drinking, Gambling, and Making Merry: Waguih Ghali's Search for Cosmopolitan Agency," *Companion to the Arab Novel in English: The Politics of Anglo Arab and Arab American Literature and Culture*, ed. Nouri Gana (Edinburgh: Edinburgh UP, 2013) 106-26.

102   Jabra Ibrahim Jabra, *Al-bahth 'an Walid Mas'ud* (Beirut: Dar al-Adab, 1978). English translation: *In Search of Walid Masoud: A Novel*, trans. Roger Allen and Adnan Haydar (Syracuse: Syracuse UP, 2000).

103   Jabra Ibrahim Jabra and 'Abd al-Rahman Munif, *'Alam bi-la khara'it* [World without maps] (Beirut: Mu'assasa al-'Arabiyya li-d-Dirasat wa-n-Nashr, 1982).

104   See Sonja Mejcher-Atassi, *Reading Across Modern Arabic Literature and Art* (Wiesbaden: Reichert, 2012) 63-75.

105   Muhsin Jassim al-Musawi, *Al-riwaya al-'arabiyya* [The Arabic Novel] (Beirut: Dar al-Adab, 1988) 282; quoted from Mejcher-Atassi, *Reading Across Modern Arabic Literature and Art* 74.

With a view to Anglophone Arab artistic practice, however, I would like to offer a close reading of Jabra's 1978 novel. The story of an Iraqi writer's narrative investigation of the main protagonist's mysterious disappearance is particularly important regarding its transgeneric incorporation of non-literary intertexts. The first-person narrator, Jawad Husni is in search of the Palestinian Baghdadi Walid Masoud. The latter, according to divergent rumors, has emigrated to Australia or Canada or is said to have been killed variously as a resistance fighter in Palestine or during the Lebanese civil war in Beirut. For his undertaking, Husni draws on a recorded tape found in a small Japanese cassette player in Walid's empty car at the Iraqi-Syrian border, letters and other written documents, stories told by friends, and on his own fragmented memory. Although the hyper-investigative project has little success in terms of reconstructing a coherent factual line of events, it demonstrates the metafictional power of imaginative research as artistic research. The "balance" between rough humanist idealism and the real problems of humanity in a "world of terror, murder, hunger, and hatred" that Walid "had talked about all his life"[106] cannot be found. The "'search' would [...] often go to extremes of rumor and conjecture, and in the end true and false would be so intermingled that it would be impossible to distinguish between the two."[107] Instead of objective, quasi-statistical approximations to Walid's secret truth, we are offered a non-conclusive mosaic of a man's life's re-emplotment, the narrative modes of which by far exceed this man's ultimate text. The writer-narrator-researcher finally accepts the many unresolved contradictions between competing versions of Walid Masoud's life. He understands that these contradictions result from the inevitable fact that his life has been framed and emplotted by and in other persons' life texts:

> I ought to sift through all the facts and data, eliminate the false trails and fabrications and delusions, then try to reach a conclusion that will entail the least degree of contradiction possible. But my sense of responsibility as a researcher won't let me do that. Even fabrications and delusions about a man have their own particular importance; why would they be invented otherwise, and where would they come from?[108]

Tayeb Salih's *Mawsim al-hijra ila-sh-shamal* in many ways reverses the representational dynamics described in the case of Jabra's *Hunters in a Narrow Street*. The novel was first published in Beirut in 1967; its English translation by Denys Johnson-Davies appeared less than two years later. In my view, it is important to point out that not only was *Season of Migration to the North* published in London, but the Arabic original was also written in London. Salih studied political science in the British

---

106   Jabra, *In Search of Walid Masoud* 3.
107   Jabra, *In Search of Walid Masoud* 47.
108   Jabra, *In Search of Walid Masoud* 288-89.

capital city, and he spent most of his professional life as a writer and BBC journalist there, where he lived with his Scottish wife.[109] Since he wrote *Season* in Arabic, he obviously had an Arab readership in mind. In other words, this novel, which begins and ends with a Sudanese frame setting and which sends its Sudanese anti-hero, Mustafa Sa'eed, to London into a deadly love-hate relationship of mutual exoticist desire and desperate revenge, was meant to be sent from London to Khartoum, Cairo, or Baghdad. It is both a postcolonial and a metropolitan novel.

Salih could not have foreseen that his work would fall victim to censorship in most Arab countries and that *Mawsim al-hijra ila-sh-shamal* would for a long time only be available in Beirut. Therefore, most Anglophone Arab readers will have come across this text first in English translation. Whereas the novel has long been incorporated into the canon of postcolonial literatures, the details of its Anglo-Arabic genesis are rarely known. The contrapuntal interpretation of *Season* as a resistant mimetic reciprocation of Joseph Conrad's turn-of-the-century classic, *Heart of Darkness*,[110] as well as its related symbolic use as a paradigmatic example of what has been variously termed "writing back"[111] or "voyage in"[112] rather evoke that Salih wrote back from his native Sudan and that his text has traveled into the Western discourse from some distant African over-there. The implicit insistence on an authentic non-Western voice speaking to the West is not without ambivalence. With a view to the novel's critique of the (neo-)colonial practice of cross-cultural othering and its simultaneous deconstruction of the (formerly) colonized systematic self-othering, it carries an almost tragic irony.

At this point, I cannot possibly do justice to the topical density and metafictional complexity of this tremendously beautiful narrative. In what follows, I simply want to explain why this Arabic novel in translation might be an important matrix and almost inexhaustible tool-kit for interpretively grasping contemporary Anglophone Arab poetics and ethics. According to Geoffrey Nash, *Season* can function as "an important intertext for our reading of later Anglophone writing by Arabs;"[113] and I agree with that. The British literary critic's both hermeneutic and teleological investigation stresses the genuine proto-postcolonial quality of *Season* regarding its content and form. But whereas he wants to see in it a pioneering prototypical

---

109 Constance E. Berkley and Osman Hassan Ahmed, eds. and trans., *Tayeb Salih Speaks: Four Interviews with the Sudanese Novelist* (Washington: Office of the Cultural Counsellor, Embassy of the Democratic Republic of the Sudan, 1982) I, 5, 12.

110 Edward W. Said, *Culture and Imperialism* (1993; New York: Vintage, 1994) 210-39. The novella was first serialized in three parts in 1899 in the pro-colonial *Blackwood's Magazine*; it was first published in book form in 1902, Joseph Conrad, *Heart of Darkness* (London: Penguin, 1994).

111 Bill Ashcroft, Gareth Griffiths, and Helen Tiffin, eds., *The Empire Writes Back: Theory and Practice in Post-Colonial Literatures* (London: Routledge, 1989).

112 Said, *Culture and Imperialism* 216.

113 Nash, *The Anglo-Arab Encounter* 62.

text that offers "the raw materials"[114] for the following generations' writing of the
Anglo-Arab encounter (i.e. the presence of hybrid protagonists placed in juxtaposed
West-Eastern setting, the cross-cultural merging of literary references and poetic
modes, or the anti-Orientalist re-writing of shared histories),[115] I prefer to concentrate on *Season*'s literary negotiation and ambivalent justification of what I call
counter-lies.

In my view, this Arab-British novel, both in Arabic and in English translation,
does not so much counter Western lies with non-Western truths but rather exposes the relational dynamics of Western lies and non-Western strategies of self-
assertion developed under conflictual conditions in which honesty and truthfulness
cease to be veritable virtues. I argue that the foremost quality of this novel is not the
representation of a national or regional literary tradition from which it supposedly
comes as a self-image of Arab Africa or the story of an authentic Sudanese experience of the Anglo-Arab encounter; it is rather the depiction of the tremendous bi-
directional effects of Europe's constant denial of the non-Europeans' humanity and
its symptomatic accompaniment: namely, the violation of the idealist humanist notion of communicative reason. There can be a gap, in other words, between what
certain nativist or multiculturalist readers may expect when they pick up the book
and what they are actually confronted with when reading *Season of Migration to the
North*. I am not saying that one has to approach the text as a piece of extra-moral
philosophy; it is, quite obviously, a work of fiction. But, it is one that narratively
elaborates, and thus transforms, the concept of lying with nearly obsessive self-
consciousness. It imagines lies and counter-lies as speech acts intrinsically linked
to the colonial and postcolonial appropriation of cross-cultural authority, and it
asks for the chances and pitfalls of lying as a transgressive activity of resisting the
ideology of Western truthfulness. As a work of literary art, *Season* performs an aesthetic transformation of its own ethical determination and thus transgresses the
given (neo-)colonial discourse of universal consistency. With a view to its idiosyn-
crasy as a postcolonial work of post-moral transgression, Salih's novel is indeed an
original and particularly important intertext for contemporary Anglophone Arab
representations.

It is no paradox, therefore, to see in Conrad's partial affirmation of colonialist-
racist ethics in *Heart of Darkness* an antecedent of *Season*'s anti-imperialist project.
Although the exiled Polish writer firmly believed that "fiction is nearer to truth"[116]
than any historiographical representation could ever be, his own novelistic writing
constantly urges its readers to ask themselves whether they are being lied to by narrative voices who regularly repress what they believe is unspeakable. Benita Parry

---

114   Nash, *The Anglo-Arab Encounter* 60.
115   Nash, *The Anglo-Arab Encounter* 57-63.
116   Joseph Conrad, *Notes on Life and Letters* (1921; London: Dent, 1949).

correctly argues that the historical truths of Conrad's imperial imaginary rather lie in what remains unspoken. According to Parry, such truths can therefore be quasi ex-negativo distilled from the novel's remarkable silence regarding the dark side of Europe's civilizational mission and its progressivist promise. First and foremost, they lie in its subversive "estrangement of colonialist perceptions and misconceptions."[117] Postcolonial critics writing in the wake of Edward Said's reading of *Heart of Darkness* as "both anti-imperialist and imperialist"[118] have variously stressed the novella's implicit critique of or dishonest complicity with an ideology that tried to cover the violent horrors of "the conquest of the earth"[119] with the idea of economic development and civilizational progress. Whether they see the novella as the work of "a bloody racist"[120] writer or as a dystopian critique of colonial hypocrisy, they almost all agree that this narrative does not provide a realistic image of colonized Africa and that the novel therefore cannot be grasped as a "mimetic transcription"[121] of the colonizers' experience. Although Marlow's recollection of his voyage into the brutal reality of colonial blessings repeats the traditional Eurocentric association of whiteness with "truth, probity and purity",[122] it deploys the imperial project's constitutive white lies to evoke what is withheld from the dominant narrative.

Marlow's complicit-passion not to disrupt the "unbound power of [Kurtz's ideological] eloquence" or "to interrupt the magic current of [his racist] phrases"[123] reaches its colonial Gothic peak when he returns to the metropolitan heart of darkness after Kurtz's death. Although his visit to Kurtz's Intended is overshadowed by the memory of the famous "whispered cry" of a dying man who represented all evils of Europe—"The horror! The horror!"[124]—Marlow does not grant him the honest justice that he wanted. With every lie spoken about "a remarkable man"[125] to whom other men looked up and upon "his goodness" that "shone in every act,"[126] Kurtz's monstrous shadow grows, and the dark memory of his colonial regime deepens. Instead of telling the Intended his true last words, Marlow saves her illusions and symbolically preserves the colonial lies of Europe's dishonest home culture: "I could not tell her. It would have been too dark—too dark altogether ..."[127]

---

117 Benita Parry, *Postcolonial Studies: A Materialist Critique* (London: Routledge, 2004) 107.

118 Said, *Culture and Imperialism* xviii.

119 Conrad, *Heart of Darkness* 10.

120 Chinua Achebe, "An Image of Africa," *Literary Criticism*, spec. issue of *Research in African Literatures*, 9.1 (1978): 9. First presented as a lecture at the University of Massachusetts, Amherst in February 1975.

121 Parry, *Postcolonial Studies. A Materialist Critique* 133.

122 Parry, *Postcolonial Studies. A Materialist Critique* 135.

123 Conrad, *Heart of Darkness* 72.

124 Conrad, *Heart of Darkness* 106.

125 Conrad, *Heart of Darkness* 107.

126 Conrad, *Heart of Darkness* 109.

127 Conrad, *Heart of Darkness* 111.

As John Kucich demonstrates in *The Power of Lies*,[128] long before Conrad, Victorian writers questioned the official bourgeois notions of truthfulness as a cornerstone of British national character. In my view, *Heart of Darkness* is significant for its questioning of the nation's ideological discourse of colonialism. Whereas Kucich mentions Conrad only in passing, Jil Larson's study on *Ethics and Narrative in the English Novel*[129] focuses on his 1911 novel, *Under Western Eyes*. The "linguistic pessimism"[130] that Larson stresses exists at the foundation of Conrad's narrative ethics applies as well to *Heart of Darkness*. Although the narrator lays bare the ideological traps of an intrinsically amoral colonial situation in which speaking and narrating necessarily become ways to lie, to manipulate, and to coerce, he "retains the distinction between truth telling as virtuous and lying as harmful, both to self and others."[131] One does not have to agree with Chinua Achebe, who interprets Conrad's retrieve into the tyrannical narrowness of tropical discourse as the intentional drawing of "a *cordon sanitaire* between himself and the moral and psychological malaise of his narrator,"[132] to see that *Heart of Darkness* is primarily concerned with the deterioration of the European mind and not with the anti-colonial revision of European lies. Marlow himself supposes that his reluctance to revise these white lies "was an impulse of unconscious loyalty"[133] to Kurtz. Perhaps it would be unfair to psychoanalytically interpret Benita Parry's false quotation of Marlow's self-apology as a similar expression of her unconscious loyalty to one of her favorite writers, Joseph Conrad. Substituting his original word choice, "life-sensation,"[134] with the term "lie-sensation," she reads into *Heart of Darkness* a critical awareness of the incommensurability of colonialism and morality that cannot be proved in the novella. Here I quote Parry mis-quoting Conrad: "'...No it is impossible, it is impossible to convey the **lie**-sensation of any given epoch of one's existence—that which makes its truth, its meaning'."[135] Even if we take for granted that this is simply a typo, one wonders from whence the meta-ethical evocation of a certain immanent, almost Nietzschean, critique of modernity's discourse of universal truth concealed in Conrad's prose fiction comes.

The materialist critic Parry is not alone in her assessment that in *Heart of Darkness* "Conrad [...] reconfigured imperialism's lust after power" by transcending "ideological determination of the milieu within which it was written."[136] In fact, one

---

128   John Kucich, *The Power of Lies: Transgression in Victorian Fiction* (Ithaca: Cornell UP, 1994).

129   Jil Larson, *Ethics and Narrative in the English Novel, 1880–1914* (Cambridge: Cambridge UP, 2001).

130   Larson, *Ethics and Narrative in the English Novel, 1880–1914* 136.

131   Larson, *Ethics and Narrative in the English Novel, 1880–1914* 131.

132   Achebe, "An Image of Africa," 7.

133   Conrad, *Heart of Darkness* 105.

134   Conrad, *Heart of Darkness* 39.

135   Conrad, as quoted by Parry, *Postcolonial Studies: A Materialist Critique* 138, emphasis mine.

136   Parry, *Postcolonial Studies: A Materialist Critique* 139.

gets the impression that such quasi-loyal reading is shared by the majority of white postcolonial critics. It was first the avowed Conradolator, Edward Said, who already in 1976 compared the novelist's work to Nietzsche's radical transvaluation of our learned notions of truth and lie and, thereby, suggested looking closely at Conrad's literary contention of the alliance of colonial language with power.[137] For re-reading Salih's *Season of Migration to the North* as an important intertext for our understanding of contemporary Anglophone Arab representations, one does not have to fully agree with Said's comparison of *Heart of Darkness* and Nietzsche's corpus of extramoral ethics.[138]

Season is not concerned with lying as a merely linguistic dilemma or a problem regarding some general moralizing manner. The novel depicts the verbal act of lying as a given practice under the socio-historical condition of coloniality. The story of Mustafa Sa'eed's emigration and remigration is told from Sudan by a man, who has just returned from his studies in England at the dawn of Sudanese independence in the mid-1960s. Back in his native village, the estranged returnee meets an even more uncanny stranger who is said to have come from the city and about whom not much is known. When the stranger one night drunkenly recites an English war poem in an "impeccable accent,"[139] the returnee's curiosity is aroused. He decides to find out more about the secrets concealed by Mustafa Sa'eed: "Wouldn't it be better if you told me the truth?'"[140] Mustafa gives in and starts narrating his long life story. He does so not without clarifying that he "'won't tell [him] everything. [...]'"[141] At an early point in his narration, he adds: "'I don't ask you to believe what I tell you. [...]'"[142] Before Mustafa disappears, the narrator, and with him the reader, listens to the life story of a highly talented half-orphan's educational transmigration. His migrational travails lead the twelve-year-old Mustafa from Khartoum to a secondary school in Cairo and from there to London and then Oxford University. The Sudanese's migration to the north culminates in a private, professional, and legal catastrophe. The enframed narrative begins in the early 20th century with Mustafa's decision to go to public school. It ends in the late 1950s or early 1960s with his remigration to Sudan after a seven-year imprisonment in England. After Mustafa's disappearance, the first person narrator does not give up researching the

---

137 Edward W. Said, "Conrad and Nietzsche," *Reflections on Exile and other Essays*, by Edward Said (2000; Cambridge: Harvard UP, 2001) 70-82.

138 See, for instance, Friedrich Nietzsche, "On Truth and Lies in a Nonmoral Sense," *Art and Interpretation: An Anthology of Readings in Aesthetics and the Philosophy of Art*, ed. Eric Dayton (Peterborough, ON: Broadview P, 1998) 116-24.

139 Salih, *Season of Migration to the North* 14.

140 Salih, *Season of Migration to the North* 15.

141 Salih, *Season of Migration to the North* 19.

142 Salih, *Season of Migration to the North* 21.

secrets of his diachronic alter-ego's true life. He does so in conversations with people who knew him personally as well as on the basis of what Mustafa has left in his house's hidden Victorian-style drawing room: a library full of English books, notebooks and autobiographical fragments, theoretical manuscripts, scraps of paper with handwritten poetry on it, photographs, and other private documents. While he is professionally involved in governmental development projects, the private researcher-narrator takes care of Mustafa's Sudanese family. Finally, the unnamed narrator attempts to commit suicide and, in the final words of the novel, possibly decides to survive.

Mustafa's life-story is indeed a *lie*-story. From the very beginning, he is lied to, and he lies to others. The many seemingly helping hands that are given to him rarely honor their pledges. School does not turn out to be the promised entrance card to becoming an official in the colonial government, a cleric's astonishment regarding his fluency in English is not at all an expression of respect, and his first European foster-mother's loving embrace does not come without the childless woman's oedipal claim of lust and power. In Cairo, she calls him "Mr. Sa'eed"[143] and in turn desires to be called "Elizabeth,"[144] while Mustafa insists on calling her with her married name. When she later writes to the adult, she addresses him with the infantilizing pet name, "Moozi."[145] In fact, the "sensation of panic"[146] that the twelve-year-old Mustafa feels when he gazes at Mrs. Robinson's armpits for the first time not only relates to his own anxiety of cross-cultural erotics but, in a psychological reading, hints at the threat of sexual abuse. Symbolically, this early gendered encounter already anticipates the discriminating exploitation of a man who has lost his father(-land) in the over-embracing arms of the colonial motherland.

In London, the brilliant student and excellent young lecturer, Sa'eed, marries Jean Morris and has several affairs with English women who yearn "for tropical climes, cruel suns, purple horizons."[147] These women project their phantasies of "a thirsty desert" or "a wilderness of southern desires" onto Mustafa, thereby perceptually transforming him "into a naked, primitive creature, a spear in one hand and arrows in the other, hunting elephants and lions in the jungles."[148] While they turn the immigrant into a symbolic personification of their own truths of cultural and racial alterity, Mustafa Sa'eed is well aware of the dynamics of misperception and hyper-affirmatively reciprocates the women's expectations. In his Orientalized "bedroom where the smell of burning sandalwood and incense"[149] fills the lungs of

---

143   Salih, *Season of Migration to the North* 25.
144   Salih, *Season of Migration to the North* 28.
145   Salih, *Season of Migration to the North* 147.
146   Salih, *Season of Migration to the North* 26.
147   Salih, *Season of Migration to the North* 30.
148   Salih, *Season of Migration to the North* 38.
149   Salih, *Season of Migration to the North* 42.

his exoticist partners with what these women imagine is "the smell of rotting leaves in the jungles of Africa,"[150] he variously plays the role of the "African demon," the "black god,"[151] or the Arab "master" of ever-changing "slave girl[s]."[152] The Oriental-ized room in London functions as a reversed doubling of the essentialist cultural paradigms represented in the secret anglicized room which Mustafa Sa'eed builds back in Sudan.

The sardonically ironic role-play is both parts masochistic and sadistic. Mustafa's deadly love affairs with English women are characterized by mutual desire and disgust, racialized stereotyping and cultural misperceptions, as well as by feelings of guilt, hate, and vengeance. The open performance of Orientalist lies and the secret acting out of counter-Orientalist revenge take the form of physical and/or psychological terror. The dynamic of gendered violence inevitably leads to liberating acts of murderous self-defense and self-destruction. With his "mind [...] like a sharp knife,"[153] the Black Arab Englishman kills his wife and brings other women to suicide. Mustafa actively participates in his own performative racialization and sexual exploitation and does not see himself as a victim. He comes to England as "a conqueror,"[154] as a hyper-masculine reverse "colonizer" and "intruder"[155]—as "a drop of the poison which you [the British, the Europeans] have injected into the veins of history."[156] As the president of the London "Society for the Struggle for African Freedom," he is known for the slogan "'I'll liberate Africa with my penis.'"[157] If Mustafa Sa'eed comes from the heart of darkness, he imagines himself penetrating the "belly of the darkness"[158] from within. As an academic, he makes himself a name as a leftist Fabian economist of colonial capitalism. The titles of his own published studies clearly signal the anti-colonial impetus of his scholarly activism: "*The Economics of Colonialism* [...]. *Colonialism and Monopoly* [...]. *The Cross and Gunpowder* [...]. *The Rape of Africa* [...]."[159]

The tragedy of Mustafa Sa'eed's life in the well-ordered world of Europe is not that he performs lies but rather that he mostly lies according to an archive of melo-dramatic colonial-racist lies that has been arranged by others. All of Europe's hack-neyed lies have participated in the making of what he has become. He knows that he directly relates his lies to prefabricated Western stories. Therefore, the killing of Jean Morris is presented as an inescapable self-punishing and yet liberating act:

---

150   Salih, *Season of Migration to the North* 142.
151   Salih, *Season of Migration to the North* 106.
152   Salih, *Season of Migration to the North* 146.
153   Salih, *Season of Migration to the North* 31.
154   Salih, *Season of Migration to the North* 60.
155   Salih, *Season of Migration to the North* 94.
156   Salih, *Season of Migration to the North* 95.
157   Salih, *Season of Migration to the North* 120.
158   Salih, *Season of Migration to the North* 93.
159   Salih, *Season of Migration to the North* 137.

"Everything which happened before my meeting her was a premonition; everything I did after I killed her was an apology, not for killing her, but for the lie that was my life."[160] The relation to and murder of Jean Morris is central to the novel's meta-ethical ambivalence. From their very first encounter, she humiliates Mustafa with her "look of arrogance [and] coldness."[161] Unlike other English women, she intentionally humiliates him with blatant racism—"You're a savage bull that does not weary of the chase,'"[162] "'I've never seen an uglier face than yours."[163]—and publicly expresses her discriminating views regarding his cultural inferiority. Although Mustafa swears early on that he "would one day make her pay for that,"[164] he nevertheless falls in love with Jean and makes her his wife. Because she openly lies to Mustafa and thus speaks some truth, and precisely because she refuses to pretend that he can possess her, the course of emotions gets successively out of control. Even when he explicitly threatens to kill Jean, she does not give up provoking his violent aggression of bashed honor: "'What's stopping you from killing me? What are you waiting for? Perhaps you're waiting till you find a man lying on top of me, and even then I don't think you'd do anything."[165] There are rare moments of partial truthfulness between the two. When Mustafa shouts at Jean that he hates her, she answers: "'I too, my sweet, hate you. I shall hate you until death."[166]

The night of Jean's murder is not only "the night of truth and of tragedy"[167] but also the night of ultimate lies. While Mustafa presses his dagger into her breast and blood gushes from the chest of the very woman that he so much desires, the two confess their mutual love for the first and the last time. The murder of Jean Morris marks a turning point in Mustafa's life. It symbolically reverses the colonial imagination of the feminized or castrated native Arab by turning him into the hyper-potent agent of the conquest of European women. Only those who consider the extremely destructive part of the economy of human lust can interpret this violent gesture of power as one of sexual conquest. One can hardly speak of an anti-colonial act of political liberation. But that seems to be precisely Mustafa Sa'eed's perception of what happens that night. In the courtroom, he relives his own pre-murder identity as "an illusion, a lie."[168] While the accused is exhibited as an "example of the fact that our civilizing mission in Africa is of no avail,"[169] he

---

160   Salih, *Season of Migration to the North* 29.
161   Salih, *Season of Migration to the North* 29.
162   Salih, *Season of Migration to the North* 33.
163   Salih, *Season of Migration to the North* 30.
164   Salih, *Season of Migration to the North* 30.
165   Salih, *Season of Migration to the North* 162.
166   Salih, *Season of Migration to the North* 159.
167   Salih, *Season of Migration to the North* 163.
168   Salih, *Season of Migration to the North* 32.
169   Salih, *Season of Migration to the North* 93.

himself has a "feeling of superiority."[170] There is the triumph of rebellion, rather than redemption, in his emotions. Dignity and happiness for him are not choices but must be achieved in a painful struggle. It seems that the West's violation of the idea of shared humanity has been countered by an equally violent strategy. This practice might not be legitimate from a strictly normative point of view, but it can be justified by Mustafa.

As Muhsin al-Musawi in my view correctly argues, Mustafa of *Season of Migration to the North* can easily be mistaken for the theoretician of racism and anti-colonial critic, Frantz Fanon.[171] Musawi draws in particular on the Fanon of *Black Skin, White Masks*.[172] Seen through this psychoanalytical lens, one can indeed interpret Mustafa as an abandoned neurotic whose attitude is to not truly love the racial other in order to avoid being abandoned on racist grounds. Accordingly, his tragically impossible love story would demonstrate how the colonial-racist discourse of superiority and inferiority is embodied in both sexual desire and neurotic discontent. In this line of argument, the drama of Mustafa's sexual preoccupation with white women represents the painful breaking of an internalized racist taboo.[173] His emotional and physical violence against white women would be the direct expression of his neurotic need for revenge. Mustafa's "quest for white flesh,"[174] in other words, would be that of an alienated psyche.

An alternative view of looking at Mustafa's performance might be offered in Fanon's theory of anti-colonial violence as articulated in *The Wretched of the Earth*.[175] In his reflections on violence, Fanon not only argues that colonialism, at the outset, "is violence in its natural state, and it will only yield when confronted with greater violence,"[176] but he also acknowledges that the "native replies to the living lie of the colonial situation by an equal falsehood."[177] Fanon's consideration of truth and lie in the context of violence stresses that anti-colonial truth is simply that which makes the break-up of the colonialist-racist regime possible. Just as he sees violence inherent in the colonial order, he argues that there are necessarily lies at work in the disciplining judgment and classification of non-white people.[178] Now, while Fanon acknowledges that the entrenchment of violence in individual and collective life makes revolutionary violence necessary, he does not explain how the vicious circle

170   Salih, *Season of Migration to the North* 94.
171   Al-Musawi, *The Postcolonial Arabic Novel: Debating Ambivalence* 195.
172   Frantz Fanon, *Black Skin, White Masks*, trans. Charles Lam Markmann (1967; London : Pluto P, 2008), orig. *Peau noire, masques blancs* (Paris : Ed. du Seuil, 1952).
173   Fanon, *Black Skin, White Masks* 52-54.
174   Fanon, *Black Skin, White Masks* 59.
175   Frantz Fanon, *The Wretched of the Earth*, trans. Constance Farrington (1967; London : Penguin, 2001), orig. *Les damnés de la terre* (Paris : Maspero, 1961).
176   Fanon, *The Wretched of the Earth* 61.
177   Fanon, *The Wretched of the Earth* 50.
178   Fanon, *The Wretched of the Earth* 46.

of colonial lies can be broken. Could one argue that, if lying is the discursive standard of the colonialist-racist order, then this order will only yield when confronted
with greater lies? Could one, in other words, see in Mustafa Sa'eed's lies a resistive
strategy of counter-lies?

The tragic end of Mustafa's transmigration actually counters the idea that using
lies may be his way to avoid being lied to. Even after his return to his native country,
he remains trapped in the violence and the lies he has both inflicted and suffered.
Until the narrator forces Mustafa to tell the lies of his life, he hides his secrets
and his memories in his concealed drawing room as in the attic of a Gothic horror
novel. Against this background, the revolutionary insistence on the Sudanese people's right to lie does not signal a "denial of historical agency"[179] or a mystification
of the true urgencies of the unfinished liberationist struggle, as critics like Waïl S.
Hassan want to have it. In my view, the self-confident statement rather anticipates
a literary meta-ethics which, instead of morally condemning acts of lying, rehabilitates the strategic use of partial truth, lies, and counter-lies as justifiable forms of
political agency—an agency that, in a similar way, guides the transgressive syntax
and correlational narrative techniques of Anglophone Arab truth-making: "Once
again we shall be as we were—ordinary people—and if we are lies we shall be lies
of our own making."[180]

Mustafa Sa'eed's lies do not always, or at least not ultimately, lead to the destruction of himself or of others. When he delivers a lecture at Oxford on the Abbasid poet, Abu Nuwas, for instance, he claims that the poet, known for his homo-
erotic Bacchic poems,[181] was an Islamic mystic and that, therefore, wine functions
in his poetry as a symbol of his "spiritual yearnings" and his "longing for self-oblit-
eration in the Divine."[182] What he presents to the illustrious audience is basically
"all arrant nonsense with no basis of fact."[183] After he reads out some poems "in a
comic oratorical style which [he] claimed was how Arabic poetry used to be recited
in the Abbasid era," the lecturer Mustafa Sa'eed is quite inspired and finds "the
lies tripping off [his] tongue like sublime truths."[184] It is on this occasion, after his
extravagant academic show, that he first meets Ann Hammond, a young Oxford
student of Arabic literature and a fetishist regarding all things Oriental. She finds
him "beautiful beyond description."[185] He calls her Sausan and pretends to know
her from their shared time in Baghdad during the days of the caliph El-Ma'amoun.

179   Waïl S. Hassan, *Tayeb Salih: Ideology and the Craft of Fiction* (Syracuse: Syracuse UP, 2003) 122.

180   Salih, *Season of Migration to the North* 50.

181   See, on Abu Nuwas's controversial place in Arab discourse, Joseph A. Massad, *Desiring Arabs*
       (Chicago: U of Chicago P, 2007) 77-98.

182   Salih, *Season of Migration to the North* 143.

183   Salih, *Season of Migration to the North* 143.

184   Salih, *Season of Migration to the North* 143.

185   Salih, *Season of Migration to the North* 143.

She is enamored by the evening's Abbasid flair. Together, they drive to London. When he takes his new girlfriend to his house to recite Abu Nuwas to her privately, she takes on the role of his slave girl. Mustafa does not hesitate to act the part of the master: "It was as if she and I were on a stage."[186] Whereas the novelistic scene stresses the importance of performativity both on the story level and with a view to the narrator's act of narration, and although the performative determination of the remembered sexual encounter is openly acknowledged by Mustafa, he recounts the evening as a rare moment of *not-honest-yet-true* ecstasy:

> Though I realized I was lying, I felt that somehow I meant what I was saying and that she too, despite her lying, was telling the truth. It was one of those rare moments of ecstasy for which I would sell my whole life; a moment in which, before your very eyes, lies are turned into truth, history becomes a pimp, and the jester is turned into a sultan.[187]

It is not so much the stage-like situation but rather these words of Mustafa that will remind the Shakespearean scholar of the rhyming couplet of the English bard's Sonnet 138, which ambiguously plays out the flattering erotic of mutual lying: "Therefore I lie with her, and she with me, / And in our faults by lies we flattered be."[188]

   There are in fact several allusions to Shakespeare's work in *Seasons of Migration to the North*. When Mustafa Sa'eed is obstinately debriefed regarding his precise biological race by Isabella Seymour during one of his rather short affairs, he answers: "'I am like Othello—Arab-African.'"[189] However, in the courtroom, he wishes he had shouted at the jury: "I am no Othello. I am a lie.'"[190] Later, he renounces both his self-identification and acting according to the European imaginary of racial blackness as well as the mimetic representativeness of the very dramatic character functioning as this imaginary's key reference: "'I am no Othello. Othello was a lie.'"[191] As I have repeatedly pointed out over the course of this study, modern Arabic and Anglophone Arab literatures participated in the anti- and postcolonial re-reading or re-writing of the Western and Arabic canonical texts. And perhaps there is no text in the English canon that "shows better the exploitation of race and color prejudice than *Othello*."[192] If it is true that, due to its Moorish hero, this tragic play touches the

186 Salih, *Season of Migration to the North* 144.
187 Salih, *Season of Migration to the North* 144.
188 William Shakespeare, Sonnet 138, *The Riverside Shakespeare*, ed. G. Blakemore Evans (Boston: Houghton Mifflin, 1974) 1774.
189 Salih, *Season of Migration to the North* 38.
190 Salih, *Season of Migration to the North* 33.
191 Salih, *Season of Migration to the North* 95.
192 wa Thiong'o, *Globalectics: Theory and the Politics of Knowing* 21.

"chords of Arab sensibility and identity"[193] more than other Shakespearean works, one cannot be surprised to find Tayeb Salih using the dramatic character as an intertextual foil to underline the lies involved in the encounter between the Afro-Arab man of color and the white European woman and to test the universal or timeless validity of the Othello-type imaginary. The narrative of the assumingly prodigal Sudanese who kills his English wife in a moment of violent ecstasy has been variously interpreted as *Heart of Darkness* in reverse, an *Arabian Nights* in reverse, or as a story of a modern-day Othello.[194] However, as Barbara Harlow reminds us regarding the last of these comparisons, it is important to see that Salih's novel is a "re-shaping of the tragic figure of the Moor."[195] Mustafa Sa'eed not only rejects the identification with Shakespeare's essentially non-European outsider, but he also rejects the act of killing himself after he has killed the Desdemona-like Jean Morris. The anti-Othello narrative assimilates the classic play without fully integrating into the dramatic sub-genre of tragedy. There is no hamartia, no inherent tragic flaw, no mistake of judgment in the hero. What is rather the inherent defect or shortcoming is the dominant racist perception of him. Neither he nor his narrating alter-ego end in full adversity. Anticipating something else beyond the catastrophe of the endless repetitions of Western lies, their life stories do not simply purge the reader of pity. This utopian and maybe revolutionary anticipation turns the sentimental presentation of cultural otherness into a cross-cultural allegory. Unlike Othello, who accepts his role as an army general fighting on behalf of Europe, Mustafa finally refuses to act according to the role assigned to him by the early modern European hypotext. What fails is the role of the Moor, not the 20th century Arab acting it. Contemporary Anglophone Arabs cannot afford to read or perform Shakespeare while colorblind.[196] In my view, *Season of Migration to the North* must be read as the attempt to partially revise *Othello* through the prism of a (formerly) colonized person of color. It seems that such Arab re-reading only looks into the classic play to critically face its own racialized image as an object of alterity before counter-discursively adjusting the borrowed representation according to its own political typologies.

I have mentioned *Don Quixote* and the *Nights* alongside the Bible and the Quran as important intertexts of Anglophone Arab representations. One cannot but add Shakespeare to this open-ended list. To point out that the work of "the icon of

---

193   Ferial J. Ghazoul, "The Arabization of Othello," *Comparative Literature*, 50.1 (1998): 1.

194   Denys Johnson-Davies, Translator's Introduction, *Season of Migration to the North*, by Tayeb Salih (New York: Kesend, 1989).

195   Barbara Harlow, "Sentimental Orientalism: Season of Migration to the North and Othello," *Tayeb Salih's Season of Migration to the North: A Critical Casebook*, ed. Mona Takieddine Amyuni (Beirut: American U of Beirut P, 1985) 75-79.

196   Cf. Ayanna Thompson, ed., *Colorblind Shakespeare: New Perspectives on Race and Performance* (New York: Routledge, 2006).

genius of British imperial culture"[197] also forms an important referential corpus in this particular cultural field is almost redundant. In fact, the same may be said for virtually all 20th-century writings in English. However, contemporary Arabic and Anglophone Arab representations not only testify "the large extent to which we are [all] possessed by him [Shakespeare],"[198] but also the extent to which Shakespeare's work has been seized by Arab writers and artists.

This process of assimilation and multiple revisions began with the first translation and production of *Othello* in Egypt in 1884,[199] and it is continuing in the Arab productions of the 2012 World Shakespeare Festival in London or the many plays written and produced during and after the so-called Arab Spring.[200] At this point, one should note that the author of the above-mentioned novels, *Hunters in a Narrow Street* and *In Search of Walid Masoud*, is considered among the most important Arabic translators of Shakespeare's plays.[201] When writing his 1978 novel, Jabra in fact undertook the translation of *Othello*.[202] It is significant that he re-Arabized Othello's name and, by extension, the title of the play into *'Utayl* while he transliterated all other characters' names to reflect their English pronunciation.[203] Whereas *Othello* often functions as a paradigmatic matrix for the critique of Orientalist discrimination and gendered violence, *The Tempest* has rarely been read in Arab discourse as a more "comprehensive allegory"[204] of the violent dialectics of the colonial master-slave relation and the importance of language as a power tool in the colonial encounter. If Arabic or Anglophone Arab writers revisit at all the wretched situation of Shakespeare's savage chained to a rock, they hardly do so to write back to Western possessors of repressive book magic. The "almost iconic status"[205] that the cursing character, Caliban, has arisen to in South American and Caribbean literatures cannot be diagnosed for the Arabic and Anglophone Arab discourse. To my knowledge, there exists no Arabic or Anglophone Arabic work comparable to Aimé Césaire's *Une Tempête*, although it is worth noting that the anti-colonial Martiniquan

197   wa Thiong'o, *Globalectics: Theory and the Politics of Knowing* 21.
198   Harry Levin, General Introduction, *The Riverside Shakespeare*, ed. G. Blakemore Evans (Boston: Houghton Mifflin, 1974) 25.
199   Muhammad Mustafa Badawi, "Shakespeare and the Arabs," *Cairo Studies in English* 26-27 (1964/1965): 183.
200   Margaret Litvin, Saffron Walkling, and Raphael Cormack, ""Full of Noises: When 'World Shakespeare' met the 'Arab Spring,'" *Shakespeare* 12.3 (2016): 300-15.
201   See Mejcher-Atassi, *Reading Across Modern Arabic Literature and Art* 51. Among Jabra's translations of Shakespeare's plays are those of *Hamlet, King Lear, Coriolanus, Othello, The Tempest*, and *Macbeth*; see ibd. 145-46.
202   Ghazoul, "The Arabization of Othello," 6.
203   Jabra Ibrahim Jabra, *'Util* [Shakespeare's *Othello*] (Kuwait: Wizarat al-I'lam, 1978).
204   Bill Ashcroft, *Caliban's Voice: The Transformation of English in Post-Colonial Literatures* (London: Routledge, 2009) 16.
205   Ashcroft, *Caliban's Voice: The Transformation of English in Post-Colonial Literatures* 17.

poet and politician's French-language play was first performed at an international festival in Hammamet, Tunisia, in 1969.[206]

Modern Arabic cultural debates and literary practice have been particularly concerned with the fate of the Danish Prince Hamlet. Dramatic adaptations and other appropriations of *Hamlet* have become a constant feature of the region's postcolonial cultural discourse. It seems that, particularly since the 1967 Arab defeat, this play has proved suitable for exploring and criticizing the rotten internal situation in many Arab nations. As Margaret Litvin demonstrates, *Hamlet's Arab Journey*[207] is closely related to the political presence and ghostly afterlife of Gamal Abdel Nasser's (failed) revolutionary promise. The deployment and negotiation of *Hamlet* is not primarily concerned with questions of resistance against Western hegemony but can be grasped as the "Hamletization of the Arab Muslim political hero."[208] Against the background of earlier ideological adaptations of Shakespeare's play as self-empowering expressions of the emerging nation's pan-Arab aspirations in the 1950s, the more recent Hamlet rhetoric serves the inward interrogation of those postheroic regimes which proved to be unable to fix what is obviously *out of joint* inside the Arab world. While Hamlet was mobilized against Claudius-like corrupt military leaders, feudal dictators, and neoliberal autocrats of the late 1960s and early 1970s, he has in more recent decades developed into a tragic and sometimes ironic anti-hero of unarticulated passivity, political ineffectuality, and the bitter laugher of those hoping for democratic change on the basis of human rights.[209] In 2000, the Syrian philosopher and prominent critic of what he coined "istishraq ma'akusan" [Orientalism in reverse],[210] Sadiq al-Azm, directly related the unrelieved tragedy of 20th-century Arab societies to their hesitating oscillation and failed reconciliation between sentimental recourses to a glorious past and coming to terms with the present reality as the necessary condition for holding oneself responsible for the future. Al-Azm sees in the contemporary Arab intellectual's search for a modern identity in the cultural and religious heritage of classical Islamic empires a subconscious fetishistic procrastination: one that, according to him, prevents awareness of the all-too-evident everyday actualities of de-facto Arab sociopolitical and economic impotence. It is precisely this presumption of the deficit of insight regarding the de-facto historical agency of the region's people that leads him to compare them

---

206 Philip Crispin, "Césaire's *Une Tempête* at The Gate," *'The Tempest' and Its Travels*, eds. Peter Hulme and William Howard Sherman (London: Reaction Books, 2000) 149.

207 Margaret Litvin, *Hamlet's Arab Journey: Shakespeare's Prince and Nasser's Ghost* (Princeton: Princeton UP, 2011).

208 Litvin, *Hamlet's Arab Journey: Shakespeare's Prince and Nasser's Ghost* 90.

209 See, on this transformation, Margaret Litvin, "Vanishing Intertexts in the Arab '*Hamlet* Tradition'," *Arab Shakespeare*, spec. issue of *Critical Survey* 19.3 (2007): 74-97.

210 Sadik Jalal al-Azm, "Al-istishraq wa-l-istishraq ma'akusan," [Orientalism and Orientalism in reverse] *Hayat al-Jadida* 1.3 (1981): 7-51.

to Shakespeare's Danish prince: "[M]odern Arabs are truly the Hamlet of the 20th century."[211] One does not have to agree entirely with al-Azm's pessimistic diagnosis to see the ramifications of his polemical intervention; the popular uprisings of the early 21st century in many Arab countries allow, at least partly, for more optimistic estimations. However, the equally Orientalist and Arab nationalist notion of Arabs who are caught between religious tradition and secular modernity was and continues to be a very powerful narrative throughout the 20th century, and Hamlet is one of its key allegorical tropes.

I must draw once again on Rihani to show that the Hamletian trope has entered Anglophone Arab representations very early on, perhaps even before it became a part of internal Arabic discourses. My case in point is once more *The Book of Khalid*. When the young immigrant Khalid oscillates between assimilating into the materialistic order of his host country and thus corrupting himself or staying true to his immanent morality and, in so doing, revolting against the American cash registers—"To trade, or not to trade"—the editor-narrator describes his anti-hero as "Hamlet-Khalid."[212] This novel, whose author allegedly ran away from his father's US business at the age of eighteen to join a traveling Shakespeare company called the Henry Jewett Players,[213] pleads quite ambivalently for a revolt against the ruling spirit of his time. Rihani does so with a view to both the dominant tendencies of his native Arab and his adopted Western locations. It is my argument that Anglophone Arab writers have not given up this project of relational opposing and cross-cultural transgression. Rihani's turn-of-the-century novel, like most of the works discussed in the previous chapters, suggests that the proper intertextual study of any Anglophone Arab representation requires familiarity with virtually all artistic practices and critical discourses of potentially every temporal and geographical space on which the individual work draws. This, of course, is not a task for a single scholar of comparative literature, relational diasporic studies, or cross-cultural theory. To accomplish such an endeavor, one would rather need a transcultural community of polymaths.

---

211   Sadik Jalal al-Azm, "Owning the Future: Modern Arabs and Hamlet," *ISIM Newsletter* 5 (2000): 11.
212   Rihani, *The Book of Khalid* 127.
213   Fine, Afterword, *The Book of Khalid* 318.

4.2   Edward Said in Anglophone Arab Works and in this Study

> "What are the East and the West? If you
> ask me, I don't know. We must settle for
> approximations."[214]

At the beginning of this chapter, I introduced the Shahrazadian trope as a key reference for my understanding of Anglophone Arab poetics. I have further argued that this trope stands for the critical project of permitting and perpetuating marginalized voices and can thus function as a narrative model for anti-hegemonic resistance and counter-discursive strategies of emancipation. Although the significance of the *Nights* for Anglophone Arab discourse concerns narratological and metafictional dimensions in equal measure, the Shahrazadian discourse's particular relevance for contemporary fictocritical practice first and foremost concerns its subversive insights into the relation between power and narrative.

It is this very relation that forms the core of Edward Said's literary and cultural critique—a critical corpus known for its analysis of colonial discourses as well as for his contrapuntal readings of imperialism, a textual corpus that 17 years after Said's death seems to be well preserved in the everyday curriculum of international criticism. The name of the author of the seminal 1978 study, *Orientalism*, has almost advanced to a critical trope in his own right. At the same time, one can get the impression that the Saidian trope has been subdued to a standardized scholarly tool and compulsory reference of instant postcolonialism. Speaking of a Saidian trope in relation to Anglophone Arab nocturnal discourses, I do not argue at all that Said's critique should be read as a direct reverberation of the Shahrazadian discourse. Actually, his work shows little interest in the narrative structure and metafictional implications of the *Nights*. If he addresses the tales, they are treated primarily as either uninspired or tendentious translations by Burton and Lane, as examples of Orientalist mis-representation.[215] However, for my purpose of re-reading the Saidian text as both an Anglophone Arab intertext and an Anglophone Arab text, one can easily point out several structural and meta-critical similarities between Shahrazad's narrative subversion of the king's truth-regime and Said's critical project of *Speaking Truth to Power*.[216] According to Paul Bové, it is this self-imposed strategic task of "speaking truth *against* power and building the severe poetic institutions of freedom and justice"[217] that sets Said's critique apart from the work of other academic critics of his time. While, for Shahrazad, storytelling is a quasi-

---

214   Borges, "The Thousand and One Nights," 564.

215   See Said, *Orientalism* 164, 176.

216   Paul A. Bové, *Edward Said and the Work of the Critic: Speaking Truth to Power* (Durham: Duke UP, 2000).

217   Bové, *Edward Said and the Work of the Critic: Speaking Truth to Power* 6.

political form of resistance and subversion, Said's criticism posits storytelling as so powerful "that he urges it as a form of political action and testimony."[218] His critique of grand narratives—most obviously those of empire, Orientalism, and the clash of cultures—as a condition for dialogue and justice stresses the central nexus between history, narrative power, and politics. Like Shahrazad, Said has somehow narratively reinvented himself as the agent of a critique that is directed against the very set of discursive rules that perceive him as a passive Oriental object. For him, as for her, the "Permission to Narrate"[219] is the inevitable condition for non-violent resistance as a practice of narrating one's own (his)stories within and against the discourse of power. While her storytelling is directed against patriarchal power, his critical narrative first and foremost aims at countering colonial-Orientalist representations. Both struggle unrelentingly against their silencing and the silencing of those marginalized groups with which they affiliated. Both texts take the liberty to include diverse narratives from discrepant historical and cultural contexts. And Said's almost classical critique, like the *Nights*, is constantly fraught with a mixture of need and rejection by its competing recipients.

That his work is important as an intertext for contemporary Anglophone Arab representations cannot come as a surprise. In fact, these narrative, audio-visual, or performative attempts at uncovering dominances, at articulating what has not been articulated, and at showing what has been made invisible are often inspired by direct or indirect encounters with Said's critique. Some of the most prominent Anglophone Arab writers, artists, and critics, such as Ahdaf Soueif, Emily Jacir, or Ferial Ghazoul, were students of Said. For many others, the internationally renowned scholar was a mentor. It would be difficult to exaggerate the intellectual impact of his critique of Western Orientalist representations. Hardly any book in recent history has managed to draw such complex simultaneous reactions, both positive and negative, across the disciplines on a truly global level as did *Orientalism*. Arab and Anglophone Arab readers were a significant share of these reactions, from both inside and outside the academy. But they do not at all form a homogenous audience. Sure, Said's role for the resurgence and development of Anglophone Arab writing "cannot be underestimated."[220] Yet, the spectrum of this impact is extremely heterogeneous and cannot possibly be narrowed down to strictly affirmative voices.

In other words, one should not underestimate the number of those writers, artists, and critics who were long "sick and tired of having only Edward Said speak-

---

218   Bové, *Edward Said and the Work of the Critic: Speaking Truth to Power* 2.

219   Edward W. Said, "Permission to Narrate," *Journal of Palestine Studies* 13.3 (1984): 27-48.

220   Hassan, *Immigrant Narratives: Orientalism and Cultural Translation in Arab American and Arab British Literature* 28.

ing"[221] on their behalf or who made him responsible for generations of Arab students who "spend their time and intellectual energy critiquing Western stereotypes and images of Empire in the novels of George Eliot, rather than actually looking at and analyzing contemporary artistic production in the Arab world."[222] Yes, Said was there before to make us "believe, if just for a moment, that academia is not pointless."[223] He was and still is an icon for many Anglophone Arabs. However, people tend to kill their idols if they want to press on and do something new. Anglophone Arab artists and critics are no exception in this regard: "He demonstrated that Orientalism does indeed exist, as an overpowering discursive contraption, brilliant, surreptitious, and monumental at once, thoroughly conservative and yet incredibly mobilizing, a tenuous abstraction with very tangible effects. Not unlike Said himself."[224]

I have elsewhere explored at length the genesis and multidirectional impact of Said's work beyond the spheres of literary and cultural studies. My 2008 book, *Kulturkritik ohne Zentrum*, traces the importance of Arab pre-texts and receptions of Said's criticism (Middle Eastern as well as diasporian) for our understanding of his traveling oeuvre, with a particular focus on its impact on critical Arab debates and his own adaptations of Arabic criticism. The book also demonstrates that Middle Eastern studies have been enduringly altered and often divided into opposing camps by Said's critique of the academic discipline. This long-time project must surely have fed into my readings of Anglophone Arab representation. For that reason, Said's emphasis on the struggle over representations of competing histories, overlapping spatial constructions, and identity was of relevance for the genesis of my present study, as well.

Nevertheless, I attempt to spare neither Said's thinking nor my own previous reception of his work's rigorous critical revision. While acknowledging the importance of the historical analysis of Orientalist power-knowledge, I do question some of his historical tracings (i.e., his focus on the post-Enlightenment era) and intentionally subvert his privileging of the Anglo-American canon as well as controvert the pessoptimist's humanistic notion of harmony. In addition, I have found myself repeatedly questioning the critic's responsibility to disenchant and the idealist notion of historical truth and truth-speaking as the inescapable condition of effective

---

221   Statement by an anonymous artist during the conference *Ashghal Daakhaliya – Homeworks*, 2–7 Apr. 2002, City Theatre of Beirut. The international conference and artistic forum, the first of its kind, was organized by the artist association, *Ashkal Alwan*.

222   Walid Sadik, quoted by Stephen Wright, "Tel un espion dans l'époque qui naît: la situation de l'artiste à Beyrouth aujourd'hui / Like a Spy in a Nascent Era: On the Situation of the Artist in Beirut Today," *Parachute, Beyrouth_Beirut* 108 (2002): 25.

223   Tirdad Zolghadr, "Thanks God He Wasn't French: Notes on Edward Said (1935–2003)," *Bidoun* 5 (2005): 41.

224   Zolghadr, "Thanks God He Wasn't French: Notes on Edward Said (1935–2003)," 41.

cultural resistance. I think Said's latent social elitism and conservatism as well as his admirable insistence on the value of the human allowed him to sometimes forget the dialectic commonplace of the critique of ideology that even truths are not timeless. While I can perfectly see the strategic need to hold on to the illusion of candor, I do not want to deny Anglophone Arab representations' critical capacity to lie strategically, to utilize sub-harmonic aesthetics, or to contradict themselves intentionally. My interest in dissonant set-ups of (maybe, but not necessarily) mutually correcting cultural archives, in other words, draws on many of Said's insights and yet is bound to go beyond his notion of contrapuntal harmonics. I regard the Saidian corpus as belonging to both Western academia and to a broader Anglophone Arab diasporic discourse. Numerous diasporic scholars of Arab (af)filiation anticipated Said's work, and this work in turn participated in the formation of "a critical Middle Eastern/Arab diasporic studies project,"[225] a project in which I place my own study. According to Ella Shohat, "Said's *Orientalism* can also be regarded as an Arab American Studies text," a project that aims to institutionalize an interdisciplinary "polylogue" that transcends ethnic studies and area studies approaches alike.[226]

Let me illustrate my relational reading and decentering of Said's text by revisiting *Orientalism*'s "being in the world"[227] and by looking at the critic Said in his capacities as a reader, writer, and politically engaged person instead of synthesizing his ambivalent position and relegating him to a depoliticized sphere of theoretical transculturality or postcoloniality. If I underline the particular Arab conditions determining the emergence and acceptance of Said's work, it is not to prove that this work is an Anglophone Arab one and indeed part of Anglophone Arab studies—I take that for granted. I rather wish to sensitize my reader to the fact that this work was produced by a person whose chosen identity was based on the secular political commitment to being Palestinian. In my view, re-reading Said's Anglophone work via selected Arab(ic) readings can also provide a critical counterpoint to interpretive strategies of theoretically domesticating a work that has in fact traveled through many locations and histories and that, in turn, was affected by those many worlds. Willful ignorance of the dynamics that transformed Said's literary criticism into a project with political change as its purpose (and vice versa) not only misses the critic's concrete involvement in the Palestinian liberation movement but in addition excludes what is supposedly one of Said's most obvious interpretive communities: (Anglophone) Arab readers, writers, and artists.

If one evaluates those situations in which Said's text enters into a relationship with concrete socio-political issues and theoretical positions within the Mid-

---

225   Shohat, "The Sephardi-Moorish Atlantic: Between Orientalism and Occidentalism," 46.
226   Shohat, "The Sephardi-Moorish Atlantic: Between Orientalism and Occidentalism," 46.
227   Edward W. Said, *The World, the Text, and the Critic* (Cambridge: Harvard UP, 1983) 35.

dle East, thus playing a role itself in the worldliness of which it speaks, then Said's self-description as an Arab by choice can be grasped as a transgressive act that aims at connecting or at least relating two spheres that are all too often mutually ghettoized: his own preeminence in the postcolonial field and the Palestinian struggle for self-determination. The 1975 meta-theoretical essay, *Beginnings: Intention and Method*,[228] can already be evaluated as a first intentional step to integrate his political life into his academic praxis. Anticipating the discussion of themes such as eurocentrism, colonialism, and racism into Western literary theory, as later carried out in *Orientalism* (1978) and *Culture and Imperialism* (1993), it marks a key turning point in Said's "unsettled intellectual way" from a doctoral Conrad scholar firmly rooted in the phenomenological strains of New Criticism to the politicized inaugurator of colonial discourse analysis.[229] Already in this early book's conclusion, he calls for challenging the secret networks and ideological pre-figurations of institutional information "as a first turning back of power."[230] His notion of criticism insists on methodologically uniting theory with a moral and practical need for political change. While *Beginnings* does not provide a direct worldly reference for this project, thus leaving the reader with some metaphorical emptiness, it clearly opened up possible questions for Said's future research projects: "the question of the cultural domination of one intellectual or national domain over another (one culture is more 'developed' than—having begun earlier and 'arrived' before—another); and the questions of liberty, or freedom, or originality."[231] Following Hayden White's reading of *Beginnings* as an instance of "Criticism as Cultural politics,"[232] one can assume that the crucial point of departure for writing this study lies outside the system of Western literary criticism. To locate these other points of departure, it seems advisable to revisit the historical circumstances and individual experiences that informed the transformation of Said's critical practice. To this end, I look first at Said's second birth as a political agent.

Before the setback of the Arab-Israeli war of June 1967, the literary scholar consistently tried to exclude his Arab background from his professional life at Columbia University. Suddenly, however, his life could no longer be lived in separate parts. To be an Arab in the US during and after the 1967 war was an experience of collective racist stigmatization and personal humiliation.[233] At the same time, the emergence of the Palestinian Liberation Organization (PLO) as a

---

228   Edward W. Said, *Beginnings: Intention and Method* (New York: Columbia UP; Basic, 1975).
229   Subhy Hadidy, "Idward sa'id wa mufhum al-bidaya," [Edward Said and the meaning of beginning] *Al-Mulhaq ath-Thaqafi/An-Nahar* 28 Nov. 1998: 16.
230   Said, *Beginnings* 379.
231   Said, *Beginnings* 381.
232   Hayden White, "Criticism as Cultural Politics," *Diacritics* 6.3 (1976): 8-13.
233   Nubar Hovsepian, "Connections with Palestine," *Edward Said: A Critical Reader*, ed. Michael Sprinker (Oxford: Blackwell, 1992) 8.

political organization independent from other Arab regimes made it possible for a growing number of Palestinians in exile to identify themselves as belonging to one people and nation.[234] While Said's childhood experience of 1948 Cairo was a materially fortunate and "scarcely conscious"[235] one, the events of 1967 in the distant Palestinian world of his frequent family visits led to a fundamental identity crisis: "I was no longer the same person after 1967."[236] During the late 1960s and early 1970s, Said not only committed himself to a re-education in Arabic but also got involved in Palestinian intellectual debates and politics. He was introduced to Fatah-leader Yasser Arafat as early as 1969.[237] In 1971, the latter addressed the Palestinian academic diaspora in the West with a quite suggestive rhetoric: "How do you contribute to the liberation of Palestine?"[238] When Said spent his sabbatical in Beirut in 1972, he came into personal contact with other key actors of the PLO, which was located in the Lebanese capital at that time. Within a few years, in which Said produced an innovative study on the discursive predicaments of a socially responsible criticism,[239] he became a Palestinian activist scholar. If it was his personal intention to become a politically involved Palestinian and to act against the constraints of freedom and justice in Palestine, *Beginnings* is the first, but by no means Said's last, step toward its fulfillment.

While Said took on the role of a high-profile intellectual in the Middle East during the 1990s, the question of his identity remains controversial to this day. Can one really decide to be an Arab? The intense intra-Arab reactions to his memoir *Out of Place* (1999)—an Anglophone Arab auto-fictional work in its own right in which Said tries to make sense of his life by placing himself into Arabic history as a formerly colonized and Orientalized subject—are an impressive illustration of Said's ambivalent location within contemporary Arab cultural debates. To a large extent, these reactions are re-receptions of the attempt by non-Arab critics to contest the validity and symbolic implications of Said's auto-narration.[240] While some Arab readers discover their own feeling of alienation from the dominant Arab discourse

---

234 This is not at all to say that there was no distinct national Palestinian identity before 1967. See Rashid Khalidi, *Palestinian Identity: The Construction of Modern National Consciousness* (New York: Columbia UP, 1997).

235 Edward W. Said, *Out of Place: A Memoir* (New York: Knopf, 1999) 114.

236 Said, *Out of Place* 293.

237 *Power, Politics, and Culture: Interviews with Edward W. Said*, ed. Gauri Viswanathan (New York: Pantheon, 2001) 209.

238 Arafat as quoted by Hisham Ahmed-Fararjeh and Ibrahim Abu-Lughod, *Resistance, Exile, and Return* (The Ibrahim Abu-Lughod Institute of International Studies, Birzeit: Birzeit UP, 2003) 115.

239 "The kernel-essay of *Beginnings* was written during the winter of 1967–8; more of it developed in 1968 and 1969, and by winter 1972–3 most of it was completed." (Said, *Beginnings* xi.)

240 Justus Reid Weiner, "'My Beautiful Old House' and other Fabrications by Edward Said," *Commentary* 108.2 (1999): 23-31.

in this personal historiography, most critics defend the book as both a proof of the autobiographer's Arab identity and a representative Palestinian national statement on the will to narrate the Palestinian story and to claim the right of return from exile to an independent homeland.[241] As a response to this hyper-patriotic debate, Said, in September 2000, provocatively presented himself as "'arabi bi-l-ikhtiyar,"[242] as an Arab by choice. The essay "To Write is an Act of Memento and Oblivion"[243] was published in the Lebanese daily *An-Nahar* and is also the preface to the Arabic edition of his memoir. Here, Said stresses the narrative genesis of his Arab-Palestinian identity and explains the act of postcolonial identification as the strategic substitution of certain external inscriptions with other, more empowering self-interpretations. He underlines the need for intentionally beginning a new meaning instead of arguing for a return to an authentic origin. For Said, Arab-Palestinian identity by choice is first and foremost a political commitment of solidarity, and it is closely related to the aim of universalizing Palestinian human rights claims.[244]

In this context, it is important to remind ourselves that, although it is true that *Orientalism* does not amount to a coherent resistance theory, Said's most prominent work did not come out of some isolated hyper-discursive turns within the French and US academy or from a series of exclusively metropolitan struggles over civil rights, black power, third worldism, and anti-imperialism. Just like *The Question of Palestine* (1979) or *After the Last Sky* (1986), which explicitly aim at undermining the Western and Israeli practice of blocking the Palestinian presence by providing a narrative grounded in Palestinian experiences, Said's more scholarly works can also be seen as immediate responses to his active involvement in Palestinian politics. This activist dimension of his academic criticism is influenced by longstanding personal friendships and continuing collaborations with Palestinian and pro-Palestinian intellectuals, such as Ibrahim Abu-Lughod, Shafiq al-Hout, Jean Genet, Elias Khoury, Mahmoud Darwish, and Eqbal Ahmad.

Said cherished Abu-Lughod as his mentor and intellectual "guru."[245] Abu-Lughod was a key figure for the early formation and consolidation of a Palestinian-

241   See for example Fakhri Saleh, *difa'an idward sa'id* [In defense of Edward Said] (Beirut: Al-Mu'assasa al-'Arabiya li-d-Dirasat wa-n-Nashr, 2000) and Schmitz, *Kulturkritik ohne Zentrum* 54-58.

242   Edward Said, "al-kitaba fi'l tadhakkar wa nisyan," [To write is an act of memento and oblivion], *Al-Mulhaq ath-Thaqafi/An-Nahar* 16 Sept. 2000: 10. Here quoted from the preface to the Arabic translation of *Out of Place: kharij al-makan. mudhakkirat*, trans. Fawwaz Traboulsi (Beirut: Dar al-Adab, 2000) 9.

243   Said, "al-kitaba fi'l tadhakkar wa nisyan," 10.

244   Elias Khoury, "Wulidat filastin fi-l-'alam tahta qalamihi. idward sa'id: awwal al-'a'din," [Palestine came into being on a global level through/under his pen. Edward Said: The first returnee] *Al-Mulhaq ath-Thaqafi/An-Nahar* 28 Sept. 2003: 15.

245   Edward Said, "My Guru," *London Review of Books* 13 Dec. 2001: 19-20.

American academic activist network in the US.[246] It was he who introduced Said to the political actuality of the Palestinian liberation struggle, and it was he who, in 1967, asked his young colleague to write an article on the image of the Arab world in American mass media; "The Arab Portrayed"[247] is the first essay in a long series of shorter studies on the Western manipulation, distortion, and exclusion of Arab experiences that finally culminates in the publication of *Orientalism*.

Eqbal Ahmad worked for the information office of the Algerian *Front de Libéra-tion Nationale* under Frantz Fanon in the early 1960s. After having returned to the US, he became one of the most prominent figures of the so-called New Left. From the beginning of the 1970s onward, he mounted a local Palestinian resistance strat-egy of non-violent aggressiveness paired with a campaign for human rights in the West. In addition, Ahmad was an important personal link and epistemological agent between Fanon's anticolonial theory of resistance and Said's conception of a decolonized, culturally decentered, and contrapuntally reformed humanism.[248] It is to Abu-Lughod and Ahmad, and not to Michel Foucault, Fredric Jameson, Hayden White, or any other exponent of so-called Western high theory, that Said dedicated his two most influential books *Orientalism* and *Culture and Imperialism*.[249]

One cannot overlook the fact that Said's studies on the correlation between overseas practices of colonial domination and metropolitan forms of cultural rep-resentation are, even if not exclusively, also the instrument of a battle for political liberation whose setting happens to lie outside of Western academia. Produced un-der cover of literary criticism, they are meant to integrate the Palestinian struggle into Western platforms of representation. In this regard, Said's project of liberat-ing the academy can be directly linked to Ghassan Kanafani's trans-local resistance strategy.[250] At the same time, it places itself within a much broader critical move-ment within Anglophone Arab criticism since the late 1960s that historian Hisham Sharabi characterizes as the rejection and replacement of "the hegemonic West-ern discourse regarding the Other."[251] Against this discursive background, it seems indeed legitimate to call *Orientalism* "a partisan book."[252] It is both a foundational

246   Jamal R. Nassar, "Ibrahim Abu-Lughod: The Legacy of an Activist Scholar and Teacher," *Arab Studies Quarterly* 26.4 (2004): 23-24.

247   Edward W. Said, "The Arab Portrayed," *The Arab-Israeli Confrontation of June 1967: An Arab Per-spective*, ed. Ibrahim Abu-Lughod (Evanston: Northwestern UP, 1970) 1-9.

248   Radwa Ashour, "as-saut: frantz fanun, iqbal ahmad, idward sa'id," [The voice: Frantz Fanon, Eqbal Ahmad, Edward Said] *Alif* 25 (2005): 79.

249   *Orientalism* is dedicated to Abu-Lughod, *Culture and Imperialism* to Ahmad.

250   Barbara Harlow, "The Palestinian Intellectual and the Liberation of the Academy," *Edward Said: A Critical Reader*, ed. Michael Sprinker (Oxford: Blackwell, 1992) 173-93.

251   Hisham Sharabi, "The Scholarly Point of View: Politics, Perspective, Paradigm," *Theory, Politics and the Arab World: Critical Responses*, ed. Hisham Sharabi (London: Routledge, 1990) 21.

252   Said, *Orientalism* 340.

work of colonial discourse analysis and a Palestinian political intervention, without either project over-determining the other.

Orientalism, as an Anglophone Arab and Anglophone Arab studies text, represents many of the ambivalences that one comes across regularly when reading Anglophone Arab representations. Reviewing the by now seminal 1984 Essex Conference on the sociology of literature,[253] the Egyptian political scientist and human rights activist, Ahmed Abdalla, already brought the implications of Said's notion of alterity to the attention of his Arab readers. He pointed out that the concept of otherness propagated within the emerging field of postcolonial studies not only affirms a neo-imperialist possessive claim of dependency but primarily refers to Arabs and Muslims: "Europe's Others; these others—that's us."[254]

Said's significance was initially restricted to inner-Palestinian debates and to a relatively small group of writers and literary theorists, most of whom had studied in Europe or the US. It was only with _Orientalism_, however, that Said reached a larger audience. Translated into Arabic by Kamal Abu-Deeb in 1981,[255] it did not elicit purely positive reactions. From the outset, it has been used selectively to both maximize cultural difference strategically and to negate that very difference categorically. To this day, the book and its author's name are exploited as a canvas for projecting Islamanic and Islamophobic positions. Marxist and liberal Arab intellectuals, in particular, view the categorical denunciation of the Western modernity model by local academic elites as an intellectual cul-de-sac, partly blaming Said for this reverse orientalist trend.[256] But religious scholars also find it difficult to relate the historical formation and continuing effects of power relations analyzed by Said to their own cognitive procedures of explaining man's place in the world.[257] Turning a blind eye to his general critique of the idea of authentic origins and forced filiations, many critics initially questioned Said's cultural and ethnic belonging and his right to speak for the Arab world when his theoretical texts were first crossing West-Eastern borders.[258] Until well into the 1990s, the majority of his Arab critics regarded him as a representative of the American cultural industry. Long before the publication of Aijaz Ahmad's _In Theory_,[259] Arab intellectuals blamed Said for

253   Francis Barker, Peter Hulme, Margaret Iverson, and Diane Loxley, eds., _Europe and its Others: Proceedings of the Essex Conference on the Sociology of Literature, July 1984_ (Colchester: U of Essex, 1985).

254   Ahmed Abdalla, "uruba wa-l-akharun 'nahnu'" [Europe and the others 'we'], _Al-'Arab_ 24 July 1984: 5.

255   Edward W. Said, _al-istishraq: al-ma'rifa, as-sulta, al-insha'_ [Orientalism: the knowledge, the power, the discourse], trans. Kamal Abu-Deeb (Beirut: Mu'assasa al-Abhath al-'Arabiya, 1981).

256   For a prominent example, see Sadik Jalal al-Azm, "Orientalism and Orientalism in Reverse," _Khamsin_ 8 (1981): 5-26.

257   Schmitz, _Kulturkritik ohne Zentrum_ 230-37.

258   For the following, see the detailed analysis in my _Kulturkritik ohne Zentrum_ 307-59.

259   Aijaz Ahmad, _In Theory: Classes, Nations, Literatures_ (London: Verso, 1992).

privileging the Western metropolitan university as a virtually exclusive location of postcolonial pedagogy. Already in 1982, the leftist critic, Nadim al-Bitar, accused him of ignoring the material conditions of criticism in the Middle East and impeding the free articulation of cultural difference without Eurocentric hierarchy, thus reproducing the unequal international streams of capital and dependence relationships generated by colonialism.[260] The contrapuntal method formulated in *Culture and Imperialism* was seen as only a limited response to this accusation, its essential frame of reference still consisting of the classics of European cultural history. To many Arab critics, the notion of Arabness by choice appears less than suitable, given the oppressive conditions of their everyday work which rarely allow for free choices. Said's attempt to release the shackles of nationalist cohesion along with the discriminating fixations of colonial racist identifications has encountered (and still encounters) considerable resistance.

The reception of Said's work gradually shifted to the affirmative with his active involvement in public debates on the post-Oslo future of Palestine and his regular contributions to discussions on the role of the intellectual in relation to Arab civil society. However, in his political writings composed with a primarily Arab readership in mind,[261] but published bi-weekly in Arabic as well as in English,[262] the tension between national solidarity and critical insistence emerges openly. Criticizing the modalities of the so-called peace process as a betrayal of civil resistance and accusing Arafat of establishing a cleptocratic regime, the dissident in exile becomes a spokesperson for secular Palestinians disillusioned by the repressive implementation of the Oslo Agreement. As a co-founder of the *Al-Mubadara*, the *Palestinian National Initiative*, Said was an active commentator and participant in the expanding regional debate on civil and human rights, gaining influence over democracy movements in Palestine and in other Arab states. In his last decade, Said's presence within Arab critical debates grew significantly, with television appearances and other forays into the field of political journalism and public culture, and most of his scholarly works were translated into Arabic. He was a public intellectual in the Middle East, and this positionality in turn contributed to a wider appreciation of his more academic criticism. Many saw him as an alternative role model for contemporary Arab activist-intellectuals who found themselves pressed between

---

260 Nadim al-Bitar, "min al-istishraq al-gharbi ila-l-istishraq l-'arabi" [From Western Orientalism to Arabic Orientalism], *hudud al-huwiya al-qaumiya* [The limits of national identity], by Nadim al-Bitar (Beirut: dar al-wahda, 1982) 151-69.

261 Edward W. Said, *ghazza - ariha: salam amriki* [Gaza-Jericho: An American peace] (Cairo: Dar al-Mustaqbal, 1994) 15.

262 For the English versions, see *Peace and Its Discontents* (London: Vintage, 1995), *The End of the Peace Process: Oslo and After* (New York: Pantheon, 2000), and *From Oslo to Iraq and the Road Map* (New York: Pantheon; Toronto: Random, 2004).

the desires of illegitimate regimes to co-opt them and their marginalization as a consequence of the rise of political Islam.

This other Said might not be well known among most Western scholars of post-colonialism. However, the literary and cultural critic's ambivalent role as an Arab activist-intellectual during at least the last decade of his life gained growing importance with a view to his reception among Anglophone Arab writers, artists, and critics. It is, therefore, this Saidian text, perhaps more than the strictly academic texts of the internationally recognized inaugurator of colonial discourse analysis and postcolonial theory, that one needs to consider as an important intertext when reading Anglophone Arab representations. Said's text does not speak for Arabs or Anglophone Arabs in the diaspora. Yet his speech acts participated in the formation of that very discourse, perhaps more than many others. His strategic identification with the Arab American community, with Palestine, or with the Arab world often consciously flattened identificatory differences to secure political agency. The inherent essentialism of such identifications has been criticized by some and instrumentalized by others. Arabic or Anglophone Arab critics who claim his work or his name for creating the impression of ethnic coherence or natural unity risk the marginalization of those voices within the respective, already marginalized communities who do not (want to) exhibit readily observable signs of such group belonging. The double bind of Said's strategic essentialism would then be replicated in a kind of double marginalization,[263] and the anti-essentialist critique of *Orientalism* would be "simply an ephemeral pastime."[264]

---

263   See, on this particular dynamics of cultural identity politics, Gary C. David, "The Creation of 'Arab American': Political Activism and Ethnic (Dis)Unity," *Critical Sociology* 33.5-6 (2007): 833-62.

264   Edward W. Said, "Orientalism Reconsidered," *Cultural Critique* 1 (1985): 107.

5. Reading Anglophone Arab Enunciations Across Genres: Narrative Display, Performative Evidence, and the Parafiction of Theory

In the following, I will discuss selected Anglophone Arab enunciations that deal with the complex nexus of blocked and forced visibility, discrepant concepts of (non-)belonging and identity, competing representational modes of alterity, mutually excluding archives, and the limits of enunciability. Although the present discussion begins with an auto-fictional text, a popular narrative, and a fictocritical-theoretical discourse which either arise from the Arab ethnic situation of the US or were produced by intellectuals who strictly do not identify themselves with Arab Americans, the cultural sphere that my readings explore is a culture of transnational relations rather than one of ethnic identifications. Whereas I consider local conditions, such as the Palestinian situation in relation to the Anglophone Palestinian discourse, seriously, I pay particular attention to strategies and effects of critical revisions and artistic or literary re-significations under the condition of global migrations and cross-cultural encounters.

The Anglophone Arab articulations selected for this chapter have a particularly decentering and sometimes disorienting quality. Although their genesis is often tied to the experience of belonging to a stigmatized diasporic and/or otherwise marginalized group, they cannot be grasped simply as acts of translation between different cultures. These works transgress both the dominant image-repertoire of the Western archives and the leading representational modes of local Arab culture. They represent the recursive blurring effects of continuous crossovers. These effects have direct consequences for our understanding of taxonomic boundaries. By choosing the audiovisual arts, traveling literatures, and the sphere of theory as the subject matter of my cross-cultural analysis, the following readings are intended to go beyond the current predominant focus on Anglophone Arab literature. At the same time, my choices underline the continuing topical and structural overlaps across genre divides. In fact, the strict differentiation between works of literature and art, on the one hand, and the spheres of research and theory, on the other, is decisively questioned by some of the works which I discuss here. The overlap of the abstract formal and the socio-political, epistemic ideological in the artistic, literary, and cultural productions that I interpret here partly results from the importance of the hegemonic gaze of the anticipated Western reader, watcher, or listener. However, the genesis, functioning, and effects of narrative modes, artistic forms, or visual images cannot be grasped as sheer counter-discursive reactions. These works' critical inquiries and heterodox provocations do not just counter what passes for representation by Westerners but also challenge Occidentalist sureties. Their relational agency, in other words, is as self-questioning as it is self-determining.

While it is true that the literary and artistic works discussed here are more preoccupied with the seductiveness of critical practices and the effectiveness of their political poetics than with the creation of new aesthetic forms, the impetus of countering dominant lies can also lead to the innovative transgression of learned aesthetics. Although these works form themselves by reverting to dominant conventions of expression, they regularly express what has not yet been expressed. As social phenomena, they are produced at concrete historical moments, and as such, they speak to the worldly realities of their own conditionality. However, as works of art, they also chart new directions of aesthetic display. To explain Anglophone Arab representations as imaginaries of critical correlations, I demonstrate that these works do not simply counter Western representations by telling non-Western truths.

In my view, the spheres of concept and performance art sometimes offer more critical insight than works of literature or theory. If we understand works of concept and performance art as acts of artistic research, then these acts not only produce new narratives and images but also contribute to the exploration of alternative epistemologies and theories in transnational art, literatures, and comparative cultural criticism. They test out alternative ways of seeing, hearing, reading, narrating, and thinking and sometimes enable the remaking of the many worlds from which they derive, simultaneously within and against each other. Maybe more directly than works of other creative genres, they invite us to grasp Anglophone Arab representations as socio-cultural articulations shaped by but also requiring the representational norms that they anticipate. They do so by performing and thus illustrating that cultural signifiers do not necessarily relate to a stable signified; instead, they are by definition contested in cross-cultural correlations.

Whether I am dealing with literary narratives, artistic documents and audiovisual imageries, or works of theory and criticism, I approach Anglophone Arab representations both as scraps of historical evidence and as representations that (willingly or not) make visible the performative production of their own source materials and truth claims. I believe that the works I have chosen for this chapter explicitly admit to being shaped by the representational norms which they anticipate and that they openly perform the mechanisms of their own adjustment of meaning. Many of the works discussed represent what might be described as a particular parafictional strand of Anglophone Arab representations. They can be considered as examples of a representational practice that relies on the multiplicity of deception and the seriousness of doubt. Such doubts are directed at both the truth claims of hegemonic statements and the reliability of their own messages. Nevertheless, they do not end up in a celebration of skepticism. If these representations question their own performative reliability, they do so first and foremost with a view to their operational capability. They worry about their agency of enunciation rather than their moral integrity. It is on the basis of such extra-moral self-positioning that Anglophone Arab representations can transgress one-sided truths claims. And it is from here that they can imagine lies that tell other truths.

5.1 The Horrors of Assimilation, Uncanny Transferences, and the End of the Roots-Talk

> "I expel *myself*, I spit *myself* out, I abject *myself* within the same motion through which 'I' claim to establish *myself*."[1]

When the late Clifford Geertz critically reviewed several newly published, highly reductionist, crash-course-style books designed to explain Islam and the Arabs to the English-speaking world in June 2003, the anthropologist illustrated the long history of America's "casual mixture of ignorance and indifference"[2] by referring to a 1938 cartoon by Peter Arno. "Which way to Mecca?"—the title of Geertz's two-part review essay—quotes directly from Arno's short caption. The original drawing shows a pith-hatted tourist leaning out of his car to ask a turbaned man praying by the side of the road for the way to the holy city of Islam. Geertz demonstrates that post-9/11 attempts to produce and circulate a "public-square image of 'Islam'"[3] while being caught up in the know-your-enemy excitement of the present war on terror regularly draw on a long-established Orientalist tradition of standard accounts, ideological assumptions, and xenophobic symbolizations. One of the key examples of such new-old, cultural-essentialist, us-versus-them narratives is the controversial Middle East historian, Bernard Lewis. Lewis's public exposure reached new heights in the aftermath of the events of September 11, 2001. Although much of the

---

1   Julia Kristeva, *Powers of Horror: An Essay on Abjection*, trans. Leon S. Roudiez (New York: Columbia UP, 1982) 3.

2   Clifford Geertz, "Which Way to Mecca?," *Life Among Anthros and Other Essays*, by Clifford Geertz, ed. Fred Inglis (Princeton: Princeton UP, 2010) 135; the two-part review essay was first published in *The New York Review of Books* 50.10 (12 June 2003) and 50.11 (3 July 2003).

3   Geertz, "Which Way to Mecca?" 135.

book deals with the history of the late Ottoman Empire, his 2002 study *What Went Wrong?*[4] immediately acquired enormous popularity within and beyond the circles of academics and policymakers. In order to explain why the commercially successful decision to publish this book soon after the terror attacks went right for Lewis, one might look at the revised subtitle of the Weidenfeld & Nicolson edition *of the same year: The Clash Between Islam and Modernity in the Middle East.*[5] The Huntingtonian evocation of a clash between modern Western culture and Islamic tradition cannot be missed here. According to Lewis, the central intrinsic problem of Islamic religious and political thinking is its totalitarian character: hence, the conflict with the democratic West.

What is unprecedented in the American post-9/11 experience according to Geertz is that the construction of Arab-Muslim alterity as "an alien phenomenon, obscure and worrisome"[6] for the first time openly enters the American homeland's mainstream discourse. He argues that Americans can newly directly see the process of re-presenting the Arab-Muslim Other instead of just subcutaneously feeling or pop-culturally experiencing the uncanny results of that very process. If one believes Geertz's retrospective assertion, then the inner-worldly nexus of stereotypical representation and discriminating practices was not directly observable with regard to Arabs and Muslims before 9/11. One does not have to agree with the anthropologist's general argument regarding the newness of the situation to evaluate the experiences of the early 21st century as a further occasion for rethinking and critically revisiting the substantial "line between writing and the world."[7] That is what I intend to do in this sub-chapter.

Placing particular emphasis on the discourse of assimilation, I will selectively re-read the writings of two Americans whose works have little in common and whose relevance for and positionality within and outside of the Anglophone Arab discourse is quite controversial. By reading the novelist and screenplay writer, William Peter Blatty, side by side with the literary theoretician, Ihab Hassan, in a study like this one, I do not assume any shared Arab origin of the two writers; nor do I claim to trace a hidden exchange between their respective texts. I rather use, and perhaps misuse, selected writings by the two men to ask what went wrong in the process of cross-cultural exchange and mutual assimilation between the West and the Arab world. Instead of drawing on academic experts of the Middle East, like Lewis, or ideological prophets of Arabs' failed integration into the Westernized

---

4   Bernard Lewis, *What Went Wrong? Western Impact and Middle Eastern Response* (Oxford: Oxford UP, 2002).

5   Bernard Lewis, *What Went Wrong? The Clash Between Islam and Modernity in the Middle East* (London: Weidenfeld & Nicolson, 2002).

6   Geertz, "Which Way to Mecca?" 138.

7   Geertz, "Which Way to Mecca?" 156.

world order, like Samuel Huntington,[8] my interpretive search for meaning starts from the literary afterlife of Arno's cartoon, published on the eve of World War II.

5.1.1 The Laughter and Slaughter of Subjection

A woman with a stylish pillbox hat is a passenger in an American convertible racing through a landscape marked as Middle Eastern by a village with a minaret and a dome (fig. 15). The driver, her pith-helmet husband, barks at the praying man dressed in Muslim clothes and racially tagged as a hook-nosed Arab. The drawing depicts a haughty drive-through rather than a self-deprecating stopover. Without really breaking and waiting for the local's answer, the driver speeds on in a direction that he does not know. As we understand today, he drives into a Middle Eastern future that would soon be invaded by other American vehicles, with drivers wearing helmets of steel.[9]

In 1958, twenty years after this cartoon's first appearance in *The New Yorker*, the second generation Arab American immigrant writer, William Peter Blatty, best known for his 1971 bestseller, *The Exorcist*,[10] entitled his first auto-fictional narrative *Which Way to Mecca, Jack?*[11] Whereas neither the famous horror novel depicting the demonic possession of an 11-year-old, all-American girl nor its successful 1973 filmic adaptation is considered a work of Anglophone Arab representation, the 1958 book is also rarely included in serious discussions of Anglophone Arab writing. If it receives critical attention at all, it is usually instrumentalized as proof of the quiescence, stagnation, or even degeneration of Arab-American literature during the 1930s, 1940s, and 1950s. This period has been described by scholars of Arab-American history and Arab ethnic literature as one of heavily assimilationist pressures.[12] The 1924 Johnson-Reed Quota Act had drastically limited numbers of new Arab immigrants. Those who made their way to the US found themselves forced to quickly assimilate into mainstream society. As Lisa Suhair Majaj puts it, Arab Americans were "in danger of assimilating themselves out of existence [...]."[13] According to Majaj, writers of this generation regarded their Arab background as something to either disavow or ironically distance themselves from.

---

8   Samuel Huntington, "The Clash of Civilizations?," *Foreign Affairs* 72.3 (1993): 22–50.
9   On this cartoon, see also Oren, *Power, Faith, and Fantasy: America in the Middle East: 1776 to the present* 267-68.
10   William Peter Blatty, *The Exorcist* (1971; New York: Harper Paperbacks, 1994).
11   William Peter Blatty, *Which Way to Mecca, Jack?* (1958; New York: Bernard Geis Assoc./Random, 1960).
12   See Naff, *Becoming American. The Early Arab Immigrant Experience*, and Al Maleh, "Anglophone Arab Literature: An Overview," 6.
13   Majaj, "Arab-American Literature: Origins and Developments," 63.

Figure 15: Cartoon by Peter Arno, published in The New Yorker, April 9, 1938.

"*Hey, Jack, which way to Mecca?*"

Which Way to Mecca, Jack? is predominantly read as a paradigmatic product of such self-distancing dynamics. According to literary critic Evelyn Shakir, Blatty's narrative turns the pain of discrimination and exclusion into an almost "burlesque"[14] mocking of himself and his Arab family background. Reading the text as an autobiography instead of looking closely at the fictional ways in which the supposedly humoristic writing deals with the painful experience of racist discrimination and the conflicts of West-Eastern image repertoires, Shakir sees

---

14 Evelyn Shakir, "Arab Mothers, American Sons: Woman in Arab-American Autobiographies," *MELUS* 17.3 (1991–92): 9.

the author's individual experience of humiliation as the central motive for writing a self-denigrating piece of slap-stick humor. Although Nicole Waller follows Shakir's generic location, she correctly argues that the "self-mocking parody" at work in *Which Way to Mecca, Jack?* does not simply affirm the vagrant American stereotypes of Arabs and the Arab world but instead "sends both his Arab and his American characters into an endless loop of distorted looks."[15] Whereas Waller sets particular focus on the narrative's capacity to address the historical pretexts leading into contemporary cross-cultural conflicts, I am more interested in the text's auto-fictional engagement in the psychology of impossible assimilation and its narrative strategies of resisting the assimilationist paradigm of identification:

> My mother is an Arab, which would make me half Arab, except that my father was an Arab too. But already I digress. What I actually meant to say was that my parents were born in Lebanon, but I was born within sight of American Legion Post #804 in Manhattan and that's your, cue, Dr. Freud—I'm all yours.[16]

The auto-narrator pretends to tell the life story of the second-generation Arab immigrant, William Blatty. Abandoned by his father at the age of seven, he grows up alone with his brothers and his Lebanese mother in the extremely discriminatory and assimilationist surroundings of Manhattan's Lower East Side and Brooklyn. Born to become a "Sheik" one day, according to his oedipal mother's plans, "Will-*yam*['s]" earliest attempts at "*rapprochement* with the pale-faced children in that neighborhood" end in what he calls "Arab exile."[17] His mother's rigorous termination of his short affair with the colored girl, Frankie, *of course* "had nothing to do with race"[18] and further deepens his feeling of isolation. As a victim of daily racist humiliation, the Arab American boy's desire to be seen as belonging to the American mainstream grows constantly. The ambivalent identification with whiteness expresses itself in his recurrent dream "of waking up some morning and finding myself an Irishman."[19] What seems to be a clear desire to assimilate into the dominant discourse of racial whiteness could also be seen as the subconscious psychic transference of the wish to become white discursively—the way the earlier immigrant group of black Celtics succeeded in being perceived as white in the US. The fact that, indeed, William later marries the Irish Peggy and learns of a "rare racial theory, the general drift of which was that the Irish were descendants of the Arabs,"[20] further complicates the interpretation of the boy's dream.

---

15   Nicole Waller, "Arabs Looking Back: William Peter Blatty's Autobiographical Writing," *Transnational American Memories*, ed. Udo J. Hebel (Berlin: De Gruyter, 2009) 131.

16   Blatty, *Which Way to Mecca, Jack?* 13.

17   Blatty, *Which Way to Mecca, Jack?* 21.

18   Blatty, *Which Way to Mecca, Jack?* 21.

19   Blatty, *Which Way to Mecca, Jack?* 29.

20   Blatty, *Which Way to Mecca, Jack?* 211.

William's everyday "boyhood nightmares"[21] of being the target of discrimination as non-White in white America do not resolve at all as he becomes increasingly more Americanized. While his older brothers enter the Army or the Navy, his brother Mike copies Hamlet's "feigned insanity" to escape from reality. Before he becomes a Shakespearean actor and fully escapes from the immigrant family, Mike writes adaptations of Shakespeare's plays "for dogs."[22] Following his brother's example, William tries to engage in the prep school's extracurricular acting class to perform with a sword that was mightier than his "sense of being an 'Arab alone.'"[23] On stage, he is discriminated against for the shape of his nose. Finding himself excluded from his classmates' community once again, he is then cast by his mother "in her own production of 'Only in Arabia.'"[24] This quasi-racial recasting is later reciprocated when William is rejected by Hollywood agents on the grounds of either not being "The Type!"[25] wanted in American mainstream cinema or because his blue eyes collide with the demands for minor roles in Biblical films. This is how William grows up, and this is how he becomes the adult "Arab expert"[26] drafted by the United States Information Service (USIS) after college.

After a short "brainwashing" training at the USIS's Washington overseas headquarters, William is assigned to Lebanon. There he quickly finds out that he is not at all the Arab expert he thought: "There was trouble ahead. Big trouble."[27] Whereas William seeks to prove his "worthiness as an American by being an Arab [informant],"[28] his new surroundings hardly see him as anything other than a non-Arab foreigner. Feeling like an "outcast among Americans *and* Arabs," he imagines himself registering for the "Tibetan Secret Service. Or maybe Conrad Hilton ...."[29] Since William's man in the Washington headquarters is "dissatisfied with the lack of sex"[30] in his agent's reports and insists on being informed "on every aspect of Arab mores that might radically differ"[31] from American values, William starts searching for what could be considered exotic by Americans. Since neither the reality of Lebanese youth leisure time entertainment nor the Beirut red light district have anything particularly exotic to offer, he invents "a night club act featuring a 'thousand and one nights tableau,' in which two live camels participated"[32] in one of

---

21   Blatty, *Which Way to Mecca, Jack?* 32.
22   Blatty, *Which Way to Mecca, Jack?* 37.
23   Blatty, *Which Way to Mecca, Jack?* 38.
24   Blatty, *Which Way to Mecca, Jack?* 39.
25   Blatty, *Which Way to Mecca, Jack?* 55.
26   Blatty, *Which Way to Mecca, Jack?* 39.
27   Blatty, *Which Way to Mecca, Jack?* 82.
28   Blatty, *Which Way to Mecca, Jack?* 87.
29   Blatty, *Which Way to Mecca, Jack?* 129.
30   Blatty, *Which Way to Mecca, Jack?* 154.
31   Blatty, *Which Way to Mecca, Jack?* 154-55.
32   Blatty, *Which Way to Mecca, Jack?* 162.

his next reports. The Washington reader of the fake memorandum slightly misunderstands the image of a show involving a camel population and comes to Beirut to see what he imagines to be a "Camel copulation!"[33] With the help of a petty criminal trickster and a former student of the American University of Beirut disenchanted by his personal Arab-American dream, William brings the Agency officer to the "Club Yimken"[34] without explaining to him that the Arabic term *yimken* means "could be." The arranged night club turns out to be a small tent somewhere in a non-existent desert close to Beirut. It is filled with actors from "Hajji Hasheesh's Jidda Jazzcats"[35] who are paid to perform in Oriental-style costumes. At this nocturnal location, the Washington man is systematically intoxicated with Arak, a potent local liquor. When what is explained to him as a quasi-religious Muslim ritual is supposed to start, the lights are switched off and the American falls asleep. The club guest misses a performance that never happens. Instead of presenting the *sodomia islamis*-show the American longed for in his dreams, the Jazzcats perform a variation of "When the Saints Come Marchin' In,"[36] and the semi-comatose man is taken back to his tourist hotel.

The narrative only indirectly places the Arab American encounter into the wider political context of neo-imperialism and capitalist expansion. And it rarely offers correctives to the dominant American perception of the Middle East. The many lies of William's reports and his bi-directional split-performance create a double mirror that lays bare those imagined identities denied to him by Arabs and Americans alike. His designated role of an Arab-American interlocutor further alienates him from his earlier visions of a fully assimilated Arab American.

Critical strategies of returning the Orientalist-racist gaze are evoked rather than inscribed on the narrative level. The depiction of a cocktail party organized by William and his wife for the American Embassy staff in Beirut is a rare moment of such counter-discursive quality: The party's host furnishes his guests with binoculars so that they can look into the windows of the Lebanese residents in the buildings around them. Spying on Arab lives is described as the favorite pastime of expat-Americans in Beirut. This practice symbolically reciprocates USIS activities in the region, but it is also associated with the much older Orientalist fantasy of uncovering the veiled Muslim's body. Consequently, Blatty recommends that his American guests peek through the windows at a Saudi Arabian man who is said to live with four wives. However, something unexpected disrupts the party guests' pleasures of hierarchical observation. Suddenly, one of them claims to have made a troubling discovery in another window: "He handed over the binoculars and I

---

33   Blatty, *Which Way to Mecca, Jack?* 163.
34   Blatty, *Which Way to Mecca, Jack?* 169.
35   Blatty, *Which Way to Mecca, Jack?* 173.
36   Blatty, *Which Way to Mecca, Jack?* 173.

squinted at where he was pointing. I saw nothing but the old Arab in the night-shirt on the sixth floor, which wasn't too unusual at all, except that he was training a pair of binoculars on *us!*"[37] The switched positions of those gazing and those gazed upon cause reactions of anxiety and aggression: "See what happens when you edu-cate the beggars?" one of the Americans shouts. Meanwhile, the Arab man and his friends enjoy the uproar their act of looking back has created: "With my naked eye, I could see the old man in the nightshirt jumping up and down on his balcony, and the men who usually played Boardless Monopoly soon joined him and were passing the binoculars back and forth."[38]

Refuting his own double position as a potential spy and un-loyal Arab, the nar-rator's staging of Arabs returning the gaze neither asserts Orientalist stereotypes nor replaces them with a more truthful version of Arab private lives. Arab-American relations in Lebanon are just one more foil on which the narrator projects his own instable positionality between competing claims of Arabness and Americanness.

After his return from Beirut, William is examined by a psychiatrist to make sure that he does not suffer from a "cultural shock" related to his two-year overseas stay. He easily convinces the psychiatrist that he has lost his mind among the Arabs and cannot resume his service in the USIS. William instead goes to Los Angeles for a second time to cure himself of his old complex of not being "the Type." To this end, he becomes his own "Favorite Prince."[39] The ridiculous revenge on Hollywood is presented as an act of performative pseudo-catharsis through cultural travesty. Re-inaugurating himself to America as the Saudi Arabian prince "Khairallah el Aswad al Xeer,"[40] he finally gains access to those film studios formerly barred to the blue-eyed Arab American with a talent for acting.

Which Way to Mecca, Jack? was written in the late 1950s, a time dominated by the social pressures and false promises of gradual assimilation. Instead of affirming this ideology, the narrative's endless loops of mimicry and mockery are directed at both American self-images and American perceptions of Arabness. Somewhere in-between these loops, one can discern a hidden man who is deeply hurt from the multiple discriminations he has suffered. With biting irony, this man is tum-bling in search of a position and an agency that has more to offer than the painful laughter of mocking revenge. The narrator's regular allusions to the long history of conflictual encounters between the West and the Arab world can only adum-brate the violence involved in that tumbling. I believe it is this invisible violence resulting from the horrors of discriminatory assimilation that can function as a missing link between *Which Way to Mecca, Jack?* and the 1971 novel, *The Exorcist*, on

---

37   Blatty, *Which Way to Mecca, Jack?* 213.
38   Blatty, *Which Way to Mecca, Jack?* 213.
39   Blatty, *Which Way to Mecca, Jack?* 240.
40   Blatty, *Which Way to Mecca, Jack?* 242.

which Blatty's success as an American mainstream writer is based. I argue that this novelistic representation can also be related to the history of Arab-American immigration, anti-Arab discrimination, and assimilation. One finds indeed several intra- and extra-textual hints that suggest reading it as an allegorical expression, not only of the paranoid nationalist desire to cleanse the American nation from an internal threat but also of a much more horrific and ambivalent intra-psychic struggle related to the assimilationist pressure to exorcise the Arab within oneself.

The Exorcist is best known for its 1973 filmic adaption of the same title.[41] Directed by William Friedkin, the screenplay was written by Blatty himself. The film became one of the most controversial and most successful horror films of all time, and it has significant influence on the popular genre to this day. While early critics searching for *The Exorcist*'s true meaning repeatedly noted that the film's overriding theme of good versus evil, depending on the applied interpretive approach, allows for various theological, psychological, or sociopolitical specifications of the demonic evil's source and identity, they strangely shied away from identifying the invading demon as an ethnic Other, especially a Middle Eastern or Arab one.[42]

For those who have watched the movie, this reluctance must come as a surprise. The filmic prologue's Iraqi setting puzzles a perplexed audience, which expects a story exclusively set in America's suburbia: The movie opens with a close shot of an archaeologist leading a project in the deserts of Northern Iraq. The man (played by Max von Sydow), who becomes an exorcist upon his return to the US, is brought to a nearby digging site where a small stone head personifying the ancient Assyrian demigod, Pazuzu, has been found. He then visits the ruins of an ancient temple watched over by a man-sized Pazuzu statue. When a strong wind begins to blow, the statue, with raptor-like wings and a massive phallus, suddenly rises from its lithic sleep (fig. 16).

A close-up shows Merrin trying to avert his gaze before a cut inaugurates a two-shot of savage desert dogs fighting in the swirling wind. After another short cut to an ominous Bedouin guard observing the scene, Merrin returns his gaze to Pazuzu. As the sand storm intensifies, the statue is increasingly obscured by red dust. Sonically accompanied by a Muslim muezzin's call to prayer, the following crossfade transposes the audience from the blood-red Iraqi sunset to a fresh, blue sunrise over Georgetown in Washington, D.C. Slowly zooming down on the city, the camera leads us into Chris MacNeil's suburban house. Chris enters her 11-year-old daughter Regan's bedroom and opens the window. A soft breeze ruffles the curtains. The camera's pan goes from the window to Regan. The Oriental demon has

---

41   *The Exorcist*, dir. William Friedkin, screenplay William Peter Blatty, perf. Linda Blair, Ellen Burstyn, Jason Miller, and Max von Sydow, Warner Bros, 1973.

42   See, for instance, Janice Schuetz, "'The Exorcist': Images of Good and Evil," *Western Speech Communication* 39.2 (1975): 92–101.

Figure 16: Merrin facing Pazuzu in Iraq. Film still from the prologue's cross(-cultural) fade; The Exorcist, 1973.

already invaded the girl, and the distant horror gradually enters the filmic home-setting.

The Iraqi prologue and the following cross-cultural fade are not reciprocated on the main plot's visual level. The only reference to the opening image and its ultimate connotation to the evil spirit of the Arab Orient is the repeated, symbolic use of blowing wind. In this regard, Timothy Pittides's movie poster, (fig. 17) designed for a three-year-anniversary screening in San Antonio, Texas, is a rare exception. It not only directly illustrates the prologue's setting of the Iraqi digging site but also imagines the perspective of the Oriental demon, Pazuzu, hidden in a cave. The fact that the cave of the pre-Islamic demigod is vested with a broken, Aladdin-style wander lamp is quite telling regarding the designer's cultural associations. The decorative use of seemingly randomly arranged Arabic characters does not even add up to any meaning.

As the movie's first sequence sets the tone and subconscious frame for the rest of the filmic narrative, the novel's prologue also ends with an unnamed old man in khaki clothes who "hastened toward Mosul and his train, his heart encased in the icy conviction that soon he would be hunted by an ancient enemy."[43] In North Iraq, this man has met the limestone statue of the demon Pazuzu and maybe other demons. We learn that the demon "is the personification of the southwest wind"

---

43   Blatty, *The Exorcist* 8.

Figure 17: Movie poster by Timothy Pittides, 1976. Designed for the three-year-anniversary screening of William Friedkin's filmic adaptation of The Exorcist.

and that "its dominion was sickness and disease."[44] The local Arab characters placed in a surrounding blazed by an inexorable sun seem to be the living embodiments of Pazuzu's execration. They are represented as an "ancient debt."[45] Grinning with their "damply bleached"[46] eyes, "rotted teeth," and "sagging cheeks," they make the "*chawaga* [the Western foreigner]" feel "strangely alone".[47] But even as he "fixed his gaze on a speck of boiled chick-pea nestled in a corner of the Arab's mouth,"[48] the American is interested in something "totally other."[49] What he is looking for is "that Other who ravaged his dreams."[50] The demon which possesses the American girl Regan and which Merrin tries to exorcise is precisely that Other.

The images of contamination and disease used to describe Regan's corrupted body are directly linked to the original Arab sickness that Merrin first faced in Iraq. The girl's "desire for repugnant foods" and her "foul breath,"[51] diagnosed as symptoms of possession, are reminiscent features of those remains of local cuisine witnessed by Merrin in Arab mouths. Even the Arabic language, the meaning of which the American could not grasp, and the "yappings of savage dog packs"[52] of the Iraqi desert seem to return in the mysterious "gibberish" of "meaningless syllables" and "guttural tones"[53] muttered by the possessed girl. The supposedly

---

44   Blatty, *The Exorcist* 6.
45   Blatty, *The Exorcist* 4.
46   Blatty, *The Exorcist* 4.
47   Blatty, *The Exorcist* 5.
48   Blatty, *The Exorcist* 7.
49   Blatty, *The Exorcist* 4.
50   Blatty, *The Exorcist* 8.
51   Blatty, *The Exorcist* 249.
52   Blatty, *The Exorcist* 8.
53   Blatty, *The Exorcist* 123.

"foreign language"[54] turns out to be English spoken backwards, just like Arabic is read from right to left. The voice speaking through Regan's body announces itself as "Nowonmai" (I am no won/one) and claims to come from "dog" (god).[55] The agent of possession is signified as foreign, non-Western, and Arab.

It is intriguing to see that, after the attacks of September 11, 2001, white American literary and cultural critics, in particular, under the impression of the ongoing war against terror abroad and at home, began re-reading *The Exorcist* as both a timeless and at the same time very timely piece of narrative fiction. For Larrie Dudenhoeffer, the book and its filmic adaptation are "more relevant than ever since the collapse of the World Trade Center."[56] Taking up a contemporary American mainstream perspective on homeland security and foreign military, Regan's struggle with the Arab demon can be compared to the US's fight against Islamic terrorism.[57] Others, like Philip L. Simpson or Tim Jon Semmerling, take a slightly more critical stance. While Semmerling is first and foremost interested in the racialized threat to American family and community values which the Arab demon symbolically represents,[58] Simpson not only reads the novel as the anticipation of "geopolitical hostilities to come"[59] but, in addition, interprets it as "an enduring supernatural melodrama of the impossibility of assimilation."[60] In this view, *The Exorcist* demonstrates "the deep-seated American fear of the invasive Middle Eastern Other."[61] Although his is the most elaborated reading with regard to the question of assimilation, Simpson's allegorical reference to the events and aftermath of 9/11 runs the risk of reducing the novel's binary structure of good versus evil to an anticipation of the post-9/11 politics of alterity. The critical impetus of his interpretation repeatedly results in seeing Blatty's novel as "a caricature conforming to [...] Orientalist stereotypes"[62] or in stating the immediate need of bridging cultural differences. When the scholar of horror studies argues that the novel demonstrates America's vulnerability to "attacks from within by a Middle Eastern force that tran-

---

54   Blatty, *The Exorcist* 141.

55   Blatty, *The Exorcist* 141.

56   Larrie Dudenhoeffer, "'Evil against Evil': The Parabolic Structure and Thematics of William Friedkin's *The Exorcist*," *Horror Studies* 1.1 (2010): 74.

57   Dudenhoeffer, "'Evil against Evil': The Parabolic Structure and Thematics of William Friedkin's *The Exorcist*," 85-86.

58   Tim Jon Semmerling, *"Evil" Arabs in American Popular Film: Orientalist Fear* (Austin: U of Texas P, 2006) 30-50.

59   Philip L. Simpson, "Fear of the Assimilation of the Foreign Other in *The Exorcist*," *American Exorcist: Critical Essays on William Peter Blatty*, ed. Benjamin Szumskyj (Jefferson, NC: McFarland & Co, 2008) 29.

60   Simpson, "Fear of the Assimilation of the Foreign Other in *The Exorcist*," 42.

61   Simpson, "Fear of the Assimilation of the Foreign Other in *The Exorcist*," 26.

62   Simpson, "Fear of the Assimilation of the Foreign Other in *The Exorcist*," 27.

scends the cultural and national boundaries of its place of origin,"[63] he implicitly affirms the very juxtaposition of West versus East of which he disapproves at other points. According to such a reading, the novel and its filmic adaptation basically exploit a paranoid anxiety about cultural assimilation held by the mainstream audience in order to enjoy larger reception. The Exorcist, then, is little more than a piece of horror thriller cum Orientalist pulp fiction. I believe that this is principally true and probably one of the reasons for its international success. However, against the background of my reading of Which Way to Mecca, Jack?, I want to add an alternative interpretive perspective. Taking up the position of an imagined Arab reader and drawing on the image of the "ocean liner"[64] introduced by Father Karras, Merrin's co-exorcist, as a psychoanalytical metaphor of the self, I delve into this ocean liner's "crew [...] down below decks."[65]

If one imagines Merrin and Pazuzu as alter egos, as competing parts of the same disputed self under the condition of racist discrimination and forced assimilation, the narrative isn't simply about foreign elements in the American self that must be exorcized without bargaining and without negotiation. The Exorcist also carries the unsettling suggestion that the act of exorcism is directed at those who must be assimilated: at the Arab within oneself. In such a reading, Regan would be the object of an affective transference. The concept of transference (Übertragung), as introduced in its psychoanalytical sense in 1893 by Josef Breuer and Sigmund Freud,[66] is tinged with numerous connotations. Many of the implications in the original German are insufficiently transposed by the English term. They range from translocation, translation, and metaphoric transfer to the transmission of a disease.[67] All of these meanings are of relevance when designating the various processes involved on the different psycho-symbolic levels of the horror narrative. The connotations of physical translocation and disease transmission seem particularly important when re-reading The Exorcist as a reaction to the horrors of racist discrimination and assimilationist repression.

The object of my investigation here is the printed book, The Exorcist, and not its author, William Blatty. However, if one—let's say in a gesture of radical deconstruction—undoes the structuralist binary distinction between literary text and

---

63   Simpson, "Fear of the Assimilation of the Foreign Other in The Exorcist," 38.

64   Blatty, The Exorcist 239.

65   Blatty, The Exorcist 240.

66   Josef Breuer and Sigmund Freud, "On the Psychical Mechanism of Hysterical Phenomena: Preliminary Communication [1893]," Studies on Hysteria, by Josef Breuer and Sigmund Freud, ed. and trans. James Strachey, in collab. with Anna Freud (New York: Basic Books, 2000) 3-17.

67   Gerhard Fichtner, "Übertragung: Zur Archäologie eines Freudschen Begriffs," Jahrbuch der Psychoanalyse: Beiträge zur Theorie, Praxis und Geschichte, eds. Claudia Frank, Ludger M. Hermanns, and Helmut Hinz, 53 (2006): 93-116.

lived text for a moment, one can begin to read the 1971 novel as the violent repetition or redirection of feelings and desires unconsciously retained from the William of *Which Way to Mecca, Jack?* It is my hypothesis that the object upon which the repressed traumatic experiences of assimilation were directed becomes the subject of a new novelistic text with *The Exorcist*. The demon itself accuses Merrin of abusing Regan for divesting his internal struggle between devotion and self-assertion:

> *"Hypocrite!* You care nothing at *all* for the pig. You care *nothing!* You have *made her a contest between us!"*
> *"... I humbly ..."*
> "Liar! Lying bastard! Tell us, where is your humility, Merrin? In the desert? In the ruins? [...]"[68]

In my view, this can be read as an instance of self-accusation. The words evoke the derogatory suspicion of a dubious Arab origin in the narrative's symbolic self. At another point, it becomes obvious that Merrin sees himself as the demon's real target. The words that he uses to describe the horrific (self-)devaluating effects of the demon's presence almost amount to a catalogue of the worst dehumanizing effects of the racist-assimilationist discourse. At the same time, they are reminiscent of the internalized, racist self-denigration and sense of unworthiness of the autofictional character, William, in *Which Way to Mecca, Jack?*:

> And yet I think the demon's target is not the possessed; it is us ... the observers ...every person in this house. And I think—I think the point is to make us despair; to reject our own humanity, Damien: to see ourselves as ultimately bestial, vile and putrescent; without dignity, ugly, unworthy.[69]

At this point, two possible objections regarding my interpretive use of the concept of transference need to be considered. The critic should be aware that her or his own act of criticism is not taking place outside the dynamics of psychic redirection or counter transference. It is impossible to strictly separate what comes into my reading from my part and what comes into it from the investigated text. Moreover, such reading always risks treating the Anglophone Arab text as a hysterical, hence pathological, symptom. However, I do believe that no interpretive approach can fully escape from the psychodynamics of narcissism and transference.

Hence, let me further elaborate on my reading of *The Exorcist* as an Anglophone Arab Gothic allegory of the horrors of Arab experiences of assimilation in the West. To this end, Julia Kristeva's notion of abjection, as introduced in her seminal 1980

---

68   Blatty, *The Exorcist* 347.
69   Blatty, *The Exorcist* 351.

essay, *Pouvoirs de l'horreur*,[70] can function as an additional foundation for speculatively grasping the novel's quasi-affective, pre- or post-discursive, almost bodily expressions of less palpable and more insidious forms of racist discrimination. The enunciations of the institutionalized violence of the assimilationist structures of oppression appear underneath the level of the main narrative discourse. Kristeva's concept of abjection combines Lacanian psychoanalysis with semiotics, and literary theory to explain the psychic dialectics of internalized and externalized alterity. Selectively drawing on her arguments, I understand the Western discourse of assimilation as one that forces those defined as in need of assimilation to identify a realm of disgust regarding their own otherness inside themselves. Constructed as subjects overtaken by the very abject that they are to others, their discourse of selving is therefore motivated by fear. The horror resulting from such quasi-self-repellent otherness cannot be easily directed at the realm outside the self onto an imagined other because any potential foil of projection functions at the same time as the representation of a normative self. In other words, the very realm of the abject is almost object-less. In order to overcome the fear of never-ending racist abjection, an even more violent act of self-expulsion is evoked. Thus, the psychic procedure of assimilation can take the form of self-exorcism. *The Exorcist* can be read as a representation of such self-exorcism.

Focusing on the psychic density and eruptive quality of the novel's hidden subtext, one might gain a better understanding of the exorcising dynamics of subjection under the conditions of anti-Arab discrimination and the racist pressures of assimilation. Although the novel's main narrative body does not employ the axioms of race, racism, discrimination, and assimilation in its first place, there is more than a simple assimilationist sentiment at work in *The Exorcist*. I argue that the racist discourse of assimilation understood as a discourse over the production of a socially reformed subject through the destruction of this future subject's object status frames the novelistic text in an equally uncanny and powerful way. The imaginary of an exorcist's laboratory in an affluent neighborhood of Washington D.C. is only on its surface about the regeneration of Regan. Its deeper allegorical meaning relates to the assimilationist concept of subject-constitution as an exorcising act. The process of becoming American is presented as a violent identitarian engineering that first abjects every Arab origin and then forces the body to spit out the Arab portions of the self. The newly created (assimilated) subject is symbolically cleansed of its previous monstrous-exotic Arabness. The Arab is humanized (i.e. Westernized) by the ultimate act of integrative violence.

It is important to remind ourselves that the horror story ends with the deaths of both Pazuzu and Merrin. In terms of the narrative's inner psychic logic, the Arab as the future self's demonic part is killed so that the Americanized remains

---

70   Julia Kristeva, *Pouvoirs de l'horreur : essai sur l'abjection* (Paris : Éd. du Seuil, 1980).

can live on. However, read through a Kristevan lens, *The Exorcist* also symbolically represents the reverse convolutions of those who, in racist transference, have been perceived as void by the self-proclaimed homelanders. Accordingly, the novel can be interpreted as a particular Anglophone Arab variety of a general literary meta-theme "where identities (subject/object, etc.) do not exist, or barely so—double, fuzzy, heterogeneous, animal, metamorphosed, altered, abject."[71] Using the power of the literary trope of the demonic and the evil, the novel unveils the horrors of Arab-American being: that is, being under constant assimilationist supervision. I suggest re-reading *The Exorcist* as a subconsciously self-exorcising reaction to the dominant discourse of assimilation by a narrative sub-voice which is possessed by racist abjection.[72]

The horrors of assimilation are an almost impossible object of direct representation. They are either expressed in the dominant group's repressive integrationist legal framework and their fantasies of desire and denial, or they are at work in the self-annihilating nightmares as well as in the resistive visions and actions of those who are expected to assimilate themselves. In these situations, the boundaries between the ego and its negation, between beauty and horror or life and death, can easily be turned inside out. To hesitate between staying outside as Other or getting inside through the negation of one's otherness is a difficult and regularly criminalized undertaking.[73] In such moments, the dominant moral and legal codes purify repression. Blatty's *The Exorcist*, however, indicates that none of us (Arabs and non-Arabs alike!) can fully escape from the return of the repressed horrors of assimilation. I believe the imaginary of such an inevitable return is constitutive of many Anglophone Arab representations. These representations' reifying or queering of identity across cultures remains a fragile undertaking. Without necessarily representing themselves as abjects, most Anglophone Arab writers and artists know very well that they are subject to the braided horrors of abjection, and they incorporate this knowledge into their representational strategies.

An allegorical reading of *The Exorcist* as a post-colonial Gothic narrative does not necessarily link it to early imperial Gothic writings or even explore its nocturnal traces. Although the occult narrative of an innocent American girl invaded (hence penetrated) by an Oriental demon who turns the peaceful American home into a scene of horror clearly draws on the fears of reverse colonization and miscegenation, both common motives of the imperial Gothic,[74] the bloodthirsty story's

---

71   Kristeva, *Powers of Horror: An Essay on Abjection* 207.

72   Derek Hook, "Racism as Abjection: A Psychoanalytic Conceptualisation for a Post-Apartheid South Africa," *South African Journal of Psychology*, 34.4 (2004): 672-703.

73   Kristeva, *Powers of Horror: An Essay on Abjection* 155.

74   Andrew Smith and William Hughes, eds., *Empire and the Gothic: The Politics of Genre* (Basingstoke: Palgrave Macmillan, 2003).

symbolic synonymizing of racial, cultural, and national identity/alterity works perfectly without any prior knowledge of inter-texts such as Mary Shelley's *Frankenstein* (1818) or Bram Stoker's *Dracula* (1897). Thus, the novel's epilogue might include a post-Gothic hint through a statement made by Chris MacNeil's new partner, Dyer. Invited for the screening of a filmic adaptation of Emily Brontë's *Wuthering Heights* (1847)—the story of the assimilation procedure of the dark-skinned adoptee, Heathcliff, which comes to a tragic end—Dyer refuses without an expression on his face: "'I have seen it.'"[75]

Sure, one cannot read *The Exorcist* without remembering that the discourses of racism and imperialism are part of the general cultural text of the 19th and 20th centuries. But the way the novel reproduces the discursive axioms of imperialism is not neatly framed by meanings of text and intertext. My allegorical reading tries to reveal a fear beyond the level of the narrator and the narration, beyond the text itself. The horrors of assimilation and self-exorcism perhaps even step outside the text and enter the reader's (non-)assimilated worldliness and psychic states. Opening the violent fractures of the assimilationist discourse, my reading of *The Exorcist* wishes to extend the novel's meaning outside the tradition of the Gothic novel or the popular horror genre and to negotiate a critique that resists the terror of assimilation in past and present.

5.1.2   Being Non-Arab and the Anxiety of Re-Filiation

I read Blatty's 1971 novel as an Anglophone Arab text. By doing so, I might have acted against the author's intention. One might even argue that I participate in the commodification and writing of Anglophone Arab identities instead of allowing these identities to articulate themselves. I have no excuses. My reading simply relates this piece of narrative fiction to a discourse that, in my opinion, is haunted and continues to haunt Arab lives in the Anglophone West. It is not my intention to turn the individual author, William Blatty, into a representative of Arab victimhood. The same is true for my following reading.

At least since the late 1960s, Arab writers in the West have grappled with their quest for anti-assimilationist self-identification. Poets, in particular, such as Sam Hazo, Sam Hamod, Jack Marshall, or Naomi Shihab Nye, began to recover creatively what was supposed to have been lost during generations of assimilation and anti-Arab self-exorcism: names, memories, heritages, histories, identities. Many Anglophone Arab writers and activist-scholars also engaged in strong critiques of Western foreign policies and the sociopolitical conditions within the Arab world. Such bidirectional, cross-cultural critique based on varying forms of ethnic identification with one's culture of origin or one's Arab diasporic community forms an

---

75   Blatty, *The Exorcist* 385.

important element in contemporary Anglophone Arab discourse to this day. There was probably no other intellectual of Arab descent writing in English who refuted ethnic identification so rigorously and self-consciously than the late Ihab Hassan. Born in Cairo in 1925, he arrived in the United States in 1946 on an Egyptian government fellowship to study electrical engineering. Instead, he earned a PhD in English and American literature and never returned to his native Egypt. Hassan died in 2015. Over the final four decades of his life, he not only advanced to a leading figure of postmodern literary theory but, at the same time, became one of the most provocative (Arab) critics of postcolonial identity politics. I want to revisit this theoretical farewell to the Anglophone Arab roots-talk from a relational Arab studies perspective. In doing so, I am not reclaiming Hassan's theoretical work for the corpus of Anglophone Arab studies. Nevertheless, I find it at least intriguing to ask for the (perhaps hidden) Arab contiguities of postmodernism.

Hassan's list of publications is too long and the spectrum of topics, ranging from postwar American fiction to the literature of travel, too wide to be discussed exhaustively within the framework of this chapter. His oeuvre includes 16 books and an almost unmanageable amount of essays. Among his theoretical contributions are such seminal studies as *The Dismemberment of Orpheus*,[76] *Paracriticisms*,[77] *The Postmodern Turn*,[78] and *Rumors of Change*.[79] To seriously grasp his literary criticism and theory production of fifty years, one would indeed need, as he puts it, "a library of books, written and burned."[80] A key notion in most of Hassan's writings is that of *indetermanence*. First coined in a 1977/78 essay entitled "Culture, Indeterminacy, and Immanence: Margins of the (Postmodern) Age,"[81] the term is a combination of indeterminacy and immanence. In Hassan's view, both stand for two disparate yet central tendencies within literary and extra-literary postmodernism. Directly related to the material conditionality of technological immanence and capitalist individuation, the two non-dialectical trends form the quasi-ethos and post-moral episteme of our postmodern present without being resolved into

---

76   Ihab Hassan, *The Dismemberment of Orpheus: Toward a Postmodern Literature* (1971; Madison: U of Wisconsin P, 1982).

77   Ihab Hassan, *Paracriticisms: Seven Speculations of the Times* (Urbana: U of Illinois P, 1975).

78   Ihab Hassan, *The Postmodern Turn: Essays in Postmodern Theory and Culture* (Columbus: Ohio State UP, 1987).

79   Ihab Hassan, *Rumors of Change: Essays of Five Decades* (Tuscaloosa: U of Alabama P, 1995).

80   Ihab Hassan, "Postmodernism, etc.: An Interview with Frank L. Cioffi," *Postmodernism and Other Distractions: Situations and Directions for Critical Theory*, ed. David Gorman, *Style* 33.3 (1999): 361. On Hassan's work, see also Klaus Stierstorfer, ed. *Return to Postmodernism: Theory—Travel Writing—Autobiography: Festschrift in Honour of Ihab Hassan* (Heidelberg: Winter, 2005).

81   Ihab Hassan, "Culture, Indeterminacy, and Immanence: Margins of the (Postmodern) Age," reprinted in Ihab Hassan, *The Postmodern Turn: Essays in Postmodern Theory and Culture* (Columbus: Ohio State UP, 1987) 46-83.

a higher synthesis. The decisively anti-Marxist notion of the human mind forming its own reality, dependent and at the same time independent of its material being, suggests that we are witnessing a radical transformation of man who has the capacity to generalize his mind for the first time in history. Hassan knows the ironies and identitarian insecurities resulting from the indeterminacies of such postmodern processes of selving. But instead of lamenting the assumingly empty subject or warning of the risk of total absorption (assimilation), he insists on the liberating power of individual human beings and art to make reality. Whereas, according to Hassan, traditional notions of *selves* are consequently *at risk*,[82] the literary and artistic techniques of play, parody, and pastiche can help us to "empty ourselves out of self-concern."[83] There is a thoroughly positive notion of self-marginalization at work in such an engagement with identity that comes close to a kind of liberal-optimist nihilism in its ignorance of questions about subalternity, identity politics, or political agency in the broadest sense. Although he acknowledges that the socio-historical discourses of class, race, and gender participate in the construction of differences, he insists on man's fundamental capacity for self-creation. Hassan's reluctance to reduce human beings to their specific material and political conditionality likewise applies to questions of ethnicity and cultural descent. The self-marginalized and yet fully assimilated loner represents himself neither as a hyphenated American nor as an Arab.

Given this chapter's main concern with the question of assimilation, I am particularly interested in Hassan's writings at the intersection of fiction and theory. These are writings that exhibit his poetics and ethics of self-concern perhaps more than others. Such a cross-generic quality by definition applies to most of his academic work as a postmodern theoretician. Yet, in his *Out of Egypt: Fragments of an Autobiography*,[84] this quality advances to the text's distinctive constitutive feature. Hassan's auto-fictional I presented here differs significantly from the William of *Which Way to Mecca, Jack?*, who is sent back to the Arab world and Arab identification against his will. The first-person narrator cannot be compared to the remembering I in Edward Said's memoir *Out of Place* (1999), which re-(af)filiates with the non-Edward part of a divided self, formed during his Egyptian-Palestinian-Lebanese childhood, or to André Aciman, who recollects his own and his Jewish family's memories of living in and their exodus from Alexandria in *Out of Egypt*[85] (1994). Hassan's auto-fictional self seems instead to represent an identitarian coun-

---

82   Ihab Hassan, *Selves at Risk: Patterns of Quest in Contemporary American Letters* (Madison: U of Wisconsin P, 1990).

83   Hassan, "Postmodernism, etc.: An Interview with Frank L. Cioffi," 364.

84   Ihab Hassan, *Out of Egypt: Fragments of an Autobiography* (Carbondale: Southern Illinois UP, 1986).

85   André Aciman, *Out of Egypt: A Memoir* (New York: Farrar, Straus & Giroux, 1994).

terpoint to the invisible self that exorcises the Arab parts of itself in Blatty's *The Exorcist*.

Ihab Hassan left Egypt behind, never to return and barely looking back again. The both autobiographical and metafictional telling of his escape-journey out of the country of his birth appeared in 1986, ten years before Aciman's memoir of the same title was published. Hassan's *Out of Egypt* is a uniquely radical—some would say contradictory—auto-narrative by an Anglophone writer of outstripped Arab background on precisely that background. The auto-narrator, "I.H.," at no point claims to be Ihab Hassan. Interviewed in many interludes by an anonymous "Autobiographer," he presents his life story fundamentally as a self-made story. From the beginning, the notion of origin and ancestral predetermination is decidedly rejected: "Roots, everyone speaks of roots. I have cared for none".[86] Already before he left what is depicted as the claustrophobic place of his early life to find success in the academia of the free world, Hassan shows a talent for inventing the self that he wants to be. But his self-emplotment comes full circle only by drawing on the classic narrative pattern of the American immigrant track record.

The scholar of American literature pretends to follow "the country's autobiographers" who "have told us usually optimistic stories, in which they praised the power of the individual."[87] Placing his private *texture* firmly into this overall storyline, the narrative act is released in the form of an almost mythical reenactment of earlier immigrants' life stories. Instead of embracing his country of birth retrospectively, I.H. embraces the place where he arrived to find himself. The relevant source for the formation of this self is America, not Egypt: "I am in the American grain, a tradition of men and women who crossed an ocean to reinvent themselves."[88] The identitarian self-location's reference to William Carlos Williams's equally selective and Eurocentric historical account of famous American immigrants, *In the American Grain*,[89] is significant for I.H.'s project. First published in 1925, ironically the year of Hassan's birth, it begins with Columbus's *discovery* of the West Indies and moves on through Cotton Mather, George Washington, and Benjamin Franklin to Edgar Allan Poe and Abraham Lincoln. Williams's collection of micro-histories poetically reconstructs American lives to reveal a national strain of human endeavor and human tragedy.[90] Although failure is as much a part of this strain as is success, the belief in the capacity of the individual dominates. I.H.'s hint stresses his own confidence in the autonomy of man's individual creativity. Similarly to Williams's insistence

---

86   Hassan, *Out of Egypt: Fragments of an Autobiography* 4.

87   Hassan, *Out of Egypt: Fragments of an Autobiography* 12.

88   Hassan, *Out of Egypt: Fragments of an Autobiography* 251.

89   William Carlos Williams, *In the American Grain* (New York: New Directions, 1956).

90   See also Alan Holder, "In the American Grain: William Carlos Williams on the American Past," *American Quarterly* 19.3 (1967): 499-515.

upon his artistic insight that individual lives cannot be explained by "mere acci-
dents of geography and climate,"[91] the auto-narrator of *Out of Egypt* rejects the idea
that his life and identity are forcibly reduced to external determinants. He is not
possessed by his Arab history but possesses the only country he is willing to call
home. I.H.'s almost fetishistic assertion of chosen Americanness triggers his son
Geoffrey's skeptical questions regarding the true reasons for re-writing a childhood that apparently does not matter. Why dig up something he has rigorously left
behind? I.H. self-critically re-poses the question to himself without providing an
answer: "Is autobiography my own warrant for American self-exile?"[92]

Instead, he explains his escape from Egypt as an escape from a dysfunctional
family, both in a literal and a metaphorical sense. "Self-recreation," he explains to
himself, his son, the autobiographer, and the readers, "helped me slip through my
birthrights: language and the clutching blood."[93] However, the slippery use of the
trivializing verbal form "to slip" apparently cannot denote the remembered pain felt
before the liberating outcome: "Slip? We tear ourselves free. We learn murder in the
family, as the ancient Greeks knew, and rehearse the pride of Oedipus before the
Sphinx."[94] The image of Oedipus encountering the Sphinx does not only evoke the
oedipal experience of violence. I.H. comes from a background of landowners and
ministers. He received an education in English and French. His relatively privileged
childhood, however, is confused by the suffocating constrictions of his direct social environment. I.H's hint at the antique myth and its everyday rehearsal within
the family also carries the notions of a more fundamental liminality of intellectual
autonomy and the risk of human hubris. In ancient mythology, the Sphinx figure
marks the binaries of human/animal, masculine/feminine, and Egyptian (Oriental-
Arab/Greek-Occidental). The constellation of Oedipus standing before the Sphinx
"is a figuration of unparalleled indeterminacy and ambiguity" from Sophocles's
early version to Freud.[95] I.H.'s identification with Oedipus shares this ambiguity
of the threshold. The tragic auto-fictional hero faces an Other who could be his double but decides against any mirroring identification. The Oedipus-Sphinx passage
finds its symbolic analogue in the veritable armory of guns, swords, and knives
that supplies many of the family incidents of I.H.'s memory. Cutting himself off
from a violent family and repressive surroundings that seem resistant to change,
he searches for "scope, an openness of time, a more viable history. I also looked for

91   Williams, *In the American Grain* 188.
92   Hassan, *Out of Egypt: Fragments of an Autobiography* 106.
93   Hassan, *Out of Egypt: Fragments of an Autobiography* 6.
94   Hassan, *Out of Egypt: Fragments of an Autobiography* 6.
95   Almut-Barbara Renger, *Oedipus and the Sphinx: The Threshold Myth from Sophocles through Freud
     to Cocteau*, trans. Duncan Smart, John T Hamilton, and David G Rice (Chicago: U of Chicago P,
     2013) 44.

some private space wherein to change, grow; for I had not liked what I foresaw of my life in Eternal Egypt."[96]

I.H. does not evoke any diasporic feeling of loss. He does not suffer from being separated from his Egyptian family, his place of origin, or from Arab culture and language, for that matter. Instead, he is haunted by the anxiety of re-filiation and return:

> For a long time after leaving Egypt, I had a bad, recurrent dream. I dreamt that I was compelled to go back, complete some trivial task—close a door left ajar, feed a canary, whisper a message. There was terror in the banal dream, terror and necessity, and also the sense, within the dream itself, that I had dreamt it before, and within that a feeling that each time I dreamt the dream, something would work out: I would no longer need to go back.[97]

His repeated compulsion to close the door might conceal or "whisper" a subconscious message regarding the psychic inconsistency of rigorous indeterminacy and total dissociation from his Arab past. In this view, the act of writing an autobiography would amount to just one more neurotic closing of the door. Although the auto-narrator openly expresses his discomfort with being pushed to relate himself to his Arab background, he reveals his uncertainties regarding the re-verse effects of his auto-writing at some points: "Do my words re-colonize the fellah, who will never read them, as do all these learned [Egyptologist] books I read?"[98] I.H.'s rejection of Egypt and his Egyptian past excludes self-wounding through the rigorous negation of any collective interdependence. He opts for emancipating his self from the claims of belonging, of roots, and of collective memory. He insists on his right to re-invent himself in the West, free from Anglo-Arab identity discourses. *Out of Egypt* is confidently devoid of nostalgic diasporic sentiments. It voices an unapologetic rejection of Egypt and declares I.H.'s, and maybe Hassan's, disowning of any Arab heritage.

The absence of Arab group solidarity or at least of a strategic commitment to Arab identity politics can come as a provocation for diasporic Arab activist intellectuals who see themselves as fighting for their respective immigrant communities, for human rights and democracy in their countries of origin, or for just and peaceful relations between the West and the Middle East. The image of happy cultural orphans, cut off from any feeling of Arab belonging thanks to a one-way transatlantic escape, does not fit into the Anglophone Arab discourse of critical commitment. Although his auto-narrative shares a lot with other exilic and/or diasporic narratives of multiple, sometimes contradictory, and often shifting personal texts,

---

96   Hassan, *Out of Egypt: Fragments of an Autobiography* 107.
97   Hassan, *Out of Egypt: Fragments of an Autobiography* 108-09.
98   Hassan, *Out of Egypt: Fragments of an Autobiography* 48.

Hassan's insistence on indetermanence suspends the possibility of ethnic alliances based on shared national or cultural roots. The absence of any ethnic political "we" in Hassan's writing has direct implications for the ethics of postcolonial criticism. One might even argue that this absence goes as far as to question the allegation of an Arab "we" in my own readings of Blatty's *Which Way to Mecca, Jack?* and *The Exorcist*. I believe that it is precisely these decentering effects of Hassan's farewell to the Arab ethnic roots-talk that make his work an important contribution to the relational diasporic study of Anglophone Arab representations and to postcolonial theory more generally.

Hassan's "Queries for Postcolonial Studies"[99] are posed in a 1998 essay of the same title. These queries are often arbitrary, sometimes cynical, and consistently polemical. But they are not at all pointless. Constantly reminding us that "we" is not a singular pronoun, he radically questions any moral authority that claims partisanship of shared political traits and emancipatory horizons while at the same time celebrating cultural difference. Hassan criticizes what he perceives as the field's inherent epistemo-ideological progressivism, which makes thorough self-criticism impossible and instead produces a self-congratulatory jargon. In his view, the emphasis on imperialist politics and economic exploitation in postcolonial studies selectively moralizes history and overlooks the "benefits [...] of cultural interaction."[100] According to Hassan, postcolonial critics tend to overhastily exclude the non-oppressive dynamics of sameness and to underestimate the individual's capacity to voluntarily choose "soft-universals."[101] In turn, they totalize the image of an integral capitalist-imperialist West. Hassan advocates leaving behind what he sees as a "colonial complex," characterized by him as "a deep malady and sinister disease, mixing anger with self-contempt."[102] The repetitive insistence on this demand has an openly exterminatory, almost exorcizing tone. In my view, it is not without ambivalence regarding his own denunciation of the ethnic roots talk: "Root it out, root out the colonial complex from the mind, the heart, the gut, and learn to look at the world with level gaze."[103] Instead of lamenting material injustice in the world, Hassan calls for the spiritual transcending of selves and cultures to involve what he coins "spiritual interculturalism."[104] Whereas this neo-transcendentalist and late romantic rather than postmodern project is not further specified, Hassan, the literary philosopher of the mind, repeats his disregard for the simple truths of postcolonial morality in a 2005 essay.

---

99   Ihab Hassan, "Queries for Postcolonial Studies," *Philosophy and Literature* 22.2 (1998): 329-30.
100 Hassan, "Queries for Postcolonial Studies," 333.
101 Hassan, "Queries for Postcolonial Studies," 336.
102 Hassan, "Queries for Postcolonial Studies," 338.
103 Hassan, "Queries for Postcolonial Studies," 339.
104 Hassan, "Queries for Postcolonial Studies," 341.

The essay is composed as an imagined dialogue between three competing voices. Its main topic is the changing perception of America by the world and by Hassan himself at the beginning of the 20th century. Partly affirming a national crisis of international legitimacy in the wake of the Iraq war, Abu Ghraib, and Guantanamo, he strongly argues against what he interprets as Occidentalist anti-Americanism. Hassan sees no alternative to the American model of liberal democracy: "Thoughtful visitants to the planet would agree: America needs to do better, somehow, by itself and the world. The visitants do not specify how."[105] In part, Hassan seems to identify postcolonial critics with these imagined extraterrestrial visitors who criticize without specifying alternatives. He particularly attacks the postcolonialists' all too often raw (and in his view narcissistic) equation of truth with power. Directly drawing on Said's notion of speaking truth to power, Hassan advises that postcolonial intellectuals attempt "the harder task, telling truth to themselves, or harder still, telling truth *against* themselves."[106] There is a certain pre-postmodern mythic essentialism at work in this critique of the Saidian "rowdy counterpoint."[107] Hassan apparently believes in the need for speaking "equably, mindful of truth in all its shades."[108] But he is not willing to fully give up the idealist notion of truth. In his view, reducing truth to naïve, one-sided perception over-generalizes ambiguity and turns truth into something "simply pluralist and conflictual." Against such an understanding, he brings forward the self-heedless and self-dispossessing approximation to truth in "human kenosis."[109]

In a paper presented during a 2013 conference on *Diasporic Constructions of Home and Belonging*[110] at Münster University, Hassan once more returned to his self-exilic conception of relinquishing identification. But at this time, the notion of a self-transcending human mind was supplemented with a very physical dimension: "the individual human body."[111] The event was characterized by an uncanny ghostly atmosphere—not only because the keynote lecture was read out by the conference

---

105   Ihab Hassan, "The Eagle, the Olive Branch, and the Dream: Changing Perceptions of America in the World," *Georgia Review* 59.2 (2005): 342.

106   Hassan, "The Eagle, the Olive Branch, and the Dream: Changing Perceptions of America in the World," 328-29.

107   Hassan, "The Eagle, the Olive Branch, and the Dream: Changing Perceptions of America in the World," 331.

108   Hassan, "The Eagle, the Olive Branch, and the Dream: Changing Perceptions of America in the World," 332.

109   Hassan, "The Eagle, the Olive Branch, and the Dream: Changing Perceptions of America in the World," 337.

110   Florian Kläger and Klaus Stierstorfer, eds., *Diasporic Constructions of Home and Belonging* (Berlin: De Gruyter, 2015).

111   Ihab Hassan, "Extraterritorial: Exile, Diaspora, and the Ground under Your Feet," *Diasporic Constructions of Home and Belonging*, eds. Florian Kläger and Klaus Stierstorfer (Berlin: De Gruyter, 2015) 22.

convener due to the absence of the seriously ill body-in-flesh of Hassan. The title of the ventriloquial talk, "Extraterritorial: Exile, Diaspora, and the Ground Under Your Feet," did not really embody its content. Using Toni Morrison's work as a point of departure, Hassan specified the body as the basis of our intimate, private, and socio-historical experiences, as man's real and final home. Accordingly, it is not exilic sentiment or diasporic longing but our individual being in the world that shapes the process of identification.

Again, Hassan's own partial memory of decisively not being in Egypt helps to illustrate his general theoretical argument. In addition, language functions a second, quasi-extraterritorial[112] home sphere. Since, in the case of Hassan, this language is clearly English, a phone call by an Arabic-speaking Egyptian General Consul after the so-called Arab Spring of 2011 led to a temporary identitarian dislocation and disorientation. The short non-conversation (imagined and/or remembered) marks the beginning of the kernel of the talk. Hassan is suddenly haunted by his Arab roots. When he who cared for none is informed about the fact that the Egyptian state considered him dead, he not only promptly hung up the phone and rejected Egypt as always but suddenly discovered his anger at Egypt's rejection of him.

From this symbolic encounter with his Arab past, Hassan moved to his personal "disappointment at the consequences of Tahrir Square."[113] The *Midan at-Tahrir* was the Egyptian democracy movement's public and symbolic center, located in downtown Cairo. For Hassan, the Arab Spring merely marked a brief interlude "heralding yet another ice age."[114] To lighten his deep "frustration with his native culture,"[115] he imagines a dialogue with a person "more firmly embedded in the Arab world" than Hassan himself and who, unlike himself, identifies as Arab. The queries are obviously his own. He confronts his imagined interlocutor about the lack of democracy and intellectual responsibility in Arab countries, addresses issues of corruption, patriarchy, and sexism, and brings forward the question of violence, anti-Semitism, Arab-Israeli relations, and Islamic terrorism. The answers are basically presented as self-apologetic, nativist justifications of the current state of things and sometimes as ironic excuses. His generalizing description of the Middle East as a "serpents' nest of irredentist passion"[116] subsumes and thus discriminates diverse contemporary local, national, and regional struggles as one coherent backward-oriented reclaiming of a long lost past. Hassan's reductionist matrix of Arab culture is characterized exclusively by attributes of negative indication. They include "misogyny,

---

112   Here Hassan draws on George Steiner, *Extraterritorial: Papers on Literature and the Language Revolution* (New York: Atheneum, 1971).
113   Hassan, "Extraterritorial: Exile, Diaspora, and the Ground under Your Feet," 27.
114   Hassan, "Extraterritorial: Exile, Diaspora, and the Ground under Your Feet," 27.
115   Hassan, "Extraterritorial: Exile, Diaspora, and the Ground under Your Feet," 30.
116   Hassan, "Extraterritorial: Exile, Diaspora, and the Ground under Your Feet," 31.

poverty, illiteracy, irresponsible elites, a taste for inflated rhetoric" as well as a "lack of critical spirit, a tendency to see the world without nuances, and a postcolonial mood."[117] In typical ironic manner, Hassan shows himself to be fully aware of his harsh critique of a "people whose 'blood'—so to speak—runs in my veins."[118] Whereas he does not explain on what grounds (under his feet) and on which worldly experiences he judges more than 400 million individuals living in what he imagines as the Arab world, Hassan does not simply leave the distant audience puzzled by the open enunciation of his willingly politically incorrect anti-Arab polemics. Explaining the direction of his Orientalist-racist generalizations with his learned "distrust in so-called 'roots'," he provocatively insists on his right to lay bare and thus to cultivate his self-constitutive anti-Arab stereotypes: "In any case, I never promised to extirpate, only to sublimate, my prejudices."[119]

I have decided to abstain from a psychoanalytical interpretation at this point. Although Hassan claims to place his identity within the ongoing challenges of unfinished arrivals rather than in sorrows of loss, his repeated use of tropes of extirpation and extermination for the rhetorical defense of his Arab non-self seems to indicate a reverse-rootedness. The fact that he at the same time brings in the notion of sublimation lets one question what a poetics of prejudices might look like. What is, however, evident is that Hassan's ethics, in so far as we can speak of such a normative moral system, do not harmonize with the dominant strands of Anglophone Arab discourse.

Against this background, it is all the more significant (or should I say worrying?) that, five years after the failed revolution of 2011, a new generation of Egyptians who read and write English turn to Hassan's *Out of Egypt* in order to engage with their own crisis of Egyptianness. Living in an extremely repressive and dangerous atmosphere of religious-cum-nationalist authoritarianism, many writers, including Tarek Ghanem, feel the desperate need to rethink "what it means to be Egyptian and how to deal with psychological or physical exile."[120] Due to either lack of hope and fear of prosecution, numerous activists of the January 25, 2011 generation have long left or decided to leave the country. Those who stayed sense that they no longer have anything left to lose and often find themselves strangers in their own land. In his recent review of Hassan's *Out of Egypt* for the independent counter-journalist net-magazine, *Mada Masr*, Ghanem describes the current situation as follows:

---

117   Hassan, "Extraterritorial: Exile, Diaspora, and the Ground under Your Feet," 31.
118   Hassan, "Extraterritorial: Exile, Diaspora, and the Ground under Your Feet," 32.
119   Hassan, "Extraterritorial: Exile, Diaspora, and the Ground under Your Feet," 32.
120   Tarek Ghanem, "Literary Gems: On Being Egyptian and Ihab Hassan's *Out of Egypt*," *Mada Masr* 19 Feb. 2016, 3 Mar. 2016, <https://madamasr.com/en/2016/02/19/feature/culture/literary-gems-%E2%80%8Bon-being-egyptian-and-ihab-hassans-out-of-egypt-%E2%80%8B/>.

For many, in the past five years being Egyptian has become more of a psycholog-ical syndrome than an identity. The social suffering, the fantastically Orwellian news, the difficulties of the most mundane interactions, the continuous clamping down on freedoms and critical thought, and the rise of xenophobic and fascistic public sentiments are all alienating. Those who believed in change have become cultural orphans, cut off from true feelings of belonging.[121]

In this situation, the young activist blogger and literary reviewer, Ghanem, rec-ommends reading *Out of Egypt* side by side with the latest prison writings by the Egyptian blogger, Alaa Abd El Fattah. His essay written on the occasion of the fifth anniversary of the January 25 uprisings is particularly telling. Abd El Fattah, who served a five-year prison sentence for his political commitment, articulates in the English language what is painfully obvious for many of those aspiring to self-re-alization with their feet on Egyptian ground: "I have nothing to say: no hopes, no dreams, no fears, no warnings, no insights, nothing, absolutely nothing."[122] Corre-lational readings of Anglophone Arab representations can lead to strange encoun-ters, unexpected side-by-side-readings, and shattering insights.

5.2   Blurred Archives and Queered (Hi-)Stories: Literary Writing and Art Work in Transmigration

> "Yes, our story is tragic, yes, it is sordid, but you have to remember that it is first and foremost a story."[123]

Anglophone Arab imaginaries can travel. When Arab narratives and images travel overseas and back again or when Western representations migrate to the Middle East, the individual cultural sign can change in ways that are more insidious than the literary critics, the curators, or even the writers and artists themselves could have predicted. Sometimes, this process leads to a radical questioning of the act of narrating or representing itself. In such moments, it is not only the act of lit-erary and audio-visual representation that is explored and re-conceptualized. The

---

121   Ghanem, "Literary Gems: On Being Egyptian and Ihab Hassan's *Out of Egypt.*" *Mada Masr* is a Cairo-based news website that attempts to provide a platform for dislocated counter-journal-ist practices. The website started publishing on June 30, 2013 in the midst of popular protests and increasing censorship.
122   Alaa Abd El Fattah, "Jan 25, 5 years on: The only words I can write are about losing my words," *Mada Masr* 24 Jan. 2016, 3 Mar. 2016 <https://madamasr.com/en/2016/01/24/opinion/u/jan-25-5-years-on-the-only-words-i-can-write-are-about-losing-my-words/>.
123   *Hostage: The Bachar Tapes (English Version)*, Tape #17, dir. Souheil Bachar, The Atlas Group in collab. with c-hundred film corp., 2000, 2:33-2:45 min. DVD.

re-vision of representational procedures themselves can be turned into an object of critical imagination by writers and artists. If this happens, the boundaries between fiction, metafiction, and parafiction become blurred. Narratologies are fictionalized alongside histories, and facts are approached not only in their crude facticity but also with a view toward the complicated mediations by which they acquire their immediacy. This chapter focuses on such equally fictocritical and performative dynamics in the contemporary production of Anglophone Arab evidence.

The Anglophone Arab cultural sphere explored selectively in the present discussion is a culture of decisively transnational and transmigrant identifications rather than a hyphenated immigrant culture. Contrary to received ideal types of international migration, such as immigration, re-migration, and diasporic migration, the transmigration approach shall be used as in transnational migration studies—to interpret cultural representations that travel discursively across multiple national and cultural borders. The concept of transmigration was first employed in the mid-1990s by Nina Glick Schiller, Linda Basch, and Cristina Szanton Blanc as an analytical point of entry into the examination of key processes in a world that is increasingly restructured by economic globalization and transnational migration.[124] In social anthropology, transmigrants are usually seen as individuals whose continuing migratory movements transcend the boundaries of nation-states and whose complex socio-economic relationships challenge the traditional isomorphism of people, territory, and belonging. The dominant focus in transmigration research on the social and economic dimensions of the globalization of capital often fails to grasp its effects on the reformulation or transformation of cultural articulation.

My discussion here is concerned with the literary and artistic practices of transmigrants. It adapts the paradigm of transmigration as an open explanatory model without screening out the material clashes between specific and frequently polarized mono-localities. Using the literary writings of Rabih Alameddine and the concept and performance art of Walid Raad as examples, I address the representations of two Anglophone Arab intellectuals who, although both are based in the US, are not at all afraid of regularly returning to their place of upbringing. However, I do not aim at tracing a clear nexus between the individual cultural producers' transmigrant lives and their respective creative work. In other words, I am less interested in the intellectuals' physical crossovers than in the effects of these crossovers on their specific representational poetics and aesthetics. Reading contemporary Anglophone poetics across the boundaries of what we are used to imagine as stable morality, factual history, and sexual normativity, my discussion hopes to shed light on the sordid details and anger of tragic memories as well as the fragile beauty and wisdom of unstable truths and contested love:

---

124   Nina Glick Schiller, Linda Basch, and Cristina Szanton Blanc, "From Immigrant to Transmigrant: Theorizing Transnational Migration," *Anthropological Quarterly* 68.1 (1995): 48-63.

"I can't think straight anymore. I should not have said that. I try never saying the word *straight*. Let's say I can't concentrate."[125] This is Mohammad speaking, the main narrator among many narrative voices in Rabih Alameddine's 1998 debut novel, *Koolaids: The Art of War*. He refuses to straighten his thoughts, to arrange his narrative in a straight order. Alameddine grew up in Lebanon, attended secondary school in England, and has academic degrees from UCLA and the University of San Francisco. Today, he divides his time between San Francisco and Beirut. His debut novel was quite successful in the US and became a bestseller in Beirut in 2001, as well. However, the publication of the Arabic translation fell victim to Lebanese censorship. Therefore, his novel represents both an Anglophone Arab transmigrant's work and a traveling text. Nevertheless, it is first and foremost a transgressive narrative.

While dying from AIDS in San Francisco, the main narrator of *Koolaids*, Mohammad, remembers his and other people's lives: stories related to the AIDS epidemic in the US, the so-called civil war in Beirut, stories set in the 1980s and 1990s, stories about death, sex, and the meaning of love and anger between worlds. Mohammad's refusal to think straight is expressed after a short apocalyptic hallucination on the novel's first page. We also learn that the man suffering and lying in a hospital bed cannot think in English anymore, the language in which he felt at home for the longest time. What is presented to us is an Anglophone narrative that refuses a stable mode of emplotment in order to transpose a loose collection of Arabic thoughts, memories, and dreams. Competing first-person narrators provide a polyphonic mosaic of diary entries, memories, and hallucinations, news reports, abortive book projects, and hilarious short plays. While the literary figures in *Koolaids* fit in America without belonging there, they conversely belong in Lebanon without fitting into Lebanese society. This uneasy fact of always being somehow out of place constantly forces the protagonists to situate their own displaced subjectivities in relation to dominant fixations of history, identity, and culture, thus questioning habitual representations of the Arab world and the West in both the US and Lebanon.

Mohammad is an artist who clearly locates himself outside ethnic and national unities of belonging and filiation. Distancing himself from "naïve and dumb" Americans as well as from "arrogant" Lebanese who are "too busy judging everybody else's life to live their own,"[126] he cannot escape being perceived by others through the straight parameters of mutually excluding cultures. This man apparently struggled for the longest part of his life with getting rid of those reductive stereotypes that recognize him as someone he is not or does not want to be:

---

125   Alameddine, *Koolaids: The Art of War* 1.
126   Alameddine, *Koolaids. The Art of War* 243.

The happiest day in my life was when I got my American citizenship and was able to tear up my Lebanese passport. That was great. Then I got to hate Americans. And I really do. [...] I tried so hard to rid myself of anything Lebanese. [...] The harder I tried, the more it showed up in the unlikeliest places. [...] Would people think of me as a painter or a Lebanese painter?[127]

The many narrative fragments and voices of the novel are intertwined. The multiple narrators do not substitute the narrative claims of the respective other voices, but rather complement and correct singular claims of narrative authority. They do not form a higher unit. Associating competing representations of living and dying in the Lebanese war and living with and dying from AIDS in the US, *Koolaids* relates situational settings of physical deterioration to graphic depictions of bodily love and juxtaposes public mediations with private musings: Gunfire erupts in moments of deflowering; the Pope's solidarity with the Christian victims of the Lebanese war is related to Cervantes's musings on historical truths; the Beatles song, "Revolution," is playing on a record player while a Syrian shell kills the father of a boy who, in turn, blames Yoko Ono; Lebanese reports on the killing of civilians are moved to the newspapers' back pages while Western media forgets those dying of AIDS; Tom Cruise assures his fans that he is not homosexual, while the mystic Krishnamurti and the writer Julio Cortázar lay bare the impossibility of expressing the unity of an individual life.

If I had to confess my true, spontaneous aesthetic experience and inter-medial association when reading Alameddine's queer-fictional work in terms of its narrative strategies, I would have to go beyond the primary topical framework of Arab-American encounters in the sphere of literature to stress this work's secret alliance with Pedro Almodóvar's camp-cinematic art of telling (other) stories. But I am afraid a solid comparative grounding of this association is not possible within the scope of this chapter.[128] Therefore, let me return to my primary script.

Koolaids can be conceived of as a narrative about the drafting and re-drafting of a book "where all the characters died in the beginning"; a project that "never went beyond the incipit."[129] The Borgesian structure of draft and re-draft, of copy and re-copy, seems to dominate the novel's narrative direction. This technique will advance to the decisive structure for Alameddine's second novelistic project, *I, the Divine*.[130]

127 Alameddine, *Koolaids. The Art of War* 244.
128 For a first starting out in the interpretive direction indicated here, see: Monica Lopez Lerma, "Law in High Heels: Performativity, Alterity, and Aesthetics," *Southern California Interdisciplinary Law Journal* 20.2 (2011): 289-324 and Stefanie Knauss, "Excess, Artifice, Sentimentality: Almodóvar's Camp Cinema as a Challenge for Theological Aesthetics," *Journal of Religion, Media & Digital Culture* 3.1 (2014): 31-55.
129 Alameddine, *Koolaids. The Art of War* 18.
130 Rabih Alameddine, *I, The Divine: A Novel in First Chapters* (London: Weidenfeld & Nicolson, 2002).

In the 2001 novel, the Lebanese Druze-American narrator, Sarah, starts and re-starts anew to tell her as well as her family's transnational life stories. Her endless attempts at inventing, revising, and re-inventing herself culminate in a willingly self-contradictory narrative conglomerate that forms *A Novel in First Chapters*.[131]

Among the many aborted projects collected in *Koolaids* is a piece of pulp fiction, which turns out to be a slightly queered variation of already published books on ruthless Arabs kidnapping innocent Westerners:

> I wanted to write a book [. . .]. A stunningly beautiful American woman with perky breasts is sold as a slave to an Arab prince. He, on the other hand, is an incredibly successful American corporate executive pretending to be an Arab prince, for what American would fantasize about being seduced by an Arab.[132]

Koolaids is regularly placed within the genre of (multi-)ethnic literature by scholars of Arab American literature and presented as an example of the experimental articulation of the predicament of cultural and national in-betweenness.[133] If critics see "a milestone in the modern Arab American literary tradition"[134] in this novel, as Steven Salaita does in his 2007 study, they stress its transgression of sexual taboos, especially in view of the way Alameddine's narrative treats Arab homosexuality. In my view, homosexuality is only on its surface a major theme of *Koolaids*. In fact, the stories presented in this novel query the inherent stability of normative identifications, sexual and extra-sexual alike. These queries and queerings include gendered classifications of desire as well as racialized constructions of cultural or national belonging. They assert the narrative and performative create-ability of identities.[135] Although Mohammed basically represents himself as a gay character, he at one

---

131   On *I, the Divine*, see also Michelle Hartman, "Rabih Alameddine's I, the Divine: A Druze Novel as World Literature?" *The Edinburgh Companion to the Arab Novel in English: The Politics of Anglo Arab and Arab American Literature and Culture*, ed. Nouri Gana (Edinburgh: Edinburgh UP, 2013) 339-59 as well as Carol Fadda-Conrey, "Transnational Diaspora and the Search for Home in Rabih Alameddine's I, the Divine: A Novel in first Chapters," *Arab Voices in Diaspora: Critical Perspectives on Anglophone Arab Literature*, ed. Layla Al Maleh (Amsterdam: Rodopi, 2009) 163-85 and Cristina Garrigós, "The Dynamics of Intercultural Dislocation. Hybridity in Rabih Alameddine's I, The Divine," 187-201.

132   Alameddine, *Koolaids. The Art of War* 117.

133   See, for instance, Susan Muaddi Darraj, "Arab American Novel," *The Greenwood Encyclopedia of Multiethnic American Literature: A-C*, ed. Emmanuel S. Nelson (Westport, CT: Greenwood P, 2005) 179-82 and Hassan, *Immigrant Narratives: Orientalism and Cultural Translation in Arab American and Arab British Literature* 206-09.

134   Steven Salaita, *Arab American Literary Fictions, Cultures, and Politics* (Basingstoke: Palgrave Macmillan, 2007) 73.

135   Judith Butler, *Gender Trouble: Feminism and the Subversion of Identity* (New York: Routledge, 1990).

point draws on the Kantian argument that "nothing entirely straight can be carved" to seriously ask whether "something entirely gay can be carved."[136]

The literary characters in *Koolaids* are very fragile bodies with equally fragile social identities always in the process of becoming and losing themselves. Similarly, Mohammad's concern with religious metanarratives appears heretic. He does not drink the Kool-Aid: he does not become a firm believer, and he does not commit suicide.[137] He questions the biblical and quranic narrative of Lot as a story of a patriarchal prophet who not only is "pimping his two virgin daughters"[138] in Sodom but later also is sleeping with them and who "doesn't remember anything the next day. This is the common pattern among straight men. They always forget what happened the night before while they were drunk."[139]

The Revelation of John is turned into a symbolic matrix of the narrative "Queer A/theology."[140] The dialogue of the four horsemen of the apocalypse[141] is presented in four variations. The novel opens and ends with it. In the opening passage, the fourth rider (Jesus) refuses to take "a non-Christian homosexual" with knowledge of war, plague, and death with him: "You brought me all the way out here for a fucking fag, a heathen. I didn't die for this dingbat's sins."[142] In a later variation, the first, second, and third horsemen chant from the Quran instead of the biblical scripture. Their diversion from the Christian script triggers a severe identity crisis in the fourth horseman (Jesus): "Those are not my words. I never said that."[143] The last encounter develops into a flirt with the vision of queer love across sexual, gendered, religious, racial, or cultural divides. Jesus finally says "'I love you, Mohammad.'"[144] The latter is led away by the rider of the white horse.

Shortly before his death, Mohammad remembers a skyjacking scene from the famous 1986 Hollywood action movie, *The Delta Force*.[145] The passage not only addresses the dominant Arab screen image of the hostage-taking terrorist[146] but at the same time criticizes the common (neo)colonial conceptualization of the Arab

---

136 Alameddine, *Koolaids. The Art of War* 112.

137 Dervla Shannahan, "Reading Queer A/theology into Rabih Alameddine's Koolaids," *Feminist Theology* 19.2 (2011): 133.

138 Alameddine, *Koolaids. The Art of War* 63.

139 Alameddine, *Koolaids. The Art of War* 64.

140 Shannahan, "Reading Queer A/theology into Rabih Alameddine's Koolaids," 129-42.

141 John J. Collins, *The Apocalyptic Imagination: An Introduction to the Jewish Matrix of Christianity* (New York: Crossroad, 1984).

142 Alameddine, *Koolaids: The Art of War* 1.

143 Alameddine, *Koolaids: The Art of War* 99.

144 Alameddine, *Koolaids: The Art of War* 245.

145 *The Delta Force*, dir. Menahem Golan, screenplay James Bruner and Menahem Golan, perf. Chuck Norris, Lee Marvin et al., Cannon Films, 1986.

146 Jack G. Shaheen, *Reel Bad Arabs: How Hollywood Vilifies a People* (New York: Olive Branch P, 2001).

world as an exterritorial playground and world-historical stage of Western civilization—a perception that reduces cities like Cairo and Beirut to mere copies, extensions, or appendices of the Western metropolis. In the early 20th century, the Egyptian metropole was described by Europeans as Paris on the Nile, while the Lebanese capital city was known as the Paris of the Middle East. Moreover, until the so-called civil war, Lebanon was represented in Western mass media as the Switzerland of the Arab world. Now Mohammad imagines this:

> One of the hijackers in the movie tells the hostages that the *New Jersey* bombed Lebanon. The priest, one of the hostages, denies it. He says Americans never bombed Beirut. There is no rebuttal. When the hijacked plane lands in Beirut, one of the passengers said this used to be a wonderful city. You could do whatever you want. I couldn't believe what he said next. Beirut used to be the Las Vegas of the Middle East. Now that's fucking insulting.[147]

Koolaids strongly erodes our cultural flight data. It queers the referential system by which we used to position ourselves against others. The narrative not only unsettles heteronormative convictions and one-sided, cross-cultural identifications but also questions our own geographic, historiographic, and epistemic self-locations. Alameddine's third novel, *The Hakawati* (2008), shares this radically disorienting strategy of crossing up dividing lines of belonging and non-belonging. But in this novel, the heretical narrative act comes with an even stronger metanarrative emphasis.

"Listen. Allow me to be your god. Let me take you on a journey beyond imagining. Let me tell you a story."[148] This opening address marks the beginning of a saga of four generations of a Lebanese family, at the heart of which is a hakawati (storyteller) of such dubious origins—a bastard Armenian whose father was an American missionary and who escaped the 1915 genocide in Turkey—that his employer and patron, a Lebanese nobleman, gives him the surname al-Kharrat (the liar). Within one generation, the storyteller's oral profession is subsequently replaced by mundane commerce, and a family empire is spawned. The only person to continue the patriarch's survival strategy of spinning tales within tales is the first-person narrator of the frame-story and main protagonist, the hakawati's grandson, Osama. He returns to his country from California for his own father's deathbed as a family outsider: "I was a tourist in a bizarre land. I was home."[149]

The Hakawati is simultaneously a book about an American Lebanese's coming home, about the modern history of Beirut, and a metafiction about storytelling—a fictionalized narrative that reflects on the conditions for the (im)possibility of

---

147   Alameddine, *Koolaids: The Art of War* 244.
148   Rabih Alameddine, *The Hakawati* (New York: Knopf, 2008) 5.
149   Alameddine, *The Hakawati* 7.

telling true stories. By adapting the narrating-against-death motive and poly-phonic structure of *The Arabian Nights* side by side with the stereotypes of the Western Orientalist archive, it uses both the counter-narrative power and the hegemonic commodifications of the Shahrazadian trope. Reflecting these for-merly separated and now interwoven representational modes in the broken mirror of our postcolonial present, the novel lays bare the complex narrative precedents of cross-cultural (mis-)understanding.

The main subject of *The Hakawati* is first announced in the American-Arab hy-brid title. The reader learns that a hakawati is a professional storyteller. And in case one loses the novel's narratological focus, each of its four sub-books opens with a series of epigraphs testifying to the power of storytelling from sources as diverse as the Quran, Hannah Arendt's *The Human Condition* (1958), or literary works by Fer-nando Pessoa and Emile Habibi. While the ever-shifting narrative does not allow the reader to form an immediate, strong attachment to any of the characters of the many subplots, each individual story sets its hook, giving her or him just enough of a deathbed scene, piece of family history, or fantastic tale to draw her/him further in: Thousands of Arabian desert miles are traveled in a sentence, historic battles are fought in a paragraph, and an encounter with jinns receives only a minimal-ist description. This illustrative bareness explores and thereby exposes the limits of what the (Western) reader needs to get hooked to the frame story. At the same time, the multiplying dissection of the Kharrat's family story provides a template for *The Hakawati*'s larger experiment, namely, to question the ways in which we understand ourselves and our worlds. Mythic stories of the heroic Islamic Sultan, Baybars, who fights the European crusaders, are interposed with stories of Osama's personal history and the stories of his family. The reader learns about the mythical twinned lovers, Shams and Layla, against snippets from Osama's intoxicant under-graduate years in California or his grandfather's birth. In other sections, we find references to Western and Middle Eastern mass media. Each of the narrative frag-ments participates in building Osama's self, whether by illuminating his family's complex genealogy or his personal cross-cultural past. For this novelistic process of narrative identification, the story of how his grandparents first met is as important as the story of a jinn having sex with a human being.

The individual ego that the novel narrates is made up of many intertwined sto-ries, canonized representations of pivotal historical moments, as well as fleeting personal experiences. As Osama's grandfather explains, each story's power comes not from any causal importance or intrinsic logic but from the fact that it is being told: "Events matter little, only stories of those events affect us."[150] It is this insight that guides the novel's narrative structure. Coherent historical events or linear bio-graphical strands are as irrelevant as authentic authorship or narrative originality.

---

150   Alameddine, *The Hakawati* 450.

Instead, *The Hakawati* focuses on the selective procedure of making meaning and listening. None of the many narrators has the authority of a historical chronicler: "'Never trust the teller,' [...]. 'Trust the tale.'"[151] This phrase is reminiscent of D.H. Lawrence's famous 1923 essay, "The Spirit of Place," in which he warns his reader: "Never trust the artist. Trust the tale."[152] Whereas Lawrence argues that the proper function of a literary critic "is to save the tale from the artist who created it,"[153] Alameddine's novel seems to evoke more fundamental skepticism regarding the narrative capacity to represent factual truth. Most of Osama's stories are about other people and told by other people. However, these are the stories that make up Osama's self because they prefigure how other people perceive him. In cross-cultural perspective, the transmigrant Osama's intimate reflection on his difficult personal relation to his dying father in the final section of the novel can be read as an allegorical comment on the mutual ignorance between the West and the Arab world. In such a reading, the relation between the two men symbolizes the collective history of Orientalist and Occidentalist (mis)representations: "what happens is of little significance compared with the stories we tell ourselves about what happens. [...] My father and I may have shared numerous experiences, but, as I was constantly finding out, we rarely shared their stories."[154]

The narrational relation between Osama and his father in many ways reciprocates the narrative frame situation of Elias Khoury's anti-heroic epic, *Bab ash-Shams* (*Gate of the Sun*). Whereas the Palestinian exile, Khaleel, talks to the dying freedom fighter, Yunis, to delay death and fight forgetfulness, Osama's re-construction of memories seems to be strictly privately grounded, at least at first sight. Like his grandfather, he has remarkable skills of storytelling as an endless spiral of inaugurating further enframed narrative voices with even greater narrative skills. His quasi-nocturnal discourse, like Khaleel's, uses narrative gaps and absences in dominant representations to open up a metafictional, almost metahistorical space for reflecting the archival limits of telling his own and his family's (hi-)stories. But no final resolution or harmonizing reconciliation between the competing modalities of enunciation is offered.

The enduring dilemma of unresolved dissonances is metaphorically emplotted in a sub-story on a love-hate relationship between an Arabic 'oud and a Western electric guitar. Osama learns and loves to play the traditional, pear-shaped Arabic stringed instrument at a young age. However, at a certain point, he decides to learn to play the e-guitar to attract the Beiruti girls around him who prefer Western pop music. Many years later, as a student in Los Angeles, he tries to play a maqam,

---

151 Alameddine, *The Hakawati* 206.
152 D. H. Lawrence, "The Spirit of Place," *Studies in Classic American Literature*, by D. H. Lawrence, ed. Ezra Greenspan, Lindeth Vasey, and John Worthen (Cambridge: Cambridge UP, 2003) 14.
153 D. H. Lawrence, "The Spirit of Place," 14.
154 Alameddine, *The Hakawati* 450.

a particular Arabic modality or genre related to scale and mood of music, for his roommates in his university's dormitory on his brand-new Gibson J-200. While his fingers still remember to play the Arabic way, the Western guitar frets' prefiguring of the instrument's fixed chordal tonality get in the way. He improvises and his roommates look dazed: "'That was different'," one of them says. "You shouldn't play anything but that'."[155] However, Osama himself feels that he cannot make the guitar produce the sounds he re-imagines. Finally, he knows what is wrong and what to do:

> I walked out of the room and into the common kitchen. I unstrung my guitar and put it on the Formica counter. I searched the drawers for the right tool, but could come up with nothing better than a steak knife to defret my J200. The steak knife was too flimsy, so I tried a bread knife. Without its frets, my guitar would sound better, more me. The bread knife didn't work, either. I plugged in the carving knife, and the current jerked it into life. I went to work. The sound of the knife's tiny motor grew deafening, but I persisted. I went too deep with the first fret, not so much with the second. I'd figured out how to operate by the third and fourth, but I stopped at the fifth. I stared at the dying instrument before me and left it. I returned to my dorm room and lay down, my head buzzing.[156]

There is no higher unity of polyphony or harmonic contrapuntality foreseen in this story. The sounds of the guitar and the 'oud establish dissonant cross-cultural counterpoints. Assumed consonance is deconstructed through a violent skip, and dissonance is metaphorically depicted as more than simply a transitory state to be overcome in dialogue. Aesthetic harmony gives way to the painful expression of conflicting voices. Nevertheless, some critics discovered in *The Hakawati* a potential "to transcend the mountain of polemic, historical inquiry, policy analysis and reportage that stands between the Western reader and the Arab soul."[157] So here it comes again: the Arab soul. No wonder Alameddine's next book project avoided easy Orientalizing connotations.

The 2013 novel, *An Unnecessary Woman*, presents an elderly heroine that resists all things exotic. The story of the solitary Beiruti eccentric armed with a typing machine and a pistol who produces translations of Western books that nobody knows about at several points risks ending up in a metafictional contribution to the studies of translation and intertextuality. It definitely succeeds in preventing any evocation of ethnic or cultural representation. While the translator, Aliya, knows

155   Alameddine, *The Hakawati* 342.
156   Alameddine, *The Hakawati* 342-43.
157   Lorraine Adams, "Once Upon Many Times," Rev. of *The Hakawati*, by Rabih Alameddine, *The New York Times*, nytimes.com 18 May 2008, 13 Feb. 2015 <http://www.nytimes.com/2008/05/18/books/review/Adams-t.html?_r=0>.

that we all "lie down with hope and wake up with lies,"[158] Alameddine apparently optimistically did not give up believing in his readers' capacity for unprejudiced expectations: "If I am supposed to represent the Arabs, we're in deep shit."[159] Yet, the pessimistic or rather realistic quasi-dialogic anticipation of these very readers' impertinent demands for ethnic authenticity and cultural representativity never ceased to inform his literary work.[160]

The cross-cultural conflict between musical instruments imagined by Alameddine reminds us that the conflict between competing representational modes takes place not only on the level of text and narrative. Whereas *The Hakawati*'s sub-plot draws on musical (sonic) tropes, the broader cultural sphere with which I am concerned here involves textual narrative, performance, images, and sounds in equal measure. If one considers the complex nexus of invisibility and blocked visibility or forced visibility, of mutually excluding images/stereotypes, as well as the struggle of voicing these experiences, one cannot be surprised that Anglophone Arab intellectuals have increasingly turned to the sphere of audio-visual arts. Many diasporic transmigrant artists from the late 1990s onwards directly participated in the formation of independent projects, galleries, and festivals within the Middle East. The art scene in Cairo and Beirut, in particular, offered new platforms beyond the state-controlled cultural spaces of phobocratic censorship. At the same time, Anglophone Arab concept and performance artists are increasingly present(ed) at international art shows in Venice, Kassel, New York, or Abu Dhabi.[161] At this point, I want to turn to these audio-visual and performative spheres of Anglophone Arab cultural production.

Contemporary Anglophone Arab concept and performance artists have a particularly intense interest in the archive, both in a literal and in a metaphorical sense. This archival impulse and documentary turn within Anglophone Arab representations raises several questions regarding the possibilities and impossibilities of telling individual Arab truths or providing collective testimony. These artists work through the archival materiality in order to rethink and transform the representational conditions of their own present positionalities. Their art is both an archival and a counter-archival art. It is at work in the archive, and it at the same time works against competing archives.

---

158   Alameddine, An *Unnecessary Woman* 44.

159   Dwyer Murphy, "This is also my world," Interview with Rabih Alameddine, *Guernica* 3 Mar. 2014, 13 Feb. 2015 <https://www.guernicamag.com/interviews/this-is-also-my-world/>.

160   This *pessoptimist* double anticipation is particularly true for his latest novel, which in many ways can be read as a sequel to *Koolaids*; see Rabih Alameddine, *The Angel of History* (New York: Atlantic Monthly P, 2016).

161   Kaelen Wilson-Goldie, "Off the Map: Contemporary Art in the Middle East," *The Future of Tradition—The Tradition of Future*, ed. Chris Dercon, León Krempel, and Avinoam Shalem (Munich: Haus der Kunst, 2010) 62-63.

A significant example of the artistic practice of calling into question stories and histories in Anglophone Arab representations is Walid Raad's brainchild, the Atlas Group project. Founded in 1999, the Atlas Group forms the constant basis for Raad's multimedia performances. The pseudo-scientific laboratory mimics and thereby exposes the mechanisms of the archive as a place where the production of historical knowledge happens.[162] When the Atlas Group first appeared on the Lebanese art scene, it was immediately afforded a space in high-profile international venues such as Documenta, the Whitney Biennale, and the Venice Biennale. Today, artist and Cooper Union School of Arts teacher Raad is based between Brooklyn and Beirut. His work is particularly concerned with selections and representations of knowledge of the Middle East. His specific approach to the accumulation of documents related to Lebanon's recent history has all the trappings of the documentary genre. A typical Atlas Group production involves press photographs, news clippings, interview transcripts, video footage, graphics, elements of collage, and video art—all rolled up in the framework of the artist's talk or lecture. The most important bases for any production or publication are the documents collected and the ordered files of the Atlas Group Archives.

The use of the term *Atlas* is no accident. It refers to and re-claims one of the most important representational constituents of imperial power. At the same time, it alludes to a particular archival tradition of art history, cultural studies, and art practice ranging from Aby Warburg's *Mnemosyne Atlas* to Gerhard Richter's famous artistic collection of photographs, newspaper cuttings, and drawings.[163] The Atlas Group represents many things at the same time. It refers to the work of an individual artist, to his imaginary foundation established in 1976, or to a real foundation established in 1976 by someone called Maha Traboulsi. On various occasions and in various locations, Raad has stated that the Atlas Group is a nonprofit foundation established in Beirut in 1967, or in New York in 2000, or in Beirut in 2002. The information circulated depends on the artist's considerations with regard to the specific pre-knowledge of the audience.

Although Raad's performances, exhibitions, and publications explain that the Atlas Group documents are produced and that he attributed them to various imaginary individuals, the international audience long failed to grasp the imaginary nature of the Atlas Group, its archives, and its documents. This confirms the weighty associations of authority and authenticity that certain modes of address (the lecture, the conference) and display (the white walls of a museum or gallery, the picture frame, the museum catalogue) automatically carry. The performative adjustment of authority is particularly evident in the Atlas Group's lectures, which look

---

162   Sarah Rogers, "Forging History, Performing Memory: Walid Raad's The Atlas Project," *Parachute (Beyrouth_Beirut)* 108 (2002): 68-79.

163   Benjamin H. D. Buchloh, "Gerhard Richter's 'Atlas'," *October* 88 (1999): 117-45.

and sound like a college lecture or an academic conference presentation. Raad sits behind a rectangular table facing the audience and shows slides and videotapes on a screen. He speaks into a microphone. A glass of water, a notebook, a pen, and a lamp lay on the table. He wears a light shirt and dark dress pants. The earliest manifestations of this kind of performance authority happened in the context of an academic conference in Beirut in 1999, and the second occurred in the context of an artist talk at the Ayloul Festival in Beirut shortly thereafter.[164]

A file with the title "Missing Lebanese Wars" contains a richly illustrated notebook by Dr. Fadl Fakhouri (fig. 18). It is about historians who spend their wartime gambling at Beirut's horse-race track. These historians, however, do not bet—as one might expect—on the winning horse but on the distance between the winning horse and the finish line that would be captured in the published photo-finish photograph. Against the background of competing versions of the so-called civil war and the roles or responsibilities along the lines of different sectarian and political groups, this work can be interpreted as a direct comment on the unresolved inner-Lebanese struggle over historical representation (for instance, in schoolbooks) and reconciliation. At the same time, it can be read as a translocal metaphor for the production and control of historical evidence through acts of deferment and extension of meaning. These acts or counter-acts of controlling the distance between a signified thing or event (here the winning horse's running-in) and its signification (the published photo) are at the core of Walid Raad's artistic practice.

The crucial implication of "Missing Lebanese Wars" is that it is impossible to coherently reconstruct a history of the civil war without an abstraction. Shedding light on some of the unexamined dimensions of the war, the Atlas Group does not speak of the Lebanese Civil War but sensitizes the audience for the plurality of wartime experiences as they are conditioned by manifold religious, class, ideological, and gender locations. Dr. Fadl Fakhouri's notebook raises the troubling question of the possibilities and limits of writing any history of the wars in Lebanon. Only on the surface does the project recount the story of some Lebanese historians who were betting on photo-finish horse-race photographs. It also allegorically forces the audience to consider whether the violent events represented were actually experienced by those who lived them.

The cross-cultural implications of this radical questioning of archival truth become obvious when watching the so-called *Bachar Tapes*. The fifty-three videotapes form another file of the Atlas Group archives. Only two are available to a Western audience. They serve as a testimony to the experiences of Souheil Bachar, a Lebanese man claiming to be a sixth hostage held in captivity with five American men in Lebanon during the hostage crisis of the early 1980s (fig. 19 and 20).

---

164   Walid Ra'ad, Interview with Alan Gilbert, *BOMB Magazine* 81 (2002), 24 Nov. 2016 <http://bombmagazine.org/article/2504/walid-ra-ad>.

Figure 18: Walid Raad/The Atlas Group, Notebook Volume 72:
Missing Lebanese Wars, 1999.

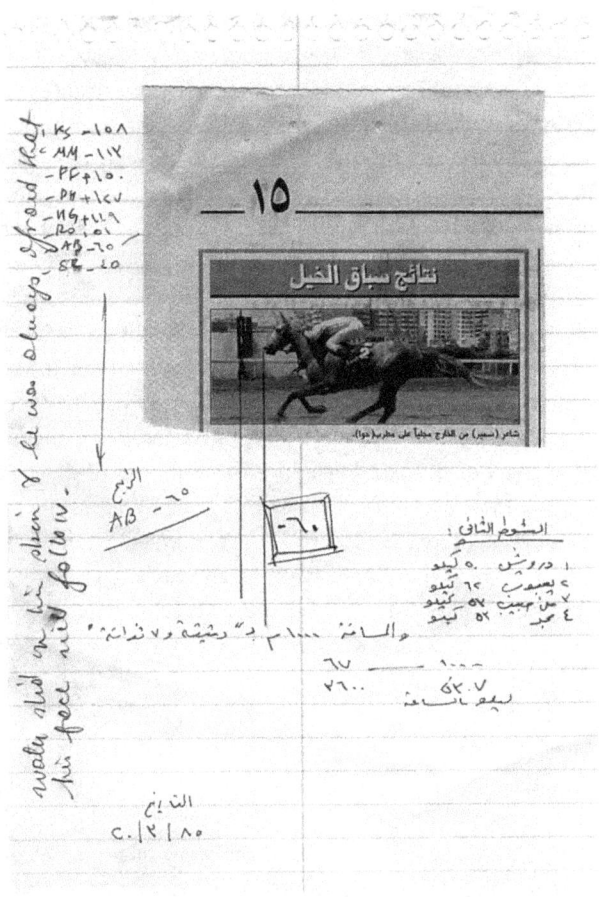

Whereas the captivity memoirs written by American ex-hostages, such as Terry A.
Anderson's *Den of Lions* (1994)[165] or Tom Sutherland's *At Your Own Risk* (1996),[166] primarily represent the experience of captivity as a completely depoliticized individual
phenomenon without prequel, Bachar insists on laying bare the concrete pretexts
and contexts of the American presence in the Middle East as well as the motives of

165   Terry A. Anderson, *Den of Lions: Memoirs of Seven Years* (1993; New York: Ballantine, 1994).
166   Tom Sutherland, *At Your Own Risk: An American Chronicle of Crisis and Captivity in the Middle East*
      (Golden, CO: Fulcrum, 1996).

the hostage-takers. He wants to demonstrate that geopolitical and regional backgrounds, such as the Reagan administration's military support of the Israeli army during its occupation of Lebanon, are displaced systematically in Western representations. Bachar explains his counter-discursive approach of using the gaps and blind spots of Western narratives as starting points to set off his own narrative as follows:

> My interest today is how this kind of experience can be documented and represented. I am convinced that the Americans have failed miserably in this regard but that in their failure they have revealed much to us about the possibilities and limits of representing the experience of captivity.[167]

At the same time, he wants to demonstrate that the human tragedy of captivity was first and foremost a Lebanese experience. The unnamed "pest" who is described by Anderson as "worth nothing as a bargaining chip" and at whom he reports to "have snapped several times"[168] or the fellow-hostage christened "the Arab"[169] in Sutherland's account suddenly gets a face.

Although Bachar presents himself as a reliable ex-hostage, a Lebanese or Arab audience would immediately recognize him as the well-known Lebanese TV soap actor, Fadi Abi Samra. The casting of a prominent Arab actor stresses the perceptual divide between a Western and an Arab audience. Hence, one cannot be surprised that Bachar, despite aesthetic hints and explicit statements signaling fictionality, has often been taken as a factual historical person by the Western art audience. Inventing a man who insists to tell his true story, Raad reciprocates the scripted nature of the Western hostage narrative. The clearest trope of doubling or countering the representational authority of the Western archive happens through the excessive use of dubbing and subtitling. Bachar speaks Arabic but makes clear with his first words how the narrative should be edited. Echoing the biblical creation trope, his dictates are immediately set into practice. He controls the (mis-)translation of his text into English and insists on a neutral, CNN-style female voice. The Orientalist image of the Arab as a passive, feminized other who cannot speak for himself is affirmed and, at the same time, subverted. The Arab, equally abhorred and desired, speaks through his female voice-over (the voice of the paradigmatic other, if you'd like) to the Western audience and thus seems to confirm that audience's perception. However, the American hostages who asserted their straight identity and moral superiority in their own narratives are represented here according to

---

167   Souheil Bachar [Walid Raad], "Civilizationally, We Do Not Dig Holes To Bury Ourselves," Interview with The Atlas Group/Walid Raad, *Tamáss: Contemporary Arab Representations Beirut/Lebanon 1*, ed. Catherine David (Barcelona: Fundació Antoni Tàpies, 2002) 136.
168   Anderson, *Den of Lions: Memoirs of Seven Years* 120.
169   Sutherland, *At Your Own Risk: An American Chronicle of Crisis and Captivity in the Middle East* 167.

Figure 19: Souheil Bachar, film still (7:11 min.) from Hostage: The Bachar Tapes (English Version), Tape #17, dir. Souheil Bachar, The Atlas Group in collab. with c-hundred film corp, 2000.

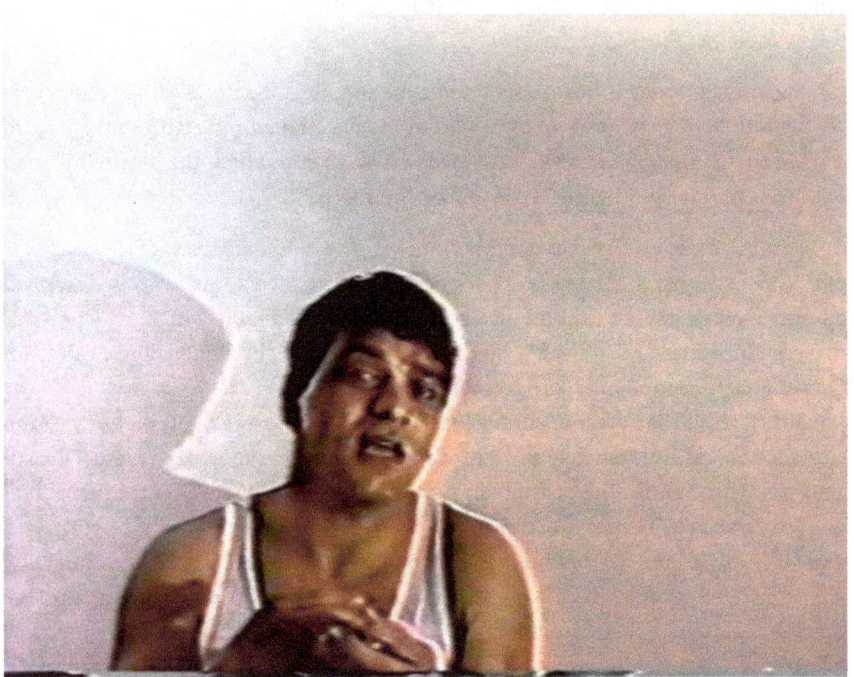

Bachar's script. Mistranslations are only evident to a bi-lingual Arabic-speaking audience. Only they can follow the reversal of symbolic power when, for instance, Bachar's Arabic voice reports to have penetrated Anderson while his English voice-over explains that Anderson aroused Bachar and then punched him. The disclosure of his editorial control not only displaces truth claims but also draws attention to the act of displacement. The performative reversal of translational power is repeat-edly exhibited and underlined by Raad. Asked by the artist-researcher-archivist about the reliability of his translations and their obvious contradictions, Bachar defensively answers: "Yes, I do my own translations. I have nothing to say about the second part of your second question."[170]

Raad's project does not approach facts in their crude facticity but through the complicated mediations by which they acquire their immediacy. The Atlas Group

---

170   Bachar, "Civilizationally, We Do Not Dig Holes To Bury Ourselves," Interview with The Atlas Group/Walid Raad, 125.

Figure 20: Film still (06:27 min) from Hostage: The Bachar Tapes (English Version), Tape #17, dir. Souheil Bachar, The Atlas Group in collab. with c-hundred film corp, 2000.

produces and collects objects and stories that cannot be examined through the conventional binary of fiction and nonfiction. It demonstrates that the way we con-struct our cross-cultural imaginaries does not do justice to the complex experiences of those imagined. Furthermore, Raad urges us to see his documents not as based on any one person's actual memories but on "fantasies erected from the material of collective memories."[171] These documents do not function as scraps of historical evidence. The faked documents are presented as *art-facts* rather than as artefacts. Functioning as artistic traces between what is known to be true and what has to be believed from a certain political, ideological, or cultural point of view, Raad's art exposes the performative genesis of (cross-cultural) meaning: "It is also important for us to note that the truth of the documents we research does not depend solely on their factual accuracy. We are concerned with facts, but we do not view facts as self-evident objects that are already present in the world."[172]

In recent years, Walid Raad's art practice has expanded upon this research-based method of the Atlas Group. The project, *Scratching on Things I Could Disavow* (2007–ongoing), or the more recent work, *Preface to the First Edition* (2013–ongoing), radically questions the current dominant mode of representation and perception of

---

171   Gilbert, Interview with Walid Ra'ad.
172   Gilbert, Interview with Walid Ra'ad.

art in and from the Arab world. These projects explore the relation between the ideological, economic, and political dimensions of the global art market phenomenon. They ask whether and how the recent hype around and commodification of Arab and Islamic art can really help to establish representational spaces that are defined by Arab or Muslim artists and not by Western consumers. As virtual micro-expositions, they imagine and thus function as model platforms for alternative future art shows. Such artistic-curatorial platforms are explained by Raad himself as "stage-sets from a forthcoming play."[173] The artist Raad uses the conventions of display and the modes of address associated with an authoritative curatorial voice to destabilize and to challenge dominant Western modes of representing non-Western art. He leans on and at the same time plays with these modes.

Rabih Alameddine and Walid Raad share an interest in the narrative discourse of (hi)storytelling. Their narrations take the form of a tragedy, comedy, or farce and often combine other modes of telling stories. In the two transmigrants' works, narration is not treated as a neutral discursive form. Far from being a medium in which events, whether imaginary or real, can be represented in transparency and reliability, the narrative or performative act is presented as an expression in discourse. Their representations do not carry a message without at the same time reflecting the competing modes of experiences, the structural conditions, and the archival precedents that determine these representations. The experience of *life across* is narrated from inside and outside of the eventualities upon which these transmigrant intellectuals draw. The ideological nature of storytelling is turned into a metafictional parallel text that constantly considers the recognizability and discursive authority of the story-type chosen. The question of authenticity, originality, or truthfulness is at least postponed. Both the writer and the artist know that single archives and closed structural systems of enunciations have the tendency to (re-)produce (hetero-)normative stories, no matter how idiosyncratic and supposedly overarching they are. Exploring the mnemonic power of narrative queer-steps or audio-visual snapshots, they multiply archival dissonance. At the same time, their praxeology of narrative truth goes decisively beyond what has been variously described as the counter-discursive or dialogical imagination. Foucault's notion of the archive and his celebration of modern literature and art as counter-discourse[174] cannot sufficiently explain the particular cross-cultural practice at work here. Neither can it be fully grasped with Bakhtin's important evidence that in novelistic

---

173   "Walid Ra'ad—Scratching on Things I Could Disavow," *Kunstaspekte* July 2007, 22 Sept. 2011 <http://www.kunstaspekte.de/index.php?action=termin&tid=52070>.

174   Michel Foucault, *Archeology of Knowledge*, trans. A.M. Sheridan Smith (*L'archéologie du savoir*, 1969; tr. 1972; London: Routledge, 2002) 142-50 and Michel Foucault, *The Order of Things: Archaeology of the Human Sciences* (*Les mots et les choses: Une archéologie des sciences humaines*, 1966; trans. 1970; London: Routledge, 2002) 48.

writing "every word is directed toward an *answer* and cannot escape the profound influence of the answering word that it anticipates."[175]

In my view, any archaeology of the dialogic production and dissemination of Anglophone Arab meaning must consider the specific relational dynamics constricting the interpretation of words and images when the Arab subject speaks. Therefore, if one wants to name a specific Anglophone Arab stamping of the general *Archive Fever*[176] in contemporary literature and the arts, it probably lies in a poetics that incorporates the ideological and moral ambiguity of working across archives, Arab and non-Arab alike. It is my argument that such poetics can help one to allegorically imagine the as of yet all too often unimaginable correlation of mutually excluding archives.

5.3   Palestinian *Parkours*–Matters of (F)Act: Occupation, Deterritorialization, and Cultural Resistance

Emily Jacir is a Palestinian activist-artist. Born in 1970 in Bethlehem, in the occupied Palestinian territories, she grew up in Saudi Arabia, Italy, and the US, where she received a degree from the Memphis College of Art. Since 2006, she has taught at the International Academy of Art Palestine in Ramallah. Today she divides her time between Rome, Ramallah, and New York City. The transmigrant artist grew up well aware of the representations and misrepresentations of the Palestinian people, of their individual life stories, and collective history. Like other transmigrant Palestinian intellectuals, Jacir incorporates the insights gained from her experience of the cross-cultural dissemination of meaning into her own mode of artistic production. Therefore, the dilemma of mutually excluding systems of evidence (of competing archives) is at the core of her work.

Jacir first caused a stir in the New York City art scene when, in 2000, she placed her Christmas postcards (fig. 21) in Manhattan's small stationery stores, thus smuggling the continuing actuality of military occupation into the aesthetics of the US Christmas industry, and again in 2001, with her refugee tent project *Memorial to 418 Palestinian Villages* (fig. 22), which traced the depopulation of Palestine in both a historical and a contemporary context. In the meantime, her art was afforded a space in high-profile international venues such as the Documenta, the Whitney Biennale, and the Venice Biennale.

Since 2005, Jacir has worked on the long-term concept and performance project, *Material for a Film*. The multimedia work is dedicated to the remembrance

---

175   Mikhail M. Bakhtin, "Discourse in the Novel," 280.
176   Jacques Derrida, *Archive Fever: A Freudian Impression*, trans. Eric Prenowitz (Chicago: U of Chicago P, 1995).

Figure 21: Emily Jacir, Christmas 2000, Christmas greeting card, c-print, 2000.

of the Palestinian activist, poet, writer, and translator, Wael Zuaiter (fig. 23), who was killed at the age of 38 by Mossad agents in Rome on October 16, 1972. While the PLO representative himself had always renounced political violence against civilians, he was suspected of being a member of the militant group, Black September, responsible for the Munich massacre of Israeli athletes during the 1972 Summer Olympics. His murder marked the beginning of a series of secret retaliation attacks and assassinations perpetrated by Israeli intelligence against Palestinian activists in the Western diaspora. The details of what really happened in Rome have never been clarified.

Although the Israeli journalist, Aaron J. Klein, stated in his 2005 publication, *Striking Back*, that Zuaiter was seen by the Mossad as a terrorist merely posing as

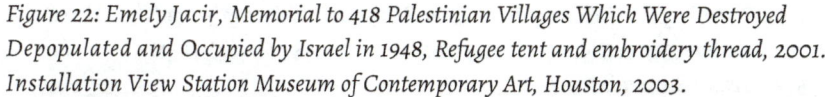

Figure 22: Emely Jacir, Memorial to 418 Palestinian Villages Which Were Destroyed Depopulated and Occupied by Israel in 1948, Refugee tent and embroidery thread, 2001. Installation View Station Museum of Contemporary Art, Houston, 2003.

a moderate intellectual and that he consequently became the so-called "first man down"[177] of the Mossad's counter-terrorism operations, the Israeli government has to this day denied any involvement. It was neither Klein's real-life spy drama of Zuaiter's murder nor its random filmic visualization in Steven Spielberg's 2005 movie, *Munich*,[178] that spurred Jacir to present a Palestinian narrative but rather these as well as other Western depictions' lack of detail and background regarding Zuaiter's actual life. The main source and conceptual starting point of her documentary allegory is *Per un palestinese*,[179] an Italian anthology of tribute essays, poems, interviews, memoirs, and drawings edited in 1979 by Zuaiter's spouse, Janet

---

177 Aaron J. Klein, *Striking Back: The 1972 Munich Olympics Massacre and Israel's Deadly Response* (New York: Random House, 2005) 117.

178 *Munich*, dir. Steven Spielberg, screenplay Tony Kushner, Eric Roth, Universal Pictures & DreamWorks Pictures, 2005.Warner Bros, 1973.

179 Janet Venn-Brown, ed., *Per un palestinese. Dediche a più voci a Wael Zuaiter* (Milano: Mazzotta, 1979).

Figure 23: Portrait of Wael Zuaiter, detail from Emily Jacir's Material for a Film. Mixed media installation, 2005–ongoing. Here, installation at the Central Pavilion at the Giardini, 52nd Venice Biennial, 2007.

Venn-Brown. The anthology's English translation was published in 1984.[180] In one of its chapters, Elio Petri, a neorealist film director, and Ugo Pirro, a novelist and screenplay writer, elaborate on their plan to produce a documentary about Zuaiter's life. They present their scripts of conversations with persons who knew Zuaiter in Rome under the title "Material for a Film."[181] The writers, artists, filmmakers, and journalists interviewed consistently assert that he categorically rejected violence. In fact, Zuaiter was never conclusively linked to the Olympics' murders. It seems that he was eliminated rather because he was a pioneer in trying to tell the Palestinian story to the world from a Palestinian point of view, an eloquent and well-connected spokesperson for the Palestinian cause in Europe. Pirro's premature death brought the film project to an end; it was never realized.

---

180   Janet Venn-Brown, ed., *For a Palestinian: A Memorial to Wael Zuaiter* (London: Kegan Paul, 1984).

181   Elio Petri and Ugo Pirro, "Material for a Film," *For a Palestinian: A Memorial to Wael Zuaiter*, ed. Janet Venn-Brown (London: Kegan Paul, 1984) 75-116.

Almost thirty years later, coinciding with the 35th commemoration of Zuaiter's assassination, a diasporic Palestinian investigation that takes up Pirro's idea of shedding light on the lost and obscured fragments of Zuaiter's life was awarded the Venice Biennale's prestigious Golden Lion. At first glance, Jacir's ongoing artistic research simply collects and exhibits historical documents with the aim of narrating an individual life story that has not been told. Her installations combine Zuaiter's private items, press photographs, news clippings, interview transcripts, video footage, as well as a film sequence of Zuaiter's featured part in Peter Sellers's 1963 movie, *The Pink Panther*. At the same time, this ongoing homage stands for the claims of memory related to the marginalized experiences of numerous Palestinian exiles.[182] Material for a Film is as much about the Palestinian people as it is about one man.

I do, however, believe that there is more at stake in this project: Jacir's accumulation of documents related to Zuaiter's life story has all the trappings of the documentary genre. While each of her objects sheds light on another biographical fragment or contextual aspect, her retelling of the personal history willingly exposes the archival violence involved in the production of historical evidence. This particular quality of Jacir's work can be best illustrated with her 2006 performance at the Sydney Biennale. When Zuaiter was assassinated in Rome, he carried with him the second volume of an Arab edition of the *Arabian Nights* (fig. 24, 25). Since all available Italian editions were translations from European versions, the Palestinian intellectual was working on a new, direct Italian translation of the Arabic classic. According to the artist, Zuaiter's Arabic copy was perforated by a 22-caliber bullet. The Sydney performance of *Material for a Film* picks up precisely this deadly end to a failed cross-cultural transfer of the *Nights*—the failed translation of a text that has influenced Western misrepresentations and perceptions of the Arab world probably more than any other narrative.

During her Sydney performance, Jacir fired a gun at 1,000 blank-paged books (fig. 26). In the installation that followed, she exhibited these perforated empty carriers of meaning together with the single pages ripped out of what was presented as Zuaiter's original copy. The 1,000 blank pages clearly symbolize the thousands of Palestinian stories that have not been written (fig. 27). However, beyond the particular tragedy of Zuaiter's murder and other Palestinians' cruel fates, the performance work addresses the complex interrelation between physical power and representational validity in the Palestinian-Israeli conflict. The failed translation of *Arabian Nights* reminds us that the cross-cultural translation of stories, just like telling histories, is by no means an ideologically neutral undertaking. As Jorge Borges elaborates in his 1936 essay on "The Translators of *The Thousand and One*

---

182   Ahmad H. Sa'di and Lila Abu-Lughod, eds., *Nakba: Palestine, 1948, and the Claims of Memory* (New York: Columbia UP, 2007).

Figure 24: Wael Zuaiter's corpse after his assassination in Rome on 16 October 1972; detail from Jacir's mixed media Installation Material for a Film, 2005– ongoing.

Nights,"[183] translation (any translation) is necessarily a mistranslation: a polemical act of translating against other translations, of imposing one's interpretation over another and thus outdoing other translators. In this view, Jacir's performance symbolically re-enacts the violent prevention of a strategic and, maybe, polemic Palestinian translation. It performs the deadly prevention of the resistive appropriation of the *Nights* by a Palestinian activist-intellectual. The particular symbolism at work here combines the Palestinian experience of violence with the Shahrazadian trope of resistance and the Borgesian notion of translating against.

Re-enacting the violent suspension of an emancipatory Palestinian self-representation, the Sydney performance broaches an issue that is at the core of the Palestinian experience: the denial of Palestinians' memory, the erasure of their archives, and the silencing of their voices. In this context, it is worth recalling that Edward Said's seminal 1984 essay, "Permission to Narrate,"[184] was written as a direct consequence of Israel's invasion of Lebanon and the destruction of the PLO research center and archives in Beirut. According to Said, Palestinian history has been oc-

---

183   Jorge Luis Borges, "The Translators of *The Thousand and One Nights*," 92-109.
184   Edward Said, "Permission to Narrate," *Journal of Palestine Studies* 13.3 (1984): 27-48.

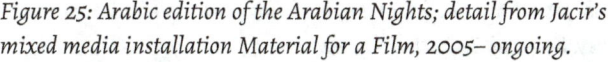

Figure 25: Arabic edition of the Arabian Nights; detail from Jacir's mixed media installation Material for a Film, 2005– ongoing.

cluded to the point that Palestinians "are invisible people."[185] Therefore, the very act of creating and circulating a narrative or an image that proves the existence of Palestinians becomes a form of political resistance: "Facts do not at all speak for themselves, but require a socially acceptable narrative to absorb, sustain, and circulate them."[186] Said's argument has inspired numerous writers and film makers, who created what Hamid Dabashi coined Palestinian "aesthetic of the invisible."[187] Ma-

185 "A One-State Solution, KGNU, Boulder, Colorado, February 8, 1999," *Culture and Resistance: Conversations with Edward W. Said,* by David Barsamian and Edward Said (Cambridge, MA: South End P, 2003) 20.

186 Said, "Permission to Narrate," 34.

187 Hamid Dabashi, Introduction, *Dreams of a Nation* (London: Verso, 2006) 18.

Figure 26: Emily Jacir, Material for a Film, performance 1000 blank books shot, 2006. Bi-
ennale of Sydney, Zones of Contact, 8 June–27 August 2006.

terial for a Film is influenced by this aesthetic attempt to make visible what has been
hidden. In addition, Jacir's project can be linked to the trans-local resistance strategy of the Palestinian novelist and theorist, Ghassan Kanafani. Until his murder in
1972, the editor of the Beirut-based magazine, *Al-Hadaf*, called upon Palestinians
to first analyze how representational regulations affect the almost unconditional
acceptance of military occupation and to then take the local struggle for liberation into the civic domain of Western representation. Jacir's work draws on both
Kanafani's concept of resistance literature (*adab al-muqawama*) and Said's permis-
sion-to-narrate imperative. It documents, preserves, and narrates the Palestinian
experience.

However, as a work of performance art, *Material for a Film* transgresses the
morality of counter-truth that dominates the traditional Palestinian resistance
paradigm of writing or narrating back. It resists the dominant demand to explain
to the world who or what Palestinians really are, to show to the world that they
exist. Similar to the documents of the Atlas Group, Jacir's documents do not

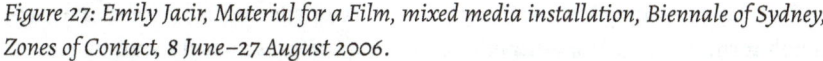

Figure 27: Emily Jacir, Material for a Film, mixed media installation, Biennale of Sydney, Zones of Contact, 8 June–27 August 2006.

function simply as scraps of historical truth. Having witnessed the performative production of the perforated blank pages, we cannot know if the artist is manipulating her other materials as well. In order to interpret this work, one needs to acknowledge first of all that one is confronted with *matters of act* rather than with matters of fact, with *Tat-Sachen*, in German, rather than with *Tatsachen*. The Sydney performance explicitly stages the difference between the two. Jacir's work does not simply narrate Palestinian truths against hegemonic histories, thus leading to the contrapuntal harmony of an extended archive. Archival dissonance is not dissolved into any higher order. Her performative acts and conceptual exhibitions function as reminders that real experiences sometimes need to be re-formed or even perforated in order to be believed by others. The project creatively adapts and then extends the Saidian insight that facts do not speak for themselves: It explores both the procedures of memory and the strategies of making meaningful statements. The respective performative approach in an attempt to arrive at an *objective* view of a lost or obscured truth is not that of maximum detachment, in the Freudian sense, but of personal and subjective re-attachment.

Jacir seems to be more preoccupied with the modality of art as a fictocritical practice that constantly tests the capacity of art to control and extend meaning through form making. Her aesthetics of resistive re-presentation simultaneously functions as a poetics of artistic research.[188] It explores the representational regulation of a socio-political and historical phenomenon (the Palestinian cause) rather than its aesthetic display. Her aesthetics is an aesthetics of *formativity*,[189] not of form. It sets focus on the performative invention and production of forms that can or cannot tell the truth. It does not search for the beauty of truth but requires a dynamic rethinking and interpreting of our all too often static certainties regarding what is true and beautiful. In such artistic production, there is almost no vision outside the forming action itself.

Occasionally, Jacir's performative acts of controlling the relation between a historical event and its signification come along with an angry or even violent mood. Some might interpret her Sydney shooting as an act of artistic revenge. At other times, one gets the impression that the artist herself implicitly argues for a post-moralistic understanding of lies, as if she is saying that, within the Palestinian struggle, the powerful Israeli and Western lies need to be countered by lies of the Palestinians' own making. One should not forget that *Material for a Film* not only traces history but performs acute expressions within a concrete historical moment. Given the continuity of military occupation, settlement, and refugee tragedies, the project seems to argue that (factual historical) events matter little and that only stories of these events affect the world. The project indicates the emergence of new Palestinian strategies of cultural resistance. It allegorically suggests that what is assumingly *indeed* can only have an emancipatory effect in the world after it has been turned into an activity—only when it is *in deed*.[190]

This should not be misinterpreted as an artistic call to arms. Nevertheless, *Material for a Film* might encourage a post-moral understanding of strategic lies and a refusal to be repressed by what the London activist poet Sean Bonney calls "police re-

---

188 On the artist as researcher, see Janneke Wesseling, ed., *See it Again, Say it Again: The Artist as Researcher* (Amsterdam: Valiz, 2011).

189 I borrow the notion of formativity (*formatività*) from Luigi Pareyson's theory of artistic production. See Luigi Pareyson, "Art: Performance and Interpretation," *Existence, Interpretation, Freedom: Selected Writings*, by Luigi Pareyson, ed. Paolo Diego Bubbio, trans. Anna Mattei (Aurora, CO: Davies Group, 2009) 114-40. On Pareyson's concept of performativity, see also Umberto Eco, *The Open Work*, trans. Anna Cacogni (Cambridge: Harvard UP, 1989) 158-60 and Edward Arthur Lippman, Rev. of *Estetica. Teoria della formatività*, by Luigi Pareyson, *The Journal of Philosophy* 52.25 (1955): 791-96.

190 I borrow the fine but important differentiation between the meaning of "indeed" and "in deed" from Shakespeare's *Antony and Cleopatra*, Scene I.V. 6-16. Here, the eunuch Mardian has not "in deed" affections because he can do nothing. See *The Riverside Shakespeare* 1353. I thank Marga Munkelt for this hint!

ality."[191] When Ugo Pirro asked Janet Venn-Brown about her assassinated partner's reliability—"Did he also tell lies? Perhaps poetic ones?"—she answered in a quite evasive, yet significant way: "I wouldn't call them lies; let us say romanticisms."[192] Against the background of this statement, it seems legitimate to argue that Jacir's project encapsulates a poetics of post-romantic lies rather than an ethic of counter-truths. Such poetics is romantic in so far as it draws on the radical impulses of romanticisms (note the plural form!). *Material for a Film* is carried by a poetics of an equally active *and* activist romanticism.[193]

The concept and performance project can be placed within a particular strand of cultural resistance that struggles against invisibility and that can be traced back at least to the resistance literature of the 1960s. It is spurred by a lack of exposure regarding one Palestinian's life. Although it is concerned with exploring the collective meaning of this individual tragedy artistically, *Material for a Film* aims at more than charting spaces for speaking Palestinian truths to power or narrating a collective experience against the hegemonic Western/Israeli denial of that very experience. This is an archival documentary allegory which explores the dense relation between power and representational validity—a relation that prefigures the Palestinians' present struggle for justice. It is precisely this double-movement of shifting a local emancipatory struggle to the global (art) market while at the same time exploring the conditions of the (im)possibility of effectively doing so that is characteristic for the recent transformation within transnational cultural resistance. Whether from within or from outside Palestine, this conceptual shift is carried decisively by many recent Anglophone works, the approaches of which go beyond older notions of resistance represented by activist-intellectuals such as Ghassan Kanafani or Edward Said.

I want to use the remaining pages of this chapter to selectively explore these works' inherent frictions of truth and fiction with a particular focus on the questions of space, place, and (im)mobility. A spatial or geocritical approach to contemporary Anglophone Palestinian representation is almost inevitable. Given the geography of occupation and the spatial politics of its implementation,[194] a blind

---

191   Sean Bonney, "'Minds do exist to agitate and provoke / this is the reason I do not conform'—Anna Mendelssohn," *The Poetry Project Newsletter* (Feb./Mar. 2011): 17, <http://poetryproject.org/wp-content/uploads/PP_Newsletter_226_reduced.pdf>.

192   Janet Venn-Brown, "Material for a Film," Interview with Elio Petri and Ugo Pirro, *For a Palestinian: A Memorial to Wael Zuaiter*, ed. Janet Venn-Brown (London: Kegan Paul, 1984) 80.

193   On the notion of active romanticism in the context of poetry, see Julie Carr and Jeffrey C. Robinson, "Introduction: Active Romanticism," *Active Romanticism: The Radical Impulse in Nineteenth Century and Contemporary Poetic Practice*, eds. Julie Carr and Jeffrey C. Robinson (Tuscaloosa: U of Alabama P, 2015) 1-16.

194   On how the land of occupied Palestine has been hollowed out by Israel's politics of space, see Eyal Weizman, *Hollow Land: Israel's Architecture of Occupation* (London: Verso, 2007).

celebration of cultural mobility in the age of globalization is in every sense of the words out of place.[195] Instead, there is an urgent need to blatantly address the violently adjusted fixity and rigid compartmentalization of Palestinian lives under occupation. The literary and artistic representations that I discuss in the following pages do exactly that. But they do so without accepting the given spatial order and its social impacts as a permanent state. While it is true that Israel's politics of occupation implement the separation of human space, one cannot talk about contemporary cultural resistance without also considering the artistic invention of alternative spaces and new ways of crossing borders: spaces of local and global transgression, real spaces of representation, as well as spatial imaginaries that question the logics of separation, resistive walks, unexpected routes, and courageous *parkours*:

> A man going on a *sarha* wanders aimlessly, not restricted by time and place, going where his spirit takes him to nourish his soul and rejuvenate himself. But not any excursion would qualify as a *sarha*. Going on a *sarha* implies letting go. It is a drug-free high, Palestinian style.[196]

Raja Shehadeh's *Palestinian Walks: Notes on a Vanishing Landscape* was published in 2007. Shehadeh is a Palestinian lawyer, writer, and human rights activist who lives in the West Bank city of Ramallah. In 1979, after returning from his studies in England, he co-founded *Al-Haq* [truth, law, right of property, claim], an independent Palestinian non-governmental human rights organization based in Ramallah. He worked with *Al-Haq* as co-director until 1991, when he left the organization to pursue a literary career. Shehadeh is the author of several non-fictional studies on international law, humanitarian law, and the question of Palestine, such as *The West Bank and the Rule of Law* (1980), *Occupier's Law: Israel and the West Bank* (1985), and *From Occupation to Interim Accords: Israel and the Palestinian Territories* (1997). He was awarded the Orwell Prize in 2008 for his *Palestinian Walks*.

As I have mentioned earlier in this book, among the first Palestinian writers who decided to write in English in order to reach a global audience, to globalize the Palestinian question, was Jabra Ibrahim Jabra. From the late 1960s onwards, an increasing number of autobiographies, memoirs, and other sub-genres of self-narration have told the Palestinian story to the West in English, with or without the claim of collective representativeness, ranging from Fawaz Turki's *The Disinherited* (1972)[197] to Edward W. Said's *Out of Place* (1999). Shehadeh's *Palestinian Walks* can be placed within this tradition of Anglophone Palestinian writing. At the same

---

195   See, on this over-totalizing trend, for instance, Stephen Greenblatt et al., *Cultural Mobility: A Manifesto* (Cambridge: Cambridge UP, 2010).

196   Raja Shehadeh, *Palestinian Walks: Notes on a Vanishing Landscape* (London: Profile Books, 2007) 2.

197   Fawaz Turki, *The Disinherited. Journal of a Palestinian Exile* (New York: Monthly Review P, 1972).

time, however, it marks a unique generic transgression. The text is a hybrid of a mimicry of the travel guide, an impossible travel memoir, a personal (anti-)travelogue, transporting the English-speaking reader into Palestine's shrinking geography of occupation, and a collection of political meditations commenting on the pitfall of the so-called peace process and its aftermath. The account of six essayistic-literary *sarhat* [walks; plural form of sarha] takes the reader on a hike through what remains of Palestine to expose the increasing impossibility of unrestricted wandering in the occupied territories.

Palestinian Walks is both fictional and documentary in style. With his personal journal, *The Third Way*,[198] published in 1980, Shehadeh had already crossed the genre borders between non-fiction and auto-fiction. Arguing that the occupation's ultimate aim is to encourage Palestinians to leave and to be replaced by Israeli settlers, he concludes that, as a precaution, Palestinians have to do everything, despite all material difficulties, to stay put on the land. He calls this *as-sumud*, which translates as perseverance, steadfastness, or simply staying in place. Derived from the verbal form *samada* [to proudly raise one's head], the term, as used in Palestinian national discourse, designates a non-violent strategy of resisting occupation by staying in Palestine and keeping daily life going, thus physically and morally affirming the collective Palestinian presence and future claims. In the realms of cultural practice and education, it refers to the relentless persistence of narrating the Palestinian experience, preserving its heritage, and struggling for human dignity.

Palestinian Walks can be read as precisely such an act of *sumud*. Using the Western genre of travel memoirs as a negative matrix, the auto-narrator of real, impossible, and imagined walks knows well that Palestine was long seen by Europeans and Americans as a desolate land without a people. As he is fully aware that Palestine has been constantly reinvented in Western travelogues, with devastating consequences for its inhabitants, he also knows that the justification for and legitimization of its colonization was laid down in so-called Holy Land travel accounts: British, German, and American pilgrimage narratives written in the 19th and early 20th centuries.[199] Shehadeh's accounts attempt to refuse these imperial spatial ideologies.

His travels cross no continents. The narrator of *Palestinian Walks* hardly manages to cross hills and valleys. Searching for Palestine's present space-time, Shehadeh's text runs counter to the world of imperial maps, military maps, or tourist maps, for that matter. The text itself resembles a *sarha*, meandering from the hills of Ramallah to family history, into the Palestinian past, and finally into the present situation. Unlike space in the accounts of past travel writers, Shehadeh's space is full

198   See Raja Shehadeh, *The Third Way: A Journal of Life in the West Bank* (London: Quartet, 1982).
199   Mona Kattaya, "Writing the 'Real Jerusalem': British and American Travel Accounts in the Nineteenth Century," *Jerusalem Quarterly* 44 (2010): 14-27.

of people. Each sarha *walks* the reader through different and multifaceted aspects of occupation, from the draining of the Dead Sea for the irrigation of settlement lands to the pouring of concrete over the hills to support Israel's expanding industrial zones to the wall that not only isolates communities but also destroys land and livelihood. The social landscape, thus robbed of natural innocence, provides solace only next to grief, freedom only coupled with imprisonment, and sanctity never without danger.

One such walk begins with a recapitulation of how the hills of the West Bank have been turned into Jewish settlements. It describes the scattered, noncontiguous areas of land with which Palestinians are left today that cannot possibly constitute the basis of any viable state. Closures of roads force them to use unpaved side-tracks. The large number of checkpoints and obstacles placed by the Israeli army on West Bank roads further complicates daily life. The auto-narrator describes Palestinians as a people moving surreptitiously in their own country, like unwanted strangers, constantly harassed, never feeling safe, subject to the most abusive treatment at the hands of the soldiers controlling the checkpoints. These constraints of the ghetto life experienced in the cities of the occupied territories are reinforced by the so-called security wall:

> The most destructive development, which boded only misery and spelled continued conflict for the future, was the wall being constructed by Israel. This stretched in a jagged course that was determined not only by Israeli military considerations but also by the special interests of settlers and land mafia lords, slicing through the hills, destroying their natural shape, gulping large swathes of Palestinian land.[200]

Still, the Palestinian narrator is determined that none of these humiliations is going to prevent him from taking his walks. Very good weather in spring 2006 adds further motivation. While preparing for the walk, he suddenly remembers an experience he had some months earlier when driving back from the Jordan valley and getting lost in the midst of newly built settlements and industrial zones. The further he drives in his memories, the more the reader is immersed in the narrator's claustrophobic feelings of disorientation and fear: "As a child I had a recurring nightmare in which I found myself in a strange place unable to find my way home. I would try to shout for help only to realize that I had no voice. This felt like a similar situation. I began to sweat. Where was I?"[201] He finally manages to find a way out of the settlement. The narrative leads us out of this memory back to the man's primary intention of taking a walk. However, there are other barriers to consider before the repeatedly postponed spring hike can begin. Due

---

200   Shehadeh, *Palestinian Walks: Notes on a Vanishing Landscape* 190.
201   Shehadeh, *Palestinian Walks: Notes on a Vanishing Landscape* 191.

to newly built bypass roads, finding a track "without settlers or practice shooters or army posts"[202] becomes a challenge. Reluctantly consulting an odious map, the auto-narrator finally works out a route to a hill that promises to avoid settlements and army posts alike. On his way, he reaches a beautiful natural spring site. There the Palestinian, who has tried to avoid any encounter with the occupiers, comes upon an armed settler smoking weed. A direct address by the younger Israeli man makes quickly slipping by impossible. The two get involved in a conversation which soon turns into an intense argument over questions of nature preservation, civilizational progress, ignorance and prejudice, Arab-Jewish (non-)neighborhood in past and present, mutual violence, property rights and compensation claims, and international law.

When the auto-narrator intends to leave, the settler calls after him to stop and join in a smoke: "It felt more like an order which the law, his law, gave him the power to enforce. I feared for the worse."[203] The passionate political hiker suspects a violent escalation of the situation and feels guilty of symbolic cooperation with the occupier. However, the strong opiated hashish takes effect. After the narrator is once more flooded back into the memory of another walk that ends in shootings by the police of the Palestinian Authority, the unintended Palestinian-Israeli encounter turns into an almost surreal moment of intimacy. The two seemingly agree to ignore their dissonant positions and discrepant positionalities. Yet the intoxicated vision of transgression and coexistence only lasts for a while before it is disturbed by the distant sounds of violent segregation:

> I was fully aware of the looming tragedy and war that lay ahead for both of us, Palestinian Arab and Israeli Jew. But for now, he and I could sit together for a respite, for a smoke, joined temporarily by our mutual love of the land. Shots could be heard in the distance, which made us both shiver. "Yours or ours?" I asked.[204]

There is little optimism in this auto-narrative. There is no hero who takes risks to change reality. There is no self-victimization. These are the accounts of an ordinary Palestinian man who insists on continuing his rather privileged middle-class life as a free citizen and hiker. However, the experiences that he has on his walks are the epitome of a human tragedy which has long been unfolding on his land. If there are moments of optimistic trust in the shared humanity of all individuals involved in this conflict, these moments are quickly distorted by the violence on the ground. The same is true for Shehadeh's earlier diary-based semi-fictional writings, such as

---

202 Shehadeh, *Palestinian Walks: Notes on a Vanishing Landscape* 193.
203 Shehadeh, *Palestinian Walks: Notes on a Vanishing Landscape* 205.
204 Shehadeh, *Palestinian Walks: Notes on a Vanishing Landscape* 207.

Strangers in the House (2002),[205] *The Sealed Room* (1992),[206] or *When the Birds Stopped Singing* (2003).[207]

Occupation Diaries (2012),[208] a rather recent collection of personal essays and anecdotes, can no longer modulate its inherent anger through walks, natural observations, or hashish visions. Like *Palestinian Walks*, these essays extend beyond the political domain into the private and psychological sphere. *Occupation Diaries* is an angry book that defies both standard Western liberal support for the Palestinian Authority and the Israeli agenda of occupation. It spans a two-year period, from December 2009 to December 2011, covering major events such as the 2011 Nakba Day, on which thousands of Palestinian and Syrian youths marched to the border of the occupied Syrian Golan Heights, the killing of nine solidarity activists on board the Mavi Marama in May 2010, as well as the everyday experiences of a Palestinian living in Ramallah. However, Shehadeh criticizes not only Israel's continuing policy of occupation; the Palestinian Authority is also blamed for establishing what he sees as a "police state."[209] The general fragmentation and deterioration of Palestinian civil society is related to an economic pseudo-boom fueled by international aid. Shehadeh condemns this development as a "scheme devised by European and US funders, a policy of anti-insurgency."[210] Yet, against all despair at the duplicity of repression by the Israeli army and the Palestinian Authority and the apathy of the international community, Shehadeh expresses a strong perseverance to resist and stay in Palestine: "we have no intention of going anywhere."[211]

Palestinian cultural articulations in English serve multiple functions: they are testimonies, forms of self-identification, and transnational calls for political mobilization. They are not simply about the transformative power of culture to liberate Palestine from occupation but about resisting representational annihilation. They strategically transgress the distinction between collective testimony in national literature and individual self-narration as well as the linguistic barriers between Arabic as a local idiom and English as a transnational communicational tool.

In this context, one cannot be surprised that the World Wide Web has increasingly been used by Palestinians to communicate with each other and people around the globe and thus to transgress both internal and external borders. Internet cafes

205 Raja Shehadeh, *Strangers in the House: Coming of Age in Occupied Palestine* (London: Profile, 2002).

206 Raja Shehadeh, *The Sealed Room: Selections from the Diary of a Palestinian Living Under Israeli Occupation, September 1990–August 1991* (London: Quartet, 1992).

207 Raja Shehadeh, *When the Birds Stopped Singing: Life in Ramallah Under Siege* (Hanover, NH: Steerforth P, 2003).

208 Raja Shehadeh, *Occupation Diaries* (London: Profile Books, 2012).

209 Shehadeh, *Occupation Diaries* 86.

210 Shehadeh, *Occupation Diaries* 43.

211 Shehadeh, *Occupation Diaries* 204.

exist in most Palestinian cities and refugee camps, and Palestinian counter-journalists use the internet to report their otherwise unheard news and perspectives. Many platforms are in English or are bi-lingual, allowing messages to reach a Western audience. Numerous websites have published regular eyewitness reports from the West Bank and Gaza, where Israeli forces deny journalists access to Palestinian areas under attack. The Electronic Intifada is one example of these transnational platforms of activism. It is an independent online news publication and educational resource focusing on Palestine, its people, politics, culture, and its place in the world. Founded in 2001, it is based in both Ramallah and Chicago. The Electronic Intifada has won awards and earned widespread recognition for publishing original, high-quality news and analysis and first-person accounts. Writers and journalists working for this web project include Palestinians and non-Palestinians living inside and outside Palestine and Israel. As one of its co-founders explains, the web project originated on Birzeit University's website, with Said's imperative of representational resistance in mind: "Birzeit's web team set about creating our own realisation of the 'permission to narrate'."[212] The project came to life as a direct reaction to the September 1996 uprisings, when Birzeit students not only witnessed the harsh Israeli military violence, which ultimately claimed 88 Palestinian lives, but also felt powerless regarding the misrepresentation of the events in Israeli and Western mass media. This experience gave birth to the website, *On the Ground*, and a variety of similar projects. When the Second Intifada broke out in 2000, many of those who worked on the Birzeit website regrouped to compile the *September 2000 Clashes Information Center* website; one year later, *The Electronic Intifada* was born.[213] Arjan El Fassed and his cofounders, Ali Abunimah, Laurie King-Irani, and Nigel Parry, aim at enabling a growing network of human rights and media activists to challenge the distortions about Palestinians and their rights disseminated by various official Israeli media and media outlets throughout Europe and North America. The Internet has become a key new arena of narrative resistance.

The Electronic Intifada's *Diaries: Live from Palestine* project represents one important sub-field of this arena.[214] Created in March 2002 as sub-site within the Electronic Intifada's website, it provides writers with a space in which to record their opinions and reflections on their own experiences of living under occupation. Updated regularly, this citizens' source contains on-the-ground accounts and photographs by individuals, including doctors, aid workers, human rights activists,

---

212   Nigel Parry, "Permission to Narrate: Edward Said, Palestine, and the Internet," *The Electronic Intifada* 25 Sept. 2003, 20 Jan. 2016 <https://electronicintifada.net/content/permission-narrate-edward-said-palestine-and-internet/4789>.

213   *The Electronic Intifada*, ed. Ali Abunimah, Maureen Clare Murphy, Nora Barrows-Friedman, David Cronin et al. <https://electronicintifada.net/>.

214   "Diaries: Live from Palestine," *The Electronic Intifada* 19 Jan. 2016 <https://electronicintifada.net/diaries>.

and anyone else who has managed to get access to the Internet—and this despite repeated power cuts and curfews. The entries are often personal and private, sometimes emotional and literary, and regularly pedestrian. Residents upload their entries from home or Internet cafes, making their narratives immediately available to a wider, international, English-reading audience. Instead of lobbying the media, citizens confined to their homes in Ramallah, Nablus, Bethlehem, Gaza, and other places essentially become the media. The 2003 edited volume, *Live From Palestine: International and Palestinian Direct Action Against the Israeli Occupation*, contains essays by net-activists of the Electronic Intifada as well as reprints of diary entries.[215] Among those prominent figures who, until very recently, contributed to the Diaries project is Raja Shehadeh.

Whether on the internet, in published writings, or in the audio-visual spheres of art, the struggle of representational resistance is inextricably entwined with the experience of spatial restrictions related to the Palestinian geography of occupation. The anger, restlessness, frustration, and pain of forced segregation and walled immobility is depicted in feature movies like Elia Suleiman's *Divine Intervention* (2002)[216] as well as in video-works of a younger generation of Palestinian artists. Whereas *Divine Intervention* tells the tragic-comic love story of a couple that meets at military checkpoints and can only escape from the unbearable pressures of living under occupation through surreal dreams of unobstructed border-crossings and magic imaginations of Palestinian almightiness (fig. 28),[217] the Anglophone Palestinian-Russian artist, Larissa Sansour, expresses the violent limitation of Palestinian mobility by using the German 1998 film, *Run Lola Run (Lola rennt)*, as a bitterly ironic matrix.[218] While the German Lola (played by actor Franka Potente in red-colored hair) runs in a new German capital city that finally got rid of its cold war separation wall, the red-helmeted Palestinian woman (played by the artist herself) in Sansour's 2008 short video, *Run Lara Run*,[219] is constantly forced to stop in front of the many fences and walls of the occupied West Bank (fig. 29).

Not all Palestinians have the material resources to transform the absence of freedom of movement into an act of internationally acknowledged art. The traceurs (those who practice parkour) of the Parkour Gaza Team[220] instead use their bodies

---

215   Nancy Stohlman and Laurieann Aladin, *Live from Palestine: International and Palestinian Direct Action against the Israeli Occupation* (Cambridge, MA: South End P, 2003).

216   *Divine Intervention*, dir. Elia Suleiman, screenplay Elia Suleiman, perf. Elia Suleiman, Manal Khader, Avatar Films, 2002, DVD.

217   On the cinema of Elia Suleiman, see Dabashi, *Dreams of a Nation* 131-60.

218   *Lola rennt*, dir. Tom Tykwer, screenplay Tom Tykwer, perf. Franka Potente, Moritz Bleibtreu, 1998, DVD.

219   Larissa Sansour, *Run Lara Run* (2008), *Resistance[s]: Experimental Films from the Middle East and North Africa, Vol. III* (Paris: Lowawe, CNC, 2010) DVD.

220   See the group's website, *Gaza Parkour Team*, 27 June 2015 < http://www.actionsportsfordev. org/partners/gaza-parkour-and-freerunning-gaza/>.

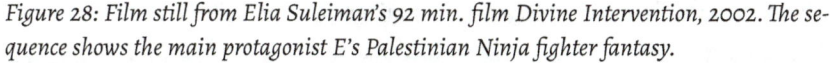

Figure 28: Film still from Elia Suleiman's 92 min. film Divine Intervention, 2002. The sequence shows the main protagonist E's Palestinian Ninja fighter fantasy.

to run free (fig. 30). Founded in 2005 after the withdrawal of the Israeli army, this is, to my knowledge, the oldest organized parkour team in Palestine. Unlike most traceurs of the Western metropoles, the group directly links its sport of overcoming obstacles in its own post-/war urban setting to the political goal of liberation. Mediated into the world via internet, its members' free-running practice adapts the free-style philosophy of getting from one point to another as quickly and efficiently as possible to a situation where free movement is virtually impossible. What is elsewhere the imitation of a matter of survival here advances to an expression of survival within the prison-like situation of the so-called Gaza strip. Drawing on military training, parkour was innovated by French free runners in the 1990s as a cultural lifestyle of athletic performance. In Palestine, this performance functions as a cultural act of *sumud*: an act that transposes a unique poiesis of resistance.[221]

Practicing parkour in Gaza might seem surreal to some. Yet it is not the act but the repressive conditions under which it takes place that make this performative practice seem unreal. In my view, it is precisely the hyper-real dimension of the Gaza Parkour team's performances that allows reading this cultural practice as one of spatial resistance. Against this background, I wish to close this chapter with an

---

221 On Parkour as a cultural practice, see Michael Atkinson, "Parkour, Anarcho-Environmentalism, and Poiesis," *Journal of Sport and Social Issues* 33.2 (2009): 169-94.

Figure 29: Film still from Larissa Sansour's 2:17 min. video, Run Lara Run, 2008.

equally extreme and sad representation of Palestinian deterritorialization, a filmic hyper-compensation of repressed powerlessness that willingly loses control over its feet on the ground.

From the outset, Larissa Sansour's 2009 mixed-media installation, *A Space Exodus*, eludes the question of whether there has ever been or will be a Palestinian on the moon. Born in Jerusalem in 1973, Sansour lived in Copenhagen for ten years and is now based in London. She regularly works in Bethlehem, Palestine. The activist-artist grew up well aware of the reductive meaning of truth when it comes to the representation of the Palestinian people and of the so-called peace process in international mass media. Her installation combines a video clip,[222] still photos from the video, and sculptures of little Palestinian astronauts (Palestinauts) taking over the installation's space. The audiovisual work presents an impossible alternative (or anti-alternative) to both the one-state and the two-state solutions. It does so at a particular historical moment, after extended interim periods and multiple interrupted roadmaps which have manifested a final status of continuing occupation and expanding settlements—a moment in which many Palestinians, in Palestine

222   Larissa Sansour, *A Space Exodus*, dir. and perf. Larissa Sansour, prod. Søren Lind, Beofilm, Laver Film, 2008 <https://www.youtube.com/watch?v=-tNAuSrp6tk>.

Figure 30: Member of Gaza Parkour performing in Gaza, 2014.

as well as in exile, have given up waiting for a just solution between equals, though the international community still speaks of the need for mutual compromises.

Sansour's extraterrestrial dystopian solution to the Palestinian question is as charmingly mischievous as it is despairing. The 5:25-minute experimental video shows the artist herself as a Palestinian astronaut landing on the moon and establishing a Palestinian exile colony (fig. 31). While *A Space Exodus* is shot and choreographed with state-of-the-art special effects, it explicitly does not look real. The video, which had its world premiere in 2008 at the Dubai festival's short-film competition, opens with a close-up of female fingers running over the controls of a space ship. "Jerusalem, we have a problem,"[223] a woman's voice says. But there is no response from the Holy City on earth. After an uncanny moment of deafening silence, a woman dressed in a spacesuit plants her foot in the moon dust as she proclaims: "That's one small step for a Palestinian, one giant leap for mankind."[224] This proclamation refers directly to the first US moon landing. The soundtrack—an Arabized variation of Richard Strauss's musical interpretation of Nietzsche's late-romantic critique of European morality, *Also sprach Zarathustra* (1896)[225]—as well as the subsequent scenes recall Stanley Kubrick's famous 1968 movie, *2001: A Space*

---

223 Sansour, *Space Exodus* 0:36–0:38 min.
224 Sansour, *Space Exodus* 1:53–2:01 min.
225 Richard Strauss, *Also sprach Zarathustra*, Op. 30 TrV 176, 1896.

Odyssey.[226] In fact, the video sometimes appears like a very brief remake of several key images from Kubrick's science-fiction classic on the pitfalls of human evolution and civilizational progress.

Figure 31: Larissa Sansour, film still (2:17 min.) from A Space Exodus, 2009.

In Sansour's *A Space Exodus*, the Palestinian flag is prominently featured, as is her Palestinian spacesuit and the uniquely designed, orientalized space-shoes. But it is the twinkling stars and the earth in the distance as well as her low-gravity gliding across the image that evoke some transcendent freedom, far from the so-called political *facts on the ground*—far from the continuing occupation of the Palestinian ground. The film takes a paradigmatic narrative of extreme technological progress and transposes it onto a situation in which a population is bound, constrained, and denied the most rudimentary rights of movement. In the final scene, the female Palestinaut waves to planet Earth (fig. 32). The camera focuses on her boots bouncing on the surface of the moon and eventually pans out as she fades away into outer space. Larissa Sansour's work leaves one grasping for meaning. The question of the work's mimetic capacity is obsolete. The work does not pretend to represent any fact of life in the West Bank or in the Gaza strip:

> I think that reality in some cases could become so fictional that the only way to address it is to make work that exaggerates it even more. I find that this is truly the case when you look at the Israeli occupation of Palestine. I feel that work that

---

226   Stanley Kubrick, dir., *2001: A Space Odyssey*, screenplay Stanley Kubrick and Arthur C. Clarke, Metro-Goldwyn-Mayer, 1968.

attempts to be rationally grounded with facts and documentation fails to deliver an adequate and genuine picture of the surreal, absurd atrocities on the ground.[227]

Mankind's dream of extraterrestrial discoveries has become a nightmare in which the moon functions as a false promise of a better future for Palestinians. The non-planet, hostile to life, is imagined as a land without a people for a people increasingly without land.

Figure 32: Larissa Sansour, Space Earth, 2009, 45 x 80 cm, c-print.

Without using a single image of a soldier, a checkpoint, a wall, or a refugee camp, *A Space Exodus* emphasizes the traumatically exilic condition of the Palestinian people, unheard by the international community and threatened to fade into nothingness. At first glance, the work seems to portray Palestinian deterritorialization and loss exclusively in outer space. By doing so, however, it directs our attention to a very real and earthly struggle. The audio-visual exodus narrative does not represent Palestinian pain and trauma as an end in itself. The project needs, rather, to be seen as an artistic act of resistance. It is simultaneously a non-violent and translocal act. By taking the local struggle for dignity into the global art market, it voices the Palestinian demand for the world to overcome ignorance and the almost unconditional acceptance of military occupation and settlements that are blatant violations of international law. In this view, the work should be

---

227   Larissa Sansour, "'Fiction and Art Practice'. Interview with Larissa Sansour 'A Space Exodus',"
       by Wafa Gabsi, *Contemporary Practices* 10 (Mar. 2012): 115.

interpreted as a metaphoric encouragement of moral and practical solidarity with those who cannot emigrate to the moon.

6. The Challenge of Anglophone Arab Studies: For a Post-Integrationist Critical Practice

I have always distrusted the Orientalist obsession with origins and roots in which seeing the Orientals' true roots is hardly anything more than a function of where the Occidental stands. This is the first reason I would have liked to skip the question of beginnings entirely. I wanted no essentialist excuses for my approach to reading Anglophone Arab works. I would have preferred being liberated from the arguable obligation to begin my study by naming selected pre- and interstices among all other possible beginnings. I wanted to approach Anglophone Arab works as self-conscious works of art and literature without any Orientalist pre-qualification and without using any culturally specific interpretive code. There would have been no beginnings and no endings, no pre-texts and no intertexts of importance, and no interpretive prefiguration. Instead, Anglophone Arab articulations would have been approached as autonomous aesthetic works with their own sense of achievement beyond their existence as Anglophone carriers of Arab culture. They would be explained right from their respective inside, and they would be approached at the moment of their individual emergence. Their unique truth would firmly stand within the self-proceeding text or image, and that truth would emerge immediately from these representations' close reading.

Yet, the noble but equally naïve wish of recognizing Anglophone Arab works by universal standards in their pure aesthetic existence and not by using any particular (Anglo-)Arab predicament as the interpretive matrix would have run the risk of ignoring these aesthetics' specific correlations, both regarding their discursive formation as well as with a view to their potential and de-facto discursive effectivity. The archival arrangement of possible Anglophone Arab statements and the terms by which we recognize the appearance of these statements—the order of Anglophone Arab discourse,[1] so to speak—is much too striking regarding its non-intentional

---

1   I am, of course, referring here to Michel Foucault's 1970 inaugural lecture of the same title, *L'ordre du discours* (Paris: Gallimard, 1971); "The Discourse on Language," Appendix of *The Archaeology of Knowledge and The Discourse on Language*, by Michel Foucault, trans. A. M. Sheridan Smith (New York, Pantheon, 1972) 215-37.

entanglements and far too complex concerning its worldly power effects to allow the critic to place herself or himself comfortably within the posed authenticities and inner certainties of any individual work.

In order to begin my undertaking seriously, I took the risk of breaking up, exploring, and, if necessary, multiplying the uncertainties of these assumingly transculturally located and closed-up works. I wanted to show that, if the doubt of clear-cut beginnings and distinctive intertexts is pursued as far as possible, it can be productively turned against itself. As a consequence, I was happily forced to accept the notion that dissonances are unavoidable in transgressive readings of Anglophone Arab representations. Now, I was no longer primarily concerned with the individual Anglophone Arab writer's or artist's heritage or her or his work's self-proclaimed identity but with the interventionist originality and symbolic quality of the respective work. I have treated the entity of the singular literary text or audio-visual representation, just like the individual author or artist, as a symbolic marker and communicative function for the general writing and re-writing (and in some cases even for the disavowed writing) of Anglophone Arab culture.

Although or maybe precisely because Khalid and other Anglophone Arab voices to which I have responded in the course of this study do not offer themselves as serious intercultural dragomans guiding the Western reader through the real Arab mind, the Arab world, or the authentic experiences of Arab immigrants to the West, they express key issues that have confounded the relations between Arabs and non-Arabs, between the so-called West and the Arab Middle East, throughout the 19th, 20th, and 21th centuries. By doing so, they critically reciprocate those experiences of physical transmigrations and correlative discursive formations that form the topical core of contemporary Anglophone Arab works: narratives of emigration, immigration, and forced assimilation; dreams of tolerance, conviviality, and cultural fusion as well as of ignorance, discrimination, failed integration, and remigration; stories of coerced identification and resistive selving caught between the claim of individual freedom and the struggle for collective liberation; movements of emancipation and unfinished revolutions, narratives of split belongings and multiplied affiliations, as well as strategic assertions of Oriental originality; issues of race and racialization and Orientalized relations of gender and sexual desire; nocturnal voyages into the powers of narrative counter-truth and illuminated experiments in revealing reality's uncanny magic; representations that manipulate and subvert normative conceptions of time, space, location, and belonging; works that elude the essentialist conceptualization of subjectivity and reality according to fixed cultural locations; and others that try to re-invent lost spaces and mobilities.

The narratives and audiovisual works I have explored are almost inescapably loaded with the challenge of competing truth claims, the denial of Arab representational authority, and the ambivalence of deploying a language, the narrative repertory of which has already defined Arab alterity. The long history of Western-Arab encounters was, and continues to be, largely characterized by power imbalances and violent acts (representational and physical alike). These conflictual encounters decisively participated in the adjustment of competing symbolic orders and referential archives that, to this day, frame Anglophone Arab narrative acts. One cannot be surprised that the producers of Anglophone Arab representations show a heightened awareness of the presence of an external receiver who does not believe them. Always anticipating the Western audience's skeptical curiosity that can easily degenerate into "vulgar inquisitiveness,"[2] they know well that they are not perceived as fully reliable representations. The Anglophone Arab narrator's story and the Anglophone Arab audiovisual artist's work always risk being assimilated into a hegemonic Western discourse that suspects Arabs of speaking the non-truth. At the same time, these representations potentially expose themselves to Arab allegations of betraying internal claims of factuality. These narratives, in other words, are not concerned, as the multiculturalists want to have it, with challenging the Arab world's intrinsic traditions within the exceptional modernity of the Western (host) culture. They rather explore the spectrum of possible strategic uses and ab-uses of what Spivak calls the "trans-contextual gifts" of our globalized modernity.[3] As they shift from forced self-exhibition to resistive opacity, or the use of half-truths, they cultivate representational strategies of disruptive translations, reversed plagiarisms, and strategic lies.

The confusion that such re-presentations can ideally produce is not the result of their intrinsically different rationalities. Their insistence on dissonances rather directly follows from these representations' narrative and performative differentiation between what is postulated as universally rational and what is reasonable according to a particular worldly situation. If the re-coding of identities triggered by such differentiations seems at times to culminate in quixotic constructions of uncanny or improper non-belongings, this possibly mirrors "the uneven diachrony of global contemporaneity."[4] It is from this contradictory present that claims of memory and future visions are articulated. And it is from here that Anglophone Arab representations are working within and against often competing cultural archives to search for untold stories, lost struggles, and unrecorded histories. In order to respond creatively to one-sided claims of exact transcription or to the epistemo-ideological critique of flawed translations, they have to question both the residual Western narrative and dominant Arab modes of representation. Anglophone Arab representations struggle with the reliability of given narratives over here *and* over

---

2   Rihani, "The Lying Oriental," 182.
3   Gayatri Chakravorty Spivak, Introduction, *An Aesthetic Education in the Era of Globalization*, by
      G. Chakravorty Spivak (Cambridge, MA: Harvard UP, 2013) 4.
4   Spivak, Introduction, 11.

there, and they willingly risk being seen as unreliable in their own search for truth or even lying on both sides of the pre-packed divide.

While it is true that these both unstable and destabilizing articulations usually wind up in the seemingly competing and mutually excluding master narratives of Orientalism and Occidentalism—how could they not?—they rarely affirm either one of the binary worldviews. The decentered representations with which I have been concerned over the course of this study instead have the capacity to disclose the secret alliance between Orientalists and Occidentalists across learned ethnic and geographical divides and thus to displace the Orient/Occident economy of reason. Anglophone Arab representations have a particular fictocritical capacity to mark out and question the established forms of systematic ordering and to blur ritualized divisions between true and false readings or between recognition and negation. These representations *in deed* (that is, *in actu*) identify themselves as intentional disruptions of dominant sureties. As discursive discontinuities in their own right, they explicitly address their own and their audience's materiality. As metafictional works, they broach questions related to the material conditionality of the cultural enunciation and reception of Anglophone Arab meaning.

Although the choice of primary works for my endeavor to trace discourses, counter-discourses, and what is in between has been selective, the genealogical treatment of the chosen works necessarily also attempts to critically question my own selection's discursive prefiguration. The study of Anglophone Arab representations does not reveal any original core or the universality of Anglophone Arab meaning. It rather brings to light distinct cultural acts as discursive events of imposing, alternating, and re-imposing meaning on Anglophone Arab encounters. Dissonances of cross-cultural encounters and inconsistencies of transmigratory identification were not only unavoidable but turned out to be of direct interpretive evidence for my undertaking. As I have shown, such dissonances and inconsistencies are explicitly addressed in the Anglophone Arab works I discuss. Their merging, equally disruptive and selective, and the constant blurring of disparate narrative and visual sequences lead to a high degree of internal distances, discordances, concurrences, and external interferences. The generic self-location of Anglophone Arab representations is often willingly unstable, as is their placement regarding the narrated time-space. Mobilizing familiar and less familiar codes, they usually escape any genuinely comparative morphology. Instead, they constantly remind us that the works and their critics (i.e., us) exist within a larger cross-cultural and trans-temporal meta-text of symbolic mediations and deviations, directly related to the long history of Western-Arab encounters. As a consequence, the scholarly obsession with stylistic purity and clear generic filiations regularly remains unsatisfied. Anglophone Arab works sometimes show resonances to medieval Arabic narratives, popular epic cycles, and folk tales—and this side by side with traces of early modern European classics, South American magical realist writings, modern North American poetry and fiction, and newer transnational genres of literature and film. They draw on the image repertoire of globalized popular culture and mass media and participate in the latest archival turn within international concept and performance arts. The theoretical frames and ideological schemes through and against which they operate are equally diverse and change significantly between the individual artists and writers.

Instead of lamenting a crisis of the cosmopolitan Arab subject in (trans-)migration or affirming the notion of worlds torn apart by clashing (post-)modernities, Anglophone Arab representations explore the correlational tensions of these binary imaginations and thus confront partial truths with other partial truths. They *push together*, but when they merge, they do not aim to resolve anything. In these works, hybridity is not a de-politicized ideology of instant postcolonial theory but a complex sociohistorical dynamic and theoretical concept. Anglophone Arab representations invite us to challenge, and maybe to unlearn, the consensual conceptions of moral and aesthetic boundaries which usually determine the limits of corporate identification. Whether we see ourselves as Arabs (by choice) or Westerners (by choice), these works urge us to question both our own subject position and that of our respective cultural other, whom we have imagined as a silent object for far too long: "No; travel not on a Cook's ticket; avoid the guides."[5]

Although many Anglophone Arab representations deploy the very narrative repertory which they challenge they creatively search for alternative documents and figments. Their performative evidence often results from the strategic invention of narrative and audiovisual modes of telling meaningful stories which anticipate, and yet manage to escape, the Western reader's overhasty answering word or penetrating gaze. While Anglophone Arab trustworthiness regularly surpasses or subverts the doubtful veracity of hegemonic Western representations and erodes the main referential systems of these representations' narratives, it can have truth effects in the world. Inventing modalities of the narrative production of a meaning that intentionally refuses to be fully translated and grasped as an intercultural translation of Arab truth, their modes of speaking for themselves are often fraught with willful untranslatability. I have interpreted this strategy as resistance to being assimilated within normative Western notions of intersubjectivity or intercultural accuracy. Refusing to be harmonized with the moral authority of exceptional Western reliability, Anglophone Arab articulations turn their discursively inscribed and, therefore, inescapable cross-cultural unreliability into a self-confident narrative act of critical validity across formerly separated representational spheres.

The metafictional contiguities of these representational acts are manifold and far-reaching: They subvert the learned culturalist assumption of originality, au-

---

5   Rihani, *The Book of Khalid* 5.

thentic belonging, and teleological itinerary still at work not only in the ideological polemics of Arab and Western nationalists but also among scholars of Middle Eastern studies and immigrant culture or minority literatures. Circumnavigating the terrain of linguistic diversity and avoiding crude intercultural recodings, Anglophone Arab representations cannot be—and indeed, often explicitly, do not want to be—considered accountable for writing/translating any presupposed original meaning. Nevertheless, they can serve as a means for the realization of individual liberation or collective emancipation. As, for instance, my readings of contemporary Palestinian practices of cultural resistance have demonstrated, the questioning of the normative adjustment of truth does not collide with the goal of bearing witness to injustice, forming collective agency, or even mobilizing transnational forms of political action. However, a relational approach to Anglophone Arab discourse can also open up perspectives on hitherto excluded individual voices like that of Ihab Hassan, whose self-identification and intellectual agency is grounded in the decisive negation of any (af-)filiation to such collectivity.

In order to explore the cross-cultural communicational structures at work in Anglophone Arab representations, one needs to combine the analysis of the individual text's narrative organization or the individual representation's visual or performative order with the study of this internal organization's external discursive prefiguration. For this, any scholar working in the field must consider the presence of dominant Western representational modes which have fixated and still fixate Arabs within a differential network of unequal relations and, therefore, form an important matrix for Anglophone Arab correlational representations. Yet, s/he needs to be equally sensitive to the fact that these representations rarely care for the notions of culturally specific literary syntax or narrative genealogies. Whoever sees herself or himself as the intended receiver of these works should be aware of the ambivalent translocations of assumingly firmly located modes of emplotment or visual frames of references at work in Anglophone Arab discourse. If it is true that these works sometimes smuggle meaning from one place to another by displacing self-totalizing truths claims and related representational modes, and if they do so by telling lies, it is important to see that they do so intentionally. The strategic decision to counter hegemonic lies by *lying back* not only destabilizes the principal Eurocentric hierarchy of cross-cultural inquiry confined by the constitutive strategies of othering and selving but ultimately gains an epistemological and moral component. The reader, listener, or viewer is rarely in the position of fully grasping the socio-historic evidence and moral consistency of the world represented. There is no easy affective attachment to the represented cultural space. Moreover, it becomes increasingly difficult to differentiate between what is authentic and what is foreign or between what has been imported from the dominant Western discourse and what is exported from the assumed internal Arab discourse. Interpretive modes related to certain linguistic signifiers associated with socio-spatial or ethno-cultural identities give way to conflictual gestures of horizontal exchange beyond intercultural translation.

The forgery of Anglophone Arab representations is by no means unidirectional. It is regularly committed against normative moralities and standardized aesthetics on both sides of the historically generated divide. Their cross-cultural contaminations, selective translational distortions, and strategic inauthenticities have unpredictable effects that exceed the institutionalized control of intercultural judgment. These works' structural and semantic correlationality disrupts both our aesthetic conventions of cultural specificity and ethical norms of universal accountability. Therefore, the (co-)relational reading of Anglophone Arab representations demands that we rethink our theories and procedures of cross-cultural comparativism. Such rethinking might lead to a meta-ethics of comparative literary and cultural criticism that, instead of morally condemning or habitually excluding acts of lying, rehabilitates the strategic use of partial truths, of lies, and of counter-lies as justifiable forms of cultural and, perhaps, political agency. In such praxeology of narrative truth, the act of interpretation goes beyond revealing what has been variously described as the counter-discursive or dialogical imagination. To interpretively grasp a poetics that incorporates the ideological and moral ambiguity of working across archives demands the imagining of the conflictual correlation of mutually excluding archives instead of the yearning for harmonizing meta-archives that are not yet in sight. In other words, such a project requires rethinking art and morality in the age of competing archives.

Although postcolonial theory has been decisively inspired by the critique of pure reason, our critical practice seems to be first and foremost concerned with the contrapuntal or counter-discursive project of speaking non-Western truths to Western powers, of narrating subaltern facts, or of writing back what has scarcely been written hitherto. While it has been sufficiently demonstrated that the civilizational promises of colonial and semi-colonial projects, the claim of Western exceptionality and superiority, or the legitimizing discourses of developmentalism and humanitarian interventionism were and still are very powerful lies, when it comes to creative works and emancipatory movements from the postcolonies of the global south or from immigrants of color within the Western metropolis, one finds an almost ethnographic inquiry aiming at the total disenchantment of other worlds and the world's Other(s). At least, in this regard, an almost idealist enlightenment paradigm and objectifying gaze seem to operate continuously in mainstream criticism. My readings of Anglophone Arab representations have shown to me and hopefully to others that such an approach is either astonishingly anachronistic in its lack of epistemological self-reflexivity or simply dishonest regarding its methodological Eurocentrism. In both cases, it contradicts the very (theoretical and political) foundations of postcolonialism. The field's preoccupation with making the invisible visible seems to aim first and foremost at recovering interpretively authentic historical agencies and at uncovering who or what is really there beyond colonial and neo-colonial ideologies of representational othering. Whereas I do agree that there are many good reasons for opening up the Western canon so that its injustices can be redressed and its inherent lies exposed, the interpretive paradigm of locating the unseen, silenced, or the unspoken in the name of emancipation can easily lead to a practice which, in its scholarly institutionalized form, replicates the binary hierarchy between those who belong to the dominant group and those to be integrated. Such a practice can—intentionally or not—establish a structural alliance with the interrogative pattern of instrumental socio-political integration and hierarchical assimilation.

Considering the ambivalent setback and hype of cross-cultural communication since 9/11, it seems important, now maybe more than ever, to look at those representational acts that go beyond the questioning of established Western truths by giving voice to alternative truths—and at this point, I no longer think exclusively of Anglophone Arab representations. If we respect the many locations and complex meanings of contemporary cultural articulations, and if we seek to respond critically to these articulations, we cannot deny the writer's, artist's, and critic's capacity to lie strategically. Paradigmatically anticipating or even morally insisting on the postcolonial subject's obligation to speak and exhibit his or her truth in literature and the arts as well as in other forms of cultural mediation and political representation, in my view, risks affirming the oppressive (neo-)colonial practice of integration under the restrictive condition of total decommissioning. The conceptual incarceration of postcolonial representations within the field's institutionalized prison of counter-truth neglects the postcolonial writer's, artist's, or activist's right to utilize sub-harmonic and post-moralistic strategies of (narcissistic) self-affirmation or individual liberation or even to contradict herself or himself, intentionally or reluctantly. A self-critical literary and cultural critique cannot afford to exclude resistive strategies and emancipatory imaginaries of the counterfactual, thus reducing its scholarly commitment to the institutionalized incorporation of the self-confessing, self-exhibiting, or self-marketing global subalterns' narratives on the postcolonial bookshelf.

The unfinished project of emancipating postcolonial dissonances and the badly needed set-up of competing and yet equitable, and hopefully mutually correcting, cultural archives is bound to go beyond the still dominant objectifying paradigms of intersubjectivity, reciprocity, and harmony. As recent archival research conducted by the Dutch musicologist Wouter Capitain in the Edward W. Said Papers at Columbia University shows, Said, while drafting his seminal *Culture and Imperialism*, in fact, seriously considered using the concept of heterophony instead of drawing on the more harmonic notion of counterpoint, but was reluctant to actually incorporate the concept into the final manuscript.[6] I propose to draw on these draft fragments preserved in the archives of unpublished postcolonial criticism to interpretively grasp the voices played off in Anglophone Arab representations heterophonically rather than contrapuntally.

The Foucauldian insight that modern arts and literatures are characterized by both a particular decision for the non-truth and a commitment to its truth-effects in evidence[7] seems to be crucial for such undertaking. From here, the assumingly contradictory impression that Anglophone Arab or other postcolonial interventions against the discriminatory foundations of colonial-racist modernity can sometimes be true—in the sense of having truth-effects in the world—if, and only if, they are false looses its oxymoronic fright. If a central precondition of the criticized academic integration procedure is honest self-exhibition of those (willing) to be integrated, how can we grasp narratives which do not offer themselves to be included into the scopic matrix of the postcolonial integration regime? How can we interpretively respond to representations that are not secured by their truth-value or moral consistency? Can we imagine an aesthetics of negative exposure or an ethics of non-knowing that includes lies which disclose mutual unknowns and competing ignorance(s)?

I believe the fictional and non-fictional works I have discussed in this study do provide multiple points of departure for such a post-moralistic re-conceptualization of postcolonial lies and for a post-integrationist approach of correlational reading. And I hope my operations of selective correlational Anglophone Arab readings can also function as an exemplary point of departure. Yet, to avoid useless recapitulations at this point, I want to transgress the theoretical and conceptual boundaries delineated throughout these pages. I believe that alternative approaches to bridging the gap between theoretical reason and practical reason in relational Anglophone Arab studies or postcolonial criticism, for that matter, can be found outside the learned system of intellectual veracity as institutionalized in literary and cultural studies. To re-think truths and lies in cultural representations as intersections which can only be grasped on a transnational and relational axis, our critical practice needs to regain a utopian dimension, if not intention. During the last decade, scholars of critical social theory and political philosophy have been increasingly concerned with the theoretical implications of new transnational social movements which articulate global objectives and thus function as careers of a utopian

---

6   I am referring here to an unpublished manuscript by Wouter Capitain, "From Counterpoint to Heterophony and Back Again: Reading Edward Said's Drafts for Culture and Imperialism," (2019). The manuscript derives from a chapter of his unfinished dissertation project "Postcolonial Polyphony: Edward Said's Work on Music" (working title) to be filed in 2020 at University of Amsterdam. I thank Wouter for kindly providing his manuscript.

7   Michel Foucault, "La vie des hommes infâmes," Les Cahiers du Chemin 29 (15 Jan. 1977): 12-29.

promise without speaking in the name of any social totality or universal truth.[8] These ecocritical, anticapitalist, or human rights movements, unlike the bourgeois worker movements of the past, are self-limited in so far as they know that there is no unified subject in history. Although they know that many unknowns, disagreements, and contradictory particularities remain, their political action to invent agency signals a sincere desire for global change. This tension between a desire for a global sense and the reasonable doubt of such a sense cannot be easily resolved. It is important to recognize that most global protests today "aren't pursuing any identifiable 'real' goal"[9] because they realize that failure may be inherent in any principle truth for which they are fighting. This insight might offer a hint into the direction of Slavoj Žižek's dialectics between the event of a truth and the truth of an event. His eventualizaton of the notion of social truth[10] assumes a certain compatriotism of mutual not-yet-knowing. Such compatriotism might not only form a new basis for a future ethics of global justice and peaceful coexistence; at the same time, it can function as a provisional horizon for a relational study of Anglophone Arab cultures in a critically revised global comparativist perspective.[11] In order to engage critically with cross-cultural transgressions related to past and present dynamics of globalization, one has to explore divided archival systems and discrepant dispositives formed out of these dynamics without dragging on within the old paradigm of mutually exclusive universal exceptionalisms. My study is an essayistic attempt to outline the contours of such literary and cultural criticism as a political event.

I have opened, I think, possibilities for myself (and hopefully for others) of an immense spectrum of future research directions in relational Anglophone Arab studies. Some of the topics to be explored include the role of Anglophone Arab and Muslim discourses within the American genesis and transnational transformation of hip-hop culture, the function of Anglophone Arab debates and agents within the so-called Arab Spring of 2011, the political ethics of (Anglophone Arab) refugee imaginaries, strategic lies in post-secular ideologies and militant movements, and postcolonial political authorities without truth-claim. These are projects to which the unpredictable sociopolitical circling of the world and our academic institutions shall hopefully offer some space.

---

8   See, for instance, Seyla Benhabib, *Another Cosmopolitanism: Hospitality, Sovereignty and Democratic Iterations* (Oxford: Oxford UP, 2006) and Seyla Benhabib, *Dignity in Adversity. Human Rights in Troubled Times* (Cambridge: Polity P, 2011).

9   Slavoj Žižek, "Trouble in Paradise," *London Review of Books* 35.14 (2013): 11.

10   Slavoj Žižek, *Event: Philosophy in Transit* (London: Penguin, 2014).

11   On postcolonial comparativism, see Rita Felski and Susan Stanford Friedman, eds., *Comparison: Theories, Approaches, Uses* (Baltimore: Johns Hopkins UP, 2013) and Aamir R. Mufti, "Global Comparativism," *Edward Said: Continuing the Conversation*, eds. Homi Bhabha and W. J. T. Mitchell (Chicago: U of Chicago P, 2005) 109-26.

One insight I certainly gained from my readings in Anglophone Arab literary and artistic representations is that Arabs (by choice or by birth) and non-Arabs (by choice or by birth) are allies, if sometimes secret, in being seekers of common truths or lies to come. Let me thus end on a positive note and recite once more—this time not as a pun on the inescapable moral predicaments of (bodily) love between woman and man but as an allegorical vision of cross-cultural coexistence between different equals—the beautiful rhyming couplet of sonnet 138 by the famous English bard whose real name, as some of us know, was Shaikh al-Pīr, an Indian mystic and saint, or Shaikh Zubair, because he was Arab or because he converted to Islam, maybe during his lost years, maybe in Al-Andalus—and that is *a* truth:

Therefore I lie with her, and she with me,
And in our faults by lies we flattered be.
(Shakespeare, Sonnet 138)

Works Cited

Abdalla, Ahmed. "'Uruba wa-l-akharun 'nahnu'" [Europe and the others 'we']. *Al-'Arab* 24 July 1984: 5.

Abu-Jaber, Diana. *Crescent.* New York: Norton, 2003.

Abu-Lughod, Ibrahim. *The Arab Rediscovery of Europe: A Study in Cultural Encounters.* Princeton, NJ: Princeton UP, 1963.

Achebe, Chinua. "An Image of Africa." *Literary Criticism.* Spec. issue of *Research in African Literatures* 9.1 (1978): 1-15.

Aciman, André. *Out of Egypt: A Memoir.* New York: Farrar, Straus & Giroux, 1994.

Adams, Lorraine. "Once Upon Many Times." Rev. of *The Hakawati.* By Rabih Alameddine. *The New York Times, nytimes.com* 18 May 2008, 13 Feb. 2015 <http://www.nytimes.com/2008/05/18/books/review/Adams-t.html?_r=0>.

Adonis. *Ash-Shir'iya al-'Arabiya.* Trans. Catherine Cobham. *An Introduction to Arab Poetics* (Cairo: AUC P, 1992).

—. "This is my Name." Trans. S. M. Toorava. *Journal of Arabic Literature* 24.1 (1993): 28-38.

—. "The Funeral of New York." *The Pages of Day and Night.* Trans. Samuel Hazo. Marlboro, VT: Marlboro P, 1994. 57-74.

—. "A Cultural Symbol." *Ameen Rihani: Bridging East and West: A Pioneering Call for Arab-American Understanding.* Eds. Nathan C. Funk and Betty J. Sitka. Lanham, MD: UP of America, 2004. xiii-xiv.

Ahmad, Aijaz. *In Theory: Classes, Nations, Literatures.* London: Verso, 1992.

Ahmed-Fararjeh, Hisham, and Ibrahim Abu-Lughod. *Resistance, Exile, and Return.* The Ibrahim Abu-Lughod Institute of International Studies, Birzeit: Birzeit UP, 2003.

Al Maleh, Layla. "Anglophone Arab Literature: An Overview." *Arab Voices in Diaspora: Critical Perspectives on Anglophone Arab Literature.* Ed. Layla Al Maleh. Amsterdam: Rodopi, 2009. 1-65.

Alameddine, Rabih. *Koolaids. The Art of War.* London: Abacus, 1998.

—. *I, The Divine. A Novel in First Chapters.* London: Weidenfeld & Nicolson, 2002.

—. *The Hakawati.* New York: Knopf, 2008.

—. *An Unnecessary Woman.* New York: Grove P, 2013.

—. *The Angel of History*. New York: Atlantic Monthly P, 2016.

Alger Jr., Horatio. *Tattered Tom, or, The Story of a Street Arab*. Boston: Loring, 1871.

Ali, Tariq. "A Patriarch of Arab Literature." *Counterpunch* 1 Feb. 2004.

Allen, Roger. *The Arabic Novel. An Historical and Critical Introduction*. 2nd ed. 1982; Syracuse: Syracuse UP, 1995.

Al-Omar, Nibras A. M. "The Self-Translator as Cultural Mediator: In Memory of Jabra Ibrahim Jabra." *Asian Social Science* 8.13 (2011): 211-19.

Alsultany, Evelyn, and Ella Shohat. "The Cultural Politics of 'the Middle East' in the Americas." *Between the Middle East and the Americas: The Cultural Politics of Diaspora*. Eds. Evelyn Alsultany and Ella Shohat. Ann Arbor: U of Michigan P, 2013. 3-41.

Ameen Rihani 18 May 2014, 23 Aug. 2014 <http://www.ameenrihani.org/index.php>.

"Ameen Rihani's Statue in the United States of America." *Ameen Rihani*. 13 Sept. 2015 <http://www.ameenrihani.org/newsevents.php?archive=bustattufts>.

Anderson, Benedict. *Imagined Communities: Reflections on the Origins of Nationalism*. London, New York: Verso, 1991.

Anderson, Terry A. *Den of Lions: Memoirs of Seven Years*. 1993; New York: Ballantine, 1994.

Appadurai, Arjun. "The Colonial Backdrop." *Afterimage* 24.5 (1997): 4-7.

Ardila, J. A. G., ed. *The Cervantean Heritage. Reception and Influence of Cervantes in Britain*. London: LEGENDA, Mod. Humanities Research Assn. and Maney Pub., 2009.

Arva, Eugene L. *The Traumatic Imagination. Histories of Violence in Magical Realist Fiction*. Amherst: Cambria P, 2011.

Asad, Talal. *Formations of the Secular: Christianity, Islam, Modernity*. Stanford: Stanford UP, 2003.

Ashcroft, Bill, Gareth Griffiths, and Helen Tiffin, eds. *The Empire Writes Back: Theory and Practice in Post-Colonial Literatures*. London: Routledge, 1989.

Ashcroft, Bill. *Caliban's Voice. The Transformation of English in Post-Colonial Literatures*. London: Routledge, 2009.

Ashour, Radwa. *Gharnata*. Cairo: Dar al-Hilal, 1994.

—. *Thulathiyat Gharnata*. Beirut: Mu'assasa al-'Arabiya lil-Dirasat wa-n-Nashr, 1998.

—. *Qit'a min Urubba*. Cairo: Dar ash-Shouruq, 2003.

—. "As-saut: frantz fanun, iqbal ahmad, idward sa'id" [The voice: Frantz Fanon, Eqbal Ahmad, Edward Said]. *Alif* 25 (2005): 79.

Asselineau, Roger, and Ed Folsom, "Whitman and Lebanon's Adonis." *Walt Whitman Quarterly Review* 15.4 (1998): 180-84.

Atkinson, Michael. "Parkour, Anarcho-Environmentalism, and Poiesis." *Journal of Sport and Social Issues* 33.2 (2009): 169-94.

Auerbach, Erich. *Mimesis: The Representation of Reality in Western Literature*. Trans. Willard R. Trask. Princeton: Princeton UP, 1953.

al-Azm, Sadik Jalal. "Al-istishraq wa-l-istishraq ma'akusan" [Orientalism and Orientalism in reverse]. *Hayat al-Jadida* 1.3 (1981): 7-51.

—. "Orientalism and Orientalism in Reverse." *Khamsin* 8 (1981): 5-26.

—. "Owning the Future: Modern Arabs and Hamlet." *ISIM Newsletter* 5 (2000): 11.

Bachar, Souheil [Walid Raad]. "Civilizationally, We Do Not Dig Holes To Bury Ourselves." Interview with The Atlas Group/Walid Raad, *Tamáss: Contemporary Arab Representations Beirut/Lebanon 1*, ed. Catherine David. Barcelona: Fundació Antoni Tàpies, 2002. 124-36.

Badawi, Muhammad Mustafa. "Shakespeare and the Arabs." *Cairo Studies in English* 26-27 (1964/1965): 181-96.

Bakhtin, Mikhail M. "Discourse in the Novel." *The Dialogic Imagination: Four Essays.* By M. M. Bakhtin. Ed. Michael Holquist. Trans. Caryl Emerson and Michael Holquist. Austin: U of Texas P, 1981. 259-422.

Banks, Marcus, and Richard Vokes. "Introduction: Anthropology, Photography, and the Archive." *History and Anthropology* 21.4 (2010): 337-49.

Barker, Francis, Peter Hulme, Margaret Iverson, and Diane Loxley, eds. *Europe and its Others: Proceedings of the Essex Conference on the Sociology of Literature, July 1984.* Colchester: U of Essex, 1985.

Barthes, Roland, and Lionel Duisit. "An Introduction to the Structural Analysis of Narrative." *New Literary History* 6.2 (1975): 237-72.

Bell, Michael. "García Márquez, Magical Realism and World Literature." *The Cambridge Companion to Gabriel García Márquez.* Ed. Philip Swanson. Cambridge: Cambridge UP, 2010. 179-95.

Benhabib, Seyla. *Another Cosmopolitanism: Hospitality, Sovereignty and Democratic Iterations.* Oxford: Oxford UP, 2006.

—. *Dignity in Adversity. Human Rights in Troubled Times.* Cambridge: Polity P, 2011.

Benjamin, Walter. "The Task of the Translator." *Walter Benjamin: Selected Writings Vol. 1, 1913-1926.* Eds. Marcus Bullock and Michael W. Jennings. 1996; Cambridge: The Belknap P of Harvard UP, 2002. 253-63.

Berkley, Constance E., and Osman Hassan Ahmed, eds. and trans. *Tayeb Salih Speaks. Four Interviews with the Sudanese Novelist.* Washington: Office of the Cultural Counsellor, Embassy of the Democratic Republic of the Sudan, 1982.

Berman, Antoine. *The Experience of the Foreign: Culture and Translation in Romantic Germany.* Trans. S. Heyvaert. Albany: SUNY P, 1992.

Berman, Jacob. "Mahjar Legacies: A Reinterpretation." *Between the Middle East and the Americas: The Cultural Politics of Diaspora,* Eds. Evelyn Alsultany and Ella Shohat. Ann Arbor: U of Michigan P, 2012. 65-79.

Bhabha, Homi. "Of Mimicry and Man: The Ambivalence of Colonial Discourse." *October. Discipleship: A Special Issue on Psychoanalysis* 28.2 (1984): 125-33.

—. "DissemiNation." *The Location of Culture.* London, New York: Routledge, 1994. 139-70.

Bilefsky, Dan, and Mona Boshnaq. "Street Artists Infiltrate 'Homeland' with Subversive Graffiti." *The New York Times* 15 Oct. 2015, 30 Oct. 2015 <http://www. nytimes.com/2015/10/16/world/europe/homeland-arabic-graffiti.html?_r=0>.

al-Bitar, Nadim. "Min al-istishraq al-gharbi ila-l-istishraq l-'arabi" [From Western Orientalism to Arabic Orientalism]. *Hudud al-huwiya al-qaumiya* [The limits of national identity]. By Nadim al-Bitar. Beirut: dar al-wahda, 1982. 151-69.

Blatty, William Peter. *Which Way to Mecca, Jack?* 1958; New York: Bernard Geis Assoc./Random, 1960.

—. *The Exorcist.* 1971; New York: Harper Paperbacks, 1994.

Bloom, Harald. *The Anxiety of Influence. A Theory of Poetry.* Oxford: Oxford UP, 1973.

Bonney, Sean. "'Minds do exist to agitate and provoke / this is the reason I do not conform'—Anna Mendelssohn." *The Poetry Project Newsletter* (Feb./Mar. 2011): 17-19. <http://poetryproject.org/wp-content/uploads/PP_ Newsletter_226_reduced.pdf>.

Boone, Joseph Allen. *The Homoerotics of Orientalism.* New York: Columbia UP, 2014.

Borges, Jorge Luis. "Partial Magic in the Quixote." *Labyrinth: Selected Stories & Other Writings.* By Jorge Luis Borges. Eds. Donald A. Yates and James E. Irby. New York: New Directions Books, 1964. 193-96.

—. "Tale of the Two Dreamers." *The Universal History of Infamy.* By Jorge Luis Borges. Trans. Norman Thomas di Giovanni. London, Penguin, 1975. 111-13.

—. "The Chamber of Statues." *The Universal History of Infamy.* By Jorge Luis Borges. Trans. Norman Thomas di Giovanni. London, Penguin, 1975. 107-10.

—. "The Thousand and One Nights." Trans. Eliot Weinberger. *The Georgian Review* (Fall 1984): 564-74.

—. "Preface to the First Edition [1935]." *A Universal History of Infamy.* 1972; New York: Penguin, 1987. 15.

—. "Pierre Menard: Author of the Quixote." *Collected Fictions.* By Jorge Luis Borges. Trans. Andrew Hurley. New York: Penguin, 1998. 88-95.

—."The Translators of *The Thousand and One Nights.*" *The Total Library. Non-Fiction 1922-1986.* By Jorge Luis Borges. Ed. Eliot Weinberger. Trans. Esther Allen, Suzanne Jill Levine, and Eliot Weinberger. London: Penguin, 1999. 92-109.

Boullata, Issa J. *Critical Perspectives on Modern Arab Literature.* Washington: Three Continents, 1980.

Bové, Paul A. Introduction. *Edward W. Said.* Ed. P. A. Bové. Spec. issue of *Boundary 2* 25. 2 (1998): 1-9.

—. *Edward Said and the Work of the Critic: Speaking Truth to Power.* Durham: Duke UP, 2000.

Breuer Josef, and Sigmund Freud. "On the Psychical Mechanism of Hysterical Phenomena: Preliminary Communication [1893]." *Studies on Hysteria.* By Josef Breuer and Sigmund Freud. Ed. and trans. James Strachey, in collab. with Anna Freud. New York: Basic Books, 2000. 3-17.

Buchloh, Benjamin H. D. "Gerhard Richter's 'Atlas'." *October* 88 (1999): 117-45.

Buck, Christopher. "The Eschatology of Globalization: The Multiple Messiahship of Bahā'u'llāh Revisited." *Studies in Modern Religions, Religious Movements and the Bābī-Bahā'ī Faiths.* Leiden: Brill, 2004. 143-78.

Burton, Richard. *The Book of Thousand and One Nights.* London: Burton Club, 1885-1888.

—. *Supplemental Nights to the Book of the Thousand Nights and a Night, with Notes Anthropological and Explanatory* (London: Burton Club, 1886).

Bush, George W. "Remarks in Abu Dhabi, United Arab Emirates, January 13, 2008." *Public Papers of the Presidents of the United States: George W. Bush 2008-2009, Book I,* Jan. 1 to June 30, 2008. Washington: United States Government Printing Office, 2012. 75-80.

Bushrui, Suheil B., and Joe Jenkins. *Kahlil Gibran: Man and Poet. A New Biography.* Oxford: Oneworld, 1998.

Bushrui, Suheil. Introduction. *The Prophet.* By Kahlil Gibran. Richmond: Oneworld, 2012. xii-xxiv.

Butler, Judith. *Gender Trouble: Feminism and the Subversion of Identity.* New York: Routledge, 1990.

Carr, Julie, and Jeffrey C. Robinson. "Introduction: Active Romanticism." *Active Romanticism: The Radical Impulse in Nineteenth Century and Contemporary Poetic Practice.* Eds. Julie Carr and Jeffrey C. Robinson. Tuscaloosa: U of Alabama P, 2015. 1-16.

Certeau, Michel de. *The Practice of Everyday Life.* Trans. Steven F. Rendall. Berkeley: U of California P, 1984.

Cervantes Saavedra, Miguel de. *Don Quixote de la Mancha.* Ed. E. C. Riley, trans. Charles Jarvis. Oxford: Oxford UP, 1992.

Childers, William. *Transnational Cervantes.* Toronto: U. of Toronto P, 2006.

Coetzee, John Maxwell. *Waiting for the Barbarians.* London: Secker & Warburg, 1980.

Collins, John J. *The Apocalyptic Imagination: An Introduction to the Jewish Matrix of Christianity.* New York: Crossroad, 1984.

Conant, Martha Pike. *The Oriental Tale in England in the Eighteenth Century.* New York: Columbia UP, 1908.

Conrad, Joseph. *Notes on Life and Letters.* 1921; London: Dent, 1949.

—. *Heart of Darkness.* 1899-1902; London: Penguin, 1994.

Cox, Harvey. *The Secular City: Secularization and Urbanization in Theological Perspective.* 1965; Princeton, NJ: Princeton UP, 2013.

Cresswell, Tim. *In Place/Out of Place: Geography, Ideology, and Transgression.* Mineapolis and London: U of Minnesota P, 1996.

—. *Place: A short Introduction.* Malden, MA: Blackwell, 2004.

Crispin, Philip. "Césaire's *Une Tempête* at The Gate." *'The Tempest' and Its Travels*. Eds. Peter Hulme and William Howard Sherman. London: Reaction Books, 2000. 149-57.

Culture and Resistance: Conversations with Edward W. Said. By David Barsamian and Edward Said. Cambridge, MA: South End P, 2003.

Czitrom, Daniel. "Underworlds and Underdogs: Big Tim Sullivan and Metropolitan Politics in New York, 1889-1913." *The Journal of American History* 78.2 (1991): 536-58.

Dabashi, Hamid. *Dreams of a Nation*. London: Verso, 2006.

D'Ancona, Matthew. *Post-Truth: The New War on Truth and How to Fight Back*. London: Ebury P, 2017.

al-Daif, Rashid. *Tistifil Meryl Streep*. Beirut: Riad al-Rayyes, 2001.

—. *Who is Afraid of Meryl Streep?* Trans. Paula Haydar and Nadine Sinno. Austin: U of Texas P, 2014.

Darraj, Susan Muaddi, ed. *Scheherazade's Legacy: Arab and Arab American Woman on Writing*. Westport, CT: Praeger, 2004.

David, Gary C. "The Creation of 'Arab American': Political Activism and Ethnic (Dis)Unity." *Critical Sociology* 33.5-6 (2007): 833-62.

Dawisha, Adeed. *Arab Nationalism in the Twentieth Century: From Triumph to Despair*. Princeton: Princeton UP, 2003.

Dawn, C. Ernest. "The Formation of Pan-Arab Ideology in the Interwar Years." *International Journal of Middle East Studies* 20.1 (1988): 67-91.

—. "The Origins of Arab Nationalism." *The Origins of Arab Nationalism*. Eds. Rashid Khalidi, Lisa Anderson, Muhammad Muslih, and Reeva S. Simon. New York: Columbia UP, 1991. 3-30.

de Man, Paul. *Blindness and Insight. Essays on the Rhetoric of Contemporary Criticism*. New York: Oxford UP, 1971

—. *Allegories of Reading: Figural Language in Rousseau, Nietzsche, Rilke, and Proust*. New Haven: Yale UP, 1979.

—. "Autobiography as De-facement." *Modern Language Notes* 94.5. (1979): 919-30.

—. "Autobiography, Theory and Practice: the Case of Al-Ayyām." *Writing the Self: Autobiographical Writing in Modern Arabic Literature*. Eds. Robin Ostle, Ed de Moor, and Stefan Wild. London: Saqi, 1998.128-138.

Derrida, Jacques. *Archive Fever: A Freudian Impression*. Trans Eric Prenowitz. Chicago: U of Chicago P, 1995.

—. "Passages—from Traumatism to Promise." *Points… Interviews 1974–1994: Jacques Derrida*. Ed. Elisabeth Weber. Trans. Peggy Kamuf et al. Stanford, CA: Stanford UP, 1995. 385-87.

Devi, Mahasweta. "Douloti the Bountiful." *Imaginary Maps: Three Stories*. By Mahasweta Devi. Trans. Gayatri Chakravorty Spivak. New York: Routledge, 1995. 19-93.

Devji, Faisal. *The Terrorist in Search of Humanity. Militant Islam and Global Politics.* London: Hurst, 2008.

Diab, Nuwar Mawlawi. "Ameen Rihani's Vision of Globalization." *Ameen Rihani: Bridging East and West: A Pioneering Call for Arab-American Understanding.* Eds. Nathan C. Funk and Betty J. Sitka. Lanham, MD: UP of America, 2004. 93-101.

Diqs, Isaak. *A Bedouin Boyhood.* London: Allen and Unwin, 1967.

Divine Intervention. Dir. Elia Suleiman, screenplay Elia Suleiman, perf. Elia Suleiman, Manal Khader, Avatar Films, 2002, DVD.

Djebar, Assia. *Fantasia: An Algerian Cavalcade.* Trans. Dorothy S. Blair. Portsmouth, NH: Heinemann, 1993.

Duala-M'bedy, Munasu. *Xenologie: Die Wissenschaft vom Fremden und die Verdrängung der Humanität in der Anthropologie.* Freiburg: Alber, 1977.

Du Bois, W. E. B. *The Souls of Black Folk.*1903; Oxford: Oxford UP, 2007.

Dudenhoeffer, Larrie. "'Evil against Evil': The Parabolic Structure and Thematics of William Friedkin's *The Exorcist.*" *Horror Studies,* 1.1 (2010): 73-88.

Dunnavent III., Walter Edward. "Rihani, Emerson, and Thoreau." *Ameen Rihani: Bridging East and West: A Pioneering Call for Arab-American Understanding.* Eds. Nathan C. Funk and Betty J. Sitka. Lanham, MD: UP of America, 2004. 55-71.

Eco, Umberto. *The Open Work.* Trans. Anna Cacogni. Cambridge: Harvard UP, 1989.

El-Enany, Rasheed. *Arab Representations of the Occident: East-West Encounters in Arabic Fiction.* New York: Routledge, 2006.

El Saadawi, Nawal. *Suqut al-Imam.* Cairo: Dar al-Mustaqbal al-'Arabi, 1987.

—. *The Fall of the Imam.* Trans. Sherif Hetata. London: Methuen, 1988.

Fadda-Conrey, Carol. "Transnational Diaspora and the Search for Home in Rabih Alameddine's *I, the Divine: A Novel in First Chapters.*" *Arab Voices in Diaspora: Critical Perspectives on Anglophone Arab Literature.* Ed. Layla Al Maleh. Amsterdam: Rodopi, 2009. 163-85.

Fahrenthold, Stacy. "Transnational Modes and Media: The Syrian Press in the *Mahjar* and Emigrant Activism during World War I." *Mashriq & Mahjar* 1.1 (2013): 30-54.

Fairbrother, Trevor. *Making a Presence: F. Holland Day in Artistic Photography.* Andover, MA: Addison Gallery of American Art, 2012.

Fanning, Patricia J. *Through an Uncommon Lens: The Life and Photography of F. Holland Day.* Amherst: U of Massachusetts P, 2008.

Fanon, Frantz. *The Wretched of the Earth.* Trans. Constance Farrington. 1967; London: Penguin, 2001.

—. *Black Skin, White Masks.* Trans. Charles Lam Markmann. 1967; London: Pluto P, 2008.

Fattah, Alaa Abd El. "Jan 25, 5 years on: The only words I can write are about losing my words." *Mada Masr* 24 Jan. 2016, 3 Mar. 2016

<http://www.madamasr.com/opinion/politics/jan-25-5-years-only-words-i-can-write-are-about-losing-my-words>.

Feldman, Keith. "The (Il)legible Arab Body and the Fantasy of National Democracy." *MELUS* 31.4 (2006): 33-53.

Felski, Rita, and Susan Stanford Friedman, eds. *Comparison: Theories, Approaches, Uses*. Baltimore: Johns Hopkins UP, 2013.

Feminist News 21 (Sept. 2002): 8-9, 16-19.

Fichtner, Gerhard. "Übertragung. Zur Archäologie eines Freudschen Begriffs." *Jahrbuch der Psychoanalyse. Beiträge zur Theorie, Praxis und Geschichte*. Eds. Claudia Frank, Ludger M. Hermanns, and Helmut Hinz, 53 (2006): 93-116.

Fieni, David. "The Language of the Other: Testimonial Exercises." Trans. Catherine Porter. *PMLA* 125.4 (2010): 1002-1019.

Fine, Todd. "'The Beginning of Arabia's Spring': The Khalid Revolution." *Middle East Institute Viewpoints: Revolution and Political Transformation in the Middle East*. Outcomes and Prospects, Vol. III. Washington: The Middle East Institute, 2011. 20-25. <http://www.mei.edu/sites/default/files/publications/RevolutionVol.III_.pdf>.

Foucault, Michel. *L'ordre du discours*. Paris: Gallimard, 1971.

—. "The Discourse on Language," Appendix of *The Archaeology of Knowledge and The Discourse on Language*. By Michel Foucault. Trans. A. M. Sheridan Smith. New York, Pantheon, 1972. 215-37.

—. "La vie des hommes infâmes." *Les Cahiers du Chemin* 29 (15 Jan. 1977): 12-29.

—. "The Ethics of the Concern for Self as a Practice of Freedom." *Ethics: Subjectivity and Truth*. The Essential Works of Michel Foucault 1954–1984, Vol. 1. Ed. Paul Rabinow. Trans. Robert Hurley. New York: The New P, 1997. 281-301.

—. *Archeology of Knowledge*. Trans. A.M. Sheridan Smith. 1972; London: Routledge, 2002.

—. *The Order of Things: Archaeology of the Human Sciences*. 1970; London: Routledge, 2002.

Funk, Nathan C., and Betty J. Sitka, eds. *Ameen Rihani: Bridging East and West: A Pioneering Call for Arab-American Understanding*. Lanham, MD: UP of America, 2004.

Gana, Nouri. "In Search of Andalusia: Reconfiguring Arabness in Diana Abu-Jaber's *Crescent*." *The Edinburgh Companion to the Arab Novel in English: The Politics of Anglo Arab and Arab American Literature and Culture*. Ed. Nouri Gana. Edinburgh: Edinburgh UP, 2013. 198-216.

—. "The Intellectual History and Contemporary Significance of The Arab Novel in English." Introduction. *The Edinburgh Companion to the Arab Novel in English: The Politics of Anglo Arab and Arab American Literature and Culture*. Ed. Nouri Gana. Edinburgh: Edinburgh UP, 2013. 9-11.

Garrigós, Cristina. "The Dynamics of Intercultural Dislocation. Hybridity in Rabih Alameddine's *I, The Divine*." *Arab Voices in Diaspora: Critical Perspectives on Anglophone Arab Literature*. Ed. Layla Al Maleh. Amsterdam: Rodopi, 2009. 187-201.

Geertz, Clifford. *After the Fact: Two Countries, Four Decades, One Anthropologist*. Cambridge, MA: Harvard UP, 1995.

—. "Which Way to Mecca?" *Life Among Anthros and Other Essays*. By Clifford Geertz. Ed. Fred Inglis. Princeton: Princeton UP, 2010. 135-56.

Genette, Gérard. *Narrative Discourse. An Essay in Method*. Trans. Jane E. Lewin. Ithaca: Cornell UP, 1980.

Ghali, Waguih. *Beer in the Snooker Club*. London: André Deutsch, 1964.

Ghanem, Tarek. "Literary gems: On being Egyptian and Ihab Hassan's *Out of Egypt*." *Mada Masr* 19 Feb. 2016, 3 Mar. 2016 <http://www.madamasr.com/sections/culture/literary-gems-%E2%80%8B-being-egyptian-and-ihab-hassan%E2%80%99s-out-egypt-%E2%80%8B>.

Ghaussy, Soheila. "A Stepmother Tongue: 'Feminine Writing' in Assia Djebar's *Fantasia: An Algerian Cavalcade*." *World Literature Today* 68.3 (1994): 457-62.

Ghazoul, Ferial J. *Nocturnal Poetics: The Arabian Nights in Contemporary Context*. Cairo: American U in Cairo P, 1996.

—. "The Arabization of Othello." *Comparative Literature* 50.1 (1998): 1-31.

Gibb, H. A. R. "Studies in Contemporary Arabic Literature." *Bulletin of the School of Oriental and African Studies* 7.1 (1933): 1-22.

Gibran, Jean, and Kahlil Gibran. *Kahlil Gibran: His Life and World*. Boston: New York Graphic Society, 1974.

Gibran, Kahlil. *The Prophet*. New annot. ed. Richmond: Oneworld, 2012.

Glick Schiller, Nina, Linda Basch, and Cristina Szanton Blanc. "Immigrant to Transmigrant: Theorizing Transnational Migration." *Anthropological Quarterly* 68.1 (1995): 48-63.

Glissant, Édouard. *Poetics of Relation*. Trans. Betsy Wing. Ann Arbor: U of Michigan P, 1997.

Gomez, Michael. *Black Crescent: The Experience and Legacy of African Muslims in the Americas*. New York: Cambridge UP, 2005.

Gordon, Murray. *Slavery in the Arab World*. New York: New Amsterdam, 1989.

Gosh, Amitav. "Petrofiction: The Oil Encounter and the Novel." *The New Republic* 2 Mar. 1992: 29-33.

Granara, William. "Nostalgia, Arab Nationalism, and the Andalusian Chronotope in the Evolution of the Modern Arabic Novel." *Journal of Arabic Literature* 36.1 (2005): 57-73.

Greenberg, Nathaniel. "Political Modernism, Jabra, and the Baghdad Modern Art Group." *CLCWeb: Comparative Literature and Culture* 12.2 (2010): 1-11, 24 Mar. 2012 <http://docs.lib.purdue.edu/clcweb/vol12/iss2/13>.

Greenblatt, Stephen, et al. *Cultural Mobility: A Manifesto* Cambridge: Cambridge UP, 2010.

Grunebaum, Gustav E. von. "Literature in the Context of Islamic Civilization." *Oriens* 20 (1967): 1-14.

Habibi, Emile. *The Secret Life of Saeed, the Ill-fated Pessoptimist: A Palestinian Who Became a Citizen of Israel.* Trans. Salma K. Jayyusi and Trevor Le Gassick. New York: Vantage P, 1982.

—. *Al-Mutasha'il: al-waqa'i' al-ghariba fi ikhtifa' sa'id abi al-nahs al-mutasha'il.* Beirut: Dar Ibn Khaldun, 1989.

Hadfield, Andrew. *Lying in Early Modern Culture: From the Oath of Supremacy to the Oath of Allegiance.* Oxford: Oxford UP, 2017.

Hadidy, Subhy. "Idward sa'id wa mufhum al-bidaya" [Edward Said and the meaning of beginning]. *Al-Mulhaq ath-Thaqafi/An-Nahar* 28 Nov. 1998: 16.

Hafez, Sabry. *The Genesis of Arabic Narrative Discourse.* London: Saqi, 1993.

—. "An Arabian Master." *New Left Review* 37 (Jan.-Feb. 2006): 39-66.

Hajjar, Nijmeh. "Ameen Rihani's Humanist Vision of Arab Nationalism." *Ameen Rihani: Bridging East and West: A Pioneering Call for Arab-American Understanding.* Eds. Nathan C. Funk and Betty J. Sitka. Lanham, MD: UP of America, 2004.134-48.

—. *The Politics and Poetics of Ameen Rihani. The Humanist Ideology of an Arab-American Intellectual and Activist.* London: Tauris Academic Studies, 2010.

Hammad, Suheir. *Born Palestinian, Born Black.* New York: Harlem River P, 1996.

Harlow, Barbara, and Mia Carter, eds. *Imperialism and Orientalism: A Documentary Sourcebook.* Walden, MA: Blackwell, 1999.

Harlow, Barbara. "Sentimental Orientalism: Season of Migration to the North and Othello." *Tayeb Salih's Season of Migration to the North: A Critical Casebook.* Ed. Mona Takieddine Amyuni. Beirut: American U of Beirut P, 1985. 75-79.

—. "The Palestinian Intellectual and the Liberation of the Academy." *Edward Said: A Critical Reader.* Ed. Michael Sprinker. Oxford: Blackwell, 1992. 173-93.

Hartman, Michelle. "Rabih Alameddine's I, the Divine: A 'Druze Novel' as World Literature?" *The Edinburgh Companion to the Arab Novel in English: The Politics of Anglo Arab and Arab American Literature and Culture.* Ed. Nouri Gana. Edinburgh: Edinburgh UP, 2013. 339-59.

Harvey, L. P. *Islamic Spain, 1250 to 1500.* Chicago: U of Chicago P, 1990.

—. *Muslims in Spain, 1500 to 1614.* Chicago: U of Chicago P, 2005.

Hassan, Ihab. *Paracriticisms: Seven Speculations of the Times.* Urbana: U of Illinois P, 1975.

—. *The Dismemberment of Orpheus: Toward a Postmodern Literature.* 1971; Madison: U of Wisconsin P, 1982.

—. *Out of Egypt: Fragments of an Autobiography.* Carbondale: Southern Illinois UP, 1986.

—. "Culture, Indeterminacy, and Immanence: Margins of the (Postmodern) Age." *The Postmodern Turn: Essays in Postmodern Theory and Culture.* By Ihab Hassan. Columbus: Ohio State UP, 1987. 46-83.

—. *Selves at Risk: Patterns of Quest in Contemporary American Letters.* Madison: U of Wisconsin P, 1990.

—. *Rumors of Change: Essays of Five Decades.* Tuscaloosa: U of Alabama P, 1995.

—. "Queries for Postcolonial Studies." *Philosophy and Literature* 22.2 (1998): 328-42.

—. "Postmodernism, etc.: An Interview with Frank Cioffi." *Postmodernism and Other Distractions: Situations and Directions for Critical Theory,* ed. David Gorman, *Style* 33.3 (1999): 357-71.

—. "The Eagle, the Olive Branch, and the Dream: Changing Perceptions of America in the World." *Georgia Review* 59.2 (2005): 327-43.

—. "Extraterritorial: Exile, Diaspora, and the Ground under Your Feet." *Diasporic Constructions of Home and Belonging.* Eds. Florian Kläger and Klaus Stierstorfer. Berlin: De Gruyter, 2015. 21-33.

Hassan, Salah, and Marcy Knopf-Newman. "Introduction." *MELUS* 31.4 (2006): 3-13.

Hassan, Salah. "Arabs, Race and the Post-September 11 National Security State." *Middle East Report* 224 (2002): 16-21.

Hassan, Waïl S. *Tayeb Salih: Ideology and the Craft of Fiction.* Syracuse: Syracuse UP, 2003.

—. "The Rise of Arab-American Literature: Orientalism and Cultural Translation in the Work of Ameen Rihani." *American Literary History* 20.1-2 (2008): 245-75.

—. "Gibran and Orientalism." *Arab Voices in Diaspora: Critical Perspectives on Anglophone Arab Literature.* Ed. Layla Al Maleh. Amsterdam: Rodopi, 2009. 65-92.

—. *Immigrant Narratives: Orientalism and Cultural Translation in Arab American and Arab British Literature.* New York: Oxford UP, 2011.

—. "The Rise of the Arab American Novel: Ameen Rihani's *The Book of Khalid.*" *The Edinburgh Companion to the Arab Novel in English: The Politics of Anglo Arab and Arab American Literature and Culture.* Ed. Nouri Gana. Edinburgh: Edinburgh UP, 2013. 39-62.

"Heba Y. Amin discusses her work in the 10th Berlin Biennale for Contemporary Art." *ARTFORUM* 5 June 2018, 11 July 2018 <https://www.artforum.com/interviews/heba-y-amin-discusses-her-work-in-the-10th-berlin-biennale-for-contemporary-art-75675>.

Hegerfeldt, Anne C. *Lies that Tell the Truth. Magical Realism Seen through Contemporary Fiction from Britain.* Amsterdam: Rodopi, 2005.

Hijazi, Muhammad, ed. *Usul al-Fikr al-'Arabi al-Hadith 'inda at-Tahtawi—Tahtawi and the Roots of Modern Arab Thought.* Cairo: Al-Hay'a al-Misriya al-'Ala lil-Kitab, 1974.

Hishmeh, Richard E. "Strategic Genius, Disidentification, and the Burden of *The Prophet* in Arab-American Poetry." *Arab Voices in Diaspora: Critical Perspectives on Anglophone Arab Literature.* Ed. Layla Al Maleh. Amsterdam: Rodopi, 2009. 93-119.

Hobsbawm, Eric J. *Nations and Nationalism since 1780: Programme, Myth, and Reality.* Cambridge: Cambridge UK, 1990.

Holder, Alan. "In the American Grain: William Carlos Williams on the American Past." *American Quarterly* 19.3 (1967): 499-515.

Homeland, season 5. Dir. Lesli Linka Glatter, Keith Gordon et al., perf. Claire Danes, Mandy Patinkin, Rupert Friend et al., 2015.

Holt, Thomas C. "The Political Uses of Alienation: W. E. B. Du Bois on Politics, Race, and Culture, 1903-1940." *American Quarterly* 42.2 (1990): 301-23.

Hook, Derek. "Racism as Abjection: A Psychoanalytic Conceptualisation for a Post-Apartheid South Africa." *South African Journal of Psychology* 34.4 (2004): 672-703.

Hostage: The Bachar Tapes (English Version), Tape #17. Dir. Souheil Bachar, The Atlas Group in collab. with c-hundred film corp., 2000. DVD.

Hourani, Albert. *Arabic Thought in the Liberal Age 1798-1939.* Cambridge: Cambridge UP, 1991.

Hovsepian, Nubar. "Connections with Palestine." *Edward Said: A Critical Reader.* Ed. Michael Sprinker. Oxford: Blackwell, 1992. 5-17.

Huntington, Samuel. "The Clash of Civilizations?" *Foreign Affairs* 72.3 (1993): 22-50.

Hussein, Taha. *Al-Ayam, 1-3.* Beirut: Dar al-Kitab al-Lubnani, 1982.

—. *The Days.* Trans. E. H. Paxton, Hilary Wayment, and Kenneth Cragg. 2nd ed. Cairo: AUC P, 2000.

Hynes, Eric. "Interview with Heba Yehia Amin, Caram Kapp, and Don Karl of 'Homeland is not a Series'." *Field of Vision* 20 Dec. 2015, 22 Dec. 2015 <https://fieldofvision.org/interview-with-heba-yehia-amin-caram-kapp-and-don-karl-of-homeland-is-not-a-series>.

Irwin, Robert. *The Arabian Nights: A Companion.* London: Allen Lane; New York: Penguin P, 1994.

Jabra, Jabra Ibrahim. "Modern Arab Literature and the West." *Journal of Arab Literature* 2 (1971): 76-91.

—. *Sayyadun fi shari' dhayyiq.* Trans. Mohammad Asfour and Jabra Ibrahim Jabra. Beirut: Dar al-Adab, 1974.

—. *Al-bahth 'an Walid Mas'ud.* Beirut: Dar al-Adab, 1978.

—. *'Util* [Shakespeare's *Othello*]. Kuwait: Wizarat al-I'lam, 1978.

—. "On Interpoetics." Interview with Najman Yasin. *The View from Within: Writers and Critics on Contemporary Arab Literature.* Eds. Ferial Ghazoul and Barbara Harlow. Cairo: American U in Cairo P, 1994. 207-12.

—. *Hunters in a Narrow Street.* 1960; Boulder: Three Continents, 1996.

—. *In Search of Walid Masoud: A Novel.* Trans. Roger Allen and Adnan Haydar. Syracuse: Syracuse UP, 2000.

Jabra, Jabra Ibrahim, and 'Abd al-Rahman Munif. *'Alam bi-la khara'it* [World without maps]. Beirut: Mu'assasa al-'Arabiyya li-d-Dirasat wa-n-Nashr, 1982.

Jacobson, Matthew Frye. *Whiteness of a Different Color: European Immigrants and the Alchemy of Race*. Cambridge, MA: Harvard UP, 1998.

Jacquemond, Richard. "Towards an Economy and Poetics of Translation from and into Arabic." *Cultural Encounters in Translation from Arabic*. Ed. Said Faiq. Clevedon, UK: Multilingual Matters, 2004. 117-27.

Jamal, Amaney A., and Nadine Christine Naber, eds. *Race and Arab Americans Before and After 9/11: From Invisible Citizens to Visible Subjects*. Syracuse: Syracuse UP, 2008.

Jarrar, Maher. "A Narration of 'Deterritorialization': Imīl Habībī's The Pessoptimist." *Middle Eastern Literatures* 5.1 (2002): 15-28.

—. "The Arabian Nights and the Contemporary Arabic Novel." *The Arabian Nights in Historical Context: Between East and West*. Eds. Saree Makdisi and Felicity Nussbaum. Oxford: Oxford UP, 2008. 297-315.

Johnson, Rebecca C. "Importing the novel. Arabic literature's forgotten foreign objects." *On the Ground: New Directions in Middle East and North African Studies*. Ed. Brian T. Edwards. Northwestern University in Qatar, 2015. n. pag. <http://ontheground.qatar.northwestern.edu/uncategorized/chapter-7-importing-the-novel-arabic-literatures-foreign-objects/>.

Johnson-Davies, Denys. Translator's Introduction. *Season of Migration to the North*. By Tayeb Salih. New York: Kesend, 1989. i-iv.

Jullien, Dominique. "In Praise of Mistranslation: The Melancholy Cosmopolitanism of Jorge Luis Borges." *Borges in the 21ˢᵗ Century*. Spec. issue of *Romanic Review* 98.2-3 (2007): 205-24.

Kaldas, Pauline, and Khaled Mattawa, eds. *Dinarzad's Children: An Anthology of Contemporary Arab American Fiction*. 2nd ed. 2004; Fayetteville: U of Arkansas P, 2009.

Kanafani, Ghassan. *Rijal fi-shams*. Beirut: Dar at-Tali'ah, 1972.

—. *Men in the Sun, and other Palestinian Stories*, trans. Hilary Kilpatrick. London: Heinemann, 1978.

Kattaya, Mona. "Writing the 'Real Jerusalem': British and American Travel Accounts in the Nineteenth Century." *Jerusalem Quarterly* 44 (2010): 14-27.

Keddie, Nikki R. "Response of Jamal al-Din to Renan." *An Islamic Response to Imperialism. Political and Religious Writings of Jamal al-Din al-Afghani*. By Nikki R. Keddie. New ed. 1968; Berkeley: U of California P, 1983. 181-89.

—. *An Islamic Response to Imperialism. Political and Religious Writings of Jamal al-Din al-Afghani*. Ed. Nikki R. Keddie. 1968; Berkeley: U of California P, 1983.

—. "Afghānī, Jamāl al-Dīn (1838–1897)." *The Oxford Encyclopedia of Philosophy, Science, and Technology in Islam*, Vol. 1. Ed. Ibrahim Kalin. Oxford: Oxford UP, 2014. 9-14.

Kerr, Malcolm H. *Islamic Reform: The Political and Legal Theories of Muhammad 'Abduh and Rashīd Ridā*. Berkeley: U of California P, 1966.

Khalidi, Rashid. "Arab Nationalism: Historical Problems of Literature." *The American Historical Review* 96.5 (1991): 1363-73.

—. *Palestinian Identity: The Construction of Modern National Consciousness*. New York: Columbia UP, 1997.

al-Khalil, Samir [Kanan Makiya]. *The Monument: Art, Vulgarity, and Responsibility in Iraq*. London: André Deutsch, 1991.

al-Kharrat, Edwar. *Rama wa-l-tinnin*. Cairo, 1979.

—. *City of Saffron*. Trans. Frances Liardet. London: Quartet, 1989.

—. *Rama and the Dragon*. Trans. Ferial Ghazoul and John Verlenden. Cairo: The American U in Cairo P, 2002.

—. *Tarubuha Za'faran*. Beirut: Dar al-Adab, 1985.

Khatibi, Abdelkébir. *La langue de l'autre*. New York: Les Mains Secrètes, 1999.

Khoury, Elias. *Al-dhakira al-mafquda: dirasat naqdiya* [The lost memory: critical studies]. Beirut: Mu'assasat al-Abhath al-Arabiya, 1989.

—. *Little Mountain*. Trans. Maia Tabet. Manchester: Carcanet P, 1989.

—. *Rihlat Ghandi as-saghir*. Beirut: Dar al-Adab, 1989.

—. *Mamlakat al-ghuraba'*. Beirut: Dar al-Adab, 1993.

—. *Majma' al-asrar* [Junction of Secrets]. Beirut: Dar al-Adab, 1994.

—. *The Journey of Little Ghandi*. Trans. Paula Haydar. Minneapolis: U of Minnesota P, 1994.

—. *The Kingdom of Strangers*. Trans. Paula Haydar. Fayetteville: U of Arkansas P, 1996.

—. "Ar-riwaya wa miraya al-waqi' al-maksur." [The novel and the broken mirror of reality] *Al-Mulhaq ath-Thaqafi* 25 May 1996: 18-19 and 1 June 1996: 18-19.

—. *Bab ash-shams*. Beirut: Dar al-Adab, 1998.

—. "Reading Arabic." *DisOrientation: Contempory Arab Artists from the Middle East*. Berlin: Haus der Kulturen der Welt, 2003. 10-13.

—. "Wulidat filastin fi-l-'alam tahta qalamihi. idward sa'id: awwal al-'a'din," [Palestine came into being on a global level through/under his pen. Edward Said: The first returnee]. *Al-Mulhaq ath-Thaqafi/An-Nahar* 28 Sept. 2003: 15.

—. *Gate of the Sun*, trans. Humphrey Davies. 2005; London: Vintage, 2006.

—. "Writing the Novel Anew: East of the Mediterranean and now and here or East of the Mediterranean once again." Ed. Sonja Mejcher-Atassi. *MIT Electronic Journal of Middle East Studies. Special Focus Writing: A 'Tool for Change': 'Abd al-Rahman Munif Remembered* 7 (2007): 70-76.

Khoury, Jamil and Stephen Combs Khoury, dirs. *Not Quite White: Arabs, Slavs, and the Contours of Contested Whiteness*. ADF/Typecast Films, 2012.

Kidwai, Abdur Raheem. *Literary Orientalism: A Companion*. New Delhi: Viva, 2009.

Kilpatrick, Hilary. "Arab Fiction in English: A Case of Dual Nationality." *New Comparison* 13 (1992): 46-55.

Kläger, Florian, and Klaus Stierstorfer, eds. *Diasporic Constructions of Home and Belonging*. Berlin: De Gruyter, 2015.

Klein, Aaron J. *Striking Back: The 1972 Munich Olympics Massacre and Israel's Deadly Response*. New York: Random House, 2005.

Klemm, Verena. *Literarisches Engagement im Nahen Osten: Konzepte und Debatten.* Würzburg: Ergon, 1998.

Knauss, Stefanie. "Excess, Artifice, Sentimentality: Almodóvar's Camp Cinema as a Challenge for Theological Aesthetics." *Journal of Religion, Media & Digital Culture* 3.1 (2014): 31-55.

Kristal, Efraín. *Invisible Work. Borges and Translation.* Nashville: Vanderbilt UP, 2002.

Kristeva, Julia. *Desire in Language: A Semiotic Approach to Literature and Art.* Ed. Leon S. Roudiez. Trans. Thomas Gora, Alice Jardine, and Leon S. Roudiez. New York: Columbia UP, 1980.

—. *Powers of Horror: An Essay on Abjection.* Trans. Leon S. Roudiez. New York: Columbia UP, 1982.

Kubrick, Stanley, dir. *2001: A Space Odyssey.* Screenplay Stanley Kubrick and Arthur C. Clarke, Metro-Goldwyn-Mayer, 1968.

Kucich, John. *The Power of Lies: Transgression in Victorian Fiction.* Ithaca: Cornell UP, 1994.

Lane, Edward William. *The Thousand and One Nights.* Ed. Edward Stanley Poole. London: Bickers, 1877.

Larson, Jil. *Ethics and Narrative in the English Novel, 1880–1914.* Cambridge: Cambridge UP, 2001.

Lawrence, D. H. "The Spirit of Place." *Studies in Classic American Literature.* By D. H. Lawrence. Ed. Ezra Greenspan, Lindeth Vasey, and John Worthen. Cambridge: Cambridge UP, 2003. 13-19.

Layoun, Mary N. "Endings and Beginnings: Reimagining the Tasks and Spaces of Comparison." *New Literary History* 40.3 (2009): 583-607.

Levin, Harry. General Introduction. *The Riverside Shakespeare.* Ed. G. Blakemore Evans. Boston: Houghton Mifflin, 1974. 1-25.

Lewis, Bernard. *Race and Slavery in the Middle East: An Historical Enquiry.* New York: Oxford UP, 1990.

—. *What Went Wrong? The Clash Between Islam and Modernity in the Middle East.* London: Weidenfeld & Nicolson, 2002.

—. *What Went Wrong? Western Impact and Middle Eastern Response.* Oxford: Oxford UP, 2002.

Lewis, David Levering. *W. E. B. Du Bois: Biography of a Race, 1868–1919.* New York: Holt, 1993.

Lippman, Edward Arthur. Rev. of *Estetica. Teoria della formatività.* By Luigi Pareyson. *The Journal of Philosophy* 52.25 (1955): 791-96.

Litvin, Margaret, Saffron Walkling, and Raphael Cormack. "Full of Noises: When 'World Shakespeare' met the 'Arab Spring.'" *Shakespeare* 12.3 (2016): 300-15.

Litvin, Margaret. "Vanishing Intertexts in the Arab '*Hamlet* Tradition'." *Arab Shakespeare.* Spec. issue of *Critical Survey* 19.3 (2007): 74-97.

—. *Hamlet's Arab Journey: Shakespeare's Prince and Nasser's Ghost*. Princeton: Princeton UP, 2011.

Lockman, Zachary. *Contending Visions of the Middle East. The History and Politics of Orientalism*. 2nd ed. Cambridge, UK: Cambridge UP, 2010.

Lola rennt. Dir. Tom Tykwer, screenplay Tom Tykwer, perf. Franka Potente, Moritz Bleibtreu, 1998, DVD.

Lopez Lerma, Monica. "Law in High Heels: Performativity, Alterity, and Aesthetics." *Southern California Interdisciplinary Law Journal* 20.2 (2011): 289-324.

Lyotard, Jean-François. *The Differend: Phrases in Dispute*. Trans. Georges Van Den Abbeele. Minneapolis, MN: U of Minnesota P, 1988.

Mahfouz, Najib. *Arabian Nights and Days*. Trans. Denys Johnson-Davis. New York: Doubleday, 1994.

—. *Layali alf Layla*. Cairo: Maktab Misr, 1978.

Majaj, Lisa Suhair. "Arab American Literature: Origins and Developments." *Arab American Literature and Culture*. Eds. Alfred Hornung and Martina Kohl. Heidelberg: Winter, 2012. 61-86.

Malti-Douglas, Fedwa. *Blindness & Autobiography: Al-Ayām of Tāhā Ḥussain*. Princeton: Princeton UP, 1988.

—. "Shahrazād Feminist." *The Thousand and One Nights in Arabic Literature and Society*. Eds. Richard G. Hovannisian and Georges Sabagh. Cambridge: Cambridge UP, 1997. 40-55.

Mancing, Howard. "Cide Hamete Benengeli vs. Miguel de Cervantes: The Metafictional Dialectic of Don Quijote." *Cervantes: Bulletin of the Cervantes Society of America* 1.1-2 (1981): 63-81.

Marmon, Shaun Elizabeth, ed. *Slavery in the Islamic Middle East*. Princeton: Wiener, 1999.

Márquez, Gabriel García. *Living to Tell a Tale*. Trans. Edith Grossman. New York: Knopf, 2003.

—. *One Hundred Years of Solitude*. Trans. Gregory Rabassa. 1970; London: Penguin, 2014.

Marzolph, Ulrich, ed. *The Arabian Nights Reader*. Detroit: Wayne State UP, 2006.

—. *The Arabian Nights in Transnational Perspective*. Detroit: Wayne State UP, 2007.

Marzolph, Ulrich, and Richard van Leeuwen, eds. *The Arabian Nights Encyclopedia*. Santa Barbara: ABC-Clio, 2004.

Massad, Joseph A. *Desiring Arabs*. Chicago: U of Chicago P, 2007.

—. "Homeland, Obama's Show." *Aljazeera Online* 25 Oct. 2012, 30 Oct. 2015 <http://www.aljazeera.com/indepth/opinion/2012/10/2012102591525809725.htm>.

Matar, Nabil I. *Islam in Britain, 1558–1685*. Cambridge: Cambridge UP, 1998.

—. *Turks, Moors and Englishmen in the Age of Discovery*. New York: Columbia UP, 1999.

—. ed. and trans. *In the Lands of Christians: Arabic Travel Writing in the Seventeenth Century*. New York: Routledge, 2003.

—. *Europe through Arab Eyes, 1578–1727.* New York: Columbia UP, 2008.

Mattawa, Khaled, and Munir Akash, eds. *Post-Gibran: Anthology of New Arab American Writing.* Syracuse, New York: Syracuse UP, 1999.

—. Introduction. *Post-Gibran: Anthology of New Arab American Writing.* Syracuse, New York: Syracuse UP, 1999. xi-xiii.

Mattawa, Khaled. "Freeways and Rest Houses. Towards an Arab Location on the American Cultural Map." *Post-Gibran: Anthology of New Arab American Writing.* Eds. Khaled Mattawa and Munir Akash. New York: Syracuse UP, 1999. 49-65.

—. "Identity, Power, and a Prayer to Our Lady of Repatriation: On Translating and Writing Poetry." *Kenyon Review Online* (Fall 2014): n. pag., 13 Mar. 2015 <http://www.kenyonreview.org/kr-online-issue/2014-fall/selections/khaled-mattawa-essay-1-656342/>.

McGurn, William. "An Arab for Ground Zero." *The Wall Street Journal* 24 May 2011, 23 Sept. 2013 <http://www.wsj.com/articles/SB100014240527023040665045763414014188827660>.

Mejcher-Atassi, Sonja. "On the Necessity of Writing the Present: Elias Khoury and the 'Birth of the Novel' in Lebanon." *Arabic Literature: Postmodern Perspectives.* Eds. Angelika Neuwirth, Andreas Pflitsch, and Barbara Winckler. London: Saqi, 2010. 87-96.

—. *Reading Across Modern Arabic Literature and Art.* Wiesbaden: Reichert, 2012. 63-75.

Montgomery, James E. *Al-Jāḥiz: In Praise of Books.* Edinburgh Studies in Classical Arabic Literature. Edinburgh: Edinburgh UP, 2013.

Moreh, Shmuel. *Modern Arabic Poetry: 1800–1970.* Leiden: Brill, 1976.

Muaddi Darraj, Susan. "Arab American Novel." *The Greenwood Encyclopedia of Multiethnic American Literature: A-C.* Ed. Emmanuel S. Nelson. Westport, CT: Greenwood P, 2005.179-82.

Mufti, Aamir R. "Global Comparativism." *Edward Said: Continuing the Conversation.* Eds. Homi Bhabha and W. J. T. Mitchell. Chicago: U of Chicago P, 2005. 109-26.

Mullan, John. "Bush Takes Camus to the Beach." *The Guardian* 17 Aug. 2006, 24 Oct. 2010 <http://www.theguardian.com/world/2006/aug/17/usa.bookscomment>.

Mulvey, Laura. "Visual Pleasure and Narrative Cinema." *Screen* 16.3 (1975): 6-18.

Munich. Dir. Steven Spielberg, screenplay Tony Kushner, Eric Roth, Universal Pictures & DreamWorks Pictures, 2005. Warner Bros., 1973.

Munif, 'Abd al-Rahman. *Sharq al-Mutawassit.* Beirut: Mu'assasa al-'Arabiyya lil-Dirasaat wal-Nashr, 1975.

—. *An-Nihayat.* Beirut: Mu'assasa al-'Arabiyya lil-Dirasat wal-Nashr, 1977.

—. *Al-Tih.* Beirut: Mu'assasa al-'Arabiyya lil-Dirasat wal-Nashr, 1984.

—. *Endings.* Trans. Roger Allen. London: Quartet, 1988.

—. *Cities of Salt (Cities of Salt, vol. 1).* Trans. Peter Theroux. 1987; New York: Vintage, 1989. *The Trench (Cities of Salt, vol. 2).* Trans. Peter Theroux. New York: Pantheon,

1991. *Variations on Night and Day (Cities of Salt, vol. 3)*. Trans. Peter Theroux. New York: Pantheon, 1993.

—. "Unpublished Munif Interview: Crisis in the Arab World—Oil, Political Islam, and Dictatorship." By Iskandar Habash. Trans. Elie Chalala. *Al-Jadid Magazine* 2003, 14 May 2015 <http://www.aljadid.com/content/unpublished-munif-interview-crisis-arab-world-%E2%80%93-oil-political-islam-and-dictatorship>.

Munkelt, Marga, Markus Schmitz, Mark Stein, and Silke Stroh. "Introduction: Directions of Translocation—Towards a Critical Spatial Thinking in Postcolonial Studies." *Postcolonial Translocations: Cultural Representation and Critical Spatial Thinking*. Eds. Marga Munkelt et al. Amsterdam: Rodopi, 2013. xiii-lxxix.

Murphy, Dwyer. "This is also my world." Interview with Rabih Alameddine. *Guernica* 3 Mar. 2014, 13 Feb. 2015 <https://www.guernicamag.com/interviews/this-is-also-my-world/>.

al-Musawi, Muhsin. *Scheherazade in England: A Study of Nineteenth-Century English Criticism of the Arabian Nights*. Washington: Three Continents P, 1981.

—. *The Postcolonial Arabic Novel: Debating Ambivalence*. Leiden: Brill, 2003.

—. "Scheherazade's Nonverbal Narratives." *Journal of Arabic Literature* 36.3 (2005): 338-362.

Naff, Alixa. *Becoming American. The Early Arab Immigrant Experience*. Carbondale: Southern Illinois P, 1985.

Naimy, Nadeem. *The Lebanese Prophets of New York*. Beirut: American U of Beirut P, 1985.

Nancy, Jean-Luc. *The Ground of the Image*. New York: Fordham UP, 2005.

Nash, Geoffrey P. *The Arab Writer in English. Arab Themes in a Metropolitan Language, 1908–1958*. Brighton: Sussex Academic P, 1998.

—. *Writing Muslim Identity*. London: Continuum, 2012.

—. "Beyond Orientalism: Khalid, the Secular City and the Transcultural Self." *The Edinburgh Companion to the Arab Novel in English: The Politics of Anglo Arab and Arab American Literature and Culture* Ed. Nouri Gana. Edinburgh: Edinburgh UP, 2013. 63-81.

Nassar, Jamal R. "Ibrahim Abu-Lughod: The Legacy of an Activist Scholar and Teacher." *Arab Studies Quarterly* 26.4 (2004): 23-24.

Nayar, Pramod K. *Postcolonial Literature: An Introduction*. Delhi: Pearson Longman, 2008.

Newman, Daniel L. *Rifā'ah Rāfi' Ṭahṭāwī. An Imam in Paris: Account of a Stay in France by an Egyptian Cleric (1826–1831)*. London: Saqi, 2004.

Ngũgĩ wa Thiong'o. *Decolonizing the Mind. The Politics of Language in African Literature*. 1986; Oxford: James Currey; Nairobi: EAEP; Portsmouth, NH: Heinemann, 2005.

—. *Globalectics: Theory and the Politics of Knowing*. 2012; New York: Columbia UP, 2014.

Nietzsche, Friedrich. *Also sprach Zarathustra. Ein Buch für Alle und Keinen*. Chemnitz, Ernst Schmeitzner, 1883–91.

—. *Ecce Homo: wie man wird, was man ist*. Leipzig: C. G. Naumann, 1889.

—. *Zur Genealogie der Moral: Eine Streitschrift*. Leipzig: C. G. Naumann, 1887.

—. "On Truth and Lies in a Nonmoral Sense [1873]." *Art and Interpretation: An Anthology of Readings in Aesthetics and the Philosophy of Art*. Ed. Eric Dayton. Peterborough, ON: Broadview P, 1998. 116-24.

Oren, Michael B. *Power, Faith, and Fantasy. America in the Middle East, 1776 to the Present*. New York: Norton, 2007.

Orfalea, Gregory. *The Arab Americans: A History*. Northampton, MA: Olive Branch P, 2006.

Oueijan, Naji. "The Formation of a Universal Self." *Ameen Rihani: Bridging East and West: A Pioneering Call for Arab-American Understanding*. Eds. Nathan C. Funk, and Betty J. Sitka. Lanham, MD: UP of America, 2004. 83-92.

Pareyson, Luigi. "Art: Performance and Interpretation." *Existence, Interpretation, Freedom: Selected Writings*. By Luigi Pareyson. Ed. Paolo Diego Bubbio. Trans. Anna Mattei. Aurora, CO: Davies Group, 2009.114-40.

Parry, Benita. *Postcolonial Studies. A Materialist Critique*. London: Routledge, 2004.

Parry, Nigel. "Permission to Narrate: Edward Said, Palestine, and the Internet." *The Electronic Intifada* 26 Sept. 2003, 20 Jan. 2016 <http://electronicintifada.net/cgi-bin/artman/exec/view.cgi/7/1975>.

Petri, Elio, and Ugo Pirro. "Material for a Film." *For a Palestinian: A Memorial to Wael Zuaiter*. Ed. Janet Venn-Brown. London: Kegan Paul, 1984. 75-116.

Poole, Deborah. "An Excess of Description: Ethnography, Race, and Visual Technologies." *Annual Review of Anthropology* 34 (2005): 159-79.

Power, Politics, and Culture. Interviews with Edward W. Said. Ed. Gauri Viswanathan. New York: Pantheon, 2001.

Ra'ad, Walid. Interview with Alan Gilbert. *BOMB Magazine* 81 (2002), 24 Nov. 2016 <http://bombmagazine.org/article/2504/walid-ra-ad>.

Ragep, Sally P., trans. *Islam and Science: A Lecture Presented at La Sorbonne 29 March 1883 by Ernest Renan*. 2nd Edition. Montreal: McGill U, 2011.

Renger, Almut-Barbara. *Oedipus and the Sphinx. The Threshold Myth from Sophocles through Freud to Cocteau*. Trans. Duncan Smart, John T. Hamilton, and David G. Rice. Chicago: U of Chicago P, 2013.

Reynolds, Dwight F., ed. *Interpreting the Self. Autobiography in the Arab Literary Tradition*. Berkeley: U of California P, 2001.

Rihani, Ameen. "The Curiosity of the Occidental." *The Path of Vision. Pocket Essays of East and West*. New York: White & CO, 1921.182-88.

—. "The Lying Oriental." *The Path of Vision. Pocket Essays of East and West*. By Ameen Rihani. New York: White & CO, 1921. 189-95.

—. *Muluk al-ʿArab au Rihla fi Bilad al-ʿArabiya* [Kings of the Arab or a voyage to the Arab world]. Beirut: Yusuf Sadir, 1924.

—. *Arabian Peak and Desert: Travels in Al-Yaman*. London: Constable, 1930.

—. *The Lore of the Arabian Nights*. Washington, DC: Platform International P, 2002.

—. *Hymns of the Valleys*. Trans. Naji B. Oueijan. Piscataway, NJ: Gorgias P, 2002.

—. *Myrtle and Myrrh*. 1905; Washington, DC: Platform Intern., 2005.

—. *Ar-Rihaniyat* [the Rihani Essays]. Beirut: Dar al-ʿIlmi, 2010.

—. *The Book of Khalid*. 1911; New York: Melville House, 2012.

Rihani, Ameen Albert. "The *Book of Khalid* and *The Prophet*. Similar Universal Concerns with Different Perspectives: A Comparative Study." *PALMA* 7.1 (2001): 31-41.

Riis, Jacob A. *How the Other Half Lives. Studies among the Tenements of New York*. New York: Charles Scriber's & Sons, 1890.

Rogers, Sarah. "Forging History, Performing Memory: Walid Raad's The Atlas Project." *Parachute (Beyrouth_Beirut)* 108 (2002): 68-79.

Rushdie, Salman. *Midnight's Children*. 1981; New York: Penguin, 1991.

—. *Two Years Eight Months and Twenty-Eight Nights*. New York: Penguin Random House, 2015.

Saʿdi, Ahmad H., and Lila Abu-Lughod, eds. *Nakba. Palestine, 1948, and the Claims of Memory*. New York: Columbia UP, 2007.

Safi, Louay M. *The Challenge of Modernity. The Quest of Authenticity in the Arab World*. Lanham, MD: UP of America, 1994.

Said, Edward W. "The Arab Portrayed." *The Arab-Israeli Confrontation of June 1967: An Arab Perspective*. Ed. Ibrahim Abu-Lughod. Evanston: Northwestern UP, 1970. 1-9.

—. *Beginnings: Intention and Method*. New York: Columbia UP, Basic, 1975.

—. *Al-istishraq: al-maʿrifa, as-sulta, al-insha'* [Orientalism: the knowledge, the power, the discourse]. Trans. Kamal Abu-Deeb. Beirut: Muʾassasa al-ʾAbhath al-ʿArabiya, 1981.

—. *The World, the Text, and the Critic*. Cambridge: Harvard UP, 1983.

—. "Permission to Narrate." *Journal of Palestine Studies* 13.3 (1984): 27-48.

—. "Orientalism Reconsidered." *Cultural Critique* 1 (1985): 89-107.

—. *Culture and Imperialism*. 1993; New York: Vintage, 1994.

—. Ghazza - ariha: salam amriki" [Gaza – Jericho: An American peace]. Cairo: Dar al-Mustaqbal, 1994.

—. *Peace and Its Discontents*. London: Vintage, 1995.

—. *Orientalism*, 4th ed. 1978; London, New York: Penguin, 1995.

—. "By Birth or by Choice?" *Al-Ahram Weekly* Oct. 28–Nov. 3, 1999: 13.

—. *Out of Place: A Memoir*. New York: Knopf, 1999.

—. "Embargoed Literature." Sept. 17, 1990. *The Best of The Nation: Selections from the Independent Magazine of Politics and Culture*. Eds. Victor Navasky and Katrina vanden Heuvel. New York: Thunder's Mouth P / Nation Books, 2000. 53-58.

—. *kharij al-makan. mudhakkirat*. Trans. Fawwaz Traboulsi. Beirut: Dar al-Adab, 2000.

—. *The End of the Peace Process: Oslo and After*. New York: Pantheon, 2000.

—. "After Mahfouz." *Reflections on Exile and Other Essays*. 2000; Cambridge: Harvard UP, 2001. 317-26.

—. "Conrad and Nietzsche." *Reflections on Exile and other Essays*. By Edward Said. 2000; Cambridge: Harvard UP, 2001. 70-82.

—. "My Guru." *London Review of Books* 13 Dec. 2001: 19-20.

—. *From Oslo to Iraq and the Road Map*. New York: Pantheon; Toronto: Random, 2004.

Salaita, Steven. *Arab American Literary Fictions, Cultures, and Politics*. Basingstoke: Palgrave Macmillan, 2007.

Saleh, Fakhri. *difa'an idward sa'id* [In defense of Edward Said]. Beirut: Al-Mu'assasa al-'Arabiya li-d-Dirasat wa-n-Nashr, 2000.

Salih, Tayeb. *Mausim al-hijra ila-sh-shamal*. 1966; Beirut: Dar al-Auwdah, 1967.

—. *Season of Migration to the North*. Trans. Denys Johnson-Davies. 1969; London: Heinemann, 2010.

Sansour, Larissa. *Space Exodus*. Dir. and perf. Larissa Sansour, prod. Søren Lind, Beofilm, Laver Film, 2008.

—. *Run Lara Run* [2008]. *Resistance[s]. Experimental Films from the Middle East and North Africa, Vol. III*. Paris: Lowawe, CNC, 2010. DVD.

—. "'Fiction and Art Practice'. Interview with Larissa Sansour 'A Space Exodus'." By Wafa Gabsi. *Contemporary Practices* 10 (Mar. 2012): 114-19.

Schmitz, Markus. "Re-Reading Said in Arabic: (Other)Worldly Counterpoints." *Edward Said's Translocations: Essays in Secular Criticism*. Eds. Tobias Döring and Mark Stein. London: Routledge, 2012. 97-113.

—. *Kulturkritik ohne Zentrum. Edward W. Said und die Kontrapunkte kritischer Dekolonisation*. Bielefeld: Transcript, 2008.

Schuetz, Janice. "'The Exorcist' Images of Good and Evil." *Western Speech Communication* 39.2 (1975): 92-101.

Selim, Samah. "The Nahdah, Popular Fiction and the Politics of Translation." *MIT Electronic Journal of Middle East Studies* 4 (2004): 71-89.

Semmerling, Tim Jon. *"Evil" Arabs in American Popular Film: Orientalist Fear*. Austin: U of Texas P, 2006.

Shahadah, 'Alik. "The History of Arab Slavery in Africa" Arab Slave Trade (2002–2005), 27 Oct. 2014 <http://www.arabslavetrade.com#convert>.

Shaheen, Jack G. *Reel Bad Arabs: How Hollywood Vilifies a People*. New York: Olive Branch P, 2001.

Shakespeare, William. Sonnet 138. *The Riverside Shakespeare*. Ed. G. Blakemore Evans. Boston: Houghton Mifflin, 1974. 1774.

Shakir, Evelyn. "Arab Mothers, American Sons: Woman in Arab-American Autobiographies." *MELUS* 17.3 (1991–92): 5-15.

—. "Coming of Age: Arab American Literature." *Ethnic Forum: Journal of Ethnic Studies and Ethnic Bibliography* 13.2/14.1 (1993–94): 63-80.

—. "Arab American Literature." *New Immigrant Literatures in the United States: A Sourcebook to Our Multicultural Heritage*. Ed. Alpana Sharma Knippling. Westport, CT: Greenwood P, 1996. 3-18.

Shannahan, Dervla. "Reading Queer A/theology into Rabih Alameddine's Koolaids." *Feminist Theology* 19.2 (2011): 129-42.

Sharabi, Hisham. *Arab Intellectuals and the West: The Formative Years, 1875–1914*. Baltimore: Johns Hopkins P, 1970.

—. "The Scholarly Point of View: Politics, Perspective, Paradigm." *Theory, Politics and the Arab World: Critical Responses*. Ed. Hisham Sharabi. London: Routledge, 1990. 1-51.

Shehadeh, Raja. *The Third Way: A Journal of Life in the West Bank*. London: Quartet, 1982.

—. *The Sealed Room: Selections from the Diary of a Palestinian Living Under Israeli Occupation, September 1990–August 1991*. London: Quartet, 1992.

—. *Strangers in the House: Coming of Age in Occupied Palestine*. London: Profile Books, 2002.

—. *Palestinian Walks: Notes on a Vanishing Landscape*. London: Profile Books, 2007.

—. *Occupation Diaries*. London: Profile Books, 2012.

Shohat, Ella. "Columbus, Palestine, and Arab-Jews: Toward a Relational Approach to Community Identity." *Cultural Readings of Imperialism: Edward Said and the Gravity of History*. Eds. Keith Ansell-Pearson, Benita Parry, and Judith Squires. New York: St. Martin's P, 1997. 88-105.

—. "Taboo Memories and Diasporic Visions: Columbus, Palestine, and Arab-Jews." *Performing Hybridity*. Eds. May Joseph and Jennifer Natalia Fink. Minneapolis: U of Minnesota P, 1999. 131-56.

—. *Taboo Memories, Diasporic Voices*. Durham: Duke UP, 2006.

—. "The Sephardi-Moorish Atlantic: Between Orientalism and Occidentalism." *Between the Middle East and the Americas: The Cultural Politics of Diaspora*. Eds. Evelyn Alsultany and Ella Shohat. Ann Arbor: U of Michigan P, 2013. 42-62.

Simmel, Georg. "The Stranger." *The Sociology of Georg Simmel*. Ed. and trans. Kurt H. Wolff. Glencoe, IL: Free P, 1950. 402-408.

—. "The Metropolis and Mental Life." *Classic Essays on the Culture of Cities*. Ed. Richard Sennett. Englewood Cliffs, NJ: Prentice-Hall, 1969. 47-60.

Simpson, Philip L. "Fear of the Assimilation of the Foreign Other in *The Exorcist.*" *American Exorcist: Critical Essays on William Peter Blatty.* Ed. Benjamin Szumskyj. Jefferson, NC: McFarland & Co, 2008. 25-44.

Smith, Andrew, and William Hughes, eds. Empire and the Gothic: The Politics of Genre. Basingstoke: Palgrave Macmillan, 2003.

Sontag, Susan. *On Photography.* 1st electronic ed. New York: Rosetta, 2005. 1-19.

Spivak, Gayatri Chakravorty. "Terror: A Speech after 9/11." *An Aesthetic Education in the Era of Globalization.* By G. Chakravorty Spivak. Cambridge, MA: Harvard UP, 2013. 372-98.

—. "Translation as Culture." *An Aesthetic Education in the Era of Globalization.* By G. Chakravorty Spivak. Cambridge, MA: Harvard UP, 2013. 241-55.

—. Introduction. *An Aesthetic Education in the Era of Globalization.* By G. Chakravorty Spivak. Cambridge, MA: Harvard UP, 2013. 1-34.

—. *Readings.* London: Seagull, 2014.

Sprinker, Michael. "Fictions of the Self: The End of Autobiography." *Autobiography: Essays Theoretical and Critical.* Ed. James Olney. Princeton: Princeton UP, 1980. 321-42.

Starr, Deborah A. "Drinking, Gambling, and Making Merry: Waguih Ghali's Search for Cosmopolitan Agency." *Companion to the Arab Novel in English: The Politics of Anglo Arab and Arab American Literature and Culture.* Ed. Nouri Gana. Edinburgh: Edinburgh UP, 2013. 106-26.

Steiner, Georg. *Extraterritorial. Papers on Literature and the Language Revolution.* 1972; New York: Atheneum, 1976.

—. *After Babel: Aspects of Language and Translation.* 3. ed. Oxford: Oxford UP, 1998.

Stierstorfer, Klaus, ed. *Return to Postmodernism: Theory – Travel Writing – Autobiography. Festschrift in Honour of Ihab Hassan.* Heidelberg: Winter, 2005.

Stohlman, Nancy, and Laurieann Aladin. *Live from Palestine: International and Palestinian Direct Action against the Israeli Occupation.* Cambridge, MA: South End P, 2003.

Suheil Bushrui, Introduction. *The Prophet.* By Kahlil Gibran. Richmond: Oneworld, 2012. xi-xxiv.

Sutherland, Tom. *At Your Own Risk: An American Chronicle of Crisis and Captivity in the Middle East.* Golden, CO: Fulcrum, 1996.

al-Tahtawi, Rifa'a. *Takhlis al-Ibriz fi Talkhis Baris.* 1834; Beirut: Mu'assasa al-'Arabiyya lil-Dirasat wal-Nashr, 2002.

The Delta Force. Dir. Menahem Golan, screenplay James Bruner and Menahem Goland, perf. Chuck Norris, Lee Marvin et al., Cannon Films, 1986.

The Electronic Intifada. Ed. Ali Abunimah, Maureen Clare Murphy, Nora Barrows-Friedman, David Cronin et al. <https://electronicintifada.net/>.

The Exorcist. Dir. William Friedkin, screenplay William Peter Blatty, perf. Linda Blair, Ellen Burstyn, Jason Miller, and Max von Sydow, Warner Bros, 1973.

Thompson, Ayanna ed. *Colorblind Shakespeare. New Perspectives on Race and Performance*. New York: Routledge, 2006.

Trilling, Lionel. *The Liberal Imagination: Essays on Literature and Society*. New York: Viking P, 1950.

Turki, Fawaz. *The Disinherited. Journal of a Palestinian Exile*. New York: Monthly Review P, 1972.

Unger, Steven. "1945, 15 October: Rebellion or Revolution?" *A New History of French Literature*. Ed. Denis Hollier. 1989; Cambridge, MA: Harvard UP, 2001. 972-77.

"Unveiling Rihani's Bust at a New Memorial in Lebanon." *Ameen Rihani*. 13 Sept. 2015 <http://www.ameenrihani.org/newsevents.php>.

Updike, John. "Satan's Work and Silted Cisterns." Rev. of *Cities of Salt*. By Abdelrahman Munif. *New Yorker* 17 Oct. 1988: 117-21.

Venn-Brown, Janet, ed. *For a Palestinian: A Memorial to Wael Zuaiter*. London: Kegan Paul, 1984.

Venuti, Lawrence. *Scandals of Translation: Towards an Ethics of Difference*. London: Routledge, 1998.

"Walid Ra'ad—Scratching on Things I Could Disavow." *Kunstaspekte* July 2007, 22 Sept. 2011 <http://www.kunstaspekte.de/index.php?action=termin&tid=52070>.

Waller, Nicole. "Arabs Looking Back: William Peter Blatty's Autobiographical Writing." *Transnational American Memories*. Ed. Udo J. Hebel. Berlin: De Gruyter, 2009. 129-44.

—. *American Encounters with Islam in the Atlantic World*. Heidelberg: Winter, 2011.

Weiner, Justus Reid. "'My Beautiful Old House' and other Fabrications by Edward Said." *Commentary* 108.2 (1999): 23-31.

Weizman, Eyal. *Hollow Land: Israel's Architecture of Occupation*. London: Verso, 2007.

Wesseling, Janneke, ed. *See it Again, Say it Again: The Artist as Researcher*. Amsterdam: Valiz, 2011.

Westphal, Bertrand. *Geocriticism. Real and Fictional Spaces*. Trans. Robert T. Tally, Jr. New York: Palgrave Macmillan, 2011.

White, Hayden. "Criticism as Cultural Politics." *Diacritics* 6.3 (1976): 8-13.

Williams, William Carlos. *In the American Grain*. New York: New Directions, 1956.

Wilson-Goldie, Kaelen. "Off the Map: Contemporary Art in the Middle East." *The Future of Tradition – The Tradition of Future*. Ed. Chris Dercon, León Krempel, and Avinoam Shalem. Munich: Haus der Kunst, 2010. 60-67.

Wright, Stephen. "Tel un espion dans l'époque qui naît: la situation de l'artiste à Beyrouth aujourd'hui / Like a Spy in a Nascent Era: On the Situation of the Artist in Beirut Today." *Parachute*, Beyrouth_Beirut 108 (2002): 13-31.

Yourcenar, Marguerite. *Mémoires d'Hadrien*. Paris: Plon, 1951.

Zamir, Shamoon. *Dark Voices: W.E. B. Du Bois and American Thought, 1888–1903*. Chicago: U of Chicago P, 1995.

Žižek, Slavoj. "Trouble in Paradise." *London Review of Books* 35.14 (2013): 11-12.

—. *Event: Philosophy in Transit*. London: Penguin, 2014.

Zolghadr, Tirdad. "Thanks God He Wasn't French. Notes on Edward Said (1935–2003)." *Bidoun* 5 (2005): 40-41.

Image Credits

Index

CPSIA information can be obtained
at www.ICGtesting.com
Printed in the USA
JSHW012046130820
7279JS00005B/30